Ancient Jomon of Japan

Junko Habu illustrates recent developments in the archaeology of the Jomon period (circa 14,500–300 BC) of Japan and presents new analyses. Unlike most prehistoric pottery-using peoples, the Jomon people are thought to have been hunter-gatherers. Evidence of plant cultivation does exist, but none of the cultigens recovered from Jomon sites seems to have been used as a staple food resource. High site density, food storage, and long-distance trade also characterize the Jomon period. Using ecological models of hunter-gatherer culture and behavior, Habu examines various aspects of Jomon culture including subsistence–settlement, rituals, crafts and trade, and presents a model of long-term change in hunter-gatherer cultural complexity. In this comprehensive analysis, Junko Habu helps to bridge the gap between largely Japanese discourse on this 10,000-year period of Japanese prehistory and the modern scientific debate on later hunter-gatherer societies. It will prove invaluable to students and researchers alike.

JUNKO HABU is Associate Professor at the Department of Anthropology, University of California at Berkeley. She has conducted fieldwork both in Japan and in North America. Her publications include *Subsistence–Settlement Systems and Intersite Variability in the Moroiso Phase of the Early Jomon Period of Japan*, International Monographs in Prehistory (2001).

Case Studies in Early Societies

Series Editor
Rita P. Wright, New York University

This series aims to introduce students to early societies that have been the subject of sustained archaeological research. Each study is also designed to demonstrate a contemporary method of archaeological analysis in action, and the authors are all specialists currently engaged in field research. The books have been planned to cover many of the same fundamental issues. Tracing long-term developments, and describing and analyzing a discrete segment in the prehistory or history of a region, they represent an invaluable tool for comparative analysis. Clear, well organized, authoritative and succinct, the case studies are an important resource for students, and for scholars in related fields, such as anthropology, ethnohistory, history and political science. They also offer the general reader accessible introductions to important archaeological sites.

Other titles in the series include:

1. *Ancient Mesopotamia*
   Susan Pollock

2. *Ancient Oaxaca*
   Richard E. Blanton, Gary M. Feinman, Stephen A. Kowalewski, Linda M. Nicholas

3. *Ancient Maya*
   Arthur Demarest

Ancient Jomon of Japan

Junko Habu

CAMBRIDGE
UNIVERSITY PRESS

PUBLISHED BY THE PRESS SYNDICATE OF THE UNIVERSITY OF CAMBRIDGE
The Pitt Building, Trumpington Street, Cambridge, United Kingdom

CAMBRIDGE UNIVERSITY PRESS
The Edinburgh Building, Cambridge, CB2 2RU, UK
40 West 20th Street, New York, NY 10011–4211, USA
477 Williamstown Road, Port Melbourne, VIC 3207, Australia
Ruiz de Alarcón 13, 28014 Madrid, Spain
Dock House, The Waterfront, Cape Town 8001, South Africa

http://www.cambridge.org

First published 2004

Printed in the United Kingdom at the University Press, Cambridge

Typeface Plantin 10/12 pt.   *System* LATEX 2ε   [TB]

A catalogue record for this book is available from the British Library

Library of Congress Cataloguing in Publication data

Habu, Junko, 1959–
    Ancient Jomon of Japan / Junko Habu.
      p.   cm. – (Case studies in early societies)
    Includes bibliographical references and index.
    ISBN 0 521 77213 3 (hb.) – ISBN 0 521 77670 8 (pbk.)
    1. Jomon culture.   2. Japan – Antiquities.   I. Title.   II. Series.

G776.3.J6H23   2004   952′.01 – dc22   2003049547

ISBN 0 521 77213 3 hardback
ISBN 0 521 77670 8 paperback

To Professor Kimio Suzuki, who first taught me the importance of active interaction between Japanese and world archaeology

Contents

Part III: Rituals, crafts, and trade

Part IV: Discussion and conclusion

Figures

Tables

Acknowledgments

Many people and institutions have helped me shape this book. First, I thank Rita Wright, the editor of the Case Studies in Early Societies series, for her warm encouragement and constructive comments. Without her I would never have finished this book. I also thank Simon Whitmore and Jessica Kuper for their thoughtful editorial assistance and their patience. Many thanks to Ken Ames, Meg Conkey, John Daehnke, Clare Fawcett, Ben Fitzhugh, Tim Gill, Mark Hall, Holly Halligan, Kari Jones, Mio Katayama, Minkoo Kim, Patrick Kirch, John Matsunaga, Paolo Pellegatti, James Savelle, Tanya Smith, Kimio Suzuki, and an anonymous reviewer, all of whom read part, or all, of earlier drafts of this book and gave me invaluable comments and suggestions. The book also benefited from discussions with Kent Lightfoot and Shuzo Koyama. Chih-hua Chiang, Jeffrey Huang, Silvia Huang, Aaron Newton, Caroline Ogasawara, Derek Shaw, and Martin Sedaghat assisted me with illustrations. John Daehnke, Mariko Idei, and Mio Katayama helped me compile the bibliography and Brian Chen, Melodi McAdams, Theresa Molano, and Gabe Rodriguez helped me compile the index. I would also like to express my gratitude to the following individuals and institutions for allowing me to reproduce photos and illustrations, or providing me with originals: Shoji Abiko, Annaka-shi Kyoiku Iinkai, Aomori-ken Kyoiku-cho Bunka-ka, Chitose-shi Kyoiku Iinkai, Shinsuke Goto, Hachinohe-shi Jomon Gakushu-kan, Hiraka-machi Kyodo Shiryo-kan, Ichihasama-machi Kyoiku Iinkai, Mineo Imamura, Akiko Inano, Yusuke Inano, Kamikita-machi Rekishi Minzoku Shiryo-kan, Kariya-shi Kyoiku Iinkai, Kitakami-shi Kyoiku Iinkai, Kita-ku Kyoiku Iinkai, Daisuke Kodama, Kodansha, Kokuritsu Rekishi Minzoku Hakubutsu-kan, Mie-ken Maizo Bunkazai Center, Naoko Matsumoto, Nagano Kenritsu Rekishi-kan, Noto-machi Kyoiku Iinkai, Odai Yamamoto I Iseki Hakkutsu Chosa-dan, Kazuyoshi Ohtsuka, Oyabe-shi Kyoiku Iinkai, Prism and Co., Rikuzentakada-shi Kyoiku Iinkai, Masaru Sasaki, Chosuke Serizawa, Togariishi Koko-kan, Tohoku Rekishi Hakubutsu-kan, Tokamachi-shi Hakubutsu-kan, Tokyo Kokuritsu Hakubutsu-kan, and Toride-shi Maizo Bunkazai Center. Finally, I would like to thank Koji and Makiko Habu, Akiko Idei, Mariko Idei, and Mark Hall for their love, support, and encouragement.

Part I

Overview

1 Introduction

Goals and scope of this book

The "fire-flame" pottery shown on the cover of this book represents the apogee of a truly remarkable artistic tradition. It was made by a Middle Jomon potter who lived on the Japanese archipelago more than 4,000 years ago. The tradition of Jomon pottery production goes back much further in time, to approximately 16,500 years ago (13,780 uncalibrated bp). It makes the Jomon people the first in the world to have mastered the technology of transforming pliable clay into hard and durable containers.

"Jomon" is the name of a prehistoric culture and period that flourished on the Japanese archipelago for more than 10,000 years. The Jomon period follows the Palaeolithic period, and precedes the agricultural Yayoi period. Unlike most prehistoric pottery-using peoples, the people of the Jomon period are thought to have been mainly hunter-gatherer-fishers.

Artistic sophistication of pottery is only one aspect of this complex hunter-gatherer culture. From many excavations, we know that some Jomon settlements were enormous, as large as modern baseball stadiums: in fact, one such settlement was discovered in northern Japan in the process of building a baseball stadium (fig. 1.1; see also chapter 4). Jomon people also engaged in extensive trade networks that included artifacts of obsidian and jade. These findings are extraordinary for early prehistoric hunter-gatherer cultures, and they provide invaluable information for our understanding of the development of cultural complexity in human history.

This book is about the life and culture of the Jomon people, including food, houses, burials, art, and crafts. Its publication is especially timely, given the large number of recent excavations. Over the past several decades, tens of thousands of Jomon sites have been excavated with systematic financial support from various levels of government. The results of these excavations are commonly available in the form of published reports. Many of these rescue excavations are also quite large in scale,

Figure 1.1 Excavation of the Early and Middle Jomon Sannai
Maruyama site, Aomori Prefecture (from Aomori-ken Kyoiku-cho
Bunka-ka 1996b: ii; permission for reproduction obtained from Aomori-
ken Kyoiku-cho Bunka-ka)

and often cover an area of tens of thousands of square meters. Because
these excavations are salvage projects, they are often conducted under
restricted research strategies; typically, time and funding constraints are
major problems. Nevertheless, the advantages of having this enormous
body of data far exceed the disadvantages of these limitations. It should
be noted, for example, that Japan is one of the few countries in the world
where regional settlement pattern analyses can be conducted through
archival research of published site reports.

Despite these exciting aspects, and despite strong interest in the
Jomon culture among Anglo-American archaeologists (i.e., archaeologists in English-speaking countries including the United States, Canada,
England, Australia, and New Zealand), relatively little of Jomon archaeology has been introduced to the English-speaking audience. This is

because most of the archaeological literature about the Jomon is written in Japanese.

My goal in this book is to bridge this gap between the academic traditions of Japanese archaeology and Anglo-American archaeology. As a Japanese archaeologist trained first in Japan and then in North America, I believe that studies of the Jomon period can contribute significantly to our understanding of hunter-gatherer behavior and variability in world prehistory. At the same time, I am convinced that active interaction between Japanese and other archaeological traditions is critical to enhance our understanding of the Jomon culture. To achieve this goal, examinations of the conditions, causes, and consequences of the development of the Jomon culture will be presented through analyses of various components of the Jomon culture, including subsistence, settlement, ritual, crafts, and exchange.

Although many of the theoretical and methodological approaches applied to Jomon data in this book have their origins in Anglo-American archaeology, it is not my intention to suggest that these theoretical and methodological approaches are superior to those of Japanese archaeology. Rather, throughout the book I will argue that the adoption of different approaches can reveal different aspects of the Jomon culture. This may then lead to new interpretations of old data, and to the discussion of the advantages and limitations of various approaches adopted by archaeologists from each of the two academic traditions.

The geographic areas covered in this book include the four main islands of the Japanese archipelago (Hokkaido, Honshu, Shikoku, and Kyushu) and smaller islands in the vicinity of these four islands (fig. 1.2). Although the four islands correspond to the principal part of the present territory of Japan, throughout this book I have tried as much as possible to avoid the words "Japan" or "Japanese" when describing the Jomon period. This is because the Jomon period was the time prior to the formation of the ancient Japanese state (for critical discussions on the concepts of "Japan" and "the Japanese," see, for example, Amino 1997). The relationship between the culture/people of the Jomon period and the contemporary Japanese culture/people will be discussed in the last section of the second chapter. The word "Japan" is retained in the title of this book "Ancient Jomon of Japan" only for the sake of simplicity.

The word "Japan" is also retained when I talk about "eastern Japan" and "western Japan" as regional units. Following the Japanese convention, "eastern Japan" refers to the northeastern half of the Japanese archipelago (Hokkaido, Tohoku, Kanto, Chubu, Hokuriku, and Tokai regions), whereas "western Japan" refers to the southwestern half (Kinki, Chugoku, Shikoku, and Kyushu regions).

Figure 1.2   Prefectures and regions of Japan

BOX 1: *English publications on Jomon archaeology*

Very few English-language publications provide comprehensive coverage of the current status of Jomon studies. While a fair number of books have been published on Japanese archaeology (e.g., Aikens and Higuchi 1982; Aikens and Rhee 1992; Akazawa and Aikens 1986; Barnes 1993; Chard 1974; Groot 1951; Hudson 1999; Kidder 1968; Mizoguchi 2002; Pearson 1992; Pearson et al. 1986a), most of them were written either during or before the 1980s, or have only a limited number of chapters on the Jomon

BOX 1: (*cont.*)

period. One of the few exceptions is Keiji Imamura's (1996) *Prehistoric Japan*. In this book, Imamura does an excellent job of summarizing the recent results of prehistoric Japanese archaeology with an emphasis on Jomon studies (see Habu 1999). However, despite its strengths, the book contains only a limited discussion of the theoretical and methodological implications of Jomon studies in the context of world archaeology.

Part of this isolation of Jomon studies in the context of world archaeology comes from the fact that the results of Jomon archaeology are published primarily within Japan and in Japanese. Even before the 1970s, when the amount of available data was relatively small, presenting the results of Jomon archaeology in non-Japanese languages was a difficult task. Today, with an overwhelming number of excavation records published in both academic and popular forms, it seems almost impossible to summarize succinctly the results of Jomon archaeology. At the same time, differences in theoretical and methodological approaches make the active interaction between Japanese and other archaeological traditions difficult (Habu 1989a). On the one hand, many Japanese archaeologists, who have been trained in the tradition of "archaeology as history," feel that Japanese prehistoric cultures, including Jomon, are historically unique. Consequently, they believe that direct comparisons with other prehistoric cultures will provide little help in interpreting Jomon data (e.g., Anazawa 1985). On the other hand, many of the non-Japanese archaeologists who are interested in Jomon archaeology are frustrated by the overemphasis on pottery typologies created by Japanese researchers, as well as by their culture-historical and/or empiricist research orientation. This frustration is particularly noticeable in the writings published by North American and British archaeologists (see, e.g., Barnes and Okita 1999; see also Bleed 1989).

Theoretical approaches

This book uses two different theoretical perspectives to achieve the goal described above. First, it analyzes hunter-gatherer cultural complexity from the perspective of an ecological model. Second, it recognizes that no archaeological practice is separate from the social contexts in which it is conducted.

An ecological approach to hunter-gatherer cultural complexity: the collector–forager model

The first theoretical perspective adopted in this book is derived from ecological anthropology, which can be briefly defined as "the study of cultural behavior in its natural and social environment, in terms of its relationship to this environment" (Jochim 1979: 77–78). Specifically, this book uses the collector–forager model, an ecologically based model developed by Binford (1980; 1982; 1983; 1990). This model posits the existence of a direct relationship between resource distribution, subsistence activities,

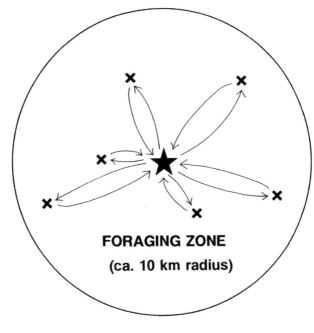

= RESIDENTIAL BASE

✗ = RESOURCE EXTRACTION LOCATION

Figure 1.3   Characterization of a forager system

and settlement patterns. According to this model, subsistence–settlement systems of hunter-gatherers can be divided into two basic types: (1) forager systems, which are characterized by high residential mobility, and (2) collector systems, which are characterized by relatively low residential mobility.

Figure 1.3 illustrates key characteristics of the forager system. In an environment where resource distribution is homogeneous, hunter-gatherers tend to acquire food and other necessary resources on a day-to-day basis near their residential base. The daily resource acquisition area is called the *foraging zone*. The radius of the foraging zone is about 10 kilometers, or two hours' walk. In this model, it is expected that when foragers exhaust food within the foraging zone, they move their residential base to a new place. Absence of food storage characterizes forager systems. Figure 1.4 illustrates an example of foragers' annual residential moves, using the data of the G/wi San of the Kalahari Desert. In this

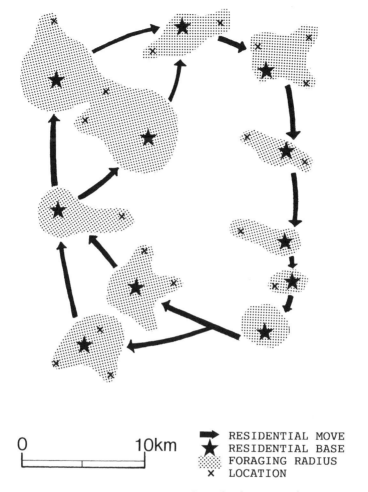

Figure 1.4   Schematic representation of a forager settlement pattern
(modified and redrawn from Binford 1980: 6)

example, a total of nine residential moves per year take place. Ethnographic data indicate that foragers move their residential bases anything
from five to forty-five times a year (Binford 1980: 7).

Compared to foragers, collectors are more sedentary. Figure 1.5 illustrates key characteristics of a collector system. When the distribution of
critical resources is spatially and/or seasonally uneven, hunter-gatherers
tend to organize their subsistence activities logistically; i.e., in addition to
daily food-gathering activities within the foraging zone, collectors send

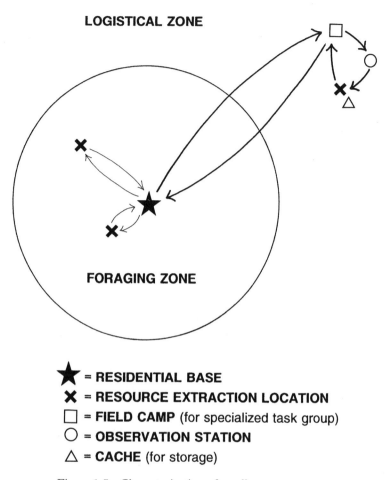

= RESIDENTIAL BASE
X = RESOURCE EXTRACTION LOCATION
☐ = FIELD CAMP (for specialized task group)
○ = OBSERVATION STATION
△ = CACHE (for storage)

Figure 1.5   Characterization of a collector system

specialized task groups to acquire food resources located outside the foraging zone (called *logistical zone*), and bring them back. Food storage is an important part of collectors' subsistence strategy. Figure 1.6 represents an example of collectors' settlement patterns using the data of the Nunamiut in Alaska. As indicated in the figure, the majority of collectors move their residential bases only a few times a year. In this example, the group forms a large residential base at settlement #1 in the figure, staying there from the fall to the spring. In the early summer, they move the whole village to settlement #2, because #2 is more convenient for

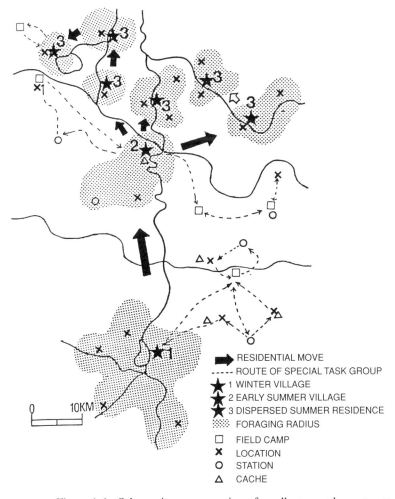

Figure 1.6   Schematic representation of a collector settlement pattern (modified and redrawn from Binford 1980: 11)

summer subsistence activities than #1. In the late summer, the group disperses to smaller residential bases at settlements #3.

According to Binford (1980: 12), forager and collector systems are not polarized types of systems but lie on a continuum from simple to complex. As these systems incorporate relatively more logistical components, the role and importance of residential mobility will change. In other words, when we examine subsistence–settlement systems of the Jomon people, it is unlikely that we will find "pure" collecting or "pure" foraging systems; most systems will be placed somewhere on the collector–forager continuum. However, the two extremes provide the necessary reference points from which I interpret actual subsistence–settlement systems of hunter-gatherers.

Although all of the ethnographic examples of collectors presented by Binford (1980; 1982) are groups with seasonal moves, theoretically collectors may stay in permanent residential bases throughout the year. In reality, such societies are rare, one of the few ethnographically documented exceptions being the Ainu in Hokkaido (H. Watanabe 1972). The settlement patterns of the Ainu people are shown in fig. 1.7; in this example, the Ainu people maintain a year-round residential base. This type of system occurs only when all the seasonally important resources are available from a single residential base. I call this type *fully sedentary collectors*.

Unlike many other ecological models of hunter-gatherer subsistence and settlement, which attempt to develop general models deductively by using ecological and economic principles, the collector–forager model is an informal model based on ethnographic examples; i.e., the model is inductive in its origin. Because of this characteristic, some Japanese archaeologists have expressed their skepticism about the usefulness of the model for the analysis of Jomon data. For example, Fujio Sasaki (1993) suggests that the collector model is not applicable to Jomon hunter-gatherers of the temperate zone since it is based on the ethnographic example of the Nunamiut, who lived in the Arctic. However, as an informal model, I find its applicability surprisingly wide. As articles in Fitzhugh and Habu (2002a) indicate, with some modifications the model is applicable to numerous archaeological and ethnographic cases from various parts of the world.

Although the collector–forager model (Binford 1980; 1982) is an ecological model, my use of it in this book does not mean that the environment is assumed to be the single causative factor of all human behavior, nor does it imply that the study of subsistence and settlement is more important than the study of social and ideological aspects of the Jomon culture. Rather, the collector–forager model is used as an explanatory device; i.e., although strong correlations between resource availability, subsistence activities, and mobility patterns are assumed, other factors are also thought to be potentially of equal influence in defining the lifeways of the Jomon people and their changes over time. For example, a case study of long-term settlement pattern changes in the Kanto and Chubu regions is presented on pages 87–108. This case study suggests that a shift from collectors to foragers in one region may have triggered a system change in another region. Although I explain these

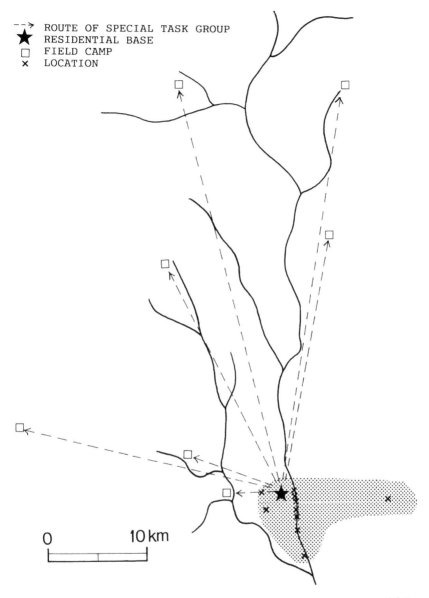

Figure 1.7   Schematic representation of a settlement pattern of fully sedentary hunter-gatherers (modified and redrawn from Hitoshi Watanabe 1972: map 2)

changes within the framework of the collector–forager model, the results of my analysis indicate that historically unique factors may be critical in understanding subsistence and settlement changes in this particular area.

The use of the collector–forager model does not imply that the Jomon people were relying exclusively on hunting-gathering-fishing. Analysis of floral remains indicates that several cultigens, including *egoma* (*Perilla frutescens* var. *japonica*) or shiso mint (*P. frutescens* var. *crispa*), bottle gourd (*Lagenaria siceraria*), and possibly barnyard millet (*Echinochloa utilis*), were present by the time of the Early Jomon period. Moreover, seven rice (*Oryza sativa*) grains were recovered from the Late Jomon Kazahari site in Aomori Prefecture (D'Andrea et al. 1995). For the moment, however, no archaeological data indicate that any of these cultigens were staple foods for the Jomon people. As Anderson's (1988) study in New Zealand reveals, hunter-gatherers can incorporate plant cultivation as a minor component of their subsistence strategies quite easily. His case study can be seen as an example of a collecting system with seasonal moves even though sweet potato cultivation was apparently part of the people's seasonal subsistence cycle. In any case, if some of the Jomon people, either in a specific region and/or in a particular time period, were relying heavily on cultivated plants, then characteristics of subsistence data and/or settlement patterns are likely to be significantly different from the collector–forager model. Thus, by identifying archaeological cases that do not fit into the collector–forager model, we may be detecting the presence of a new system with a strong emphasis on plant cultivation.

Using the collector–forager model, Part II of this book examines characteristics of Jomon subsistence and settlement. Particular attention is paid to such research topics as the development of sedentism, subsistence intensification, and changes in population density. Topics discussed in chapter 3 include the debate over possible importance of salmon fishing and plant cultivation, food storage, and maritime adaptation. Issues discussed in chapter 4 are closely related to various research topics examined in both traditional settlement archaeology (e.g., Adams 1965; Chang 1968; Flannery 1976; Trigger 1967; 1968; Willey 1953) and processual subsistence–settlement studies.

Following Part II, the two chapters in Part III examine various characteristics of Jomon cultures beyond subsistence and settlement. The collector–forager model (Binford 1980; 1982) assumes that organizational changes in subsistence and settlement would lead to a corresponding social and ideological reorientation. Rather than assuming that social behavior was necessarily structured by subsistence–settlement systems, the two chapters in Part III examine changes in Jomon rituals, crafts, and exchange networks independently. Articulations between subsistence–settlement and other factors are then discussed in chapter 7 in Part IV.

Topics discussed in chapters 3 to 6 address various issues in recent studies of hunter-gatherer cultural complexity. Characteristics of so-called "complex" hunter-gatherers typically include seasonally and/or spatially intensive subsistence strategies, food storage, sedentism, high population density, elaboration of material culture, and social inequality (Ames 1985; Lightfoot 1993; Price and Brown 1985a; Price and Feinman 1995). Of particular interest in hunter-gatherer archaeological research over the past two decades is the interplay between these cultural elements.

The ambiguity of the concept "complexity" used in hunter-gatherer archaeology has been extensively discussed (e.g., Arnold 1996a; Fitzhugh 2003; Price 2002). According to Price and Brown, "[c]omplexity refers to that which is composed of many different parts" (Price and Brown 1985a: 7, emphasis in original). This is a general perspective shared by many scholars who have been involved in the discussion of the evolution of cultural complexity, including those who are interested in the formation of state-level societies (for overviews of the archaeological study of cultural complexity, see, e.g., McGuire 1983; Tainter 1996). Following this general understanding, Price and Brown state that "we follow a general definition of cultural complexity that focuses on increases in societal size, scale and organization" (Price and Brown 1985a: 8). More recently, Price states that "there is general consensus that complexity means bigger groups, longer stays, more elaborate technology, intensified subsistence, broader resource utilization, and the like" (Price 2002: 418). According to these definitions, "cultural complexity" can be understood as a concept that includes organizational complexity in subsistence and settlement systems. That is, if we follow these definitions, collectors *sensu* Binford (1980), i.e., more logistically organized hunter-gatherers, can be legitimately called "complex" hunter-gatherers regardless of their level of social inequality.

In contrast, some researchers suggest that the word "complexity" should be reserved for those societies with hereditary social differentiation. Focusing on the control of labor by the elite, Jeanne Arnold states that "[c]omplex, as I used it here, distinguishes those societies possessing *social and labor relationships in which leaders have sustained or on-demand control over nonkin labor and social differentiation is hereditary*" (Arnold 1996a: 78; emphasis in original). She continues that "[c]omplexity, then, relates most fundamentally to two organizational features: (1) some people must perform work for others under the direction of persons outside of their kin group, and (2) some people, including leaders, are higher ranking at birth than others" (Arnold 1996a: 78). This definition, with its emphasis on labor organization, has its root in a Marxist perspective (see also Arnold 1992; 1995; 1996b).

In this book I adopt the broader definition of "cultural complexity." Following Price and Brown (1985a) and Price (2002), my definition of the concept "cultural complexity" here includes both organizational complexity in subsistence–settlement systems and social complexity. The former can be measured by the degree of the incorporation of various logistical strategies into subsistence–settlement systems, including food storage and the differentiation of site functions. The latter can be measured by the degree of vertical and horizontal social differentiation as well as the degree of the integration of the differentiated parts (Fitzhugh 2003). Under this definition, I consider social stratification as a form of social differentiation, but not necessarily the most important form in understanding the degree of social complexity.

Decoupling the concept of inequality from that of complexity allows us to examine the dynamics of long-term cultural change in human history without necessarily focusing on the development of political hierarchy. This is especially important when we examine hunter-gatherer societies that might not fit into the progressivist model of social evolution. Although the proposition that not all the hunter-gatherers are/were egalitarian or mobile gained significant support during and after the 1980s, long-term changes in hunter-gatherer subsistence, settlement, and society still tend to be interpreted from the perspective of unilinear evolution. However, with an increase in archaeological examples of hunter-gatherers from traditionally underrepresented regions, models that are capable of explaining diversity among different hunter-gatherer groups are increasingly attracting researchers' attention.

Under the broader definition of the concept of "cultural complexity," this book examines regional variability and long-term change in organizational complexity in subsistence and settlement in Part II, and variability and changes in social complexity, including social inequality, in Part III. On the basis of these analyses, the concluding chapter (chapter 7) will present a model that explains the interplay between Jomon subsistence, settlement, and society.

Social contexts of Jomon archaeology

The second perspective that underlies the discussion in this book is the recognition that no archaeological practice is free from the social contexts in which it is conducted. Although this point has been noted by many scholars with various theoretical backgrounds (e.g., Hodder 1999; Patterson 1995; Schmidt and Patterson 1995; Trigger 1995; Yoffee and

Sherratt 1993), I use the work of Kohl and Fawcett (1995a; 1995b) as my starting point for discussing the social contexts of Jomon archaeology. In the introduction of their edited volume, Kohl and Fawcett (1995a) point out the close relationship between archaeological work and its social, economic, and political contexts. A number of case studies in their edited volume reveal how archaeology in various countries has been used to support specific political perspectives favored by the politicians in power. The volume also shows the close link between archaeology and the construction of national and/or ethnic identities in each country. On the basis of various case studies, Kohl and Fawcett (1995a: 16) suggest that it is necessary to discuss explicitly the positive and negative features of nationalist archaeology and of the sociopolitical/economic contexts in which various archaeological studies are conducted.

Despite the realization of the close link between sociopolitical factors and archaeological interpretations, many authors in the Kohl and Fawcett (1995b) volume are critical of the hyperrelativist position advocated by such scholars as Shanks and Tilley (1987). Trigger (1995), for example, rejects the extreme relativist position taken by some postprocessual archaeologists, and suggests that the growing empirical database recovered by archaeologists should constrain archaeological interpretations. Citing Trigger (1995) and others, Kohl and Fawcett (1995a: 8) argue that even though only a fine line separates legitimate from questionable research, responsible archaeologists should be able to determine the *limits* of the evidence they control, what they can and cannot reconstruct with reasonable confidence from the archaeological record (see also Yoffee and Sherratt 1993; for a criticism of the perspectives of Kohl and Fawcett 1995a and others, see Hodder 1999: 16).

Following the arguments presented in Kohl and Fawcett (1995a), I suggest that particular attention should be paid to the sociopolitical, economic, and historical contexts in which archaeological studies of the Jomon period are conducted both within and outside Japan. In particular, throughout this book, the approaches of the two different academic traditions (i.e., Japanese and Anglo-American archaeology) to various research topics of Jomon archaeology are compared, and the advantages and limitations of these approaches are discussed.

In this time of increasing globalization, many archaeologists who publish primarily in English, particularly those who advocate a postprocessual (or sometimes post-postprocessual) archaeology, have begun to emphasize the importance of concepts such as multivocality and cultural diversity. For example, in his recent work, Hodder (1999) argues that a diversity of views should be espoused, with no singular and unified perspectives on the discipline. Ironically, however, these new perspectives are primarily espoused by some British and North American archaeologists whose theoretical and methodological background was formed within the Western archaeological tradition. As a result, while many of these new approaches question the validity of the Western-centered perspectives, very few archaeologists from outside the Anglo-American academic tradition are actively involved in these debates. Additionally, many advocates of these new approaches use highly specialized technical terms that are not easy to understand for even native speakers of English. The nuances of these terms are almost impossible for nonnative speakers to comprehend, making the participation of non-Anglo-American archaeologists in these debates even more difficult.

By pointing out these problems, I do not intend to suggest that the issue of multivocality and cultural diversity can be addressed only by archaeologists outside the traditions of Anglo-American archaeology. Clearly, the shift in theoretical direction in British and North American archaeology over the past couple of decades has had the positive effect of broadening theoretical diversity and flexibility. Nevertheless, just as the active participation of female archaeologists was indispensable in the development of gender/feminist archaeology in English-speaking countries in the late 1980s and 1990s (e.g., Gero and Conkey 1991; Wylie 1991; 1993), archaeologists representing a variety of non-Anglophone academic traditions should have opportunities to present their perspectives in the theoretical debates of world archaeology.

Given these circumstances, I believe that the archaeology of the Jomon period can be an interesting test case for exploring how two academic traditions can interact and benefit from each other. Since issues dealt with in Jomon archaeology include various controversial topics in Anglo-American archaeology, such as the origins of pottery and the development of hunter-gatherer cultural complexity, it would have been possible for me to write this entire book as a reinterpretation of Jomon data using a theoretical framework derived from North American archaeology. However, given the complex social and academic milieus that surround both Japanese and Anglo-American archaeologies, detaching the results of Jomon archaeology from their social and academic context and simply presenting them in English would hinder accurate understanding of the current status of Jomon studies. Discussions on various controversial issues should be evaluated without dismissing the social and academic contexts in which Jomon data have been collected, presented, and interpreted. In this regard, I do not aim to provide the reader with an "objective" interpretation of Jomon data. Rather, I try to examine what we can achieve by considering Jomon data, how we can approach various research topics using different methods, and how the study of the

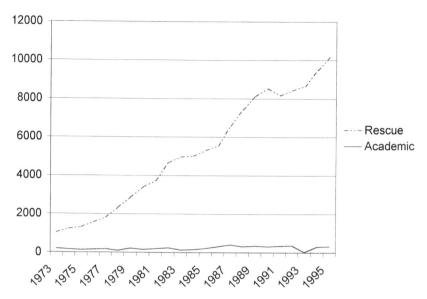

Figure 1.8 Changes over time in the number of rescue and academic excavations (raw data taken from Bunka-cho Bunkazai Hogo-bu Kinenbutsu-ka 1996: 1)

Jomon culture can make significant contributions to future developments in archaeology, especially in an international context.

To demonstrate the effects of sociopolitical factors on Jomon archaeology, I would like to discuss three factors that are particularly influential:

(1) Rescue excavations and CRM organizations First, an overwhelming abundance of archaeological data obtained through rescue excavations is a major factor that is affecting the practice of Jomon archaeology. The number of rescue excavations in Japan began to increase in the 1960s. With the rapid growth of the Japanese economy and resulting large-scale land development, the number and scale of rescue excavations increased exponentially from the 1970s through to the 1990s (e.g., Barnes 1993; Habu 1989a; Tanaka 1984). As indicated in figure 1.8 and table 1.1, the number of rescue excavations reached over 10,000 by the mid-1990s, while the number of academic excavations still remains approximately 300. Also, figure 1.9 and table 1.2 show that an extraordinary amount of money has been spent on rescue excavations over the past thirty years. While the amount began to decrease slightly after 1998, the annual spending on rescue excavations in the fiscal year 2000 was approximately 113 billion yen (approximately 1 billion dollars).

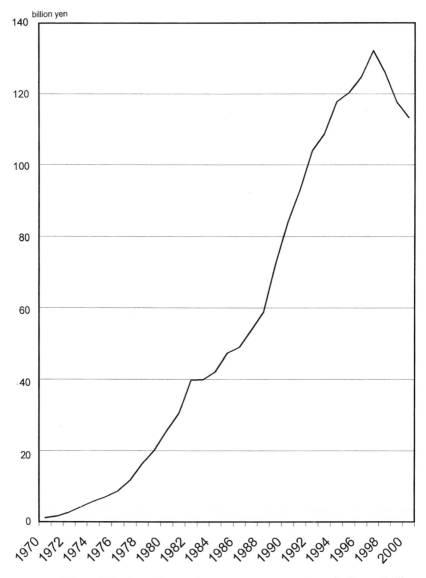

billion yen

Figure 1.9 Annual spending on rescue excavations in Japan (billion yen) (raw data taken from Nara Bunkazai Kenkyu-jo Maizo Bunkazai Center 2002: 6)

Table 1.1 *Changes over time in the number of rescue and academic excavations*

Year	Rescue	Academic
1973	1,040	203
1974	1,231	164
1975	1,318	131
1976	1,571	155
1977	1,821	184
1978	2,331	105
1979	2,858	225
1980	3,408	158
1981	3,739	196
1982	4,669	250
1983	4,968	137
1984	5,004	158
1985	5,310	223
1986	5,555	316
1987	6,598	409
1988	7,439	321
1989	8,133	354
1990	8,536	317
1991	8,168	346
1992	8,440	372
1993	8,650	32
1994	9,494	310
1995	10,164	326

Source: Bunka-cho Bunkazai Hogo-bu Kinenbutsu-ka 1996: 1.

The implication of the proliferation of rescue excavations is profound. Because Japanese archaeologists were trained in the tradition of "archaeology as history," most of them believed, and still believe, that every single archaeological site is unique and therefore should be protected as much as possible. Under the land-development policy of the Japanese government, however, the ideal of site preservation is typically substituted by systematic rescue excavation: while the site itself would be lost, at least information contained in the site is documented in the excavation record. During the 1960s and 1970s, most of these rescue excavations were conducted by civil servants of the prefectural/municipal boards of education or museums. Later, government-based CRM organizations (usually called Maizo Bunkazai Centers) were established at both the prefectural and municipal levels. Currently, approximately 7,000 archaeologists are working at these CRM organizations, prefectural/municipal boards of

Table 1.2 *Annual spending on rescue excavations in Japan (million yen)*

Year	Excavation cost
1970	1,094
1971	1,600
1972	2,686
1973	4,225
1974	5,731
1975	6,980
1976	8,599
1977	11,665
1978	16,257
1979	20,058
1980	25,551
1981	30,480
1982	39,764
1983	39,897
1984	42,023
1985	47,216
1986	48,831
1987	53,765
1988	58,830
1989	72,209
1990	83,850
1991	93,082
1992	103,930
1993	108,687
1994	117,726
1995	120,298
1996	124,694
1997	132,128
1998	125,845
1999	117,630
2000	113,231

Source: Compiled from Nara Bunkazai Kenkyu-jo Maizo Bunkazai Center 2002: 6.

education, and museums (Nara Bunkazai Kenkyu-jo Maizo Bunkazai Center 2003).

This dramatic increase in the number and scale of excavations had both positive and negative effects on Jomon archaeology. On the positive side, it not only changed the quantity of available data, but also increased the types of archaeological research possible. In particular, in the field of settlement archaeology, both inter- and intrasite spatial analyses have benefited from the rich Jomon database (see chapter 4). The greater quantity of data also made archaeologists realize the extent of regional and temporal variability in the Jomon culture.

On the negative side, this prevalence of rescue excavations resulted in an "overflow" of archaeological data. Many Japanese archaeologists are preoccupied by simply catching up with new findings. The development of CRM archaeology also resulted in the standardization of archaeological methods. Problem-oriented research was generally suppressed, and the collection of certain types of data, particularly those that are relevant to chronological studies of pottery, was encouraged. Other types of data, particularly quantitative data of faunal and floral remains, are often neglected.

In this book, I attempt to take advantage of the abundant rescue excavation data. Rather than criticizing the shortcomings of these data, I attempt to show what archaeologists can do with this large body of data, and also how the existing data may constrain archaeological interpretations. In particular, Case Study 1 in chapter 4 utilizes excavation reports of more than 1,000 Early Jomon sites as the raw data for analysis.

Since the quality of published data varies between different categories of data and for different excavations, some sections of this book (particularly those in chapter 6) are more descriptive than others. Some readers may find these sections less interesting. However, I believe that the exposition of this information is a necessary step toward conducting theory-oriented, deductive research.

(2) Jomon as the ancestors of "the Japanese"   Second, there is a strong public interest in archaeology in Japan. Japanese archaeology has a long tradition of archaeology as history (Habu 1989a; Ikawa-Smith 1980). Within this tradition, various outreach programs have identified Japanese archaeology as the study of the ancestors of "the Japanese people." At public interpretation meetings of Jomon sites, archaeologists repeatedly tell the Japanese audience that the primary purpose of Japanese archaeology is to reconstruct the lives of their own ancestors. This is in sharp contrast with "archaeology as anthropology" in the Americas, in which archaeology originally developed as the study of the past of "the other."

Large-scale rescue excavations and subsequent site report preparations funded by tax money from various levels of government would be impossible without strong support from the general public. Some Jomon sites, which were initially excavated as salvage excavations prior to construction projects, managed to escape destruction because of a great deal of public support for preservation (e.g., Okada and Habu 1995). Public interest in archaeological excavation has also been fueled by media reports since the early 1970s, when Japanese newspapers and television programs began to report archaeological discoveries in a sensational manner (Fawcett 1990; 1995).

The strong public and media interest, together with the rapid increase in the number of excavations, resulted in a "Jomon boom" in the mid-1990s (Habu and Fawcett 1999; Hudson 2003). Even though many physical anthropologists suggest that the people of the Jomon period are only partially ancestral to modern Japanese (e.g., Hanihara 1987), the Jomon people are often presented at various popular exhibitions as the ancestors of "the Japanese" or of "ourselves" (e.g., Jomon Mahoroba-haku Jikko Iinkai 1996).

In this social environment, the results of archaeological study of the Jomon culture have considerable influence on the construction of "Japanese identity." In other words, archaeology of the Jomon period provides us with an extremely interesting test case for examining the relationship between archaeological studies and contemporary society.

It is not surprising that certain types of archaeological interpretation are preferred by media reports over others. Discoveries of the so-called "oldest" or "largest" artifacts and sites are regularly reported on the front pages of newspapers. Interpretations that emphasize the high level of social complexity of the Jomon culture frequently appear in popular books and magazines, some of which even identify the Jomon culture as an "ancient civilization" and call large Jomon sites "ancient cities." Another common theme in media reports is the quest for the roots of "Japaneseness" in the Jomon people.

One of the aims of this book, therefore, is to reassess these media stereotypes of the Jomon culture and provide alternative interpretations. Although I believe that emerging cultural and social complexity should be a focus of Jomon archaeology, the nature and degree of complexity should be evaluated on the basis of case studies, rather than be assumed. Regional and temporal variability of the Jomon culture is also systematically examined, and conditions, causes, and consequences of long-term changes are discussed. From these discussions, I hope to demonstrate that the nature of the Jomon culture is multifaceted, and not as simple as presented in the popular press.

(3) Gender archaeology and the scarcity of female archaeologists
Throughout this book, the issue of gender is only minimally discussed. This is largely because feminist theories and perspectives are still virtually missing in current Jomon archaeology. I believe that this situation is closely related to the scarcity of female professional scholars in Japanese

archaeology. In 1964, women constituted 1.0 percent of the total membership of the Japanese Archaeological Association (JAA). In 1995, the percentage rose to 2.8 percent. Although the percentage almost tripled over thirty years, it is still extremely low. This unfortunate situation is certainly the major reason why gender and feminist archaeology is virtually absent in Jomon studies.

It should be noted that the scarcity of female professional scholars does not imply a scarcity of female students. Most undergraduate programs of archaeology in Japan have a significant number of female students. However, job opportunities for women, especially those in academic institutions, are still extremely limited. While this is a problem in Japanese academia in general, the percentage of women in archaeology is lower than in most other social sciences, including history.

With an increasing interaction with Anglo-American archaeology, where the issues of gender and feminism are two of the major research foci, changes in the social and academic status of women in Japanese archaeology, as well as the development of gender and feminist studies, are much anticipated. Ikawa-Smith's (2002) recent article on Jomon clay figurines may indicate that the situation is slowly changing.

Because of the fledgling nature of gender archaeology within Japanese archaeology, this topic will be only briefly touched on in the following chapters. Future areas of research would include sexual division of labor in subsistence activities, dietary differences between male and female skeletons, and the symbolic function of clay figurines and stone rods in Jomon social landscapes.

Summary

In summary, this book seeks (1) to provide up-to-date information on Jomon archaeology to an English-speaking audience, (2) to examine regional diversity in the Jomon culture and present a model of long-term changes in Jomon cultural complexity, and (3) to open a dialogue for examining the sociopolitical contexts of archaeological studies in contemporary Japanese society. Through these discussions, I hope to bridge the gap between Japanese and Anglo-American archaeology. Above all, I hope that the description of Jomon data and their interpretations presented in this book will make the readers think of various ways in which the results of Jomon archaeology can be incorporated into world archaeology. If, after reading this book, the reader, whether a student, a professional archaeologist, or an amateur, can relate the contents of this book to her/his own research interests, then its primary goal will have been achieved.

2   Background to the study: overview of the Jomon period

This chapter provides the background necessary for understanding the rest of this book, in which I examine Jomon subsistence, settlement, and society. Five topics are discussed in this chapter: (1) the origins of the Jomon culture, (2) the chronological framework of the Jomon period, (3) the environment during the Jomon period, (4) Jomon population estimates, and (5) physical anthropological studies on the relationship between Jomon peoples and modern Japanese.

Origins of the Jomon culture

The origin of the Jomon culture is a hotly debated topic. For a long time, linear-relief pottery recovered in 1960 from Fukui Cave in Nagasaki Prefecture, Kyushu (Kamaki and Serizawa 1965), was the oldest evidence of Jomon pottery with a reliable radiocarbon date. As the name indicates, linear-relief pottery (also called linear-appliqué pottery) is characterized by thin clay bands attached to the surface of pots. Linear-relief pottery recovered from Layer III at the cave (fig. 2.1) was associated with microblades and wedge-shaped microcores, and was dated to 12,700 ± 500 bp (GaK-950) (1σ: 15,850–14,250 cal BP) by a ^{14}C date from associated charcoal (Kamaki and Serizawa 1965; 1967).

BOX 2: *Calibrated and uncalibrated radiocarbon dates*

Throughout this book, lower case bp is used for uncalibrated radiocarbon dates (radiocarbon years before 1950), and upper case BP or cal BP is used for calibrated (calendrical) dates. It is known that, because the concentration levels of ^{14}C on earth fluctuated over time, radiocarbon dates do not exactly correspond with calendrical dates (Bowman 1990). Up to approximately 20,000 bp, the gap between radiocarbon dates and calendrical dates could be adjusted using the calibration curve obtained on the basis of dendrochronological and coral studies. For the calibration of radiocarbon dates from samples of marine origin (e.g., marine shells, sea mammals), a different calibration curve is used from that for samples of terrestrial origin, because past concentration levels of ^{14}C in the ocean were different from those in the atmosphere (Stuiver et al. 1998a; 1998b).

BOX 2: (*cont.*)

Jomon archaeology has been slow in adopting calibrated dates (see pp. 37–42), and most scholars working on Jomon materials still use uncalibrated dates when referring to absolute dates. Furthermore, because previous estimates of absolute dates for the six Jomon subperiods were largely based on samples measured during the 1960s and 1970s, these estimates may require major modifications in the near future. According to Mineo Imamura and Ken'ichi Kobayashi (personal communication 2003), some of the recently obtained AMS radiocarbon dates for the Kanto and Tohoku regions do not quite overlap with conventional estimates (see also Ken'ichi Kobayashi et al. 2003). Furthermore, on the basis of new AMS dates, Harunari et al. (2003) suggest that evidence for the first rice cultivation in northern Kyushu, which marks the transition from the Jomon to the Yayoi period, may be dated to several hundred years earlier (ca. 900–1000 BC) than the traditional estimate (ca. 500 BC). While the evaluation of the latter work is still controversial, it is clear that reestablishing Jomon chronology is not simply the matter of converting uncalibrated bp to calibrated BP, but it requires the reexamination of existing data and analysis of new samples.

Given the situation, this book provides both uncalibrated and calibrated radiocarbon dates. All the terrestrial and marine radiocarbon dates were calibrated using the OxCAL program and the calibration curves of Stuiver et al. 1998a (for terrestrial samples) and Stuiver et al. 1998b (for marine samples). For each radiocarbon date, the calibrated one-sigma (1σ) range (i.e., the range for 68 percent probability) is shown in parentheses. Because the calibration curve is not always smooth, sometimes the one-sigma range is split into two or more. When the discussion refers to general estimates in uncalibrated bp, rough estimates of calibrated dates are shown in parentheses.

On the basis of the associated radiocarbon date, the Fukui Cave potsherds were identified not only as the oldest Jomon pottery, but also as the oldest evidence of pottery made to function as containers in the world (e.g., Ikawa-Smith 1986; Aikens 1995). Layer II (i.e., above Layer III) of Fukui Cave, which also contained microblades and was dated to 12,400 ± 350 bp (GaK-949) (1σ: 15,350–14,050 cal BP), was characterized by another type of pottery called nail-impressed pottery. On the other hand, Layer IV (below Layer III) had microblades but no pottery. Based on these results, investigators of the site (Kamaki and Serizawa 1965) concluded that linear-relief pottery was the oldest Jomon pottery, followed by nail-impressed pottery.

Since the discovery at Fukui Cave, linear-relief pottery has been recovered from a number of sites. These include Senpukuji Cave in Nagasaki Prefecture in Kyushu (Aso 1985), Kamikuroiwa Rockshelter in Ehime Prefecture in Shikoku (Esaka et al. 1967), Tazawa Cave in Niigata Prefecture in Honshu (Serizawa and Suto 1968), and the Hanamiyama site in Kanagawa Prefecture in Honshu (Kohoku New Town Maizo Bunkazai Chosa-dan 1986; Yokohama-shi Furusato Rekishi Zaidan Maizo Bunka

Figure 2.1 Linear-relief pottery excavated from Fukui Cave. The round modified potsherd in the center was probably recycled as an ornament (scale = approximately 2/5) (photograph by courtesy of Chosuke Serizawa).

Center 1995). At Senpukuji, another type of pottery called "bean-appliqué pottery" was recovered stratigraphically below linear-relief pottery (Aso 1985). This led some researchers to believe that bean-appliqué pottery is older than linear-relief pottery. However, subsequent recoveries of bean-appliqué pottery from other sites that had yielded linear-relief pottery made many scholars believe that bean-appliqué pottery is a variety of linear-relief pottery (T. Izumi 1996a: 65). Unfortunately, apart from Fukui Cave, very few radiocarbon dates have been obtained from sites with either linear-relief or bean-appliqué pottery. Table 2.1 lists some of the representative radiocarbon dates associated with linear-relief and nail-impressed pottery.

In 1999, carbonized material adhering to the surface of pottery excavated from Layer IV of the Odai Yamamoto I site in Aomori Prefecture, northern Honshu (Odai Yamamoto I Iseki Hakkutsu Chosa-dan 1999; Taniguchi 1999a), was dated to 13,780 ± 170 bp (NUTA-6510) (Nakamura and Tsuji 1999). The calibration of this date comes to approximately 16,500 cal BP (1σ: 16,850–16,200 cal BP). A total of

Table 2.1 *Representative radiocarbon dates associated with linear-relief and nail-impressed pottery*

Site	[14]C age (bp ± 1σ)	cal BP (1σ range)[1]	Lab. no.
Fukui Cave, Layer III (linear-relief pottery)	12,700 ± 500	15,850–14,250	GaK-950
Kamikuroiwa, Layer 9 (linear-relief pottery)	12,165 ± 600	15,350–13,450	I-944
Torihama (84T, Layer 66) (linear-relief pottery)	11,830 ± 55	14,060–13,780 (53 percent) 13,700–13,590 (15 percent)	KSU-1028
Torihama (84T, Layer 66) (linear-relief pottery)	11,800 ± 55	14,050–13,500	KSU-1029
Fukui Cave, Layer II (nail-impressed pottery)	12,400 ± 350	15,350–14,050	GaK-949
Torihama (84T, Layer 62) (nail-impressed pottery)	10,770 ± 160	13,050–12,600 (65 percent) 12,500–12,400 (3 percent)	KSU-1027
Torihama (84T, Layer 86) (nail-impressed pottery)	10,290 ± 45		KSU-1017

Note: [1] Dates were calibrated using the OxCAL program and the calibration curve of Stuiver et al. 1998a.
Sources: Compiled from Fukui-ken Kyoiku Iinkai 1985; N. Watanabe 1966.

forty-six potsherds were recovered from Layers III and IV of the site. Table 2.2 lists radiocarbon dates obtained from these layers. As shown in the table, all five samples of adhesions on pottery returned dates giving ages of approximately 13,800–12,700 bp (ca. 16,500–14,900 cal BP).

Figure 2.2 (upper) shows potsherds from Layers III and IV of the Odai Yamamoto I site. The majority of these potsherds are plain pottery with no decoration. Although some of them have fine incised lines, it is more likely that these lines are not meant as decoration but are simply unintentional scratches made by the potter when he or she was smoothing the surface of the pot (Taniguchi 1999b). According to Taniguchi (1999c), who was the principal investigator of the excavation, these potsherds are associated with the so-called Chojakubo type of lithic tools, which is characterized by an abundance of end-scrapers and burins. The presence of two triangular points (fig. 2.2; lower), possibly used as arrowheads, also attracted researchers' attention, since arrowheads are considered to be characteristic of the Jomon culture, not the Palaeolithic culture (Ikawa-Smith 2000).

The discovery at the Odai Yamamoto I site has several implications for the study of the beginning of the Jomon period. First, it answers at least some of the questions that Japanese archaeologists have long been

Table 2.2 *Radiocarbon dates from the Odai Yamamoto I site*

Sample	Material	Stratum	^{14}C age (bp ± 1σ)	cal BP (1σ range)[1]	Lab. no.
F5–017	adhesion	IV	13,780 ± 170	16,850–16,200	NUTA-6510
E5–100	charred wood (conifer)	III	13,480 ± 70	16,450–15,940	Beta-125550 (RH-130)
D4–005	adhesion	III	13,210 ± 160	16,250–15,500	NUTA-6515
E4–036	adhesion	III lower	13,030 ± 170	16,100–15,250	NUTA-6507
E4–030	adhesion	III bottom	12,720 ± 160	15,650–15,050 BP (33 percent) 14,850–14,350 BP (35 percent)	NUTA-6509
E4–048	adhesion	IV top	12,680 ± 140	15,650–15,150 BP (28 percent) 14,850–14,250 BP (40 percent)	NUTA-6506
E5–011	charred wood (*Acer* sp.)	III	7710 ± 40	8540–8420	Beta-125551 (RH-131)
E2–100	charred wood (*Cephalotaxus harringtonia*)	III	7070 ± 40	7945–7840	Beta-127791 (RH-148)

Note: [1] Dates were calibrated using the OxCAL program and the calibration curve of Stuiver et al. 1998a.
Source: Nakamura and Tsuji 1999.

Figure 2.2 Potsherds (upper; scale = 2/3) and arrowheads (lower; scale = 1/1) recovered from Layers III and IV of the Odai Yamamoto I site (photographs by courtesy of Odai Yamamoto I Iseki Hakkutsu Chosa-dan [Excavation Team of the Odai Yamamoto I site])

pursuing in relation to the identification of the oldest Jomon pottery. Even though, until the mid-1990s, pottery from Layer III of the Fukui Cave was the oldest Jomon pottery with a reliable radiocarbon date, many scholars had suspected that potsherds excavated from several other sites might have been older than the Fukui Cave example. These include potsherds with "punctuated" designs from the Terao site in Kanagawa Prefecture

(Shiraishi 1980), and "plain pottery" (i.e., potsherds with no decoration) recovered at such sites as Odai Yamamoto I in Aomori Prefecture (T. Miyake 1977; 1979), Ushirono in Ibaraki Prefecture (Ushirono Iseki Chosa-dan 1976), Higashi-Rokugo 2 in Hokkaido (Sugiura 1987), and Kamino in Kanagawa Prefecture (Aida and Koike 1986). It should be noted that, although the latter group of pottery is called "plain pottery," it is not known if the pots actually had no decoration, or if the potsherds that were recovered happened to be the plain parts of decorated pots. The latter possibility is substantiated by the fact that the recovered potsherds were small fragments. Stratigraphic observations and typological analyses of associated lithic assemblages at these sites, as well as observations at several other sites with similar lithic tools, led many scholars to believe that pottery at these sites is older than linear-relief pottery. Unfortunately, however, none of these sites had radiocarbon dates. As a consequence, the debate on the oldest Jomon pottery did not make much progress for a long time. Pottery and radiocarbon dates from the Odai Yamamoto I site finally confirmed this long-unanswered question about the chronological placement of "plain pottery."

Second, the discovery at the Odai Yamamoto I site stimulated debates on the origins of Jomon pottery. After the discovery of the linear-relief pottery at Fukui Cave, some scholars suggested that Jomon pottery was invented within the Japanese archipelago (e.g., statements made by Kato and Aso in T. Kobayashi et al. 1980; Miyashita 1980). However, the majority of Japanese scholars believed, and still believe, that pottery production was first invented in mainland Asia and subsequently introduced into the Japanese archipelago (e.g., T. Kobayashi et al. 1980). Behind this assumption is the strong influence of a well-known archaeologist, Sugao Yamanouchi, who suggested that pottery was first invented in continental Asia and later diffused to the Japanese archipelago (Yamanouchi and Sato 1962; for Yamanouchi's hypothesis about the origins of Jomon pottery and its absolute dates, see K. Imamura 1996: chapter 4).

Key to solving the question of the origins of Jomon pottery is the development of early pottery in the Russian Far East and China. A series of excavations in the Amur River Basin in the 1980s and 1990s revealed that pottery in this region may be as old as, if not older than, Fukui Cave pottery (Kajiwara 1995; 1998). As shown in table 2.3, at least five sites (Khummi, Gasya, Gromatukha, Ust'Karenga, and Goncharuka) in the Amur River region have pottery associated with radiocarbon dates older than 10,000 bp (for the locations of these sites, see fig. 2.3). Among these, the oldest one is pottery from the Khummi site, which is dated to 13,260 ± 100 bp (AA-13392) (1σ: 16,250–15,600 cal BP) on the basis of the oldest associated radiocarbon date. This date is followed by pottery

Table 2.3 *Radiocarbon dates from six sites in the Amur River Basin and the Transbikal region associated with pottery*

Site	^{14}C age (bp ± 1σ)	cal BP[1] (1σ range)	Lab. no.	Materials	References
Khummi, lower layer	13,260 ± 100	16,250–15,600	AA-13392	charcoal	Kuzmin et al. 1997
Khummi, lower layer	10,345 ± 110	12,650–12,450 (15 percent) 12,400–11,900 (51 percent) 11,800–11,750 (2 percent)	AA-13391	charcoal	Kuzmin et al. 1997
Gasya, lower layer	12,960 ± 120	16,000–15,150	LE-1781	charcoal	Kuzmin et al. 1997
Gasya, lower layer	10,875 ± 90	13,110–13,090 (2 percent) 13,030–12,820 (61 percent) 12,710–12,680 (5 percent)	AA-13393	charcoal	Kuzmin et al. 1997
Gromatukha, lower layer	13,310 ± 110	16,300–15,700	AA-20940	organic temper	Kuzmin and Keally 2001
Gromatukha, lower layer	13,240 ± 85	16,200–15,600	AA-20939	organic temper	Kuzmin and Keally 2001
Gromatukha, lower layer	12,340 ± 60	15,050–14,600 (30 percent) 14,450–14,100 (38 percent)	AA-36079	charcoal	Kuzmin and Keally 2001
Gromatukha, lower layer	9,895 ± 50	11,340–11,320 (6 percent) 11,310–11,200 (62 percent)	AA-36447	charcoal	Kuzmin and Keally 2001
Novopetrovka	9,765 ± 70	11,240–11,110	AA-20937	organic temper	Kuzmin and Keally 2001
Ust'Karenga, layer 7	11,240 ± 180	13,430–13,020	GIN-8066	charcoal	Kuzmin and Keally 2001
Ust'Karenga, layer 7	11,065 ± 70	13,160–12,970	AA-38101	organic temper	Kuzmin and Keally 2001
Goncharuka 1	12,500 ± 60	15,350–15,150 (10 percent) 14,950–14,250 (58 percent)	LLNL-102169	charcoal	Kuzmin and Keally 2001
Goncharuka 1	10,590 ± 60	12,850–12,710 (29 percent) 12,670–12,610 (11 percent) 12,490–12,360 (28 percent)	LLNL-102168	charcoal	Kuzmin and Keally 2001

Note: [1] Dates were calibrated using the OxCAL program and the calibration curve of Stuiver et al. 1998a.

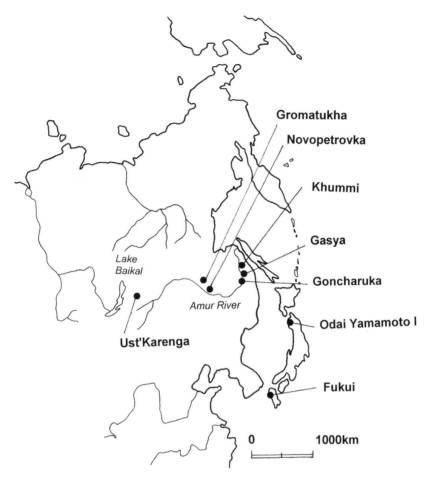

Figure 2.3   Russian Far East sites with pottery dated to older than 10,000 bp (modified and redrawn from Medvedev 1994: 14–15)

from the Gasya site, which is associated with a radiocarbon date of 12,960 ± 120 bp (LE-1781) (1σ: 16,000–15,150 cal BP) (Zhushchikhovskaya 1997). The presence of early pottery in this region, as well as similarities in lithic assemblages between the Amur River Basin and the northern part of the Japanese archipelago, seems to indicate that the origin of Jomon pottery is closely related to the pottery tradition in northeastern Eurasia. The discovery at Odai Yamamoto I in northern Honshu will further stimulate the debate on the introduction of pottery into the Japanese archipelago via northerly routes (e.g., Taniguchi 1999b). This does not necessarily imply, however, that pottery was first invented in the Amur River Basin.

For example, Kajiwara (1998) suggests that, because of the technological sophistication of pottery in the Amur River region, it is more likely that the origin of pottery production can be traced back before 13,000 bp (ca. 15,500 cal BP), probably to South China.

In terms of early pottery in China, radiocarbon dates from Nanzhuangtou, located at Xushui in Hebei Province along the Yellow River in North China (Baoding Diqu Wenwu Guanlisuo et al. 1992), and Xianren Cave (Xianrendong), located at Wannian in Jiangxi Province in the middle reaches of the Yangzi River (Jiangxi Sheng Wenwu Guanli Weiyuanhui 1963; Jiangxi Bowuguan 1976), are attracting researchers' attention (e.g., Ikawa-Smith 2000). The oldest of the seven radiocarbon dates from Nanzhuangtou accepted by the investigator (Ikawa-Smith 2000) is 10,815 ± 140 bp (1σ: 13,020–12,790 cal BP [51 percent], 12,750–12,640 cal BP [17 percent]). Pottery from Xianrendong, which was first excavated in the early 1960s, was associated with two radiocarbon dates, 8825 ± 240 bp (Zk-92; bone fragment) (1σ: 10,200–9600 cal BP) from the lower layer, and 10,870 ± 240 bp (Zk-39; shell fragment) (1σ: 12,850–11,650 cal BP) from the upper layer. Since the younger date was obtained from the lower layer, these dates were received with much skepticism. Subsequent excavations of the site, however, revealed that the site actually might be associated with pottery older than 10,000 bp (ca. 11,600 cal BP) (see Ikawa-Smith 2000). Sagawa (1998) also points out the presence of pottery at several sites in China that can be dated to 13,000–10,000 bp (ca. 15,500–11,600 cal BP). These sites include Yujiagou (Henan Province) along the Yellow River, Yuchandong (Hunan Province) in the middle reaches of the Yangzi River, and Dingshishan in Guangxi Province, South China. Based on the wide distribution of pottery dated to before 10,000 bp throughout China, Sagawa (1998) believes that, in the future, pottery dated to 13,000–10,000 bp will be found in Inner Mongolia as well as in northeast China.

Finally, the discovery at the Odai Yamamoto I site has stimulated debates on the transition from Palaeolithic to Jomon. Traditionally, Japanese archaeologists explained various subsistence–settlement changes that occurred in this transitional period as a result of warming trends at the end of "the Ice Age." They assumed that the beginning of the Jomon period roughly coincided with the end of the Pleistocene. Because the radiocarbon date for Fukui Cave was obtained in the 1960s, when the calibration of radiocarbon dates was not practiced, the radiocarbon date 12,700 bp was roughly equated with the calendar date 10,000–11,000 BC. Reluctance to incorporate radiocarbon dates actively into Jomon chronology during the 1970s and 1980s resulted in an unwillingness to use the calibrated date for Fukui Cave until the mid-1990s. The Odai Yamamoto I discovery, however, gave Japanese archaeologists a chance to reevaluate the antiquity of pottery production in the Japanese archipelago. Taniguchi (1999b) suggests that, if the pottery from Odai Yamamoto I goes back to 16,500 years ago as suggested by the calibrated date, it implies that the earliest pottery production on the Japanese archipelago occurred prior to the beginning of the warming trend in the late glacial period. Citing a wide range of radiocarbon dates associated with early pottery from eastern Russia, China, and the Japanese archipelago, Ikawa-Smith (2000: 7) also suggests that "the initial use of pottery in eastern Asia appears to have begun in the context of sudden climatic oscillation of the Final Pleistocene," and not in the context of "'gradual warming trend' that brought about 'the northward expansion of the broad-leaf forest'" as traditionally believed (see also below).

BOX 3: *Oldest Jomon pottery and terminal Palaeolithic chronology*

The quest for the oldest Jomon pottery is closely related to the study of terminal Palaeolithic stone tool assemblages. In Kyushu, microblades characterize both the last phase of the Palaeolithic period and the first two phases of the Jomon period (i.e., phases associated with linear-relief and nail-impressed pottery). Researchers believe that these microblades were primarily used as composite tools to make spear points for hunting (e.g., Serizawa 1974). On the other hand, in Honshu and Shikoku, microblades seem to have disappeared before the end of the Palaeolithic period. Linear-relief pottery in these areas is associated with tanged bifacial points (*yuzetsu-sento-ki*), not with microblades. Furthermore, researchers have suggested the so-called Mikoshiba/Chojakubo phase was present between the microblade phase and the linear-relief pottery phase in central and northern Honshu. The name comes from two sites, the Mikoshiba site in Nagano Prefecture (Fujisawa and Hayashi 1961), and the Chojakubo site in Aomori Prefecture (Yamanouchi and Sato 1967). Lithic assemblages from this phase are typically characterized by the presence of edge-ground adzes (called "Mikoshiba-type" adzes) and large spear points as well as by an abundance of such stone tools as end-scrapers and burins.

Assuming that linear-relief pottery began to be used at roughly the same time throughout the Japanese archipelago, it is likely that microblades disappeared in Hokkaido and northern and central Honshu earlier than in Kyushu. Since very few radiocarbon dates have been obtained from the terminal Palaeolithic period and the beginning of the Jomon period, chronological placement of sites from this transitional period is heavily reliant on typological chronology of lithic tools. A number of sites, which are not associated with radiocarbon dates, have been ascribed to the Mikoshiba/Chojakubo phase on the basis of lithic assemblage characteristics. In some cases, lithic assemblage characteristics are also used to verify the reliability of radiocarbon dates. For example, Cultural Layer II of the Shimomouchi site in Nagano Prefecture (N. Kondo et al. 1992), which included bifacial points and three small pottery-like fragments, is associated with an AMS (accelerator mass spectrometry) radiocarbon date of $16,250 \pm 180$ bp (1σ: 19,750–19,000 cal BP). However, Taniguchi (1999b) suggests that, because the type of bifacial points recovered

BOX 3: (*cont.*)

from the site should be chronologically placed after microblades, and because the oldest microblade assemblage in Honshu is dated no older than 15,000 bp (ca. 18,000 cal BP), the old radiocarbon date at Shimomouchi is not reliable. Some researchers also question whether the fragments were really potsherds (e.g., Taniguchi 1999b). Because the evidence is so questionable, not many Japanese scholars accept the date from Shimomouchi as the oldest pottery in the Japanese archipelago.

Chronological framework

The discovery at the Odai Yamamoto I site also stimulated debates on the reevaluation of radiocarbon dates for the Jomon period. For a long time, Japanese archaeologists' reluctance actively to use radiocarbon dates has puzzled many English-speaking archaeologists. This may be particularly intriguing given the fact that radiocarbon dates from Jomon sites obtained in the 1960s and 1970s corresponded well to the relative chronological sequence of Jomon pottery (N. Watanabe 1966; Masao Suzuki 1974a; see fig. 2.4). As a result, by the 1970s most Japanese archaeologists accepted the usefulness of the radiocarbon dating technique, with the exception of Yamanouchi (1968; 1969), Yamanouchi and Sato (1962), and their supporters (for details of this controversy, see K. Imamura 1996: 46–50). Nevertheless, there has still been no systematic use of radiocarbon dates in Jomon archaeology. This is primarily because the typological chronology of Jomon pottery is extremely fine-grained. Because of this detailed typological chronology, during the 1970s, when the total error of the radiocarbon date was relatively high (particularly when the two-sigma ranges of radiocarbon dates were often more than two hundred years), Japanese archaeologists felt that radiocarbon dates were not as useful as pottery typology for the chronological placement of archaeological data.

The skepticism about radiocarbon dates continued to dominate the field of Jomon archaeology from the 1980s to the early 1990s. During this time period, however, the errors in radiocarbon dating were considerably reduced. Also during this time period, calibration of radiocarbon dates became quite common in Western archaeology. However, neither of these developments was adopted by Japanese archaeologists. As a result, before the mid-1990s, the majority of Japanese archaeologists did not pay close attention to the progress of radiocarbon dating technology. Until a few years ago, even the use of calibrated dates was not common.

As a result of this delay in adopting new radiocarbon technologies, the primary chronological framework for Jomon studies is still heavily reliant on pottery typology. Figure 2.5 shows major chronological divisions of

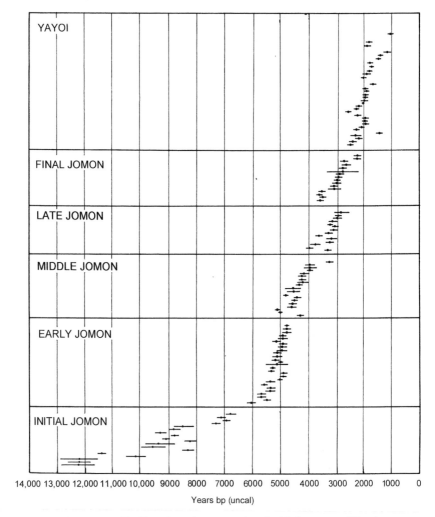

Figure 2.4 Radiocarbon dates associated with Jomon and Yayoi pottery
obtained during the 1960s and early 1970s (modified and redrawn from
N. Watanabe in Masao Suzuki 1974a: 155)

the Jomon period suggested by Abiko (1978) and T. Kobayashi (1977b)
(see also Kobayashi 1992a). As shown in this table, the Jomon period is
conventionally divided into six subperiods: Incipient, Initial, Early, Middle, Late, and Final Jomon periods (Yamanouchi 1964a). Each subperiod
is further divided into several phases (not all the phases are represented
in fig. 2.5), each of which includes several subphases (not shown in

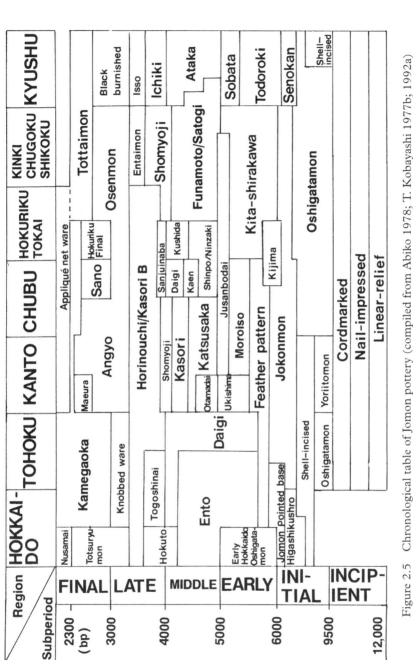

Figure 2.5   Chronological table of Jomon pottery (compiled from Abiko 1978; T. Kobayashi 1977b; 1992a)

fig. 2.5). The majority of Japanese archaeologists use the subphase as the smallest time unit for examining various cultural changes over time.

The absolute dates for the six subperiods had been estimated using only a limited number of radiocarbon dates from Jomon sites. For example, Keally and Muto (1982) indicate that, in eastern Japan, especially in the Hokkaido, Tohoku, and Kanto regions, radiocarbon dates for each of the six subperiods are internally consistent (fig. 2.6). However, there seems to be some discrepancy between Kyushu and eastern Japan in terms of the dates for the Early to Final Jomon periods (see fig. 2.6). Table 2.4 shows radiocarbon dates for the subperiods in four regions of Japan as suggested by Keally and Muto (1982). Because the number of radiocarbon dates from the Kinki, Chugoku, Shikoku, Tokai, and Chubu regions was relatively small, Keally and Muto (1982) did not suggest absolute dates for each subperiod in these regions.

It should be noted here that these estimates are based on radiocarbon dates obtained during the 1960s to the early 1980s, when the one-sigma range of radiocarbon dates was usually more than 100 years. Furthermore, some of the radiocarbon dates were obtained from marine shells excavated from shell-middens. Because of the reservoir effect, radiocarbon dates from marine products, such as shells, tend to be approximately 400–500 years older than those of terrestrial products (M. Imamura 1999; Yoshida et al. 2000). In other words, the traditional estimates are based on radiocarbon dates that include errors of one to several hundred years. Given the fact that regional variability in the reservoir effect has been reported (Hall, personal communication, 2002), the errors may be even larger.

Recently, however, the number of reliable radiocarbon dates has increased rapidly. For example, on the basis of twenty-four AMS radiocarbon dates from the Sannai Maruyama site in Aomori Prefecture, M. Imamura (1999) and Tsuji (1999) indicate that the site was occupied from approximately 5050 to 3900 bp (ca. 5900 to 4400 cal BP) (for details, see chapter 4 of this book). Comparisons between these AMS dates and chronological placement of associated pottery indicate that the relative sequences of these two sets of data are consistent with each other. Accumulation of these kinds of data will lead to more precise estimates of the duration of each Jomon subperiod, and, eventually, will allow us to determine the duration of each typological phase and/or subphase. Papers presented by T. Nakamura et al. (2000), Okuno and T. Nakamura (2000), and K. Yoshida et al. (2000) at the "Dating and Archaeology" symposium at the 17th Annual Meeting of the Japanese Society for Scientific Studies on Cultural Properties outline the current status and technical constraints of radiocarbon dating in Japanese archaeology. The

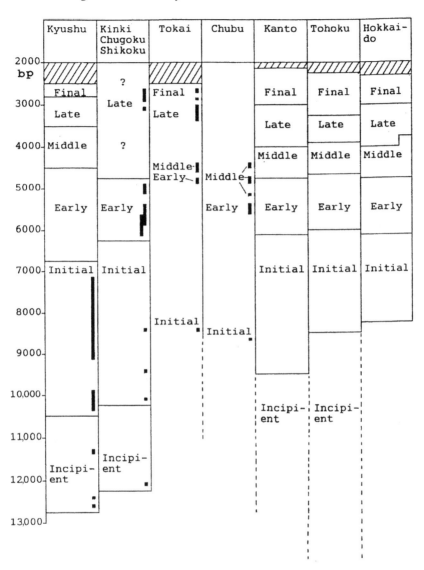

Figure 2.6   Comparison of radiocarbon dates from seven regions (modified and redrawn from Keally and Muto 1982: 252). Thick lines indicate
that radiocarbon dates from the period are only intermittently available.

Table 2.4 *Radiocarbon dates (bp) for Hokkaido, Tohoku, Kanto, and Kyushu suggested by Keally and Muto (1982)*

	Hokkaido	Tohoku	Kanto	Kyushu
Incipient				12,800–10,500
Initial	–6100	–6000	9500–6100	10,500–6900
Early	6100–4800	6000–4600	6100–4700	6900–4500
Middle	5100–4050	4600–4000	4800–4050	4500–3500
Late	4050–3000	4000–3250	4050–3050	3500–2700
Final	3000–2400	3250–2250	3050–2100	2700–2550

presenters also made useful suggestions toward the construction of an absolute Jomon chronology with high precision (repeatability) and accuracy.

Environment and climate

As discussed above, the oldest pottery from the Odai Yamamoto I site is currently dated to approximately 16,500 cal BP (ca. 14,500 BC). In the context of global climatic changes, this period can be placed toward the end of the late glacial maximum (fig. 2.7). On the basis of Greenland ice core data, it has been suggested that repeated climatic oscillation occurred between this period and the end of the Pleistocene: the Oldest Dryas (cold), Bølling (warm), Older Dryas (cold), Allerød (warm), and Younger Dryas (cold) (Stuiver et al. 1995; see also Sherratt 1997). While we do not know the full impact of this sequence of events on the Japanese archipelago, it is reasonable to assume a similar oscillation in climate. Following this rapid climatic oscillation, the first half of the Holocene was characterized by a continuous warming trend.

Along with these climatic changes, various environmental changes occurred from the Late Pleistocene to Holocene. For example, on the basis of pollen analyses, Tsukada (1986) defines seven major pollen zones from the Late Pleistocene to the present: Zones LI, LII, RIa, RIb, RII, RIIIa, and RIIIb (fig. 2.8). Of these, Zones RIa and RIb represent the warming trends, or the transition from the Final Pleistocene to the warmest part of the mid-postglacial period. These zones roughly correspond to the Initial Jomon period. The following Zone RII, which overlaps with the Early and Middle Jomon periods, represents the so-called hypsithermal interval or the "Climatic Optimum," the warmest part of the postglacial period (H. Suzuki 1974). Finally, Zone RIIIa, which

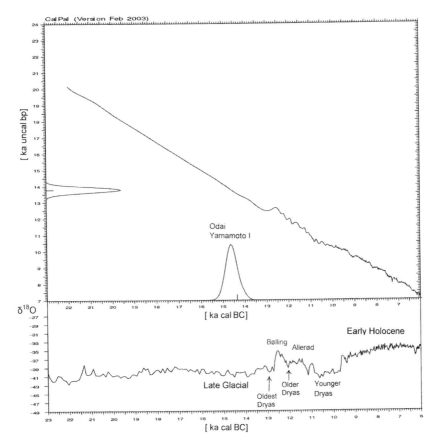

Figure 2.7   Calibration of the oldest ^{14}C date from the Odai Yamamoto I site (NUTA6510) using INTCAL 98 (Stuiver et al. 1995) (upper), and temperature fluctuations as reflected in annual ice accumulation rates in the GISP 2 ice core (lower). The diagram was created using the CalPal for Windows (Weninger et al. 2002), with oxygen isotope data from Grootes et al. 1993; Meese et al. 1994; Stuiver et al. 1995; Stuiver and Grootes 2000; Sowers et al. 1993 (these data are available from: http://www.ngdc.noaa.gov/paleo/ftp-icecore.html).

represents a cooling trend or neoglaciation, corresponds to the Late/Final Jomon, the Yayoi and part of the Kofun periods.

According to Tsukada (1986), at the time of the last glacial maximum (ca. 20,000 bp), the four main Japanese islands, as well as many other smaller islands in the Seto Inland Sea and the coastal region, were linked. The present-day Soya Strait in the north was a land bridge connected to

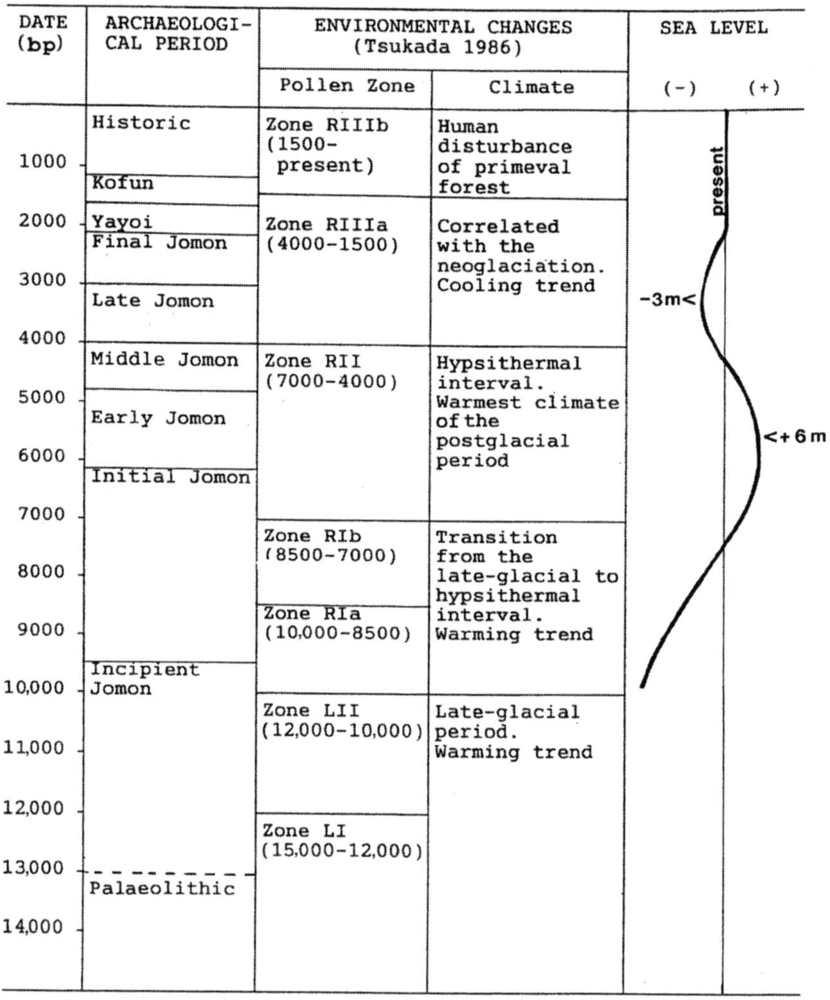

DATE (bp)	ARCHAEOLOGI-CAL PERIOD	ENVIRONMENTAL CHANGES (Tsukada 1986)		SEA LEVEL	
		Pollen Zone	Climate	(−)	(+)
1000	Historic	Zone RIIIb (1500-present)	Human disturbance of primeval forest	present	
	Kofun				
2000	Yayoi	Zone RIIIa (4000-1500)	Correlated with the neoglaciation. Cooling trend		
	Final Jomon				
3000					
	Late Jomon			−3m<	
4000					
	Middle Jomon	Zone RII (7000-4000)	Hypsithermal interval. Warmest climate of the postglacial period		
5000					
	Early Jomon				<+6 m
6000					
	Initial Jomon				
7000					
		Zone RIb (8500-7000)	Transition from the late-glacial to hypsithermal interval. Warming trend		
8000					
9000		Zone RIa (10,000-8500)			
	Incipient Jomon				
10,000		Zone LII (12,000-10,000)	Late-glacial period. Warming trend		
11,000					
12,000					
		Zone LI (15,000-12,000)			
13,000					
	Palaeolithic				
14,000					

Figure 2.8   Summary of environmental changes suggested by Tsukada (1986), and estimated sea-level changes (modified from Habu 2001: 15)

Sakhalin. During this period, most of the Japanese archipelago was covered by a boreal conifer forest and a temperate conifer forest/deciduous broadleaf forest. On the other hand, the vegetation of the Early and Middle Jomon periods was dominated by the warm-temperate deciduous forest and the evergreen broadleaf forest (also called the luciphyllous forest). These changes in vegetation not only increased the types of edible plant food, including various kinds of nuts, but they also significantly altered the habitats of terrestrial mammals. While archaeologists are still debating whether the disappearance of such large terrestrial mammals as Naumann's elephant (*Palaeoloxodon naumanni*) and Yabe's giant deer (*Sinomegaceros yabei*) during the Late Pleistocene was a result of overkill or environmental change, it is clear that, by the beginning of the Holocene, middle-sized mammals, such as sika deer (*Cervus nippon*) and boar (*Sus scrofa*), were the most commonly hunted terrestrial mammals (Harunari 1998; 2000).

The global climatic changes from the terminal Pleistocene to the Holocene also affected the sea level. Numerous studies on Holocene sea-level changes in the Japanese archipelago, however, indicate that estimating the Jomon period sea level in comparison with the present-day sea level is not easy (Stewart 1982). This is partly because isostatic changes in various parts of the Japanese archipelago were quite complex. Nevertheless, many Japanese scholars agree that the sea level reached its maximum during the "Climatic Optimum." According to Izeki (1977), for example, the sea level of the Japanese archipelago around 10,000 bp (ca. 11,600 cal BP) was approximately 20–30 meters lower than at present. The sea level continued to rise with minor oscillations during the first half of the Holocene, reaching its maximum around 6500–5000 bp (ca. 7400–5900 cal BP). This is called the Holocene or Jomon Transgression (Matsushima 1979). Ota et al. (1982) suggest that, although regional variability in the sea level caused by isostatic changes was significant, the sea level at the culmination of the Jomon Transgression was approximately 2 to 6 meters higher than at present (see also Wajima et al. 1968). After the culmination of the transgression, the coastline seems to have retreated gradually. Several lines of evidence indicate that, between 4000 and 2000 bp (ca. 4500–2000 BP), the sea level receded to 1 to 3 meters below its present level at least in some parts of the Japanese archipelago (e.g., Umitsu 1976; Toyoshima 1978).

While many researchers have argued that the sea level reached its highest point during the "Climatic Optimum," the exact timing of the maximum transgression has yet to be determined. Results of analyses of littoral molluskan collections in the southwestern Kanto region (Matsushima 1979; Matsushima and Koike 1979) indicate that the sea level reached its maximum between 6500 and 5500 bp (ca. 7400–6300 cal BP) in this region. More specifically, Fuji (1984) states that sea levels reached their maximum during the Kurohama phase (ca. 5700 bp or 6600 cal BP), the third of the five chronological phases of the Early Jomon period in the region. It should be kept in mind, however, that regional differences in isostatic changes would have affected the timing of the maximum sea level differently in each region.

Population estimates

For many scholars acquainted with the English-language literature of Japanese archaeology, the study of Jomon population estimates is a familiar field. This is because Koyama's (1978) seminal work on Jomon subsistence and population is widely read as a basic information source for Jomon archaeology. In fact, however, relatively little work has been conducted in this research field. Apart from Koyama, only two other archaeologists, Serizawa (1960) and Yamanouchi (1964a), have attempted to estimate the total Jomon population. Both scholars used population densities of ethnographic hunter-gatherer groups as a point of departure to estimate Jomon population.

Using figures for the population density estimates of the Ainu people in Hokkaido after the 1889 census, Serizawa (1960) estimated the Jomon population of Honshu to have been approximately 75,000 people, and the total Jomon population of the Japanese archipelago at about 120,000. On the other hand, Yamanouchi (1964a), who pointed out that the size of the Japanese archipelago is approximately the same as that of California, suggested that the size of the Jomon population might have been about the same as the population of the native Californians. Using Baumhoff's (1963) study of the native population in California, Yamanouchi estimated the Jomon population size to have been between 150,000 and 250,000.

Unlike the estimates presented by these two scholars, Koyama (1978; 1984) based his study on the following three sets of data: (1) the total number of Jomon sites recorded in the site database and site maps of each prefecture of Japan, (2) the total number of sites of the Haji period (usually called the Kofun, Nara, and Heian periods, ca. AD 250–1150) recorded in the site database and site maps of prefectures in the Kanto region, and (3) the eighth-century population record of the Kanto region.

Koyama's (1978; 1984) analysis was based on several assumptions. First, he assumed that each of the Initial, Early, Middle, Late, and Final Jomon periods lasted for approximately 1,000 years. This implies that the duration of each of these Jomon subperiods was roughly equal to that of the Haji period (from 250 to 1150 AD; allowing for a slight margin of error, approximately 1,000 years). Second, he assumed that the discovery rates of Jomon and Haji sites are approximately the same. Third, on the basis of these two assumptions, he suggested that, if the average settlement population of each Jomon subperiod and that of the Haji period were approximately equal, then the ratio between the total number of Haji sites and the estimated Haji population at any given time (in this case, the eighth century) should be about the same as the ratio between the number of Jomon sites from one subperiod and the population of the subperiod. However, archaeological data seem to indicate that the average number of pit-dwellings per site is much greater in Haji settlements than in Jomon settlements. After examining site size based on the number of associated pit-dwellings, Koyama estimated that the size of Early, Middle, and Late Jomon settlements was approximately 1/7 of that of Haji settlements. For Initial Jomon, Koyama used the constant of 1/20 instead of 1/7, since the average size of Initial Jomon settlements is much smaller than that of Early to Late Jomon ones.

Following these assumptions, he suggested that the Middle Jomon population in the Kanto region could be estimated using the following formula:

$$POP_{j3} = 1/7 \times T_{j3}(POP_{8c}/T_h)$$

where POP_{j3} = Middle Jomon population in the Kanto region,
   T_{j3} = total number of Middle Jomon sites in the Kanto region,
   POP_{8c} = eighth-century population in the Kanto region,
   T_h = total number of Haji sites in the Kanto region.

Using similar formulae, Koyama (1978) estimated the population of the Initial to Late Jomon periods in the Kanto region. The population of other areas was calculated using the ratio of the number of sites in that region to the number of sites in the Kanto region. He also estimated the population of the Yayoi period using the constant of 1/3. In his later work published in Japanese (Koyama 1984), Koyama added population estimates for the Final Jomon period. Neither of his publications included estimates of the Incipient Jomon.

Table 2.5 lists the population estimates presented by Koyama (1984). The population estimate for each Jomon subperiod indicates that the Jomon population increased steadily in the first half of the Jomon period. By the Middle Jomon period, the population was approximately 260,000. It then declined through the Late and Final Jomon periods. This trend is particularly characteristic of the Kanto and Chubu regions in central Honshu. Similar trends are noticeable in the Tohoku, Hokuriku, and Tokai regions, although the population decline in the Late and the Final Jomon periods in these regions is not as dramatic. In contrast, the population in western Japan (Kinki, Chugoku, Shikoku, and Kyushu regions) increased slowly and gradually from the Initial to Late Jomon period.

Table 2.5 *Population estimates by Koyama (1984) (numbers in parentheses indicate population density per km^2)*

	Initial Jomon	Early Jomon	Middle Jomon	Late Jomon	Final Jomon	Yayoi	Haji
Tohoku	2,000 (0.03)	19,200 (0.29)	46,700 (0.70)	43,800 (0.65)	39,500 (0.59)	33,400 (0.50)	288,600 (4.31)
Kanto	9,700 (0.30)	42,800 (1.34)	95,400 (2.98)	51,600 (1.61)	7,700 (0.24)	99,000 (3.09)	943,300 (29.48)
Hokuriku	400 (0.02)	4,200 (0.17)	24,600 (0.98)	15,700 (0.63)	5,100 (0.20)	20,700 (0.83)	491,800 (19.67)
Chubu	3,000 (0.10)	25,300 (0.84)	71,900 (2.40)	22,000 (0.73)	6,000 (0.20)	84,200 (2.81)	289,700 (9.66)
Tokai	2,200 (0.16)	5,000 (0.36)	13,200 (0.94)	7,600 (0.54)	6,600 (0.47)	55,300 (3.95)	298,700 (21.34)
Kinki	300 (0.01)	1,700 (0.05)	2,800 (0.09)	4,400 (0.14)	2,100 (0.07)	108,300 (3.38)	1,217,300 (38.04)
Chugoku	400 (0.01)	1,300 (0.04)	1,200 (0.04)	2,400 (0.07)	2,000 (0.06)	58,800 (1.84)	839,400 (26.23)
Shikoku	200 (0.01)	400 (0.02)	200 (0.01)	2,700 (0.14)	500 (0.03)	30,100 (1.58)	320,600 (16.87)
Kyushu	1,900 (0.05)	5,600 (0.13)	5,300 (0.13)	10100 (0.24)	6,300 (0.15)	105,100 (2.50)	710,400 (16.91)
Total	20,100 (0.07)	105,500 (0.36)	261,300 (0.89)	160,300 (0.55)	75,800 (0.26)	594,900 (2.02)	5,399,800 (18.37)

The total estimated population in western Japan is much smaller than that in eastern Japan, since the number of Jomon sites in western Japan is smaller than that in eastern Japan.

The strength of Koyama's (1978; 1984) method is that, rather than estimating the total number of simultaneously occupied sites and multiplying the number by the average site population, he used the ratio of the total number of recovered sites to a past population estimate. Estimating the total number of simultaneously occupied sites is extremely difficult for two reasons. First, as Yamanouchi (1964a) suggested, fine-grained surveys will increase the total number of recovered sites in each area. Second, because of the nature of archaeological dating, it is not possible to identify exactly which sites were simultaneously occupied; i.e., not all the sites from a specific subperiod (e.g., Middle Jomon), or even from a specific phase, are necessarily contemporaneous. By using the ratio of the number of recovered sites to population, Koyama was able to avoid these methodological problems.

It should be noted, however, that the constant 1/7 that Koyama (1978; 1984) used for his population estimates can be questioned. He regarded Jomon sites with many pit-dwellings, such as the Takanekido site in Chiba Prefecture, as typical of the Early to Late Jomon periods. However, in terms of the number of associated pit-dwellings, only a small number of Jomon settlements are as large as Takanekido. In other words, if populations are calculated using the average number of pit-dwellings per site for both Jomon and Haji sites, then the population estimates for the Jomon period will be much smaller.

Koyama's (1978; 1984) estimates are also based on the assumption that the degree of sedentism of the Jomon people was approximately the same as for the people of the Haji period (i.e., both were fully sedentary). However, as I shall indicate later in this book, it is more likely that the degree of Jomon sedentism varied considerably both regionally and temporally. If at least some of the Jomon people moved their residential bases seasonally, then the total number of Jomon settlements, on which Koyama's calculations were based, would include temporary occupation sites. This also implies that Koyama's Jomon population estimates may be too large.

Despite such caveats, many scholars suggest that Koyama's (1978; 1984) estimates generally reflect relative increases and decreases in the Jomon population over time. Koizumi (1985), for example, agrees with Koyama, and summarizes Koyama's results in the following:

[G]enerally speaking, Jomon population in eastern Japan increased gradually from the Initial to the Middle Jomon periods. The population increase stagnated in the Late Jomon period, and a significant population decrease occurred in the Final Jomon period. On the other hand, in western Japan, population increased slowly and gradually throughout the Jomon period. With the advent of the Yayoi culture associated with rice cultivation and other new cultural elements, the population of the Japanese archipelago increased dramatically. (Koizumi 1985: 231)

In Anglo-American archaeology, the issues of population increase and resulting population pressure have been discussed frequently in relation to the development of cultural complexity and changes in subsistence strategies (e.g., Price and Brown 1985a). Whether population increases naturally (i.e., with no specific causes or conditions) or not has also been a topic of archaeological debate (e.g., Cohen 1981). While very few Japanese scholars have discussed these issues in relation to Jomon population estimates, they remain key questions in any examination of the course of the development of the Jomon culture. I will address these issues later in this book.

Physical anthropological studies

Physical anthropological studies of human skeletal remains from the Jomon period are an important source of information for understanding the relationships between the people of the Jomon period and the contemporary Japanese population. Currently, many physical anthropologists think that both (1) the people of the Jomon period, and (2) the people who came to the Japanese archipelago from continental Asia (primarily via the Korean peninsula) during and after the Yayoi period are the ancestors of the modern Japanese population. This is called the "dual structure model" for the population history of the Japanese (Hanihara 1986; 1987; 1991). The model is supported by a number of physical anthropologists such as Baba (1990) and Omoto and Saitou (1997), as well as archaeologists such as Hudson (1999) and Ikawa-Smith (1995).

Figure 2.9 schematizes the outline of the dual structure model. According to this model, the Asian population can be divided into two sub-groups: archaic and new Asian populations. The archaic population originally lived in South and East Asia. Physical anthropological studies indicate that the people of the Jomon period belong to this group. The others, the new Asian population, were those who adapted to the cold, northern climate sometime during the Late Pleistocene. The majority of present-day Northeast Asian people belong to this group. According to the dual structure model, the modern Japanese population was formed as a result of the mixture of the Jomon people, who were part of the archaic Asian population, with the new Asian population, who came to

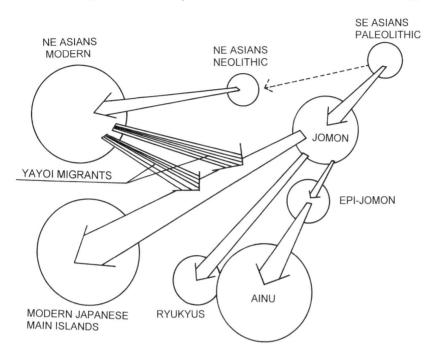

Figure 2.9   Dual structure model for the population history of the Japanese (redrawn from Hanihara 1991)

the Japanese archipelago from the continent during and after the Yayoi period.

Physical anthropologists also suggest that the degree of mixture of these two groups varies in different parts of the Japanese archipelago. In western Japan, particularly the northern Kyushu, Shikoku, Chugoku, and Kinki regions, the proportion of the "migrant" lineage is quite high. On the other hand, in eastern Japan, as well as in the Ryukyu Islands, the proportion of people of native Jomon lineage is higher. In particular, the Ainu people, an ethnic minority group who primarily live in Hokkaido, are closely related to the Jomon population.

BOX 4: *The Ainu people and cultures*

"Ainu" refers to an ethnic group who live primarily in Hokkaido, and whose cultural and linguistic traditions are different from those of the Honshu or "Mainland" Japanese (so-called *wajin*). The word "Ainu" means "human" or "people" in the Ainu language. Until quite recently, the Ainu people lived not only in Hokkaido but also in Sakhalin and the Kuril Islands. The majority of the Sakhalin Ainu, however, moved to Hokkaido

BOX 4: (*cont.*)

after World War II (Murasaki 2000). The Kuril Ainu were moved to the Shikotan Island by the Japanese government in 1884. As a result, the Kuril Ainu population decreased dramatically, and after World War II, their cultural traditions disappeared (Ogiwara 1987).

Historical documents indicate that, during the Edo period (1604–1868), the Hokkaido Ainu people's economy was based on hunting-gathering and trading with neighboring peoples. However, the Meiji Restoration (1868), which terminated the long history of the Tokugawa Shogunate (feudal government) and started the rapid westernization of Japan, forced the Ainu people to change their subsistence base in a fundamental way. A series of new laws issued by the new Japanese government severely restricted the hunting and fishing rights of the Ainu people. This was because the primary purpose of these laws was to protect the large number of *wajin* immigrants from Honshu, Shikoku, and Kyushu. Historical records indicate that, between 1886 and 1922, approximately 550,000 immigrants moved into Hokkaido from various parts of Japan. As a result, the relative percentage of the Ainu people in the Hokkaido population declined significantly (Emori 2000).

In 1899, the Japanese government issued the Hokkaido Former Aborigines Protection Act (Hokkaido Kyu-Dojin Hogo-Ho). While the name of the law includes the word "protection," the primary intention of the law was to assimilate the Ainu people (Fitzhugh and Dubreuil 1999: 26). It should also be noted that, even though the Japanese word "*dojin*" is a derogatory term for native people, the law continued to exist until 1997, when the Ainu Cultural Promotion Law (Ainu Bunka no Shinko narabi ni Ainu no Dento to ni kansuru Chishiki no Fukyu oyobi Keimo ni kansuru Horitsu) finally replaced the old law. This fact symbolizes the long history of oppression of and discrimination against the Ainu people by the Japanese government (Emori 2000).

Simply put, according to the dual structure model, the Ainu people are primarily the descendants of the Jomon people, whereas the *wajin* are a mixture of the Jomon people and the "immigrants" from the continent. However, as Baba (1990) points out, regional variability in physical characteristics among the Hokkaido Ainu indicates that the southern Hokkaido Ainu are more affected by the lineage of the new Asian population than the northern and eastern Hokkaido Ainu. In other words, just like the *wajin*, the population history of the Ainu must have been quite complex. Linguistically, the Ainu language is not closely affiliated to any other languages, and its origin is still unknown (but see Hudson 1999).

The number of so-called "immigrants" (people who moved from the continent to the Japanese archipelago during and after the Yayoi period) is a topic of debate among researchers. In a simulation study by Hanihara (1987), the estimate of the number of "immigrants" is quite high. Hanihara's work starts with Koyama's (1984) estimate of the population at the end of the Jomon period. As indicated in the previous section, Koyama (1984) suggests that the Final Jomon population in the Japanese archipelago was about 76,000, while the population at ca. AD 700 is estimated to have been approximately 5.4 million. Hanihara (1987) suggests that, if there had been no "immigrants" to Japan, then such a dramatic population increase would have involved an extremely high rate of annual population growth: 0.427 percent per year. Although this may not sound high, Hanihara (1987) points out that most agricultural societies have a growth rate of less than 0.1 percent. If the rate of 0.1 percent had been the case (i.e., if there had been no "immigrants"), then the population of AD 700 would have been only 200,000. In order to make up the 5.4 million estimated by Koyama (1984), over 3 million "immigrants" from the beginning of the Yayoi period to AD 700 are necessary. Even if we assume that the annual population growth rate was 0.2 percent, and that the Final Jomon population was 160,300 (which is the alternative population estimate in the Final Jomon period suggested by Koyama [1984]), we still need 1.3 million "immigrants."

Since Hanihara's (1987) simulation is based on several assumptions, these numbers should be evaluated with caution. Some scholars believe that Hanihara's estimate of the population growth rate for the Yayoi period is too low, and that the indigenous development was more important when the formation process of the modern Japanese population is taken into consideration. Others believe that the "immigrants" practically replaced the Jomon people. In any case, most researchers agree that the Jomon people are partially ancestral to the modern Japanese population (cf. Hudson 1999; see Habu 2002a).

Part II

Subsistence and settlement

3   Subsistence strategies

Among various subfields of Jomon archaeology, subsistence studies have traditionally been underrepresented in the Japanese-language literature. This is because the number of subsistence study specialists in Japan, including zooarchaeologists and paleoethnobotanists, has been very small when compared to the numbers of pottery, lithic, or settlement specialists. However, in terms of English-language publications, quite a few books and articles are available. Works by such scholars as Melvin Aikens (1981; Aikens and Dumond 1986; Aikens et al. 1986), Takeru Akazawa (1980; 1982a; 1982b; 1986b; 1986c; 1987), Peter Bleed (1992; Bleed and Bleed 1981; Bleed et al. 1989), Brian Chisholm (Chisholm et al. 1992), Gary Crawford (1983; 1997; Crawford et al. 1978; see also Crawford 1992a; 1992b), Hiroko Koike (1980; 1986a; 1986b; 1992), Yoshinobu Kotani (1972a; 1981), and Akira Matsui (1992; 1995; 1996) have been widely read and cited in the English-language literature.

Given this relative abundance of English-language literature on Jomon subsistence, I shall keep this chapter short. I shall first outline the history of Jomon faunal and floral remains analyses, introduce the two major hypotheses on Jomon subsistence (the "salmon hypothesis" and the "plant cultivation hypothesis"), and summarize the general characteristics of Jomon subsistence using the "Jomon calendar" developed by Tatsuo Kobayashi (1977a). The remaining part of this chapter is devoted to the review of the results of recent subsistence studies. Particular attention is paid to the issues of food storage, plant food utilization as staples, and maritime adaptation, since many researchers believe that these are closely related to the development of hunter-gatherer cultural complexity.

History of the analysis of Jomon faunal and floral remains

The history of the identification of faunal remains from Jomon sites goes back to the early twentieth century. As early as in 1911, Kishinoue, an ichthyologist, published a detailed description of fish remains recovered from Jomon sites. Naora (1938; 1941–42) and Sakatsume (1959; 1961) also contributed greatly to the field by compiling long lists of faunal remains found on Jomon sites, and discussing the potential importance of various faunal resources for the Jomon people. Beginning in the late 1950s, Kaneko and his students published a large number of Jomon faunal analyses, primarily as appendices to excavation reports. His syntheses based on these reports provide succinct summaries of Jomon faunal resource use (H. Kaneko 1965; 1967; 1969; 1976; 1979; 1982).

Since the 1970s, with the growing influence from Western archaeology, both faunal sampling methods and biological analyses of faunal remains have made significant progress. Systematic introduction of water-screening methods revealed that, without screening, small fish bones would be almost completely missed, and that these small bones often comprise the majority of Jomon faunal remains (Komiya 1976; 1980; 1981; 1983; Komiya and Suzuki 1977; Habu et al. 2001). Koike's (1973; 1979; 1980; 1983; 1986a) pioneering studies of daily growth-line analyses of clam shells also made archaeologists realize the importance of Jomon faunal analyses. Other kinds of seasonality studies, including those based on dental annuli analyses of deer and boar (Niimi 1991; Nishida 1981; Otaishi 1983) and fish body size estimates (e.g., Akazawa 1969; 1980; 1981), have also been conducted over the past several decades. Examination of relative frequencies of different anatomical parts of mammal and fish remains (Hayashi 1980; Matsui 1996; Toizumi 1998) have been used to infer such aspects as butchering patterns, game sharing, and site function. In addition, bone isotope analyses of carbon and nitrogen indicate regional variability in the Jomon people's diet (Chisholm 1985; Chisholm and Koike 1988; Chisholm et al. 1988; Koike and Chisholm 1988; Minagawa and Akazawa 1988; 1992), while lipid analyses (Sahara and Nakano 1984; Sahara et al. 1986) have helped to identify the kinds of faunal resources utilized by the Jomon people.

In spite of these investigations, the number of Jomon zooarchaeological studies that integrate the interpretation of other archaeological data is limited compared to those in many other parts of the world. Part of the problem stems from the fact that traditional Jomon studies have focused largely on the typological classification of artifacts, primarily pottery. As a result, the number of researchers working in the field is relatively small. This means that zooarchaeologists are not typically present in the field at the time of excavation, and they often end up just identifying the specimens sent from the excavators.

The history of Jomon palcoethnobotanical studies follows stages that are generally similar to those of Jomon zooarchaeology, but the scarcity of the number of researchers in this field is an even more serious problem.

One of the first attempts to provide a comprehensive list of plant remains recovered from Jomon sites was that of Sakatsume (1961). Later, Makoto Watanabe (1975) listed 39 taxa of edible plants from 208 Jomon sites. The majority of these are nut remains, such as chestnuts (*Castanea crenata*), walnuts (*Juglans sieboldiana*), buckeyes (*Aesculus turbinata*: also known as horse chestnuts), and various kinds of acorn, both deciduous (*Quercus*) and evergreen (*Cyclobalanopsis* and *Castanopsis*) (see, e.g., M. Watanabe 1973a), most of which were recovered by trowel excavations rather than through water-screening or flotation. With a few exceptions (e.g., Kotani 1972a; 1972b; 1972c; 1981), however, systematic sampling and iden-tification of small seeds did not occur until the 1980s. Nevertheless, by 1981, the total number of identified plant taxa from Jomon sites increased to 64 (Terasawa and Terasawa 1981).

The 1980s was a time of considerable progress within the field of Jomon paleoethnobotany. First, the use of the scanning electron micro-scope (SEM) improved the ability of investigators to identify small seeds. As a result, the presence of such cultigens as egoma (*Perilla frutescens* var. *japonica)* and/or shiso mint (*P. frutescens* var. *crispa*), which had remained unidentified throughout the 1970s, was finally recognized (Matsutani 1981a; 1981b; 1983; 1984; 1988). Second, an increase in the number of excavations of waterlogged sites made archaeologists realize the research potential of floral remains. For example, Masaki Nishida's (1977; 1981; 1983) pioneering work at the Torihama shell-midden revealed that systematic soil sampling and flotation can pro-vide researchers with a large number of Jomon floral remains (for the study of Torihama shell-midden in general, see also Aikens and Higuchi 1982: 127–130).

The 1980s was also a time when the majority of Jomon archaeol-ogists finally accepted the argument that at least a few domesticated plants were commonly used during and after the Early Jomon period. These cultigens include egoma and/or shiso mint, bottle gourd (*Lage-naria*), bean (Leguminosae) or green gram (*Vigna radiata*), barnyard millet (*Echinochloa*), buckwheat (*Fagopyrum*), barley (*Hordeum vulgare*), burdock (*Arctium lappa*), and rice (*Oryza sativa*). The use of SEM and water-screening/flotation methods played a significant role in increasing the numbers and kinds of identified cultigens. Subsequent excavations of several waterlogged Jomon sites, such as Mawaki (Y. Yamada 1986; Noto-machi Kyoiku Iinkai 1986; 1992) in Ishikawa Prefecture, Ondashi (Shibuya 2000) in Yamagata Prefecture, Awazu (Iba and Iwahashi 1992; Iba et al. 1999) in Shiga Prefecture, Ikenai (Akita-ken Maizo Bunkazai Center 1999) in Akita Prefecture, and Sannai Maruyama (Tsuji 1999; Habu et al. 2001), further stimulated researchers' interest in the study of floral remains. Overall, however, as in the case of zooarchaeology, problem-oriented paleoethnobotanical research with adequate sampling strategies has been relatively rare.

"Salmon hypothesis" and "plant cultivation hypothesis"

The studies of Jomon subsistence described above have been based on direct evidence: faunal and floral remains. Interestingly, however, the two influential theories on Jomon subsistence, the "salmon hypothesis" of Yamanouchi (1964a) and the "Jomon plant cultivation hypothesis" of Fujimori (1949; 1950; 1963; 1965a; 1965b; 1970), were both based on indirect lines of evidence. The former hypothesis, which Yamanouchi originally suggested in a 1947 lecture (see Yamanouchi 1964a: 144, footnote 7), became well known among Japanese archaeologists by the 1950s. He suggested that salmon fishing provided the staple food for the Jomon hunter-gatherers of eastern Japan. The source of this idea was in ethnographic analogies with California and the Ainu in Hokkaido. It is essentially a deductive hypothesis developed to explain why the Jomon cultures of eastern Japan were more prosperous than those of western Japan. According to this hypothesis, subsistence strategies in eastern Japan, which were based on both salmon fishing and deciduous acorn collecting, were able to support a larger population than those of western Japan that were primarily based on evergreen acorn collecting. Although only a small quantity of salmon remains had been recovered from Jomon sites by the 1960s, Yamanouchi (1964a) suggested that the scarcity of salmon bones from Jomon sites implies that Jomon people dried and ground salmon bones into powder. Since the publication of his article, the number of excavated salmon remains from Jomon sites has increased (Matsui 1996), but the total amount is still fairly small. As a result, the validity of this hypothesis remains a topic of debate (see Matsui 1985; 1996; A. Okamoto 1961; Obayashi 1971; M. Nishida 1983; K. Suzuki 1979; Takayama 1974; M. Watanabe 1967; 1970; 1973b).

In terms of the Jomon plant cultivation hypothesis, Fujimori (1950) argued that the large number of chipped stone axes recovered from Middle Jomon sites in the Chubu and Kanto regions were used as hoes for plant cultivation. Since no cultivated plant remains had been found from Jomon sites at the time of his publication, Fujimori used several lines of circumstantial evidence, such as changes in lithic assemblages, site size, site location, and rituals, to support his argument. Since then, several cultigens have been identified from Jomon sites (see above) but the importance of plant cultivation in overall Jomon subsistence is still hotly debated (for details of controversies over Jomon plant cultivation, see Pearson and Pearson 1978; Habu 2001: chapter 3).

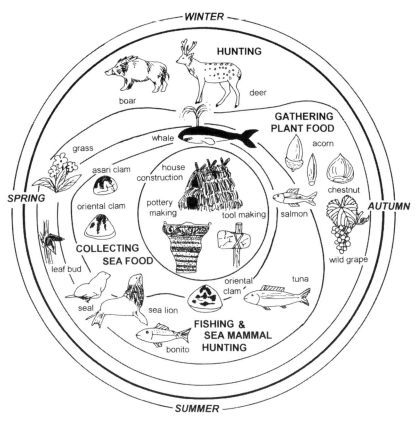

Figure 3.1 The "Jomon calendar" showing the seasonal hunting-gathering cycle (modified and redrawn from T. Kobayashi 1977a: 158)

The "Jomon calendar"

Despite these two well-known hypotheses, and despite the presence of some cultigens in Jomon floral assemblages, the majority of Jomon archaeologists still assume that the exploitation of a wide variety of wild food resources was the central part of Jomon subsistence. Figure 3.1 shows the frequently cited "Jomon calendar." It was originally developed by Tatsuo Kobayashi (1977a) to describe the seasonal cycle of food resources exploited by the Jomon people. Modified versions of this calendar have also been published by others (e.g., Aikens and Higuchi 1982: 183), but the essentials remain the same. According to this calendar, the Jomon people relied on four different kinds of subsistence activities:

fishing and marine mammal hunting primarily in the summer, plant food collecting (particularly nuts) in the autumn, terrestrial mammal hunting in the winter, and shellfish collecting in the spring. On the basis of the calendar, many Japanese archaeologists have suggested that abundant natural resources of the Japanese archipelago enabled the Jomon people to develop extremely rich cultures and societies.

Identifying major food resources and the seasons of their procurement, however, is only the first step to understanding Jomon subsistence. While the calendar does an excellent job in summarizing the general characteristics of Jomon subsistence activities, it actually raises more questions than it provides answers. First, it does not tell us about regional and temporal variability in Jomon subsistence. Since different regions were characterized by different natural environments, not all the resources shown in the calendar were available in all regions of the Japanese archipelago. In particular, the availability of seafood must have been significantly different between coastal and inland areas.

Second, establishing the seasonality of each subsistence activity is not easy. While some activities could have been conducted only in a particular season (e.g., nut collecting in the autumn), other activities might have been conducted during more than one season. For example, many Japanese archaeologists believe that winter was the best season for hunting deer and boar, because both of these animals form large herds during this season (H. Kaneko 1979; 1982). However, this does not mean that Jomon people hunted boar and deer only in the winter. In order to identify the hunting season of these animals, seasonality studies such as the analysis of dental annuli (e.g., Niimi 1991; M. Nishida 1981; Otaishi 1983) are required.

Finally, a list of major food sources does not tell us how Jomon subsistence activities were related to other aspects of the lives of the Jomon people, including mobility patterns, social organization, and religious beliefs. In order to understand Jomon subsistence systems and changes therein over time, we need to obtain various kinds of information such as the quantity of different kinds of foods and the methods of food acquisition, cooking, and storing, and interpret these data in relation to various other aspects of the Jomon people's lives (Y. Sato et al. 2002).

Jomon collectors

In summary, while previous studies provide us with a general picture of Jomon subsistence, they do not tell us how a particular subsistence system functioned in each region, nor the reason why the system developed. Traditionally, many Japanese archaeologists have suggested that the abundant natural resources of the Japanese archipelago enabled the Jomon people to exploit various kinds of food sources efficiently, which in turn allowed them to develop extremely rich cultures and societies. This interpretation is an equivalent of the "pull" or "Garden of Eden" theory in North American hunter-gatherer studies; i.e., abundant food resources allowed certain groups of hunter-gatherers to develop complex cultures and societies with intensive subsistence strategies, sedentism, and high population density. In particular, evidence of marine adaptation by the Jomon people makes this interpretation attractive, since many researchers have suggested that rich marine resources often provided an "opportunity" for hunter-gatherers to develop "complex" cultural characteristics (see, e.g., Yesner 1987; cf. Cannon 1998). Following this line of argument, some researchers suggest that the Jomon people were primarily "littoral foragers" who were heavily reliant on marine food (e.g., Barnes 1993).

The collector-forager model (Binford 1980; 1982) described in chapter 1 provides us with a slightly different picture regarding the development of sedentary lifeways and intensive food exploitation among hunter-gatherers. According to this model, the degree of sedentism and, as its corollary, residential mobility are closely related to the distribution pattern of critical resources rather than their absolute abundance. If the distribution of critical resources is homogeneous, hunter-gatherers will become residentially highly mobile with low logistical mobility (foragers). However, in an environment where the distribution of important resources is spatially and/or temporally uneven, hunter-gatherers will develop logistical mobility in order to exploit simultaneously the various resources located far away from their residential bases (collectors). Because collectors send a specially organized task group to exploit resources located away from their residential base, they tend to rely on a more limited number of resources than foragers. In other words, collectors tend to be more closely associated with intensive subsistence strategies (i.e., specialists), whereas foragers tend to be more generalists (Binford 1980; see also Winterhalder 1981).

In view of the evidence of seasonal changes in resource availability throughout the Japanese archipelago, the Jomon people in general appear to have been close to the collector end of the forager–collector spectrum. Furthermore, the faunal, floral, and other archaeological evidence described above also support the idea that, in many cases, the people of the Jomon period were not "generalists" but were "specialists," relying heavily on a limited number of resource items such as acorns, chestnuts, fish, and marine mammals.

Food storage and nut collecting

One of the key issues concerning Jomon subsistence systems from the perspective of the collector–forager model is the practice of food storage. According to the model, food storage is typical of collector systems. Because of the common presence of storage pits associated with nut remains, many researchers believe that nut storage played a critical role in Jomon subsistence strategies.

The oldest evidence of Jomon food storage comes from the Higashi-Kurotsuchida site in Kagoshima Prefecture, southern Kyushu (Kawaguchi 1982). The site is dated to the Incipient Jomon period, and is associated with a radiocarbon date of 11,300 ± 300 bp (1σ: 13,800–13,650 cal BP [7%], 13,550–12,950 cal BP [61%]). The site yielded a storage pit containing large quantities of acorn remains. The pit was about 40 centimeters in diameter, and about 25 centimeters deep. The acorn remains recovered are *Quercus*, a deciduous type of acorn, most likely *Quercus serrata* (*konara* is the Japanese common name) (T. Izumi 1996a). Since most deciduous acorns, including *Quercus serrata*, contain bitter tannic acid, they have to be soaked in water and boiled before they are eaten (M. Watanabe 1975: 136). The fact that Incipient Jomon people stored deciduous acorns indicates that, by the time of the Incipient Jomon, people had developed a sophisticated method of removing the tannic acid (T. Izumi 1996a).

Discoveries of storage pits dating to the Early Jomon and subsequent periods are quite common. These pits can be classified as wet pits and dry pits (T. Izumi 1996a). Wet storage pits are usually encountered in a wet, swampy area of a site, and often contain nut remains. Figure 3.2 (upper) shows a group of wet-type storage pits at the Middle and Late Jomon Kuribayashi site (H. Okamura 1995a; 1995b) in Nagano Prefecture. The majority of storage pits at this site contained walnut remains. The only exception was Pit no. 56, which held buckeyes. The site also produced evidence of features associated with wooden frames that were probably used to soak buckeyes or acorns in the water (fig. 3.2: lower). Similar wooden frames were associated with a buckeye midden at the Akayama Jin'ya-ato site in Saitama Prefecture (Kanabako 1996). Ethnographically, similar features are known for several areas of Japan.

Figure 3.3.1 is a schematic profile of a wet-type storage pit found at the Middle Jomon Sakanoshita site in Saga Prefecture (Saga Kenritsu Hakubutsu-kan 1975; K. Suzuki 1988). At this site, leaves, wood fragments, and clay were used to preserve acorns. Figure 3.3.2 shows the profile of another storage pit from the Late Jomon Anoh site in Shiga Prefecture (K. Suzuki 1988). Here, four different kinds of nuts – buckeyes,

Figure 3.2   Field photographs of wet storage pits (upper) and features associated with wooden frames (lower) excavated at the Kuribayashi site, Nagano Prefecture (from H. Okamura 1995b; permission for reproduction obtained from Nagano Kenritsu Rekishi-kan [Nagano Prefectural Museum of History])

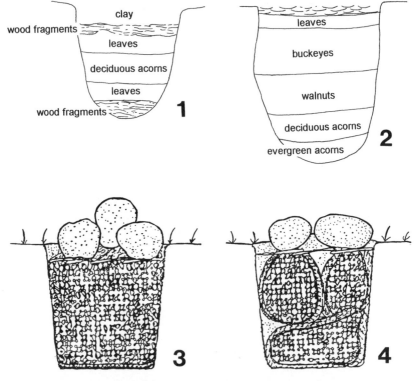

Figure 3.3   Schematic profiles of storage pit excavated at (1) the Sakanoshita site, Saga Prefecture, (2) the Anoh site, Shiga Prefecture, and (3–4) the Sobata site, Kumamoto Prefecture (modified and redrawn from K. Suzuki 1988: 62; Tsukamoto 1993: 63)

walnuts, deciduous acorns, and evergreen acorns – were recovered from a single pit, with a layer of leaves on the top of the pit. Baskets and mats were also used to store evergreen acorns in storage pits found at the Early Jomon Sobata site in Kumamoto Prefecture (fig. 3.3.3–4; Tsukamoto 1993).

The function of wet storage pits has been a matter of debate. Some archaeologists believe that they functioned as a convenient means of bleaching out the bitter tannic acid of acorns. However, K. Imamura (1996: 121) disagrees with this idea, pointing out that these wet storage pits contain naturally edible sweet acorns. In addition, wet storage pits are also frequently associated with buckeyes, which contain poisonous alkaloid constituents. Since buckeyes require even more sophisticated preparatory techniques than do deciduous acorns, simply soaking them

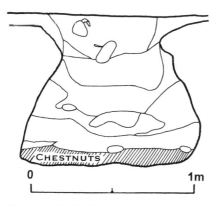

Figure 3.4 Profile of a storage pit excavated at the Nashinokizuka site, Akita Prefecture (modified and redrawn from Akita-ken Kokogaku Kyokai 1979: 31)

in water is not enough to remove the poison. Imamura believes that the purpose of these wet storage pits was to prevent the stored nuts from germinating over a long time period, even tens of years, thus ensuring a food supply in case of famine. Other researchers think that soaking nuts in the water was the most efficient way to eradicate insects (Tamada 1996).

While wet storage pits are found primarily in western Japan, dry storage pits occur more commonly in eastern Japan. This latter form of storage pit displays large variability in size and shape. Among the dry storage pits, the most well-known type is the "flask-shaped" pit (fig. 3.4). The opening of the pit is much smaller than the floor area. Some of these flask-shaped pits are quite large, measuring as much as 4 meters in floor diameter (Tsukamoto 1993: 63).

Although many archaeologists believe that large flask-shaped pits were used to store nuts and other kinds of food (e.g., Tamada 1996; Tsukamoto 1993), very few food remains have actually been recovered from these pits. Unlike wet storage pits, preservation conditions for organic remains in the dry pits are generally poor. With the exception of pits with nuts, of which there are very few (such as the Nashinokizuka site; fig. 3.4), we do not know what types of food were stored in dry storage pits. Nevertheless, many scholars assume that the flask-shaped pits were used primarily for nut storage. Tsukamoto (1993) believes that large flask-shaped pits functioned as cellars, and in many cases nuts were not stored directly on the pit floor but were put in baskets or other types of container.

In addition to these storage pits, buckeyes and chestnuts have been recovered from several burnt pit-dwellings. Based on this, some

Figure 3.5   Reconstruction of "raised-floor" storehouses at the Sannai Maruyama site, Aomori Prefecture (from Koyama et al. 1996; permission for reproduction obtained from Prism and Co.)

researchers suggest that nuts may have been stored on shelves in the ceiling of pit-houses (e.g., Tsukamoto 1993). Some researchers also think that so-called "raised-floor buildings" functioned as storehouses (for more discussions, see Ishii 1982). Figure 3.5 shows an example of the reconstruction of the feature called the raised-floor building. While this type of feature is quite similar to the raised-floor granary from the following agricultural Yayoi period, its function remains controversial.

Compared to the relatively abundant evidence of plant food storage, evidence for the storage of meat and fish is extremely scarce. Some researchers believe that a type of feature called a "fire pit with a smoke tunnel" was used for smoking meat (Kaseda-shi Kyoiku Iinkai 1998). Figure 3.6 shows a schematic diagram of the fire pit with a smoke tunnel excavated at the Kakoinohara site in Kyushu. As shown in this figure, a large main pit is associated with a smaller pit, and these two are connected by a tunnel. Results of experimental archaeology indicate that this feature is well suited for smoking meat (Kaseda-shi Kyoiku Iinkai 1998). Other archaeologists believe that fish must have been dried or smoked and stored extensively (e.g., Izumi 1996a; Matsui 1996). Finally, the common presence of large Jomon shell-middens has led some

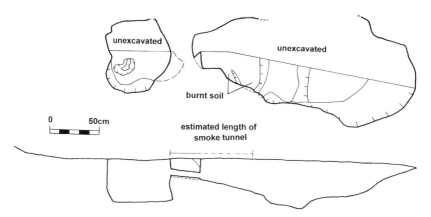

Figure 3.6   Plan and schematic profile of a fire pit with smoke tunnel excavated at the Kakoinohara site, Kagoshima Prefecture (modified and redrawn from Kaseda-shi Kyoiku Iinkai 1998: 17)

archaeologists to conclude that large quantities of shellfish were collected during a particular season of the year, dried, and stored or possibly traded with inland areas (e.g., K. Goto 1970).

It should be remembered that, since the soil in Japan is extremely acidic, the preservation of organic material in Jomon sites is generally poor. Accordingly, the scarcity of firm evidence of meat and fish storage does not necessarily mean that the storage of these food items was uncommon. Nevertheless, an abundance of nut remains from storage pits seems to indicate the relative importance of nuts as stored food in the overall subsistence strategies of the Jomon people.

From the perspective of the collector–forager model, nut storage implies collecting large quantities of nuts during the autumn for use during the winter through to early spring, thus often reducing overall residential mobility. In this regard, it is interesting to note that some scholars have suggested the possibility of artificial management of some nut trees during the Jomon period. As early as in the 1950s, Izawa (1951) and Sakatsume (1957) suggested that nut-bearing trees such as chestnut, oak, beech, and buckeye might have been tended by the Jomon people and should, therefore, be considered as potential Jomon cultigens (see also K. Imamura 1996: 105–106). Furthermore, results of recent DNA analyses of Early and Middle Jomon chestnut remains from the Sannai Maruyama site (Y. Sato et al. 2003; Yamanaka et al. 1999) also indicate the possibility of chestnut cultivation or domestication (for details, see chapter 4, p. 117). If that was in fact the case, it has significant implications for our understanding of Jomon landscapes.

Other plant foods as possible staples

Other possible staple foods for the Jomon people include various kinds of plant roots. Currently, very little direct evidence of root utilization from the Jomon period is available with the exception of the carbonized remains of a yam stalk bud excavated at the Early Jomon Matsugasaki site in Kyoto Prefecture (Anonymous 2000; Matsui, personal communication, 2000). Despite the scarcity of direct evidence, however, many researchers believe that plant roots may have been an important part of the Jomon diet. This is primarily because the so-called "chipped stone axes," which are thought to have been used for collecting plant roots, are abundant in Middle Jomon sites in the Kanto and Chubu regions. Furthermore, the Middle Jomon culture in these regions is also characterized by high site density, large site size, and a sophistication of material culture, including complex pottery decoration.

Figure 3.7 shows Keiji Imamura's (1996: 107) analysis of the distributions of Middle Jomon sites associated with a large number of chipped stone axes and sites with a large number of storage pits in the Kanto and Chubu regions. As the figure shows, the distributions of these two site types are mutually exclusive. Imamura therefore suggests that the chipped stone axes were used to collect wild roots such as yams (*Discorea japonica*), whereas storage pits were more closely related to a heavy reliance on nuts. If his interpretation is valid, then the overall subsistence–settlement systems based on these two types of archaeological remains must have been quite different from each other.

Ethnographically, yams are not the only roots heavily utilized in rural Japan. Two other taxa, *Pueraria lobata* (starchy vine [*kuzu*]) and *Pteridium aquilinum* (bracken [*warabi*]), have also been collected. The roots of these plants can be dried and ground, and then soaked in water in order to produce starchy flour (Koyama 1984). Since the method of processing these roots is quite similar to that of processing acorns and buckeyes, it is quite possible that the Jomon people actively utilized these plant roots when they were available.

In addition to nuts and plant roots, some scholars suggest the potential importance of several cultigens in the Jomon diet. As discussed above, cultigens such as egoma and/or shiso mint, bottle gourd (*Lagenaria*), bean (Leguminosae) or green gram (*Vigna radiata*), barnyard millet (*Echinochloa*), buckwheat (*Fagopyrum*), barley (*Hordeum vulgare*),

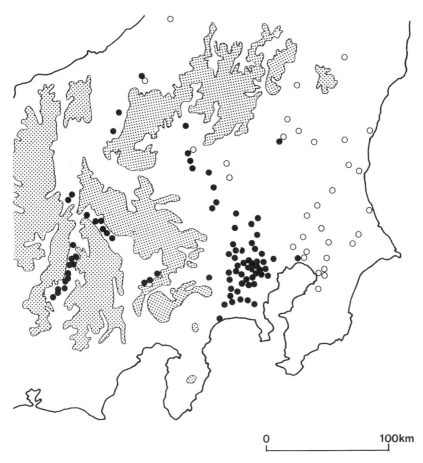

Figure 3.7   Distribution of Middle Jomon sites having a large number
of chipped stone axes (•) and sites with a large number of storage pits (○)
in the Kanto and Chubu regions (redrawn from Keiji Imamura 1996:
107)

burdock (*Arctium lappa*), and rice (*Oryza sativa*) have been identified
from Jomon sites. However, none of these recovered cultigens seems to
have been used as a staple. Bottle gourds must have been valued primarily as containers, not as food. The seeds and leaves of egoma and
shiso mint may have been used commonly as herbs, but neither of them
was valuable as a food staple. Burdock may have been a great side dish,
but the fibered texture makes it difficult to consume in large quantities. Other cultigens, such as bean, buckwheat, barley, and rice, are suitable for use as staples. So far, however, the quantities of these remains

recovered from Jomon sites are extremely small. Barnyard millet could have been used as a staple, but the results of carbon and nitrogen isotope analyses indicate otherwise; although barnyard millet is one of the few C_4 plants available as possible food for the Jomon people, carbon and nitrogen studies by Minagawa and Akazawa (1992) indicate that none of the Jomon groups examined in their studies was relying on C_4 plants (for the details of carbon and nitrogen isotope analyses, see below). Judging from these lines of evidence, Hayden's (1990) hypothesis regarding the origins of plant domestication among hunter-gatherers, which suggests that the primary importance of early domesticates was to provide prestige items for feasting, rather than to supply staples, is suggestive. Alternatively, these cultigens may have been commonly used as tertiary resources.

Maritime adaptation and development of shell-middens

While most researchers acknowledge the overall importance of plant food in Jomon diets, the contribution of marine food is more controversial. The common presence of shell-middens in various parts of the Japanese archipelago has long attracted researchers' attention. For example, as early as 1959, Sakatsume compiled a list of shell-middens that included over 4,000 sites. However, this list actually included shell-middens from other time periods as well as the Jomon period; i.e., not all of these are dated to the Jomon period. Tozawa (1989: 38) states that at least 1,108 Jomon sites known throughout the Japanese archipelago are shell-middens. While this is a rather conservative estimate, it may be close to the actual number of Jomon shell-middens.

The spatial distribution of Jomon shell-middens is quite uneven. According to Tozawa (1989: 38), of the 1,108 Jomon shell-middens, 664 (more than 60 percent) are located on the Kanto Plain. This includes the Tokyo Bay area, the east side of which is especially well known for its clusters of large shell-middens. The Pacific side of the Tohoku region, such as the Sanriku Coast and the Matsushima/Sendai Bay area, is another area in which a large number of Jomon shell-middens developed. The number of Jomon shell-middens also waxed and waned over time. While some of the famous Jomon shell-middens, such as the Natsushima shell-midden (9450 ± 400 bp; M-769) (1σ: 10,850–9550 cal BP) in Kanagawa Prefecture (see Aikens and Higuchi 1982: 114–124) and the Nishinojo shell-midden (8240 ± 190 bp; N-170) (1σ: 9470–9010 cal BP) in Chiba Prefecture (N. Watanabe 1966), are from the Initial Jomon period, the majority of Jomon shell-middens are dated to the Early through Late Jomon. In the Kanto Plain, Early Jomon shell-middens, many of which are located on the west side of Tokyo Bay, tend to be fairly small, while the Middle and Late Jomon shell-middens, especially those located in the east Tokyo Bay area, are characterized by their large size. Some of these Middle and Late Jomon shell-middens, which are often ring-shaped or horseshoe-shaped, measure over 100 meters in diameter. These shell-middens include Kasori North (Middle Jomon; 130 meters), Kasori South (Late Jomon; 170 meters) (for the details of these two middens, see Aikens and Higuchi 1982: 156–164), and Horinouchi (Late Jomon; approximately 200 meters), all of which are located in Chiba Prefecture. All of these shell-middens are associated with a large number of pit-dwellings, many of which are located beneath the shell layers.

Despite the common presence of Jomon shell-middens, researchers believe that the caloric contribution of shellfish in the overall Jomon diet must have been relatively low. On the basis of volume estimates of the Late Jomon Isarago shell-midden in Tokyo, Kimio Suzuki (1986) estimates that the maximum daily caloric intake from shellfish for an Isarago resident would have been 133.5 kcal, or approximately 7–9 percent of the average daily caloric intake. However, he points out two factors that may have significantly increased the value of shellfish in the overall Jomon diet. First, seasonality studies based on daily growth-line analyses (Koike 1981) indicate that two of the major shellfish species consumed at Isarago, *Tegillarca granosa* (granular ark) and *Meretrix lusoria* (oriental clam), were collected primarily in the spring and early summer. Other lines of evidence, such as fishing seasonality of *Acanthopagrus schlegeli* on the basis of fish-scale analyses (Ushizawa 1981), also supports the hypothesis that the site was a seasonal fishing and shellfish-collecting camp. If that was the case, the importance of shellfish in the overall Jomon diet may have been related to its seasonal abundance, since it is one of the few food items in the Japanese archipelago that are available from the late winter to early spring (Habu 2000; 2002b). Secondly, the primary importance of shellfish may need to be evaluated in terms of protein rather than caloric intake. Ethnographic studies from various parts of the world, as well as recent discussions on the role of shellfish in hunter-gatherer subsistence (e.g., Erlandson 1988), indicate that shellfish may have been more important in the protein component of the diet. Results of carbon and nitrogen isotope analysis conducted by Minagawa and Akazawa (1992), however, indicate that the contribution of shellfish in Jomon diets, at least for the Honshu Jomon people, was fairly limited even in terms of protein intake. Their simulation study (fig. 3.8) indicates that protein sources for Hokkaido and Honshu Jomon peoples were quite different

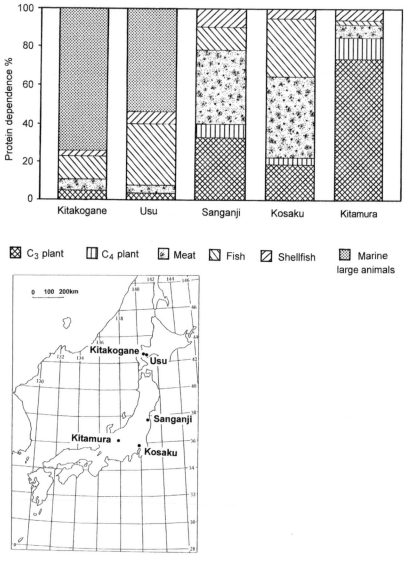

Figure 3.8 Result of a simulation study by Minagawa and Akazawa based on carbon and nitrogen isotope analysis (redrawn from Minagawa and Akazawa 1992: 60, 64)

from each other. While samples from two sites in Hokkaido indicate heavy dependence on sea mammals, samples from three Honshu sites show a greater reliance on plant food and terrestrial animals. It is especially interesting to note that even the data from two shell-midden sites in Honshu, the Sanganji site in Fukushima Prefecture and the Kosaku site in Chiba Prefecture, indicate relatively low dependence on marine food. Judging from these data, the importance of marine food, including shellfish, seems to have been quite low even in terms of protein intake.

Kimio Suzuki (1986) also suggests that the large size of shell-middens does not necessarily mean shellfish were consumed as a staple. Comparison between the Kasori South shell-midden and the Isarago shell-midden clearly demonstrates the case in point. The Kasori South shell-midden, which dates to the Late Jomon period, is known for its large extent. It is horseshoe shaped, and the diameter of the horseshoe shape measures approximately 170 meters. According to Suzuki (1986), the actual area of the Kasori South shell-midden itself is 9,453 square meters, and the volume can be estimated to be 5,463 cubic meters. While the numbers look quite large, the duration of the midden on the basis of pottery chronology is estimated to have been seven pottery phases (Shomyoji, Horinouchi I, Horinouchi II, Kasori-B_1, Kasori-B_2, Kasori-B_3, and Soya), which cover most of the Late Jomon period. On the other hand, the Isarago shell-midden, the original area of which is estimated to be approximately 700 square meters and the volume approximately 580 cubic meters, was occupied for only a single pottery phase (Horinouchi I). Judging from this evidence, Suzuki (1986) suggests that the accumulation rate for the Kasori South shell-midden was not much faster than that of smaller shell-middens such as Isarago.

Recent excavation results at the Nakazato shell-midden in Tokyo (Kita-ku Kyoiku Iinkai 2000; H. Nakajima 2000; H. Nakajima and Hosaka 1998) provide new insights into the role of shellfish in the Jomon diet. Unlike many other Jomon shell-middens that are located on hilltops, the Nakazato shell-midden is located in lowland, at the very edge of the prehistoric coastline. From the nineteenth century to the early 1990s, scholars had been debating whether the midden was artificial in origin or a natural deposit. This debate was fueled by the midden's location and the scarcity of artifacts in it. Salvage excavation of the site, which started in 1996, finally confirmed that the midden contains a small number of Middle and Late Jomon potsherds. The accumulation of shells is extremely thick (fig. 3.9), measuring as much as 4.5 meters. The excavation also revealed the presence of features with wooden frames, in which burnt cobbles, burnt shell fragments, and charcoal were identified.

Figure 3.9   Field photograph of the Nakazato shell-midden, Tokyo
(from Kita-ku Kyoiku Iinkai 1997: photo 2; permission for reproduction
obtained from Kita-ku Kyoiku Iinkai)

Hiroaki Nakajima (2000), the principal investigator of the site, suggests
that these features, as well as a number of burnt shell layers with a large
amount of charcoal, indicate steaming of oysters (*Crassostrea gigas*) and
oriental clams (*Meretrix lusoria*).

   Together with recently excavated shell-middens with only small numbers of associated artifacts, such as the Isarago shell-midden in Tokyo

(Isarago Kaizuka Iseki Chosa-dan 1981) and the Awazu shell-midden in Shiga Prefecture (Iba and Iwahashi 1992; Iba et al. 1999), Nakazato seems to represent a type of Jomon shell-midden which functioned as a special-purpose campsite to collect and process shellfish. Because the site is located at the mouth of the Arakawa River, Yoshiro Abe (2000) suggests that several residential groups along this river used the place as a shellfish-collecting camp. In order to test Abe's hypothesis, further analyses of regional settlement data need to be conducted.

Regional variability and changes through time

In summary, Jomon subsistence systems differed from region to region and over time, and a general picture of Jomon subsistence may not help us understand how individual systems in each region functioned in relation to a specific type or types of staple food. Seemingly typical sites, such as those with a large number of chipped stone axes or those associated with large shell-middens, are actually spatially and temporally constrained in their distributions. In other words, it is likely that the characteristics of Jomon subsistence strategies changed significantly over time.

Regarding regional variability in Jomon subsistence strategies, tool assemblage analyses by Akazawa (1981; 1982a; 1982b; 1986a; 1986b; 1986c; 1987) and Akazawa and Maeyama (1986) are quite suggestive. They conducted discriminant function analyses of Jomon settlements using the relative frequencies of associated bone and stone tools as variables. The results (Akazawa 1986a) indicate the possible presence of three regionally different Jomon "ecosystems": (1) a forest–freshwater ecosystem in western Japan and inland eastern Japan that is characterized by an abundance of plant-food exploitation tools, such as chipped stone axes, stone mortars, and grinding stones, and/or stone net sinkers for freshwater fishing, (2) a forest–estuary ecosystem in eastern and central Japan that is primarily associated with pottery net sinkers for estuary fishing and projectile points for terrestrial mammal hunting, and (3) a forest–Pacific Shelf littoral ecosystem in eastern Japan that is characterized by different kinds of fishing equipment, such as toggle harpoon heads and fishhooks, and secondary tools for food resource processing and tool making, including stemmed scrapers and awls. Based on these results, Akazawa suggests that marine resources, i.e., fish and shellfish, played a greater role in eastern Japan, whereas plant resources were of greater importance in western Japan. He also suggests that the forest–estuary ecosystem and the forest–Pacific Shelf littoral ecosystem provided for a more stable seasonal procurement round than did the forest–freshwater ecosystem. While the primary focus of his analyses was on adaptation to different regional environments, Akazawa (1986a) concludes that such regional variability in Jomon subsistence resulted in regional variations in receptivity to rice agriculture at the beginning of the Yayoi period.

In relation to Akazawa's (1981; 1982a; 1982b; 1986a; 1986b; 1986c; 1987) study, Soffer's (1989) interpretation of variability in Jomon subsistence is also noteworthy. In her comparative analysis of prehistoric hunter-gatherers in Eurasia, Soffer suggests that the "shelf-life" or social use value of the stored product is an important parameter in the discussion of the development of sedentism among hunter-gatherers. In her opinion, stored foods with short "use-lives," such as meat and fish, do not necessarily imply sedentism, while stored foods with long use-lives led to the development of sedentism and the ultimate rise of food production. Soffer used the Jomon as an example of the storage of long use-life products, and suggests that the storage of nuts, including acorns, was closely linked to the development of sedentism. Following Akazawa (1981; 1986b), she suggests that it is not surprising that the introduction of food production in the form of rice at the beginning of the Yayoi period occurred in western Japan, precisely in the areas whose residents traditionally relied more on stored plant products.

While I believe that stored food with long use-life played an extremely important role in the development of Jomon cultural complexity as a whole, the relationships between storage, sedentism, and the development of food production among Jomon hunter-gatherers may not be as straightforward as Akazawa (1986a; 1986b; 1987) and Soffer (1989) suggest. Storage pits with nut remains are not distributed only in western Japan; they are also quite common in northeastern and central Honshu. Furthermore, as described above, carbon and nitrogen isotope analyses by Minagawa and Akazawa (1992) indicate that plant foods formed an important part of Jomon diet for all of the three sites that they examined in northeastern and central Honshu. In other words, it is more likely that most of the Jomon people, with the exception of those in Hokkaido, were all heavily reliant on plant food, but that the type(s) of staple food were different among regions and over time.

In order to understand fully the characteristics of Jomon subsistence, additional studies that examine data from a specific time phase in a specific region are required. However, because of the generally poor preservation of organic materials in Jomon sites, it is difficult to examine characteristics of Jomon subsistence solely on the basis of faunal and floral data. Accordingly, studies of settlement patterns in relation to subsistence strategies become critical. In the next chapter, I will outline recent results of Jomon settlement archaeology, and interpret the results in the context of the collector–forager model described in the first chapter.

4   Settlement archaeology

Together with pottery chronology, settlement archaeology has been a major research focus of Jomon archaeology throughout the post-World War II period. Settlement studies have been called "*shuraku-ron* (discussions of settlements)," and they have become a distinctive field within Jomon archaeology. In particular, the rapid increase in the number of salvage excavations beginning in the 1960s has resulted in a significant increase in the amount of Jomon settlement data. On the one hand, this increase in rescue excavations has resulted in the discovery of numerous small Jomon settlements, many of which would have been missed if large-scale land development had not taken place. On the other hand, the number of large Jomon settlements that were completely excavated has also increased over the past several decades, and this has provided invaluable data for examining intrasite spatial patterns. As a result, the amount of data available for Jomon settlement analysis is incredibly rich.

This chapter first reviews the history of Jomon settlement studies, and outlines the problems of these studies. Following this review, I present two case studies on Jomon settlement pattern analyses in the context of the collector–forager model described in the first chapter.

History of Jomon settlement studies

Wajima's settlement archaeology

The majority of Jomon settlement studies conducted by Japanese archaeologists are either directly or indirectly influenced by the work of Wajima (1948; 1958; 1962), whose theoretical framework was that of classical Marxism. In his 1948 article entitled "Prehistoric settlement structure," Wajima made two major points, following a Marxist approach. First, he suggested that the Jomon society was that of a "clan community" (also called a "primitive community"). Using survey and test excavation results from several Jomon sites, Wajima suggested that the semicircular or horseshoe-shaped layout of dwellings within each settlement represents the presence of strict social rules that determined the placement of each dwelling. Since there is no evidence of social classes from the Jomon period, Wajima suggested that such strict social rules were formed under "primitive communal societies," which, according to classical Marxist theories, are defined as the first stage of social development. Second, Wajima (1948) indicated that settlement patterns from the Initial to Late Jomon periods developed gradually from mobile to more sedentary, and that the change was associated with a significant population increase. While the theory of social development was an important component of Marxist history in postwar Japan (Nagahara 1974), Wajima applied the theory not only to explain changes from the Jomon to the following Yayoi and Kofun periods, but also to understand changes over time within the Jomon period. In particular, the prominence of large settlements during the Middle Jomon period, such as the Togariishi site in Nagano Prefecture (F. Miyasaka 1946) and the Ubayama site in Chiba Prefecture, was interpreted as evidence for a high degree of sedentism of the Middle Jomon people, thus supporting his argument on increasing sedentism from the Initial to Middle Jomon periods. According to Wajima (1948), such changes were triggered by a population increase, which occurred as a result of an increase in overall productive capacity (subsistence production capacity).

BOX 5: *Wajima and Marxism in Japanese archaeology*

Wajima's interest in Marxism as a means of historical interpretation predated and continued through World War II. As early as the 1930s, he attempted to interpret archaeological data from the Japanese archipelago within the framework of Marxism. Since Marxism was severely banned in Japan before and during World War II, Wajima had to use the pen name Misawa to disguise his identity (Misawa 1936). His 1936 article was published in a volume *Textbook of Japanese History* (*Nihon Rekishi Kyotei*) edited by Yoshimichi Watanabe and others (1936).

Yoshimichi Watanabe was a member of the Japanese Communist Party, who was arrested in 1928 at the time of the March 15 Incident (a mass arrest of writers and scholars who were identified as left-wingers by the Japanese government). Furthermore, the primary objectives of this edited volume were to study the development of the ancient state in Japan and to reexamine the history of the Imperial Family through the systematic and scientific analysis of prehistoric and protohistoric societies. In other words, the main purpose of the book was to demystify the nature of so-called "national polity" (*kokutai*) defined by the Maintenance of Public Order Act (Chian Iji Ho) in order to support the proletariat and the commoners who were fighting against the ultranationalistic government (Inumaru 1976). In this regard, Wajima's attempt to study archaeological data from a perspective of historical materialism had not only academic but also political

BOX 5: (*cont.*)

connotations (Hara 1972; Ichihara 1984; for political restrictions imposed on the practice of Japanese archaeology before and during World War II, see also Habu 1989a; Habu and Fawcett 1990).

With the end of World War II in 1945, academic studies in Japan, including archaeology, entered a new stage. Marxist interpretations became not only accepted but also popular among historians and archaeologists through the late 1940s and 1950s. Thus, in the immediate postwar years, Wajima and his followers were able to concentrate on using Marxism (usually referred to as historical materialism in Japanese archaeology) to reconstruct functions of prehistoric settlements and to study how these settlements changed over time. Their primary research interests were on the increased efficiency of food production and population growth through time, as well as the division of labor, social stratification, and the formation of the ancient state.

By the 1970s, the Marxist perspective had become less popular in archaeology just as it had lost adherents in many other social sciences in Japan. However, the model of increased productivity thorough time (i.e., the notion that the transition through the various stages of hunter-gatherer to agriculturalist was one of increased efficiency of food acquisition) and the idea that the size of individual settlements gradually increased through time have continued to underlie settlement studies until today (e.g., Amakasu 1986).

Wajima's (1948) article, with its firm commitment to historical materialism and its strong emphasis on archaeological studies of intrasite settlement patterns, formed the foundation of Jomon settlement archaeology during and after the 1950s. In 1955, Wajima excavated the Nanbori shell-midden (sometimes called "Minamibori"), a large Early Jomon settlement in Kanagawa Prefecture (Wajima 1958). The result of this excavation also confirmed the presence of a horseshoe-shaped layout of pit-dwellings with an empty space at the center of the site (fig. 4.1). After this excavation, the Nanbori settlement was widely cited as the model of the "Jomon village," and the excavation strategy that Wajima adopted (i.e., to excavate the entire settlement area rather than to conduct a partial excavation by placing test pits and trenches) strongly influenced the excavation method of Jomon settlements thereafter.

Interest in "group territory" and intrasite spatial analyses

Following the excavation of the Nanbori settlement, the primary research focus of Jomon settlement archaeology from the late 1950s to the 1970s was on the "social structure" of the Jomon people, with an emphasis on the interpretation of intrasite settlement patterns. Many of the Jomon settlement studies published during this time period were influenced

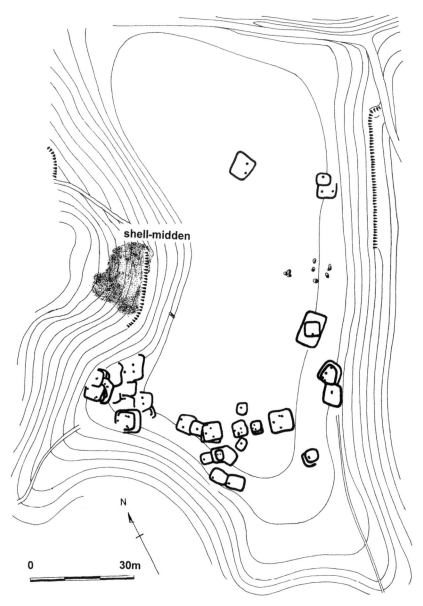

shell-midden

N

0   30m

Figure 4.1 Feature distribution at the Nanbori shell-midden site,
Kanagawa Prefecture (modified and redrawn from Wajima 1958: 37)

by Wajima's (1948) work, with an emphasis on the study of the "clan/primitive community" (e.g., Aso 1960; I. Okamoto 1975; Sugawara 1972; see also Teshigawara 1988). The works of Marxist scholars in other fields of social sciences, such as Seita Toma (1951) in history, Hisao Otsuka (1955) in social economics, and Seiichi Izumi (1962) in cultural anthropology, also influenced this research field.

The late 1950s to the 1970s was also a time when the study of "group territory" made significant progress in relation to the analysis of regional settlement patterns. For example, Ichihara (1959) studied the distribution of Middle Jomon settlements along the Oi River in Shizuoka Prefecture, and suggested that these settlements were located at a distance of at least 10 kilometers from each other. He concluded from this that the residents of each site maintained a hunting-gathering territory extending over a diameter of 10 kilometers. It is worth noting that Ichihara's work, which actually preceded the site catchment analysis of Vita-Finzi and Higgs (1970) by more than ten years, did not use an ecological approach, but instead was conducted within a Marxist framework, with an emphasis on the study of redistribution systems, division of labor, and regional social networks. Following Ichihara's study, a number of archaeologists also examined regional settlement pattern data and discussed the "activity sphere" (*seikatsu-ken*) and "group territory" (*shudan ryoiki*) of the residents of each site (Hayashi 1974; 1975; Horikoshi 1972; Mukosaka 1970; Shimizu 1973; Mamoru Takahashi 1965). While all of these studies took the natural environment into consideration, the ultimate goal was to reconstruct the "primitive community." In other words, they shared the theoretical foundation with Wajima and his followers whose primary research focus was on intrasite settlement patterns.

During the 1960s, Mizuno's (1963) intrasite spatial analysis of the Middle Jomon Yosukeone site in Nagano Prefecture also played a significant role in enhancing researchers' interests in the "social structure" of the Jomon people. According to his analyses, the basic unit of Jomon settlements comprises three pairs of pit-dwellings (i.e., six pit-dwellings); the three pairs are characterized by the presence of a large stone rod (*sekichu*), clay figurines (*dogu*), and phallic stones (*sekibo*) respectively (see also Mizuno 1968; 1969a; 1969b; 1970). Later, Kazuhito Goto (1970: 116–117) and the "Flake" Association (Fureiku Dojinkai 1971) criticized the model on the grounds that, in many cases, Mizuno manipulated archaeological data, such as the chronological identification of each pit-dwelling, so that two-dwelling "small units" and six-dwelling "large units" could be identified. Consequently, very few scholars today support Mizuno's hypothesis. Nevertheless, his analysis stimulated the development of intrasite settlement pattern analyses during and after the 1970s (e.g., Mukosaka 1970; Murata 1974; Nagasaki 1977; Obayashi 1971). In particular, citing Lévi-Strauss, Niwa (1978; 1982) attempted a structural interpretation of Jomon intrasite settlement patterns. Mizuno's work also encouraged the analysis of intrasite settlement patterns in relation to the spatial distribution of "ceremonial" artifacts such as large stone rods (phallic stones) and clay figurines (Nagasaki 1973; Tsuboi 1962).

Ecological approaches and the influence of North American settlement archaeology

As described above, the majority of Jomon settlement studies from the 1950s to the 1970s analyzed both inter- and intrasite settlement patterns in relation to the social structure of the Jomon people. Because of this emphasis, very few settlement studies incorporated subsistence data in their analyses. One of the few exceptions was the work of Hitoshi Watanabe (1964; 1986), who compared Jomon data with ethnographic examples of the Ainu in Hokkaido, and who suggested there was a need to examine the relationship between settlement patterns and subsistence strategies in the context of ecological anthropology. In addition, a series of publications by Takeru Akazawa (1980; 1981; 1982a; 1982b; 1986a; 1986b; 1986c; 1987; Akazawa and Maeyama 1986) also used explicit ecological approaches to examine Jomon settlement data. In particular, Akazawa (1981) applied the site catchment model (Vita-Finzi and Higgs 1970) in the examination of Jomon site territories, and compared characteristics of the natural environment within a 10-kilometer radius of each Jomon site with faunal remains excavated from each site. With the exception of these works, however, studies of Jomon settlements are basically separate from those of Jomon subsistence.

While the Jomon settlement studies described above essentially developed within the context of Japanese archaeology, Tatsuo Kobayashi (1973; 1980; 1986) attempted to apply the method of North American settlement archaeology, which was first introduced into Japan by Keally (1971), to regional settlement pattern data from the Tama New Town area in western Tokyo. The Tama New Town area is in the suburbs of Tokyo, where large-scale land developments took place from the 1960s to the 1980s. The Board of Education of Tokyo began surveying this area in the late 1960s. In the following two decades, more than 900 sites were excavated. Many of these sites are quite large in area, measuring between several thousand to often tens of thousands of square meters.

Using survey and excavation results from the Tama New Town area, Kobayashi (1973) classified Jomon settlements in this area into six types: (A) large settlements arranged in semicircular or horseshoe-shaped patterns; these sites are usually associated with many artifacts and features, including storage pits and burials; (B) medium-sized settlements without clear semicircular/horseshoe-shaped layouts; (C) small settlements with only one or two dwellings; (D) small sites without dwellings but with some other features; (E) small sites with a specific function, such as cemeteries, artifact depots, clay mining sites, quarries, and stone tool production sites; and (F) sporadic artifact scatters. Later in his 1980 article, Kobayashi suggested that his classifications (A) to (F) basically correspond to Campbell's ethnographic site typology of Tuluaqumiut in central Alaska (Campbell 1968).

Kobayashi's settlement pattern analysis was new in the sense that it examined various characteristics of Jomon settlements, including site location, total number of dwellings, presence or absence of storage pits and burials, feature distribution, types and quantities of artifacts, and duration of site occupation. As Kobayashi himself stated, however, it was essentially a typology of sites (Kobayashi 1973: 20), and the interpretations of site function in relation to subsistence strategies have yet to be presented.

Questions about Jomon settlement size and the degree of sedentism

It is evident from the above that the majority of Jomon settlement studies shared Wajima's (1948; 1958) interest in the reconstruction of the primitive community. Many of these studies also inherited Wajima's assumption that the degree of sedentism during the Jomon period was quite high. The presence of circular or horseshoe-shaped settlements associated with a large number of pit-dwellings has been interpreted as evidence for a high degree of Jomon sedentism. Scholars who did not share the Marxist perspective (e.g., Koyama 1978; 1984; H. Watanabe 1966; 1986) also accepted this assumption of Jomon sedentism.

By the end of the 1970s, several scholars began to question this assumption, and suggested the need to reexamine the degree of sedentism during the Jomon period. One such scholar was Ishii (1977), who published a detailed analysis of cross-sections of postmolds of Jomon pit-dwellings in the Kohoku New Town area in Kanagawa Prefecture. Based on this analysis, he suggests that, unlike previous suggestions, many Jomon pit-dwellings were occupied intermittently rather than continuously.

Other scholars suggested that the seemingly large size of Jomon settlements needed to be reexamined, and therefore the large site size should not be interpreted as evidence for full sedentism. For example, Yoshio Doi

(1985) pointed out that the majority of Jomon settlements were in fact small, and large settlement sites occurred only as a result of long-term occupation of the same place. Kuro'o (1988), who examined intrasite spatial patterns of Middle Jomon large settlement sites, suggested that the number of simultaneously occupied pit-dwellings at each subphase was actually quite small. Tatsuo Kobayashi (1986: 55) also supported the idea that most of the Jomon settlements were small, and suggested that the average number of simultaneously occupied pit-dwellings at a Jomon settlement site must have been between three and six. Such articles played a significant role in suggesting the necessity to reexamine traditional assumptions on Jomon sedentism and large settlement size. However, an alternative picture of Jomon settlements to that of Wajima (1948; 1958) has yet to be presented.

Behind these questions was the rapid increase in the number of salvage excavations in Japan beginning in the 1960s. As indicated in the case of the Tama New Town area, large-scale salvage excavations resulted in an increase in both the quality and quantity of Jomon settlement pattern data. Before the 1960s, Jomon settlement studies were based on the results of excavations of only several hundred sites. The majority of these sites were either shell-middens or large settlements, both of which were easy to identify from surface surveys. Since then, however, tens of thousands of additional Jomon sites have been discovered and excavated. A significant number of these newly excavated sites are small settlements with only one pit-dwelling, or at most a few. These small sites would never have been identified if large-scale land developments had not taken place.

The rapid increase in the number of salvage excavations, on the other hand, revealed the presence of a small number of extremely large Jomon settlements. These include the Miharada site in Gunma Prefecture (341 Middle Jomon pit-dwellings; Akayama 1982), the Sannomaru site in Kanagawa Prefecture (286 Middle Jomon pit-dwellings; Kohoku New Town Maizo Bunkazai Chosa-dan 1985), the Nakanoya Matsubara site in Gunma Prefecture (239 Early Jomon pit-dwellings; Annaka-shi Kyoiku Iinkai 1996; fig. 4.2), and the Nakano B site in Hokkaido (more than 500 Initial Jomon pit-dwellings; Izumita 1996). In particular, the discovery at the Sannai Maruyama site in Aomori Prefecture, which is associated with more than 700 Early and Middle Jomon pit-dwellings and numerous other features, attracted the attention of both researchers and the media (for details of the Sannai Maruyama study, see Case Study 2 on pp. 108–132). While some researchers interpret the presence of large settlements as evidence for full sedentism, the roles and functions of these large settlements in overall Jomon settlement systems have yet to be examined.

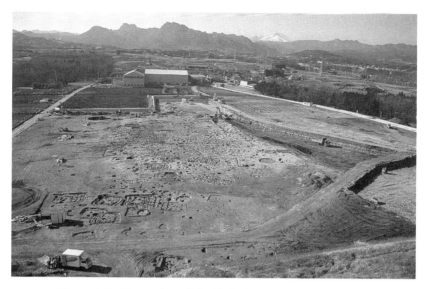

Figure 4.2 Excavation of the Early Jomon Nakanoya Matsubara site, Gunma Prefecture (from Muto 1999; permission for reproduction obtained from Annaka-shi Kyoiku Iinkai [Board of Education of Annaka City])

What became apparent through these new excavations is intersite variability in each region, as well as interregional and temporal variability in Jomon settlement patterns. Because of this large variability, outlining generalized characteristics of Jomon settlements would tell us little about the lifeways of Jomon people in different regions at different time periods. In order to understand characteristics of Jomon settlement systems as a whole, it is necessary to conduct a series of settlement pattern analyses using data from different regions and time periods, and then compare the results. Conducting systematic comparisons between the results of these analyses makes it possible to identify the extent of regional and temporal variability in Jomon settlement systems.

Case Study 1: Analysis of Early Jomon settlement data from central Japan

As the first step in approaching Jomon settlement systems, I examined intersite variability in lithic assemblages, site size, and site location from the Early Jomon Moroiso phase of the Kanto and Chubu Mountain

Table 4.1 *Expected patterns of residentially used sites*

Type	Intersite variability in lithic assemblages	Intersite variability in site size	Site distribution pattern
Fully sedentary collectors	small	small	clustered
Collectors with seasonal moves	large	large	clustered
Foragers	small	small	dispersed

regions in central Japan (for the full description of this case study, see Habu 2001).

Hypotheses

The first step I took was to formulate multiple hypotheses in which expected patterns of archaeological data for each subsistence–settlement system are suggested. Table 4.1 summarizes expected characteristics in lithic assemblage, site size, and site distribution patterns for foragers, collectors with seasonal moves, and fully sedentary collectors respectively (Habu 1996; 2000; 2001). As shown in fig. 1.6 (p. 11), collectors with seasonal moves (or relatively sedentary collectors) would have conducted seasonally different activities at seasonally different residential bases. Accordingly, comparison in lithic assemblages from these different residential sites is expected to reveal large intersite variability. Figure 1.6 also indicates that settlement patterns of relatively sedentary collectors are often characterized by seasonal amalgamation and dispersal of residential groups. In the case shown in fig. 1.6, the group formed a large residential base during the winter and early summer, but was dispersed into smaller residential bases during the late summer. Accordingly, it is expected that variability in site size among residential bases is quite large.

In contrast, all residential bases of fully sedentary collectors are occupied throughout the year (fig. 1.7; p. 13). This implies that activities conducted at each of these residential bases are relatively similar to each other. Accordingly, it is expected that variability in both lithic assemblages and site size among residential bases is relatively small. The model also assumes collectors' residential bases to be located near primary resource concentrations. Therefore, in the case of both fully and relatively sedentary collectors, it is expected that residential bases would be clustered at specific localities near resource concentrations.

Unlike collectors, who are adapted to environments in which seasonal/temporal distribution of critical resources is uneven, foragers are adapted to environments where the distribution of critical resources is homogeneous. Thus, it is likely that activities conducted at each of the foragers' residential bases are all related to exploiting a similar type of environment. Accordingly, it is expected that intersite variability in lithic assemblages and site size is relatively small. In this regard, the first and second columns of table 4.1 for both the fully sedentary collectors and the foragers are the same. However, residential bases of foragers tend to be much smaller than those of collectors. This is because (1) foragers' residential bases tend to be occupied for a relatively short time period because of their frequent seasonal movements, and (2) while collectors tend to reoccupy previously used residential bases, it is less common for foragers to reoccupy their residential bases. Finally, in terms of site distribution, it is expected that foragers' residential bases would be dispersed throughout the research area, because the distribution of critical resources, which determines the locations of residential bases, is spatially homogeneous.

Materials and methods

Using these hypotheses, I examined data from the Early Jomon Moroiso phase in the Kanto region and the Chubu region (also called the Chubu Mountain region). The Moroiso phase is the third phase of the Early Jomon period, dating to around 5000 bp (*ca*. 5900 cal BP). This phase is characterized by an abundance of pottery decorated with parallel lines and nail-shaped impressions made with half-split bamboos, as well as with thin clay bands attached to the surface of pottery. Typological chronology of Moroiso-style pottery indicates that the Moroiso phase can be divided into three subphases: Moroiso-a, Moroiso-b, and Moroiso-c from the earliest to the latest (see e.g., T. Suzuki 1989). Figure 4.3 shows typical examples of Moroiso-style pottery.

Raw data were taken from Moroiso-phase sites in six prefectures in the Kanto and Chubu regions (fig. 4.4). The study zone was divided into four areas: Areas I to IV (fig. 4.5). Areas I and II are the northwestern and southwestern parts of the Kanto region respectively. It should be mentioned that Area II includes Tokyo and the adjacent coastal area, and is characterized by an abundance of salvage excavations. Area III is the mountainous area of the Chubu region: the area was further subdivided into IIIa and IIIb for the convenience of preparing site distribution maps. Finally, Area IV covers the Izu Islands. These six prefectures cover the major distribution area of Moroiso-style pottery.

In this analysis, 1,058 Moroiso-phase sites were examined. These sites were first classified into two groups: (1) nondwelling sites, and (2)

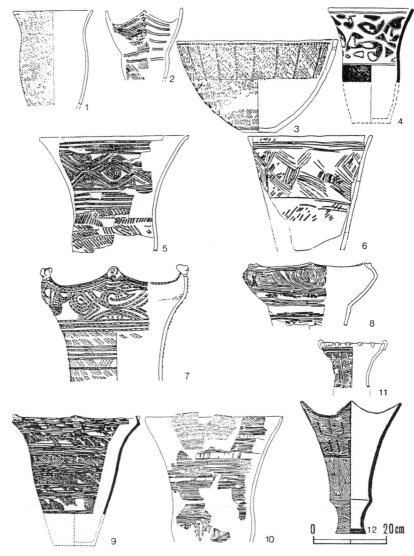

Figure 4.3   Examples of Moroiso-style pottery: 1–4. Moroiso-a style;
5–10. Moroiso-b style; 11–12. Moroiso-c style (from Habu 1988: 149)

Figure 4.4   Map of Japan showing research area. The shaded area represents the six prefectures studied (redrawn from Habu 2001: 30)

dwelling sites. A nondwelling site refers to a site in which no pit-dwellings were excavated or identified. A dwelling site refers to a site with which one or more pit-dwellings were associated. Since Jomon pit-dwellings were fairly labor-intensive, as they were constructed by digging into the ground for at least 30–40 centimeters, I assumed that the majority of these dwelling sites were used as residential bases. Of the 1,058 Moroiso-phase sites examined, 242 sites were identified as dwelling sites. All 242 dwelling sites were used for the analysis of site size variability. For the analysis of lithic assemblage variability, only 95 dwelling sites were used, because the total number of lithic tools from the remaining 147 sites was either too small for quantitative analyses, or unreported (fig. 4.6).

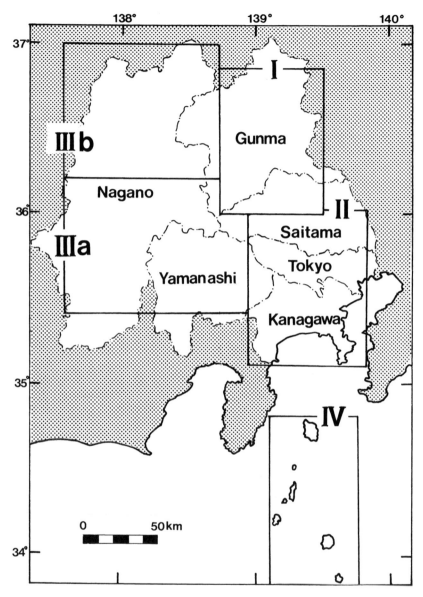

Figure 4.5   The location of Areas I to IV. The shaded area lies outside
the six prefectures studied (from Habu 2001: 31)

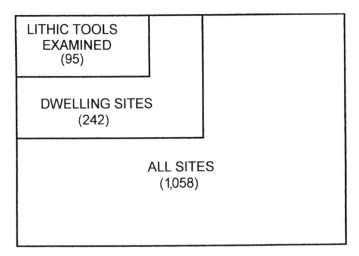

Figure 4.6   Data structure

Lithic tools from the ninety-five sites were classified into the following eleven categories (designations used in tables and figures are indicated in parentheses): (1) arrowheads (ARH), (2) stemmed scrapers (SSC), (3) awls (AWL), (4) chipped stone axes (CAX), (5) polished stone axes (PAX), (6) pebble tools (PBL), (7) stone mortars (MTR), (8) grinding stones (GRD), (9) net sinkers (NSK), (10) ornaments (ORN), and (11) others (OTH) (fig. 4.7). Relative frequencies of these eleven tool categories were calculated for each of the ninety-five sites, and used to establish site typology.

In this analysis, the ninety-five sites were first classified according to the most abundant category of lithic tools in each assemblage. Figure 4.8 shows the five site types identified as a result of this analysis. In these graphs, each line represents one site. For example, when the relative frequency of arrowheads from a site was the highest among the eleven tool categories, the site was classified into the arrowhead peak type (fig. 4.8: upper left). The majority of the ninety-five sites were identified either as arrowhead peak, chipped stone axe peak (fig. 4.8: middle left), or grinding stone peak sites (fig. 4.8: lower left). Of the remainder, two sites were classified as pebble tool peak sites (fig. 4.8: upper right), and one site was classified as a net sinker peak site (fig. 4.8: middle right).

Next, the first three of these five types (i.e., arrowhead peak, chipped stone axe peak, and grinding stone peak) were further divided into two subtypes on the basis of assemblage diversity. For example, if I look at relative frequencies of eleven categories of tools for all the arrowhead

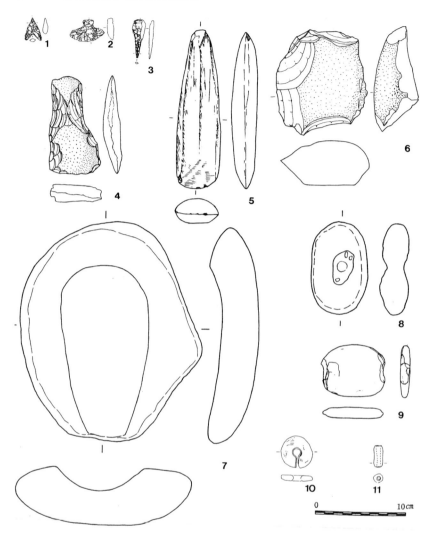

Figure 4.7   Lithic tools from Moroiso-phase sites: 1. arrowhead; 2. stemmed scraper; 3. awl; 4. chipped stone axe; 5. polished stone axe; 6. pebble tool; 7. stone mortar; 8. grinding stone; 9. net sinker; 10–11. ornaments (from Habu 2001: 33)

peak sites (fig. 4.8: upper left), some assemblages are characterized by extremely high percentages of arrowheads, as high as 85 percent. When the relative frequency of arrowheads is significantly high, relative frequencies of other tool categories are by definition low. As a result, the graph

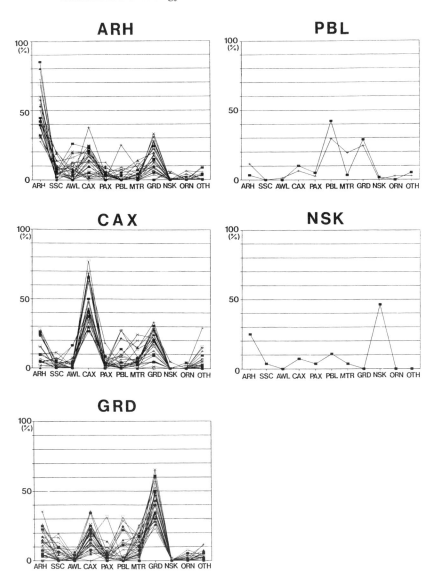

Figure 4.8   Five site types based on the highest artifact category frequency in assemblage composition (from Habu 2001: 52)

showing this type of assemblage is characterized by a single peak in the category of arrowhead. On the other hand, when the relative frequency of arrowheads is lower, the graph tends to be characterized by two or more peaks.

In my analysis, when the relative frequency of the most abundant category exceeds 50 percent of the assemblage, the site is called a "single peak site." When the highest peak accounts for less than 50 percent, the site is classified as a multiple peak site. Single peak sites are identified in three tool categories: (1) arrowheads (fig. 4.9: upper), (2) chipped stone axes (fig. 4.9: middle), and (3) grinding stones (fig. 4.9: lower).

Settlement system of the Moroiso phase

Figure 4.10 shows the distribution of the ninety-five sites according to the types and numbers of associated dwellings. The solid symbols represent multiple peak sites. The empty symbols represent single peak sites. The size of the symbols reflect site size using the maximum number of possibly simultaneously occupied dwellings in each site (1–4 dwellings = small, 5–10 dwellings = medium, and more than 10 dwellings = large).

Two things are clear from this analysis. First, dwelling sites tend to form concentrations. Such a pattern corresponds very well to the model of collectors (see table 4.1). The presence of site concentrations can be seen more clearly in enlarged maps. Figures 4.11–4.13 are enlarged maps of Areas I, II, and IIIa. In these maps, all the Moroiso-phase sites in each area are plotted. In addition to the symbols that are explained above, "S" marks represent dwelling sites for which the lithic assemblage size is too small for quantitative analysis. The "U" marks represent dwelling sites which have been already excavated, but the detailed lithic assemblage data of which are unreported. Finally, "x" marks indicate nondwelling sites (see fig. 4.13 for legend). In Area I, six site concentrations (A–F) can be identified (fig. 4.11). The large circles on this figure indicate a 10-kilometer radius, or approximate foraging radius, around each site concentration (for the definition of the foraging radius, see Binford 1980). In Area II (fig. 4.12), the Tokyo area, four site concentrations (G–J) were identified. In Area IIIa (fig. 4.13), the pattern of site concentration is not as clear as in the first two areas, but there seem to be several site concentrations (indicated as K–P in fig. 4.13). Since Area IIIa is mountainous, and less developed than the first two areas, I assume that a number of unreported sites are still hidden in this area. The sample size of Area IIIb and Area IV was too small to identify any patterns of site location.

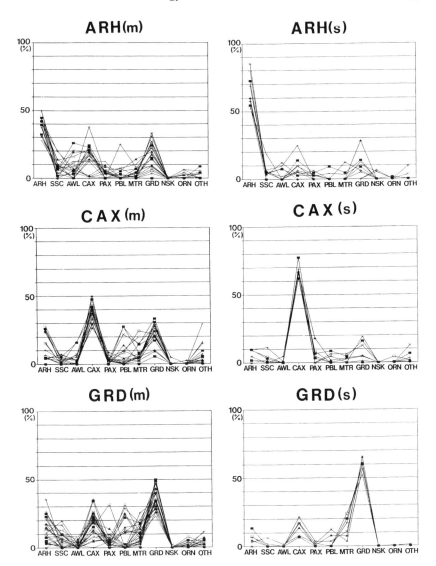

Figure 4.9   Single peak sites (s) and multiple peak sites (m) for three categories of lithic tools (from Habu 2001: 53)

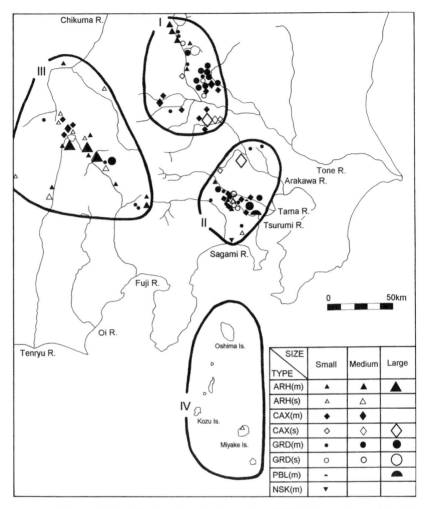

Figure 4.10   Distribution of ninety-five LTE (lithic tools examined) sites (redrawn from Habu 2001: 55)

Second, as shown in the distribution map of the ninety-five sites (fig. 4.10), there is considerable intersite variability both in site type based on lithic assemblage characteristics, and in site size. According to the hypotheses, these are characteristics of collectors who move their residential bases seasonally. Note that arrowhead peak sites (shown as triangles), chipped stone axe peak sites (diamonds), and grinding stone

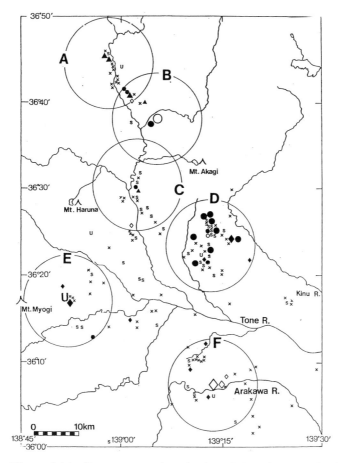

Figure 4.11   Site concentrations in Area I (see fig. 4.13 for legend [modified from Habu 2001: 61])

peak sites (circles) are never found exclusively in each of the Areas I, II, and III. Such a pattern seems to represent a wide diversity of subsistence activities practiced in the residential bases within each area.

Of the three tool types, arrowheads must have been associated with hunting. Chipped stone axes are believed to have been used as hoes for collecting plant roots, or possibly for incipient plant cultivation. Grinding stones were probably used for processing nuts, such as acorns. Given the seasonal and regional diversity in available resources in the study area, it is very likely that the differences in assemblage composition reflect seasonal

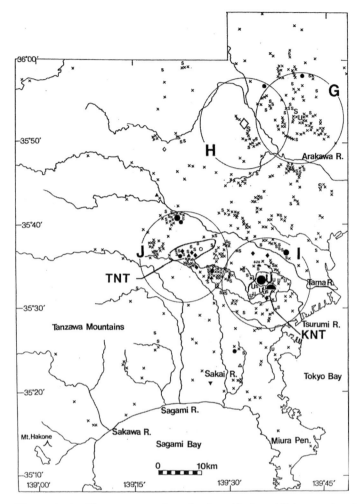

Figure 4.12   Site concentrations in Area II. In addition to the sites represented in the diagram, there are 168 nondwelling sites in the Tama New Town area (indicated as TNT) and 31 nondwelling sites in the Kohoku New Town area (indicated as KNT) respectively. See figure 4.13 for legend (modified from Habu 2001: 62)

occupations of the residential bases. Furthermore, variability in site size seems to represent seasonal dispersion and amalgamation of residential groups.

    Some of the readers of this book may think that sites with different lithic assemblage characteristics may have been occupied year-round by groups

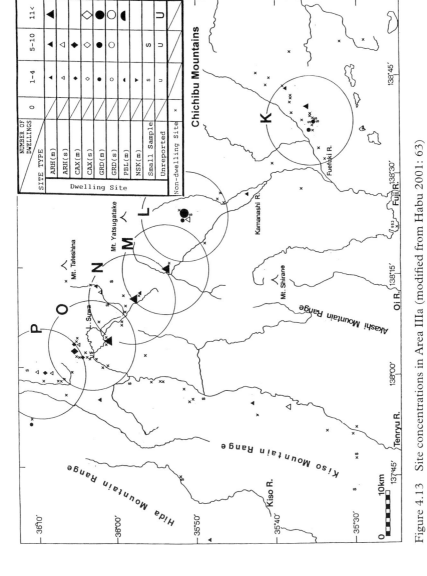

Figure 4.13   Site concentrations in Area IIIa (modified from Habu 2001: 63)

with different subsistence strategies. While this is theoretically possible, the fact that the distances between site clusters characterized by different lithic assemblages are often within the range of collectors' residential moves (i.e., approximately 10–30 kilometers; see table 1 of Kelly 1983) makes this explanation less convincing. Ethnographic examples indicate that, if different resources are seasonally available within the possible range of residential moves, hunter-gatherers tend to move their residential bases unless the area is territorially defended by another group (see for example Karok and Yurok cited in Schalk 1981). In the case of the present study, since chronological changes in site occupation patterns are evident (see below), it is unlikely that there was a long-term fixed territory during the Moroiso phase.

Changes through time within the Moroiso phase

So far, the results of my analysis support the hypothesis that the Moroiso-phase people were collectors who moved their residential bases season-ally. However, as noted above, Japanese archaeologists have divided the Moroiso phase into three subphases: Moroiso-a, -b, and -c, from the old-est to the youngest, and some of them believe that settlement patterns changed significantly within the Moroiso phase (e.g., K. Imamura 1992). If that was the case, the characteristics of intersite variability and settle-ment patterns observed above might be biased by the temporal changes throughout the Moroiso phase.

Therefore, as the next step in my analysis, I made distribution maps of each of the three subphases separately, and tested the validity of the conclusions presented above. The results were generally consistent with the conclusions discussed above with one exception, the Moroiso-c sub-phase in Area II. As described above, Area II is the coastal area, which includes present-day Tokyo. As shown in fig. 4.14, the settlement pattern of the Moroiso-c subphase in this area is characterized by a scarcity of dwelling sites; most of the sites indicated in this map are nondwelling sites, represented by "x" marks.

I suggest that these nondwelling sites might have functioned as resi-dential bases in a forager system. As the residential bases of foragers are likely to be less complex than those of collectors, it is quite possible that many of these nondwelling sites represent such residential bases. If this was the case, it can be suggested that, unlike other subphases, the people of the Moroiso-c subphase in Area II were closer to foragers than to col-lectors. This indicates that some of the Jomon people were not only not fully sedentary, but in fact may have been quite mobile.

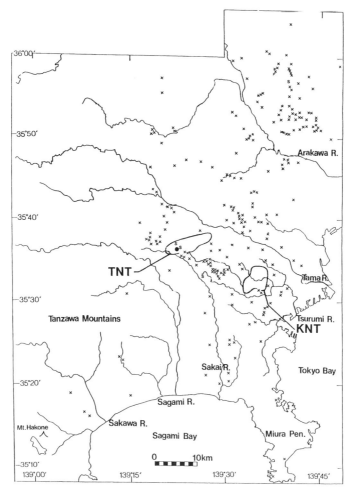

Figure 4.14 Distribution of Moroiso-c subphase sites in Area II. In addition to the sites represented in the diagram, there are 37 nondwelling sites in the Tama New Town area (indicated as TNT) and 5 nondwelling sites in the Kohoku New Town area (indicated as KNT) respectively. See figure 4.13 for legend (modified from Habu 2001: 85)

The fact that these nondwelling sites are dispersed throughout Area II also supports the hypothesis that the people of the Moroiso-c subphase in Area II were foragers. According to Binford's original model (table 1.1), collector systems occur where the distribution of critical resources is spatially or temporally uneven, whereas forager systems

Table 4.2 *Frequencies of shell-midden sites in southwestern Kanto*

	Moroiso-a	Moroiso-b	Moroiso-c
Number of all sites	273	631	278
Number of shell-midden sites	23	14	0
Percentage of shell-midden sites	8.4	2.2	0.0

are responses to environments where the distribution of resources is more homogeneous. Therefore, if there was a shift from collecting to foraging systems in Area II, we might be able to find corresponding environmental changes.

Environmental data suggest that the Moroiso phase coincides with the "Climatic Optimum," the time of maximum sea-level transgression. According to Matsushima (1979) and Matsushima and Koike (1979), the sea level in this area reached its maximum between 6500 and 5500 bp (ca. 7400–6300 cal BP). Some researchers (Fuji 1984; Sakamoto and Nakamura 1991) suggest that the sea level was at its maximum during the Kurohama phase (the phase before the Moroiso-a subphase), while others (Horiguchi 1983) believe that it occurred during the Moroiso-a subphase. In either case, it is very likely that the sea level gradually started to retreat through the Moroiso-b and -c subphases.

How did this sea-level change affect the distribution of available resources? Matsushima and Hiroko Koike (1979) suggest that in the western Kanto, especially along the Tsurumi River, sea-level retreat may have resulted in the destruction of the habitat of littoral molluskan species such as oysters (*Crassostrea gigas*) and granular ark (*Tegillarca granosa*). The frequency of shell-midden sites in southwestern Kanto shows a corresponding decrease as indicated in table 4.2: of all the Moroiso-a sites in southwestern Kanto, 8.4 percent are associated with shell-middens, whereas only 2.2 percent of the Moroiso-b sites are associated with shell-middens. No shell-middens have been reported from the Moroiso-c subphase (Habu 2001). It should be noted here that the difference in the total number of sites between subphases might reflect the difference in the duration of each subphase. In particular, the fact that the total number of sites in the Moroiso-b subphase is twice as much as that of the other two subphases may indicate that the Moroiso-b subphase lasted longer than the other two subphases. Nonetheless, the decrease in the relative proportion of shell-midden sites over time is apparent.

It is likely that the decline in the frequency of shell-middens reflects changes in the availability of shellfish resources over time. While many Jomon scholars assume that shellfish was not the most important food category for the Jomon people (e.g., K. Suzuki 1979), this decline nevertheless must have caused significant changes in the overall resource distribution patterns in Area II. Since the distribution of shellfish is spatially limited to the coastal area, and since they are key resources for hunter-gatherers during the spring when relatively few other resources are available, the decrease in the amount of shellfish would have resulted in a more homogeneous distribution of overall resources. Since Binford's original model predicts that forager systems are preferred under environments in which the distribution of resources are temporally and spatially homogeneous, the environmental data also support the interpretation that there was a change from collecting to foraging systems in Area II.

Influence of this system change on the development of the "Middle Jomon type" of system

The shift from collecting to foraging systems in Area II offers particular insights when we look at the long-term settlement pattern change from the Early to Middle Jomon periods at the interregional level (Habu 2002b). Because the shift in Area II was associated with a dramatic decrease in the total number of sites and average site size, it must have entailed a significant population decrease in this area. This can imply either a catastrophic increase in the mortality rate, or population movement to a neighboring area (or areas).

Changes in the number of sites in each region seem to indicate the possibility of population movement from Area II to Area III (the Chubu Mountain region). First, detailed analysis of settlement pattern changes in Area II indicates that the shift from the Moroiso-b to Moroiso-c subphases was heralded by a gradual shift from the Moroiso-a to Moroiso-b subphases in the concentration of site distribution from the coast to inland (Habu 2002b). Since the inland part of Area II was a gateway to Area III, such a shift in site distribution is consistent with the assumption of long-term population movement toward Area III. Second, the total number of sites in Area III increased from the Moroiso-b to Moroiso-c subphases, which is also consistent with the scenario of population movement. Third, lithic assemblage data from the Moroiso-c subphase in Area III show a new trend: several sites are characterized by an abundance of chipped stone axes for the first time. This trend continues through the remaining Early Jomon period to the Middle Jomon period.

Currently, we do not have any convincing explanations for why this major system change occurred. However, if there was population movement from Area II to Area III, that would have resulted in a significant increase in population pressure in Area III, which would provide a reason for the system change.

Because Areas II and III shared the same pottery style (the Moroiso style), the travelers may not have perceived their relocation as a permanent migration from one area to another. Rather, the change may have occurred as a result of a series of annual decisions about where to obtain food and where to establish a new camp/residential base.

Given these considerations, I have hypothesized elsewhere (Habu 2002b) that the possible population movements from Area II to III in the Moroiso-c subphase had resulted in a significant increase in population pressure within Area III, which triggered the development of a new type of a collecting system associated with a large number of chipped stone axes. This new system eventually dominated both the Kanto and Chubu regions (i.e., Areas I, II, and III) during the Middle Jomon period.

The development of a Middle Jomon settlement system with a large number of chipped stone axes in the Kanto and Chubu regions has attracted the attention of many archaeologists, since the system was associated with various unique cultural characteristics, including large settlement size and sophisticated material culture represented in the decoration of various shapes of Jomon pots and clay figurines (see for example Kamikawana 1970). It is this system that made Fujimori (1950; 1970) and others hypothesize that Middle Jomon people may have been relying on plant cultivation rather than hunting and gathering (see chapter 3). Other scholars, such as Keiji Imamura (1996), believe that the abundance of chipped stone axes represents a heavy reliance on collecting wild plant roots rather than plant cultivation.

Despite the active debates on the nature of this "Middle Jomon type" of subsistence-settlement systems, very few scholars have discussed the mechanisms of this development. The results of the settlement pattern analysis presented above indicate that interregional population movements may have been its cause. In this possible scenario, the system change in Area II can be explained within the context of the collector–forager model. However, the population movement from Area II to III and the resulting changes in the subsistence-settlement systems in Area III should be considered as historically unique events (i.e., these events occurred only as a result of a series of preceding events and regionally specific conditions). In this regard, this case study not only confirms the utility of the collector–forager model, but it also demonstrates the possible use of Jomon data to expand the original model (for theoretical implications of this case study, see Habu 2002b).

Discussion

In summary, the results of this case study indicate that intersite variability in lithic assemblages and site size, as well as site distribution patterns from the Moroiso phase, are generally consistent with those of collectors with seasonal moves, with the exception of settlement patterns from the Moroiso-c subphase of southwestern Kanto, which may represent the forager system. Since the hypothesis used in this analysis is based on several assumptions, further analysis will be necessary in order to investigate the general characteristics of the subsistence-settlement systems of the Moroiso-phase people, as well as the interrelationships between environmental changes and the possible collapse of logistically organized subsistence-settlement systems in southwestern Kanto. Nevertheless, currently available data indicate that the Moroiso-phase people were not fully sedentary. In other words, the analysis did not support the interpretation suggested by Wajima (1948; 1958) and other scholars that the people of the Jomon period were fully sedentary. The case study also demonstrated that, with its large body of archaeological data, Jomon settlement studies could contribute to the sophistication of archaeological models of hunter-gatherer behavior.

In order to determine whether the Moroiso-phase example represents a typical Jomon settlement pattern, further analysis of data from other phases and other regions will be necessary. Although detailed analyses of data from other phases have yet to be conducted, I would like to present preliminary results of site size analysis using data from three other phases. Figure 4.15 shows site size variability among dwelling sites from the Moroiso phase and three other phases of the Middle and Late Jomon periods in the Kanto region: the Katsusaka, Kasori-E, and Horinouchi phases. In this figure, site size is measured by the total number of pit-dwellings from each site. Unfortunately, lithic assemblage data from these phases are not available at this time. However, as shown in this figure, the site size data of these phases exhibit similar patterns. Based on these results, I suggest that in terms of site size variability, the Moroiso-phase case is not an anomaly among settlement pattern data from various Jomon phases.

At the same time, I believe my conclusions that the Moroiso-phase people were not fully sedentary should not automatically be generalized to all other phases of the Jomon period. Analyses of changes through the

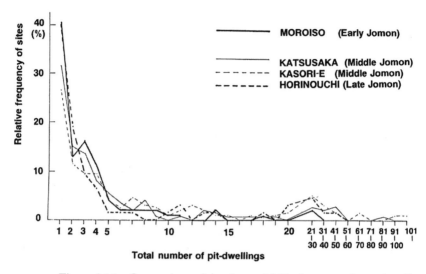

Figure 4.15   Comparison of site size variability between phases (modified and redrawn from Habu 1989b: 86; raw data from Nihon Kokogaku
Kyokai 1984)

Moroiso phase indicate that the settlement systems could change significantly in a fairly short time, even within a single phase. Furthermore, the
results of recent excavations have revealed that the regional and temporal
variability of the Jomon culture was far more diverse than archaeologists
had once assumed.

Case Study 2: The Sannai Maruyama site and its place in regional settlement systems

As I stated in the previous section, the case study described above does
not necessarily draw a picture of a "typical" Jomon settlement pattern,
because the Moroiso-phase data represent only a small part of the rich
Jomon database. Furthermore, many Japanese researchers think that the
assumption of Jomon sedentism should be tested against Middle Jomon
data, not the Early Jomon data, since the relative abundance of extremely
large settlements is particularly characteristic of the Middle Jomon period
in the Tohoku, Kanto, and Chubu regions. In other words, reexamination
of the traditional assumption of Jomon sedentism should ideally include
systematic analyses of Middle Jomon large settlements.

The recent excavation of the Sannai Maruyama site in Aomori Prefecture (fig. 1.1; for site location see fig. 4.16) provides us with an excellent

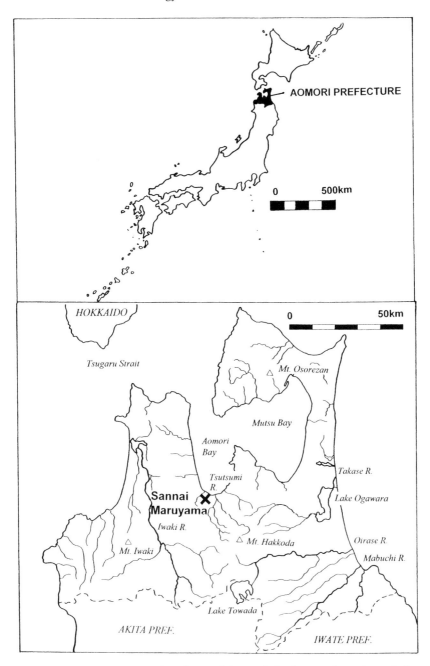

Figure 4.16 The locations of Aomori Prefecture (upper) and the Sannai Maruyama site (lower)

opportunity to examine the degree of sedentism of the Middle Jomon people in relation to site size. As mentioned in the first chapter, Sannai Maruyama is an extremely large site dated to the Early and Middle Jomon periods. The site area was originally planned as a baseball stadium, but the presence of numerous features and artifacts in the site, revealed through salvage excavations prior to the construction of the stadium, made the governor of the prefecture decide that the stadium construction should be halted for the sake of preserving the site. Subsequent test excavations indicated that the site area extends outside the Stadium Area. To date, more than 700 pit-dwellings, as well as numerous other features including long-houses, grave pits, burial jars, and "circular stone burials," have been recovered. It is currently one of the major tourist spots in Aomori Prefecture.

Overview of the Sannai Maruyama site

Figure 4.17 illustrates various excavation areas of the Sannai Maruyama site. These excavations were conducted by the Board of Education of Aomori Prefecture and the Board of Education of Aomori City from 1977 to 1999. Prior to these excavations, part of the Stadium Area was excavated by Keio University between 1953 and 1958. The two sections shaded with oblique lines (the West Parking Lot Area and the Chikano Area) indicate areas excavated during the 1970s. The excavation of the West Parking Lot Area (Aomori-ken Kyoiku Iinkai 1977) revealed the presence of fifty-six grave pits aligned in two rows in the east–west direction. The Chikano Area, on the lower right-hand corner of the figure, was originally identified as a separate site (Aomori-ken Kyoiku Iinkai 1977) but is now considered to be part of the Sannai Maruyama site complex. The coarse dots indicate areas excavated as CRM projects from 1992 to 1994 (Aomori-ken Maizo Bunkazai Chosa Center 1994a; 1994b; 1995; Aomori-ken Kyoiku-cho Bunka-ka 1996b; 1997b; 1998a; 1998b; 2000b; 2000c; 2000d; Aomori-shi Kyoiku Iinkai 1994; 1996). Among these, the large, circular area at the center of the figure is the Stadium Area, where the construction of a baseball stadium was originally planned. Finally, the areas shaded with fine dots or marked in black (Excavation Areas nos. 1–19 in fig. 4.17) represent a series of test excavations conducted after the preservation of the site was declared (i.e., during and after 1995) (Aomori-ken Kyoiku-cho Bunka-ka 1996a; 1997a; 1997b; 1998c; 1998d; 1999; 2000a; 2001; 2002a; 2002b). The primary purposes of these test excavations were to identify the areal extent of the site, and to obtain more data for intrasite spatial pattern analyses.

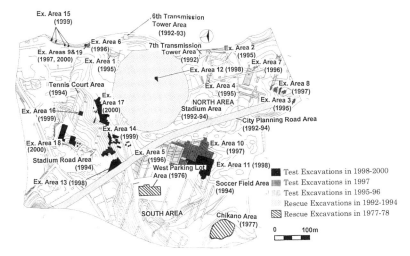

Figure 4.17 Excavation areas at the Sannai Maruyama site (modified from Aomori-ken Kyoiku-cho Bunka-ka 1998d: 12; permission for reproduction obtained from Aomori-ken Kyoiku-cho Bunka-ka)

Among these excavations, the excavation of the Stadium Area revealed particularly high concentrations of features and artifacts. Figure 4.18 illustrates the distribution of features recovered within the Stadium Area. Within this area alone, more than 500 pit-dwellings have been identified. Several clusters of features are illustrated in this figure: Early Jomon pit-dwellings are primarily clustered on the west side of the Northern Valley Midden, whereas Middle Jomon pit-dwellings are distributed throughout the Stadium Area. Middle Jomon grave pits and burial jars are located in the northeastern part of the area, and three clusters of "raised-floor buildings" can be identified in the center, northwest, and southwest quadrants (Okada 1995a). A "raised-floor building" refers to a set of six postmolds that are placed in a rectangular plan. Since there is no clear evidence of a floor associated with any of these features, most archaeologists assume that the floors of these features were constructed above the ground surface and supported by posts driven into the ground (see Miyamoto 1995).

One of these six postmold features recovered from the northwestern part of the Stadium Area was associated with particularly large postmolds. Each of the six postmolds was about 1.8 meters in diameter and more than 2 meters deep (fig. 4.19). Because the postmolds were so deep, the bases of the wooden posts were preserved. They were approximately 75 to 95 centimeters in diameter and were identified as chestnut (Okada 1995a). Some scholars suggest that these were ceremonial wooden poles such

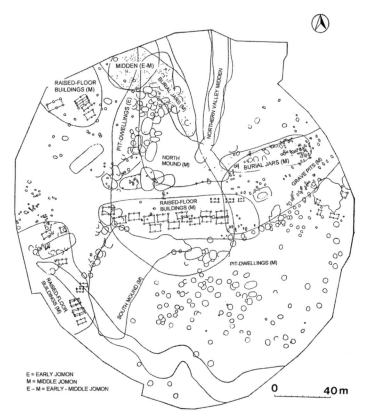

Figure 4.18   Distribution of features at the Stadium Area, the Sannai
Maruyama site (from Okada and Habu 1995)

as totem poles (e.g., T. Kobayashi 2000: 156–163). Many others (e.g.,
Okada 1995a), however, believe that the posts represent the remains of a
raised-floor building with a heavy superstructure (see Miyamoto 1995),
possibly a tower. Following this suggestion, the feature was reconstructed
as a 17-meter tower at the site near the original location.

The Northern Valley Midden indicated in the upper part of fig. 4.18
is a waterlogged midden in which a large number of potsherds as well as
abundant faunal and floral remains were recovered. The majority of these
are dated to the Early Jomon period, although the midden itself continued
to be used until the beginning of the Middle Jomon period. A similar kind
of midden deposit has also been identified along the northwestern edge
of the site, such as the Sixth Transmission Tower Area and Excavation
Area 6 (see fig. 4.17). The South and North Mounds are dated to the

Figure 4.19   Features associated with six large posts (photograph provided by courtesy of Aomori-ken Kyoiku-cho Bunka-ka)

Middle Jomon period. Although these are called "mounds," the primary
nature of these features is probably also middens, since a large number
of potsherds have been recovered from the mounds. Unlike the Northern
Valley Midden, however, the organic remains in these mounds are poorly
preserved. A similar feature from the Middle Jomon period called the
West Mound has been identified in Excavation Area 17.

The artifact assemblage excavated from the Sannai Maruyama site also
is probably the largest of any of the Jomon sites. From the Stadium Area
alone more than 40,000 cardboard boxes (approximately 40 × 30 ×
25 cm) of archaeological remains were excavated (Okada 1995b; 1997).
Since the average quantity of artifacts excavated from all the other CRM
projects within Aomori Prefecture per year fills between 800 and 1,000
cardboard boxes (Okada 1997), it is apparent that the quantity recovered
from Sannai Maruyama is extraordinary. It is estimated that these artifacts are only a small portion of all the artifacts contained within the site.
The majority of the excavated artifacts are potsherds. In particular, the
accumulation of potsherds in the Northern Valley Midden and the South
and North Mounds was extremely dense. In addition, approximately

1,500 clay figurines or figurine fragments (Ogasawara and Katsuragi 1999) have been recovered. The lithic tools recovered from the site include various kinds of hunting and food-processing tools, such as arrowheads, stemmed scrapers, grinding stones, and stone mortars. An abundance of artifacts made from organic materials, such as bone and wood, is also a characteristic of the artifact assemblage of Sannai Maruyama (Aomori-ken Maizo Bunkazai Chosa Center 1995). The majority of these organic remains were recovered from Early Jomon waterlogged middens. Various types of bone and ivory tools and ornaments, as well as wooden containers, lacquerware, basketry, cordage, and textiles, were recovered (Okada 1995a; Ozeki 1996). Finally, the abundance of exotic materials such as jade, amber, asphalt, and obsidian, in contrast to the paucity of these materials at other sites, is also a characteristic of the Sannai Maruyama site (Okada 1995a).

Chronological studies of pottery excavated from the site indicate that the site was occupied through twelve consecutive phases. They are, from the oldest to the youngest, the Lower-Ento-a, -b, -c, and -d (Early Jomon), Upper-Ento-a, -b, -c, -d, and -e, Enokibayashi, Saibana, and Daigi 10 (Middle Jomon). Based on traditional Jomon chronology, the site occupation duration was first estimated to have been from 5500 to 4000 bp (ca. 6300–4500 cal BP) (Okada 1995a; 1995b; 1997). Results of recent AMS radiocarbon dates from the site (M. Imamura 1999; Tsuji 1999; Toizumi and Tsumura 2000) indicate that the occupation of the site spanned approximately 5050 to 3900 bp (ca. 5900–4400 cal BP) (fig. 4.20). Using a computer simulation, Mineo Imamura (1999) has calculated the probability distribution of calibrated dates per ten years for each phase (fig. 4.21).

Because of the long occupational span, no scholar believes that all 700 pit-dwellings were occupied simultaneously. Okada (1995b) estimates the number of simultaneously occupied pit-dwellings to have been between 40 and 50, and, at one point in the Middle Jomon period, as many as 100. He also assumes that the average number of people in each pit-dwelling was probably 4 or 5, and suggests that approximately 200 to 500 people occupied the site continuously for over 1,500 years. Other researchers agree that the population of Sannai Maruyama could have been as large as 500 or more (see e.g., Koyama 1995; Obayashi et al. 1994; but contra M. Yamada 1997).

Analyses of faunal and floral remains from the site provide us with useful information regarding the subsistence activities of the site residents. Nishimoto (1995), who analyzed faunal remains from the Sannai Maruyama site, reports that the faunal assemblage from the site is characterized by an abundance of fish, birds, and small terrestrial mammals.

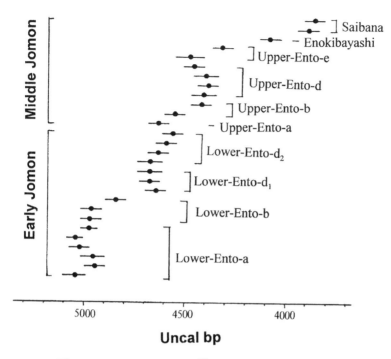

Figure 4.20   Uncalibrated ^{14}C dates from the Sannai Maruyama site.
Each dot represents one sample. The line indicates the one sigma range
for each sample. The Lower-Ento-d phase is subdivided into d_1 and
d_2 phases. No ^{14}C dates are currently available from Lower-Ento-c,
Upper-Ento-c, and Daigi 10 phases (modified and redrawn from Tsuji
1999: 36).

For example, based on the minimum number of individuals (MNI), more
than half of the terrestrial mammal assemblage from the Sixth Transmission Tower Area (see the north edge on fig. 4.17) consists of *Lepus* (rabbit)
and *Petaurista leucogenys* (flying squirrels) (Nishimoto 1998). This is in
sharp contrast with most other Jomon sites, where *Cervus nippon* (sika
deer) and *Sus scrofa* (wild boar) are the two most commonly reported terrestrial mammals. Nishimoto (1995) presents a hypothesis that the Sannai Maruyama hunters had to hunt primarily rabbits and flying squirrels
despite their low meat content since both deer and boar in this region
had been overexploited.

Analysis of fish remains recovered from the Sixth Transmission Tower
Area presented by Toizumi (1998) indicates that, in terms of MNI,
fish remains retrieved with a 4 mm mesh screen and those collected

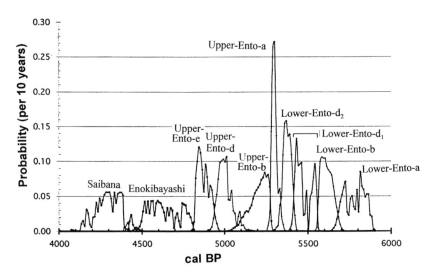

Figure 4.21   Probability distribution of calibrated dates for each phase (modified from Mineo Imamura 1999: 30; permission for reproduction obtained from Mineo Imamura)

by excavators during the fieldwork are characterized by an abundance of *Seriola* (yellow tail), Pleuronectidae (flatfish), Tetraodontidae (blowfish), *Scomber* (mackerel), Scorpaenidae (scorpion fish), *Clupea* (herring), Embiotocidae (surf perch), and Monacanthidae (file fish). In terms of the total numbers of vertebrae, the common presence of Chondrichthyes (cartilaginous fish), the majority of which are probably from several species of sharks, is also noticeable. Using these quantitative data, Toizumi (1998) discusses various aspects of fishing by the site's residents, including fishing zones, technology, butchering, trade/exchange, and seasonality. With regard to seasonality, he recorded the presence of taxa from all four seasons, although those from spring to fall are particularly abundant. Based on this evidence, he suggests that the site was occupied throughout the year (Toizumi 1998: 86). Nishimoto (1995) suggests that, while various kinds of faunal remains have been identified, the total quantity of faunal remains found at the site does not seem to be enough to support the site residents throughout the year. Accordingly, the importance of plant food should be considered seriously.

Macro floral remains identified from the Sannai Maruyama site are characterized by an abundance of nuts, such as *Castanea* (chestnut) and *Juglans* (walnut), and various kinds of fruit seeds, such as *Rubus* (raspberry), *Sambucus* (elderberry), *Morus* (mulberry), and *Vitis* (wild grape)

(Minaki 1995; Tsuji 1997a; Minaki, Saito, and Tsuji 1998; Minaki, Tsuji, and Sumita 1998). The majority of these floral remains were recovered from waterlogged Early Jomon middens, and are not carbonized. Minaki (1995) notes that the majority of walnut remains are husks, most of which are fragments and often have traces of processing in the form of hammering marks. An abundance of berries, particularly of elderberry and mulberry, has been interpreted as an indication of the brewing of fruit wine by the site residents (Minaki 1995; Tsuji 1997a; 1998). The common presence of chrysalides of Drosophilidae (fruit fly) in the concentration of these plant seeds (Y. Mori 1998a; 1998b; 1999), indicating the fruits were in the process of fermentation when they were discarded, also seems to support the fruit wine hypothesis.

Results of pollen analyses (Tsuji 1997a; Yasuda 1995; Yoshikawa and Tsuji 1998) also provide insights into understanding changes in not only the vegetation surrounding the site but also the use of plants by the site residents. According to Yoshikawa and Tsuji (1998), who analyzed pollen data from the Sixth Transmission Tower Area, chestnut pollens increased significantly at the time of the beginning of the site occupation (i.e., during the Lower-Ento-a phase) and became dominant by the time of the Lower-Ento-b through -d phases. This change seems to have been accompanied by the decline of the deciduous forest and the development of secondary vegetation near the site. Tsuji (1996) suggests that the chestnut forest, which originally developed as a result of clearing the landscape for human habitation, may have been later tended or managed by the site occupants because of its usefulness as food/lumber/fuel resources. He believes that the chestnut forest continued to dominate the landscape from the beginning of the site occupation up to at least the Upper-Ento-e phase in the middle of the Middle Jomon period. It should be mentioned, however, that pollen data provided by Yasuda (1995) indicate that the amount of chestnut pollen may have fluctuated significantly over the 1,500 years of site occupation.

The possibility of chestnut cultivation/domestication has also been suggested by Sato and Yamanaka (Y. Sato 1997; 1998; Y. Sato et al. 2003; Yamanaka et al. 1999) through DNA analyses of chestnut remains recovered from the site. According to their analyses, genetic diversity of neutral mutations (*sensu* Kimura 1968) such as isozymes and DNA fingerprint types among excavated chestnut seeds was remarkably low in comparison to that found in the wild chestnut population. Citing their previous DNA studies on rice and barley, these researchers suggest that the reduction of genetic diversity of neutral mutations is a typical occurrence in the course of domestication. Similar DNA analysis conducted on walnut remains from the Sannai Maruyama site (Kiyokawa 2000) indicates that the reduction of genetic diversity is not noticeable among walnut remains from the site.

In addition to nuts and fruit seeds, possible cultigens such as *Lagenaria* (bottle gourd), Leguminosae (bean), and *Arctium* (burdock) have also been identified (Minaki 1995; Tsuji 1996), although the quantity of these remains is extremely small. Bottle gourd seeds have been recovered from many Jomon sites, including the Early Jomon Torihama shell-midden (Fukui Prefecture) and the Early Jomon Awazu shell-midden (Shiga Prefecture). Since bottle gourds are not indigenous in the Japanese archipelago, they are believed to have been introduced from mainland Asia as a cultigen (Yoshizaki 1995). However, they were probably valued for their use as containers rather than as food. Bean remains have also been reported from many Jomon sites, but their identification has been controversial. While many of the bean remains were initially identified as green gram (*Vigta radiata*), which is a cultigen, subsequent studies indicate that it is difficult to distinguish green gram from other domesticated beans, such as *Azukia angularis* (azuki bean) and *Glycine max* (soybean), and from wild beans, such as *Azukia angularis* var. *nipponensis* (*yabutsuru azuki* in its Japanese common name), *Glycine soja* (*tsuru-mame*; wild soybean), and *Amphicarpaea edgeworthii* (hog peanut) (Yoshizaki 1995).

Finally, microscopic analysis of the clay of Middle Jomon potsherds excavated from the site revealed the presence of phytoliths of *Echinochloa crusgalli* (barnyard grass) (Fujiwara 1998), although its relative importance in the diet of the Sannai Maruyama people has been questioned (Yasuda 1995). *Echinochloa* seeds have also been reported from many sites, including the Incipient Jomon Nakano B site, the Early Jomon Hamanasuno site, and the Middle Jomon Usujiri B site in Hokkaido (Takahashi 1998), as well as from the Middle Jomon Tominosawa site in Aomori Prefecture (Yoshizaki and Tsubakisaka 1992). Yoshizaki (1995) points out that many of the *Echinochloa* seeds from these sites are larger than regular *E. crusgalli* seeds and suggests the possibility of semicultivation. Some ethnobotanists suggest that the transition from wild *E. crusgalli* to cultivated *E. utilis* (barnyard millet) occurred somewhere in northeastern Eurasia, possibly in the Japanese archipelago (e.g., Sadao Sakamoto's statement in Sasaki and Matsuyama 1988: 366).

Conventional interpretation of the site

The general picture of the Sannai Maruyama site emerging from the above description is that of a large settlement occupied by a group of extremely "affluent" hunter-gatherers, who may have carried out a little plant cultivation, for over 1,500 years. Because of its large size, many researchers have suggested that residents of the Sannai Maruyama site were fully sedentary, occupying the site throughout the year. For example, Okada (1995a; 1995b), who directed the Stadium Area excavation and who is presently the head archaeologist of the Preservation Office of the Sannai Maruyama Site (Sannai Maruyama Iseki Taisaku-shitsu; a branch office of the Cultural Affairs Section of the Agency of Education of Aomori Prefecture), suggests that the major characteristics of the site can be summarized by three key words: "large," "long," and "abundant." He suggests that all of these characteristics reflect the affluence of the lifeways of the site residents, and that the affluence was established on the basis of long-term full sedentism. Based on his intrasite spatial analysis, Okada also suggests that, because similar types of feature tend to form clusters, the location of different types of feature must have been determined under strict social control with long-term planning. Since potsherds from twelve successive phases (Early Jomon Lower-Ento-a, -b, -c, -d, and Middle Jomon Upper-Ento-a, -b, -c, -d, -e, Enokibayashi, Saibana, and Daigi 10 phases) are present at the site, Okada (1995a) suggests that the site was continuously occupied by several hundred people for approximately 1,500 years.

Koyama (1995) supports other scholars' suggestions that the site population was over 500, and suggests that this number is much larger than the population of a typical "band society" such as the Australian Aborigines and the Great Basin Shoshone. Citing ethnographic records, Koyama points out that large settlements that are similar to Sannai Maruyama are common among hunter-gatherers of the Northwest Coast of North America, where there was social differentiation between the nobles, commoners, and slaves. He also suggests that the North and South Mounds may have had a ceremonial or religious function, and that the extraordinarily large quantity of pottery and artifacts recovered from these mounds is not just debris but it may reflect some kind of ceremonial activity conducted at the mounds.

On the basis of currently available data, Koyama (1995) presents visual images of the Sannai Maruyama settlement in several drawings. In one of the drawings, the South and North Mounds are reconstructed as large trapezoidal mounds with stairways resembling the Mississippian mounds in Cahokia. According to his interpretation, the row of raised-floor store houses in the drawing represents an abundance of stored food and/or valuable goods, such as lacquerware, for exchange in long-distance trade. A long-house, which he suggests was either a shrine, communal house, or the residence of the chief, is painted with red and black, the two colors that the Jomon people used for the decoration of lacquerware and pottery. The overall image of the life of the site residents is quite sophisticated, and the advanced nature of Jomon technology and culture is emphasized.

Complexity in site structure

The images of extremely "affluent," fully sedentary hunter-gatherers occupying the site for over 1,500 years have strongly appealed not only to many archaeologists but also to the media and to the general public (Habu and Fawcett 1999). However, detailed examination of currently available data from the site suggests that the interpretation of the site may not be as straightforward as one might think (Habu et al. 2001).

It should be emphasized that there are apparent changes in the number of pit-dwellings and other kinds of features, as well as in intrasite feature distribution patterns, over time. Because these changes are quite significant, reconstructing the general picture of the site without specifying a particular occupational phase would tell us little about the lifeways of the site residents. According to Okada (1998a), in terms of feature distribution, pit-dwellings and other features from the Early Jomon period (the Lower-Ento-a, -b, -c, and -d phases) are located primarily within the central and northern parts of the Stadium Area (see fig. 4.18). By the early Middle Jomon period (the Upper-Ento-a, -b, and -c phases), they are located throughout the entire Stadium Area. The size of the settlement, measured by both the number of associated pit-dwellings and the areal extent of features, increased significantly during the middle of the Middle Jomon period (the Upper-Ento-d, Upper-Ento-e, Enokibayashi, and Saibana phases) outside the Stadium Area (see fig. 4.17). For example, the majority of pit-dwellings recovered from Excavation Areas 10 and 11, which are located immediately southeast of the Stadium Area, are dated to the Upper-Ento-d and -e phases (Hata 1998). Finally, the size of the settlement shrank dramatically at the end of the Middle Jomon period (the Daigi 10 phase, which is the last phase of the Middle Jomon period) (Okada 1998a). Thus, despite his interpretation of Sannai Maruyama being an extremely large settlement over 1,500 years, Okada acknowledges significant changes in intrasite spatial patterns through time.

Given the evidence of changes through time, I suggest that the image of a large settlement associated with an extremely large number of pit-dwellings may apply to the middle of the Middle Jomon period, but not necessarily to the other phases. Furthermore, to make things complicated, currently available faunal and floral data from the site are largely restricted to those from Early Jomon waterlogged layers. The preliminary results of faunal and macro floral analyses described above are based on the results from two middens, the Northern Valley Midden and the midden at the Sixth Transmission Tower Area, both of which are dated primarily to the Early Jomon period. In other words, results of faunal and floral analysis should not be considered fully representative when we discuss subsistence strategies of the site residents during the Middle Jomon period (i.e., the height of prosperity for the Sannai Maruyama in terms of the number of associated pit-dwellings). Faunal and floral data are invaluable sources of information as long as we keep in mind the time period with which they are associated.

Alternative approaches

To find alternative approaches, I suggest that we should go back to the collector–forager model described in the first chapter and think how we can examine subsistence and settlement practice at Sannai Maruyama within this context. In both Okada's (1995a; 1995b; 2003) and Koyama's (1995) interpretations, the large site size, the long occupational span, and the abundance of artifacts are the primary lines of archaeological evidence to suggest long-term full sedentism. However, from the perspective of hunter-gatherer studies and the collector–forager model, this interpretation is not necessarily convincing. Ethnographic examples of hunter-gatherers from California, the Northwest Coast of North America, and the Arctic indicate that large site size itself does not necessarily imply full-year occupation. As indicated in the first chapter, many hunter-gatherers with large settlements are relatively sedentary collectors, occupying large residential bases in a particular season of the year (often in the winter), while still moving their residential bases to other places in the rest of the year (see fig. 1.6). In most cases, large, seasonal residential bases are reoccupied on a multi-year basis; i.e., people came back to the same site every year in a particular season (or seasons) and reoccupied or rebuilt houses and other features (Binford 1982). As a result, in terms of typological chronology of associated artifacts, it may look as if these sites were occupied continuously. In other words, in order to determine whether a particular site was occupied by fully sedentary collectors or seasonally sedentary collectors, examination of several lines of evidence is required.

Changes in the number of pit-dwellings   The first step in understanding the settlement systems of the Sannai Maruyama residents is to understand changes over time in site characteristics so that data from different phases are not mixed up when they are being interpreted. In this regard, changes in the number of pit-dwellings from each phase show

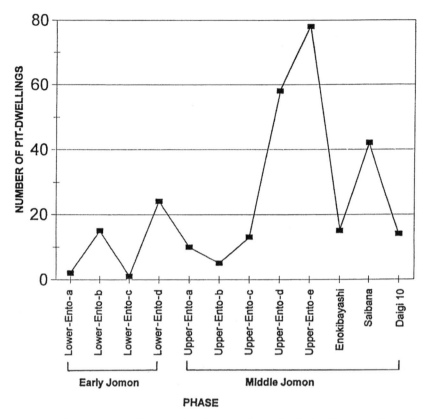

Figure 4.22 Changes in the number of pit-dwellings at Sannai Maruyama (from Habu et al. 2001: 14)

an interesting trend. Figure 4.22 indicates changes in the number of pit-dwellings identified in each phase (Habu et al. 2001; the original data illustrated in the figure were presented by Sannai Maruyama Iseki Taisaku-shitsu 1999). When possible, a specific phase was assigned to each pit-dwelling on the basis of the typological classification of associated pottery. Unfortunately, less than half of the 700 pit-dwellings were available for this analysis, since associated artifacts from the other pit-dwellings were either not diagnostic enough or they were not yet catalogued. Accordingly, the number of pit-dwellings for each phase does not represent the maximum number of pit-dwellings from the phase, nor does it represent the minimum number of simultaneously occupied pit-dwellings as many of the pit-dwellings from the same phase overlap. In other words, the number of pit-dwellings in the figure does not represent absolute population levels. Rather, the number should be seen as a possible reflection of general trends in the increase and decrease in the number of associated dwellings (Habu et al. 2001).

From this graph, several interesting characteristics can be observed. First, in terms of the number of pit-dwellings, only two phases, Upper-Ento-d and Upper-Ento-e, are associated with more than fifty pit-dwellings. In other words, for the other ten phases we have no archaeological evidence to support the image of a large settlement associated with more than fifty pit-dwellings. Second, a rapid increase in the number of pit-dwellings from the Upper-Ento-c to Upper-Ento-d phases is apparent. This may reflect major changes in site function from the earlier to the later phases of site occupation. Third, the line graph does not form a smooth and gradually increasing curve but instead is characterized by several decreases followed by sharp increases. This suggests that the size of the Sannai Maruyama settlement, measured by the number of associated pit-dwellings, not only changed through time but may also have fluctuated significantly.

Changes in dwelling size   Second, changes over time are also evident in terms of variability in the size of pit-dwellings. Figure 4.23 illustrates changes through time in pit-dwelling size variability measured by long-axis length. Data from the Lower-Ento-a and Lower-Ento-c phases are currently unavailable. Nevertheless, several trends are evident. First, the two Early Jomon phases represented in this figure (i.e., Lower-Ento-b and -d) are characterized by a relatively wide diversity in dwelling size. If we exclude pit-dwellings of more than 10 meters in length, which are usually classified as long-houses and are considered to have been communal houses, the plots are scattered primarily between 2.5 and 7 meters, but with no apparent concentrations. In other words, if we tentatively classify plots as small (less than 4 m in length), medium (4–6 m), and large (more than 6 m), we find roughly equal numbers of pit-dwellings in each category. In contrast, many of the pit-dwellings from the Middle Jomon period are relatively small, the length of the long axis being between 2.5 and 4 meters. This pattern is particularly characteristic of the Upper-Ento-d, -e, and Enokibayashi phases, from which more than 80 percent of pit-dwellings measure less than 4 meters along the long-axis length. The difference between the Early and Middle Jomon periods is also apparent from table 4.3.

The small size of pit-dwellings from the Upper-Ento-d and -e phases at Sannai Maruyama does not imply that the pit-dwelling size in this region was generally small during this time period. According to Okada (1998b), the majority of Upper-Ento-e pit-dwellings at Sannai Maruyama measure

Table 4.3 *Changes in the average length of the long axis of pit-dwellings from each phase*

Phase[1]	Mean of long-axis length (SD)[2]
Saibana (n = 13)	3.94 (± 1.04)
Enokibayashi (n = 10)	3.31 (± 0.89)
Upper-Ento-e (n = 32)	3.62 (± 0.82)
Upper-Ento-d (n = 30)	3.42 (± 0.54)
Lower-Ento-d (n = 12)	5.23 (± 1.79)
Lower-Ento-b (n = 13)	4.80 (± 1.58)

Notes:
[1] Phases with n < 10 are excluded.
[2] Excluding pit-dwellings the long axes of which measure more than 10 m.
Sources: Data were compiled from Aomori-ken Maizo Bunkazai Chosa Center 1994a, and Aomori-ken Kyoiku-cho Bunka-ka 1998b; 2000b; 2000c (modified from Habu 2002c:171).

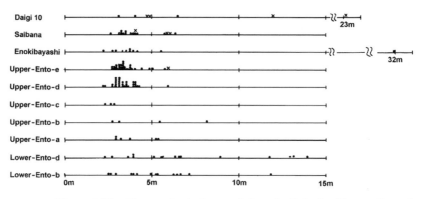

Figure 4.23   Changes in the long-axis length of pit-dwellings at Sannai Maruyama (data compiled from Aomori-ken Maizo Bunkazai Chosa Center 1994a, and Aomori-ken Kyoiku-cho Bunka-ka 1998b; 2000b; 2000c, modified from Habu 2002c: 171)

less than 10 square meters in floor area. These pit-dwellings correspond roughly to pit-dwellings with less than 4 meters in long-axis length as shown in fig. 4.23. On the other hand, measurement of floor areas of Upper-Ento-e pit-dwellings at the Tominosawa site, another large Middle Jomon settlement in Aomori Prefecture (Aomori-ken Maizo Bunkazai Chosa Center 1992a; 1992b), indicates that pit-dwellings at Tominosawa include larger ones, 10–30 square meters in floor area (see figure 1 in

Okada 1998b). This may imply that the difference in pit-dwelling size between these two sites reflects different site function.

Changes in lithic assemblages   Third, changes over time are also evident through the examination of lithic assemblage data. Figure 4.24.1 through 5 shows the percentages of eleven categories of lithic tools associated with each phase. These data were taken from pit-dwellings dated to each phase with the exception of the data for Lower-Ento-a (fig. 4.24.1; see the caption to the figure). The eleven categories of stone tools are: (1) arrowheads (ARH), (2) stemmed scrapers (SSC), (3) awls (AWL), (4) semi-circular chipped stone tools (SSC), (5) polished stone axes (PAX), (6) pebble tools (PBL), (7) stone mortars (MTR), (8) grinding stones (GRD), (9) net sinkers (NSK), (10) ornaments (ORN) and (11) others (OTH).

From these graphs, significant changes through time in lithic assemblage characteristics can be observed. The lithic assemblage of Lower-Ento-a phase is characterized by an abundance of stemmed scrapers as well as arrowheads and awls (fig. 4.24.1). Assemblages from the following Lower-Ento-b, Lower-Ento-d, and Upper-Ento-a phases are characterized by multiple peaks in the categories of arrowheads, stemmed scrapers, and grinding stones (fig. 4.24.2). The Upper-Ento-b, -c, and -d phases, on the other hand, are characterized by an abundance of grinding stones (fig. 4.24.3). Finally, the latter part of the site occupation from the Upper-Ento-e to Daigi 10 phases is generally characterized by a single peak of arrowheads (fig. 4.24.4) with the exception of the Saibana phase (multiple peaks in arrowheads, mortars, and grinding stones: fig. 4.24.5).

A life history of the Sannai Maruyama site: a model

The data analysis presented here is preliminary, since it is based on only the published results of the previous site excavations. Nevertheless, from these three lines of evidence it is apparent that the "life history" of the site may have been quite complex. In other words, we cannot assume that the function of the site remained the same over the 1,500 years of its use.

Rather than assuming a large, monofunctional settlement gradually developing and declining over 1,500 years, I suggest that the Sannai Maruyama site represents a palimpsest of multiple occupations over a long period, each of which was characterized by a different subsistence-settlement system. While the amount of currently available data is not sufficient to provide a conclusive statement regarding *the* life history of the site, I suggest that the occupational span of the site can be tentatively

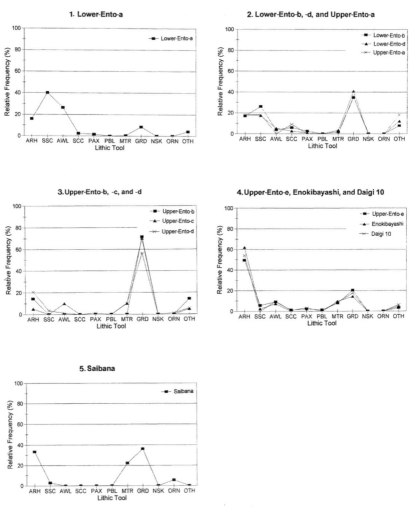

Figure 4.24   Relative frequencies of lithic tools for each category for each phase at Sannai Maruyama. For the Lower-Ento-a phase, the numbers of lithic tools from Layers VIa and VIb, which are dated to this phase, were used as raw data. For the other phases, the numbers of lithic tools associated with pit-dwellings from each phase were used. (Data compiled from Aomori-ken Maizo Bunkazai Chosa Center 1994a, and Aomori-ken Kyoikucho Bunka-ka 1998a; 1998b; 2000b; 2000c, modified from Habu 2002c: 172)

divided into the following five periods. The dates assigned to these periods are approximate estimates based on Mineo Imamura (1999) (see fig. 4.21).

Period I: Lower-Ento-a phase (ca. 5900–5650 cal BP)   This period is characterized by a scarcity of pit-dwellings. However, the presence of waterlogged midden deposits from this phase identified in the Sixth Transmission Tower and the Northern Valley areas, which are associated with a large number of faunal and floral remains, suggests that the site was actively utilized by the Jomon people during this phase. In order to understand the overall subsistence-settlement systems of the site residents during this phase, we need to examine further the seasonality of site occupation using several lines of archaeological evidence. As noted above, Toizumi (1998), who analyzed fish remains from this phase, reports the presence of fish taxa from all four seasons, and suggests the year-round occupation of the site. However, in fact only 5 percent of his samples is definitely winter fish, a fact that may indicate a relatively low level of activity during the winter. The scarcity of deer and boar remains from the middens associated with this phase, which was pointed out by Nishimoto (1995; 1998), may also reflect that the site was not actively used during the winter. According to H. Kaneko (1979), deer and boar hunting must have been conducted primarily during the winter, when both of these species form large groups. In other words, the scarcity of deer and boar remains does not necessarily indicate the depletion of these resources; it simply may be a result of seasonal site occupation. Given these lines of faunal evidence, and given the fact that the number of pit-dwellings associated with this phase is extremely small, I suggest that the site may have been used primarily during the spring to fall either as a special-purpose site (probably a field camp) or as a seasonal residential base of relatively sedentary collectors, with a short-term additional use in the winter.

Period II: Lower-Ento-b to -d phases (ca. 5650–5350 cal BP) Assuming that the number of features associated with the Lower-Ento-c phase was underestimated because of the problem of pottery chronology, we can say that this period was characterized by a relative abundance of associated pit-dwellings compared to the previous period. Various characteristics of the site from this period, including the types of associated features and relatively large variability in dwelling size, are similar to many other large Jomon sites that are believed to have functioned as residential bases (*sensu* Binford 1980). Given the substantial amount of labor investment to construct pit-dwellings, long-houses (the long axes of which measure more than 10 meters), and other features, it is likely that the residents of the sites were a "collector" type of hunter-gatherer as opposed to "foragers." Whether the site functioned as a residential base of fully sedentary collectors or seasonally sedentary ones needs to be further examined, however. The upper half of the waterlogged deposit of the Northern Valley midden is dated to the Lower-Ento-b phase, and the midden identified at Excavation Area 6 is dated to Lower-Ento-d phase. Both of these middens contain a large number of faunal and floral remains, but results of the analyses of these remains have not yet been published.

Period III: Upper-Ento-a to -c phases (ca. 5350–5050 cal BP)   The number of associated pit-dwellings for these three phases is very small. Also, because no waterlogged midden during and after this period has been recovered, currently available faunal and floral evidence from which to infer the subsistence strategies of this period is extremely limited.

Despite the scarcity of pit-dwellings from these phases, Okada (1998a) suggests that the Upper-Ento-a and -b phases represent a rapid expansion in the settlement size compared to the Early Jomon period. This is because, when we look at the distribution of features assigned to these phases, they seem to cover a larger area than they did in the previous period. Okada also indicates that these phases are characterized by the appearance of new types of feature, which were not associated with the Early Jomon period. These features include the South, North, and West Mounds, raised-floor buildings, storage pits, burial pits, and burial jars. It should be remembered, however, that dating such features as raised-floor buildings, storage pits, and burial pits is not an easy task, since usually very few datable artifacts are associated with these features. In other words, in many cases dates assigned to these features are only rough estimates and are not based on firm archaeological evidence.

Contrary to Okada's interpretation, I suggest the possibility that the scarcity of the pit-dwellings from this period may imply that the function of the site during this period was substantially different from both previous and subsequent periods. While a fair amount of pottery and some features are definitely associated with this period, overall I found no clear evidence that the site functioned as a substantial residential base. It is also unlikely that the scarcity of pit-dwellings from this period is due to the duration of this period being shorter than the others. As indicated by radiocarbon dates, the estimated duration of Period III (approximately 5350–5050 cal BP) is no shorter than the estimated duration of other periods.

It is interesting to note that the number of Jomon sites associated with pit-dwellings from Upper-Ento-a, -b, and -c phases is relatively small within the Aomori Prefecture (Murakoshi 1998). In particular, only three sites with pit-dwellings from the Upper-Ento-b phase have been reported, none of which is a large settlement. While the amount of available archaeological data is currently limited, it seems that the subsistence-settlement systems in the Aomori area during this period were characterized by a scarcity of substantial residential bases. This may imply the presence of a forager system rather than a collector system during this period.

In terms of lithic assemblage data, the characteristics of the Upper-Ento-a phase are similar to those of the Lower-Ento-b and -d phases (fig. 4.24.2). Lithic assemblage characteristics of the Upper-Ento-b and -c phases, on the other hand, resemble those of the following Upper-Ento-d phase (fig. 4.24.3). These facts may indicate the necessity of redefining the boundaries between Periods II, III, and IV. Further analyses will be necessary in order to explain the incongruity between changes in the numbers of pit-dwellings and lithic data.

Period IV: Upper-Ento-d and -e phases (ca. 5050–4800 cal BP)
Since both of these phases are associated with more than fifty pit-dwellings, this period represents the maximum site size in terms of the number of associated pit-dwellings. However, it is important to note that the majority of these pit-dwellings are small, typically measuring only between 2.5 and 4 meters in long-axis length (fig. 4.23). Furthermore, many of the pit-dwellings from this period are shallow and are associated with only a small number of postmolds. This implies that these pit-dwellings are less labor-intensive, probably constructed for short-term use (i.e., not for full-year occupation). In other words, it is very unlikely that the site functioned as a full-year residential base of fully sedentary collectors.

Although currently available archaeological data are still limited, I suggest the possibility that the site functioned as a seasonally occupied residential base and/or a trading center. An abundance of shallow, small pit-dwellings is reminiscent of summer or early fall residential bases observed among Arctic hunter-gatherers (Mathiassen 1927:133–136). Alternatively, the aggregation of a large number of people at trading centers is also commonly described in ethnographic record. For example, Spencer (1959) describes a trading center used by the Nunamiut and Tareumiut in northern Alaska as the following:

The appearance of a trading center was everywhere the same. The people had come by prearrangement and would gather to await their partners, those from the opposite ecological setting. They unloaded their umiaks, set up their tents, the nunamiut favouring the iccellik, the tareumiut the conical skin-covered kalurvik.

The tents were set up in rows, those from each community or grouping tending to congregate in one place. The umiyaks were drawn up on the bank, turned over to dry, and the goods for trade cached under them or placed on racks that might be especially built. In a few cases, families built a paameraq as a summer dwelling at the trading center. This was not generally done, however, unless they remained for a longer period and fished nearby. (Spencer 1959:199–200)

According to Spencer's description, the number of people who came to the trading center varied from year to year. For example, at Nerliq, one of the major trading centers in northern Alaska, the number was normally between 400 and 500 but sometimes as many as 600 people. The trade fair represented the height of the summer activities of these groups. The primary items traded between the groups were caribou hides from the inland group (Nunamiut), and seal and whale oil from the maritime group (Tareumiut). After the trading ended, games and dances were usually held for several days.

Since Sannai Maruyama is located at the head of the Aomori Bay, the location would have been ideal for such a large gathering from both the inland and coastal areas. Because of the relative abundance of exotic materials recovered from the site, including jade, amber, asphalt, and obsidian, some Japanese archaeologists have suggested the possible importance of trading activity among the site residents. While many of these exotic goods, which consist of both raw materials and artifacts, are currently dated roughly to the Middle Jomon period, determination of the exact phases these materials belong to will be helpful to examine further the possibility of Sannai Maruyama being a trade center at one point in its life history.

Period V: Enokibayashi, Saibana, and Daigi 10 phases (ca. 4800– 4400 cal BP)   Only a limited amount of archaeological information is available from these last three phases of site occupation. Okada (1998a) interprets these phases as the time when the site size was gradually diminishing. Data regarding the number of pit-dwellings, however, indicate that the site size in the Enokibayashi phase, measured by the total number of associated pit-dwellings, decreased dramatically relative to that in the previous Upper-Ento-e phase. The site size then increased significantly again in the Saibana phase, and declined again in the Daigi 10 phase. The slight increase in the average length of the pit-dwellings from the Enokibayashi to Saibana phases may also reflect possible differences in site function between the Enokibayashi and Saibana phases. Lithic assemblage characteristics in the Saibana phase (fig. 4.24.5) are also different from those of the other three phases in this period (fig. 4.24.4), which may indicate change in site function. In any case, by the Daigi 10 phase the size of settlement measured by the number of associated pit-dwellings had become quite small.

Future directions of research

For the moment, the interpretation presented above remains only a model. While several lines of evidence indicate the presence of certain patterns, there are still multiple ways to interpret the archaeological patterns. Nevertheless, through the discussions presented above, it became clear that the life history of the Sannai Maruyama site was much more complex than previously assumed. Given the available archaeological evidence, I suggest that the function of the site changed through time, probably between residential base and special-purpose site as defined in the collector–forager model (Binford 1980; 1982). Even if the site was functioning as a residential base throughout most of its life history, it is more likely that the primary subsistence activities conducted at the site changed significantly through time as reflected in changes in the lithic assemblages. This also implies that we cannot assume that the seasonality of site occupation and the overall subsistence-settlement systems that encompassed Sannai Maruyama remained the same during its occupational span of over 1,500 years.

Future directions of Sannai Maruyama research should include further examination of multiple lines of archaeological evidence. In particular, I suggest that the investigation of regional settlement patterns in relation to intersite variability in site size, tool assemblages, as well as faunal and floral remains, will be critical to understanding the function(s) of Sannai Maruyama. Several large Early and Middle Jomon settlements are known from the immediate vicinity of the Sannai Maruyama site. In addition, a number of smaller Jomon settlements are located within the foraging zone (approximately 10 km in radius) and the logistical zone (approximately 20 km in radius) of the Sannai Maruyama site. Many of these sites have been excavated by Aomori-ken Kyoiku Iinkai (the Board of Education of Aomori Prefecture) and other archaeological units, and the excavation results are available in the form of detailed monographs. By examining characteristics of the Sannai Maruyama site in comparison to those of other sites in its vicinity *for each phase or period* and by comparing the regional settlement patterns with general models of hunter-gatherer subsistence-settlement systems such as the collector–forager model, we will be able to infer the possible function of the Sannai Maruyama site at each phase in relation to subsistence strategies and residential mobility. Through these examinations, we will be able to discuss changes in the site function in the context of the changes in the "cultural landscape."

To suggest that Sannai Maruyama may not have been a monofunctional site, or a fully sedentary residential base throughout its life history, does not imply that I am downplaying the importance of archaeological discoveries at the site. Rather, I suggest that the site may provide us with a unique example in which changes in hunter-gatherer lifeways may not necessarily fit into the traditional assumption of unilinear cultural evolution. In the past, many hunter-gatherer archaeologists, including Japanese archaeologists studying the Jomon culture, assumed that fully sedentary hunter-gatherers are more culturally evolved or advanced than mobile hunter-gatherers. Following this view, the presence of large settlements is often interpreted as evidence of full sedentism. However, as I have suggested elsewhere (Habu 2000), the relationship between the degree of sedentism and cultural complexity among hunter-gatherers is much more complex than scholars have previously assumed. Unlike the case of hunter-gatherers in California and the Northwest Coast, where you can see steady developments in the degree of sedentism, subsistence intensification, population density, and social stratification through time, the trajectory of the prehistoric Jomon culture does not necessarily indicate that all of these aspects developed hand in hand. By examining the interrelationship between these cultural elements in both archaeological and ethnographic examples, we will be able to have a better understanding of various aspects of hunter-gatherer lifeways. In this regard, the case of Sannai Maruyama is providing us with an excellent opportunity to understand the nature of hunter-gatherer cultural complexity.

Discussion

Case Studies 1 and 2 demonstrate that the examination of Jomon settlement data from a perspective of the collector–forager model can help us understand Jomon cultural landscapes, including the degree of sedentism. Contrary to the conventional interpretation, neither of the two cases suggests the presence of fully sedentary systems. Seasonal movements of residential bases would have significantly affected the way the Jomon people perceived their surrounding environments. In this regard, the traditional assumption, in which the degree of sedentism in Jomon society was basically equated with that in small-scale agricultural societies, needs to be reexamined. These case studies also revealed wide regional and temporal variability.

These results do not necessarily imply that none of the Jomon people were fully sedentary hunter-gatherers. On the contrary, given the large regional and temporal variability observed through these studies, it would not be a surprise if some of the collector-end Jomon groups in fact practiced full sedentism. While only two case studies have been presented here, the large body of Jomon settlement data allows us to conduct similar analyses for various parts of the Japanese archipelago in each Jomon subperiod.

Ultimately, what is important here is not to determine the degree of sedentism itself, but to understand *how* the degree of sedentism was related to various other aspects of Jomon cultural landscapes, including subsistence practice, population density/pressure, and social complexity. In terms of organizational complexity in subsistence and settlement, it is likely that both the Moroiso-phase systems in central Honshu (with the exception of the Moroiso-c subphase system in the Kanto region) and Early/Middle Jomon systems in the northern Tohoku region (with the possible exception of Period III) generally represent relatively complex systems (i.e., highly logistically organized). In other words, they are likely to have been closer to the collector end of Binford's (1980; 1982) forager–collector continuum. However, what seems most interesting here is not the average degree of organizational complexity in subsistence and settlement, but the constantly changing nature of these systems.

In Case Study 1, this fluidity of the systems seems to have led to the major change from the Early to the Middle Jomon periods. In Case Study 2 at Sannai Maruyama, we do not have enough data to assess the long-term implications of the system changes from Periods I through to V, since regional settlement pattern analyses of the northern Tohoku region have yet to be conducted. Interestingly, however, many Japanese archaeologists (e.g., Kodama 2003; Okada 2003) have noted the rapid disappearance of large settlements in northern Tohoku at the end of the Middle Jomon (i.e., the period that coincides with the last phase of the Sannai Maruyama occupation). Thus, it is likely that the abandonment of the Sannai Maruyama settlement was part of a major system change in northern Tohoku from the Middle to Late Jomon.

The ever-changing nature of Jomon subsistence-settlement systems may restrict our ability to depict subsistence-settlement characteristics at a given time in each region. Nevertheless, it does not prohibit us from examining the long-term trajectory of Jomon subsistence-settlement systems. Many scholars have pointed out that Jomon site density and settlement size show a gradual increase over time, and reached their highest point during the Middle Jomon. This trend is particularly characteristic of the Kanto and Chubu regions.

Keiji Imamura (1996:93) reports that 70 percent of all excavated Jomon pit-dwellings in the Kanto and Chubu regions are dated to the

Middle Jomon, with 50 percent of all excavated pit-dwellings belonging to the latter half of this period. In these two regions, site density (based on the total number of sites) and the frequency of large settlements (sites associated with a large number of pit-dwellings) decreased significantly from the Middle to Late Jomon. The exception is the eastern half of the Tokyo Bay area, where a concentration of Late Jomon settlements associated with large shell-middens is reported. Finally, site density and the frequency of large settlements in these two regions became very low during the Final Jomon. These changes are reflected in the population estimate presented by Koyama (see table 2.5 on p. 48). Although this may partly be due to the relatively short duration of the Final Jomon period, it does not seem to be the only reason.

To a certain extent, similar trends in long-term change can be observed in the Tohoku region. The frequency of large settlements decreases significantly from the Middle to the Late/Final Jomon periods (Kodama 2003; Okada 2003). However, a decrease in site density is not as evident as in the case of the Kanto and Chubu regions (Kodama 2003). Because of the latter factor, the population estimate for Tohoku by Koyama (1984) (table 2.5) does not show as significant a decrease from the Middle through to Final Jomon as in the case of Kanto and Chubu.

High site density and a high frequency of large settlements are characteristic of collecting systems, because logistically organized strategies typically involve a number of special-purpose sites and the aggregation of people. Thus, at least in the Kanto and Chubu regions, and to a certain extent in the Tohoku region, the degree of organizational complexity in subsistence and settlement increased from the Incipient to the Middle Jomon, and then decreased through to the Late and Final Jomon periods.

This pattern of long-term change in subsistence and settlement does not fit into the unilinear model of the development of cultural complexity. Moreover, changes over time in social aspects including those reflected in mortuary/ceremonial practices, crafts, and exchange systems indicate rather different patterns. In the following two chapters, these topics are discussed.

Contrary to the patterns observed in eastern Japan, in western Japan (Kinki, Chugoku, Shikoku, and Kyushu), site density and the frequency of large settlements did not reach their highest points during the Middle Jomon. Rather, they continued to increase from the Middle to Late Jomon. The discrepancy between eastern and western Japan will be further discussed in chapter 7.

Part III

Rituals, crafts, and trade

5 Mortuary and ceremonial practices

Unlike the study of Jomon subsistence and settlement, relatively little has been published in English on Jomon mortuary and ceremonial practices. Summarizing previous analyses of burial and ritual data in a concise manner is not an easy task, primarily because very few scholars have presented interpretations of these data using explicit theoretical frameworks (see for example comments by Pearson et al. 1986b). Additionally, large regional and temporal variability in Jomon mortuary and ceremonial practices makes it difficult to provide coherent interpretations of these data. With the rapid increase in the amount of available data, however, certain patterns that were previously unnoticed have begun to be recognized. These patterns provide new lines of evidence that lead to a greater understanding of the social systems of the Jomon people, including the development of social inequality and gender/sex differences.

In Anglo-American archaeology, processual archaeologists have seen burial and ritual data as an important source of information from which to infer the social status and role of the deceased, and ultimately to understand the evolutionary development of social stratification in human history (e.g., O'Shea 1984; Peebles and Kus 1977). On the other hand, postprocessualists have criticized these approaches, suggesting that direct relationships between funeral or ceremonial practices and past social organization cannot always be assumed (e.g., McGuire 1992; Parker Pearson 1982). With these cautionary tales in mind, hunter-gatherer archaeologists over the past decade have attempted to use burial and ritual data to approach the issue of social inequality, especially hereditary or institutionalized inequality (e.g., Ames and Maschner 1999).

Parallel to the recent progress in the analysis of burials and rituals is the development of models of the origins of social inequality. Traditionally, archaeologists have tended to assume that either "pull" (such as resource abundance) or "push" (such as population pressure) factors were the direct cause of the emergence of inequality. Hayden's (1995) seminal work on the emergence of social inequality, which emphasizes the role of aspiring elites in the development of institutionalized inequality, provides an alternative view to the traditional interpretations. Feinman's (1995) distinctions between corporate-based (with an emphasis on the ties between a leader and his local faction) and network-based (with an emphasis on an individual's link to the extrafactional arena) strategies of emergent leaders suggest the possibility of dual pathways toward inequality. Arnold (1992; 1995; 1996a; 1996b), who identifies the presence of hereditary social inequality as the core of hunter-gatherer cultural complexity, proposes that organization of labor is the key to understanding the emergence of hereditary inequality.

In the context of these recent developments in Anglo-American archaeology, the Jomon culture has been cited frequently as an example of a complex hunter-gatherer culture with a certain degree of social stratification. For example, Hayden (1995: 51, 62) identifies Early and Middle Jomon cultures as "Reciprocator" communities (characterized by moderate heredity of social inequality), and the Late and Terminal (Final) Jomon cultures as "Entrepreneur" communities (characterized by strong heredity and incipient stratification) respectively. On the other hand, many Japanese archaeologists have traditionally assumed that the Jomon society was essentially an egalitarian one, in which certain people, such as shamans and skilled hunters, may have played distinguished social roles but in which no institutionalized inequality was established (e.g., I. Okamoto 1956; 1975; but see H. Watanabe 1990 and O. Nakamura 1999; 2000).

With these previous studies in mind, this chapter attempts to outline the current status of the study of Jomon mortuary and ceremonial practices, and provide possible directions for future research. Before examining currently available data, I will first review the history of the study of Jomon mortuary and ceremonial practices. Following the review, I will summarize major characteristics of three categories of Jomon data – (1) ritual artifacts, (2) burials and (3) monumental features – and examine their temporal and spatial variability. The results are discussed in the context of the study of hunter-gatherer social inequality.

History of the study of Jomon mortuary and ceremonial practices

Studies of Jomon mortuary practices by Japanese archaeologists have traditionally focused on the examination of social structure within the context of classical Marxist theory. As early as the 1950s, Isamu Okamoto (1956) suggested that the spatial patterning of burial pits within a Jomon settlement should be seen as a reflection of past social organization. Following Wajima's (1948; 1958) theoretical framework (see chapter 4), Isamu Okamoto attempted to understand the kinship structure of the Jomon "primitive community." The common presence of jar burials for babies and infants (see pp. 166–169) made him think that the mother–child tie was extremely strong. He interpreted this as indirect evidence for the presence of a matrilineal society. Clearly, he was influenced by classical Marxism, particularly by the works of Morgan and Engels, and tried to fit the Jomon data into this framework. His later work (I. Okamoto 1975) emphasized the importance of rituals in Jomon societies, which in his opinion reflects the presence of strict social rules in an egalitarian society at the "primitive community" level.

Okamoto (1975) also discussed the presence of female skeletal remains wearing a large number of shell bracelets on both wrists. Examples of these can be found at such sites as the Tsukumo shell-midden (Late and Final Jomon; Okayama Prefecture) and the Yoshigo shell-midden (Late and Final Jomon; Aichi Prefecture). Although a large number of skeletal remains have been recovered from both of these sites (170 from Tsukumo, and more than 300 from Yoshigo), only a small number of individuals wore a large number of shell bracelets. Furthermore, because these bracelets are too small to have been put on and taken off after these individuals became adults, the bracelets must have been put on their arms when the individuals were children. In other words, once these individuals grew up, it would have been impossible to remove the bracelets. Okamoto (1975) suggested that, because shell bracelets are extremely fragile, it would have been impossible for these individuals to take part in everyday chores such as collecting shellfish and gathering plant food. Based on these lines of evidence, he suggested that these individuals must have been shamans who were in charge of the ceremonial realm of Jomon societies.

Finally, Okamoto (1975) discussed a possible gendered division of labor during the Jomon period. Starting with a conventional assumption that Jomon men were primarily engaged in "heavy work" such as hunting and fishing while women conducted "light work" including food gathering and domestic chores, he assumed the presence of the "natural" division of labor based on gender (Okamoto 1975: 107–108). He also pointed out the common association of shell bracelets, earrings, and other ornaments with female skeletal remains, and waist pendants with male ones. Citing Kiyono's (1949) physical anthropological work, which showed that bone fractures (primarily right ulnas) were five times more common among Jomon men than women, Okamoto suggested that heavy work that could cause bone fractures was mainly performed by men.

During the 1960s and 1970s, various issues raised by Okamoto (1956) were examined by other Japanese scholars. Based on the generally similar size of burial pits and similar treatment of the corpses, Nishimura (1965) denied the presence of social stratification during the Jomon period. Hayashi (1965) noticed that Final Jomon burials in the Tohoku region include several infant burials with ornaments, and that these burials were often covered with red iron oxide. Since these practices can be observed only among Final Jomon burials in Tohoku, Hayashi suggested that the ideological view and social rules of the Final Jomon society of Tohoku were different from those of the other regions. Focusing on the presence of both flexed and extended burials at the Late Jomon Ubayama shell-midden, Ohtsuka (1967) suggested the presence of two social groups within a single settlement. Mizuno (1968; 1969a; 1969b) suggested that Jomon cemeteries could be spatially divided into several groups, and that these burial groups would correspond to his understanding of intrasite dwelling distribution patterns (see chapter 4). Most of these works were directly or indirectly influenced by classical Marxist perspectives. Unilinear cultural evolution through the Jomon period was either implicitly assumed or explicitly emphasized, and Marxist terms and concepts such as "the organization of labor" and "primitive communities" were frequently used in these articles. In addition, works by several cultural anthropologists (e.g., Obayashi 1971) encouraged the use of general ethnographic analogies to reconstruct intrasite social groups through the analysis of burial and settlement data.

In the 1970s and 1980s, Harunari (1973; 1974; 1979; 1982; 1986) examined patterns of Jomon tooth extraction and suggested a hypothesis regarding the rule of postmarital residence. According to his analysis of data from three Final Jomon sites in western Japan, the extraction of permanent teeth occurred "not on a single occasion but at several different points over the course of an individual's life for different reasons" (Harunari 1986: 294). Focusing particularly on the extraction patterns of lower jaw teeth, Harunari (1973) suggested that two distinctive types of tooth extraction could be identified: Type 4I (removing four lower incisors) and Type 2C (removing two lower canines). Through his examination of relative occurrences of Type 4I, Type 2C, and their variations at the three sites, he suggested that the extraction of the lower incisors and canines took place at the time of marriage. His analyses also indicated that both types occurred in each of the three sites, and for both sexes.

After analyzing (1) intrasite spatial distribution patterns of burials associated with various tooth extraction types, (2) relationships between tooth extraction types and the occurrence of artificially deformed teeth (called *Zackenfeilung,* or teeth with forklike incisions; Harunari 1986: 299), and (3) associations of ornaments with different tooth extraction types, Harunari (1982; 1986) suggested that different tooth extraction patterns may reflect "the principle of exogamy, which distinguishes the original members of the community from those who marry into it from the outside" (Harunari 1986: 303). He hypothesized that Type 4I extraction was characteristic of the original members of the society, whereas people who married into the society underwent Type 2C extraction. Applying these principles to Jomon data from various parts of the Japanese archipelago, Harunari (1979; 1982; 1986) attempted to reconstruct changes in postmarital residence rules through the Jomon period. Despite its hypothetical nature, Harunari's (1973; 1974; 1979; 1982; 1986) elegant argument on the basis of several lines of evidence (tooth extraction patterns, artificial tooth deformation, intrasite spatial distribution, and association of ornaments) attracted the attention of many Jomon researchers.

In summary, research foci in the study of Jomon mortuary practices up to the 1980s were placed on such aspects as the organization of labor, kinship structure, and rules of postmarital residence. Behind these studies were classical Marxist theories that emphasize kinship ties among "primitive communal societies." However, in many cases, Marxist perspectives were used only informally rather than explicitly applied. As a result, to the eyes of most Anglo-American archaeologists, the majority of these studies seem to lack a solid theoretical framework.

In comparison to Jomon mortuary archaeology, in which Marxist perspectives have been influential, studies of Jomon ritual artifacts and monumental features have tended to be more descriptive. An abundance of clay figurines, stone rods, and other seemingly nonutilitarian artifacts in Jomon assemblages have long attracted the attention of many scholars (see e.g., Ono 1999; Shinsuke Goto 1999). Similarly, early discoveries of large-scale features, such as the two stone circles at the Late Jomon Oyu site in Akita Prefecture in the 1950s, have made Japanese archaeologists aware of Jomon people's ability to conduct large-scale corporate work (Akimoto 1999). As a result, a significant number of review articles that list all the major findings in these research fields are available (see below). These articles are extremely useful sources of information for understanding the range of available data, but very few of them interpret the data in relation to variability and change in other aspects of the Jomon culture.

Types of ritual artifacts

Having reviewed the brief history of the study of Jomon mortuary and ceremonial practices, I suggest that we next try to understand temporal and regional variability in each category of burial and ritual data. The first category of data discussed here is the ritual artifact. The types of so-called ritual artifacts from Jomon sites are quite diverse. They include clay and stone figurines, stone rods and "swords," clay masks, and other objects. In addition, archaeologists often analyze various kinds of ornament, such as clay and stone earrings and jade beads, in the context of Jomon ceremonial practices. An abundance of ritual artifacts is particularly noticeable during and after the Middle Jomon period in eastern Japan. However, the distribution area and the time period of a particular type of ritual artifact are often restricted. As a result, an examination of the vicissitudes of each of these types reveals quite complex patterns.

Materials covered in this section do not include artifacts made of wood (including lacquered wood) and fabrics. This is because their discoveries are primarily limited to an extremely small number of waterlogged sites, and this restricts our understanding of the spatial and temporal variability of these organic artifacts. The production and use of these organic artifacts will be discussed in chapter 6.

Clay and stone figurines

The most well-known type of Jomon ritual artifact is the clay figurine. Figure 5.1 shows schematic drawings of various types of Jomon clay figurines compiled by Osaka Furitsu Yayoi Bunka Hakubutsu-kan (1998). Most Japanese scholars believe that the majority of Jomon clay figurines represent female bodies, particularly the pregnant ones, although some are skeptical that all of the figurines are representations of females. According to Nagamine (1986: 255), "the typological changes on many of the clay figurines indicate an asexual rendering of the human form," but "there are no figurines that manifest concrete male characteristics." However, Ueki (1999) and others suggest that some of the clay figurines, such as those with beard-like lines or incisions, represent males.

Scholars have also noted that very few complete figurines have been recovered from Jomon sites. Accordingly, many Japanese archaeologists have suggested that Jomon figurines were intentionally destroyed during the process of ceremonial activities (Fujimori 1966; T. Kobayashi 1977c; Kono 1929; Nagamine 1977; 1986; Mizuno 1979). Behind this argument is the common ethnographic knowledge that, in certain parts of rural Japan, figurines or dolls made of various materials were used

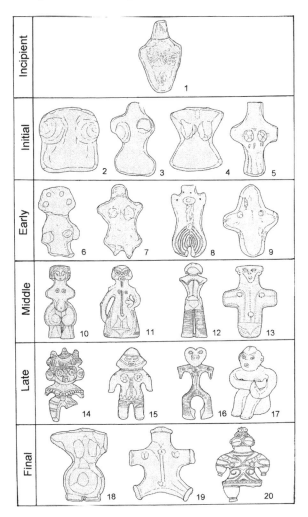

Figure 5.1   Schematic drawing of various types of clay figurines from Incipient to Final Jomon periods: 1. Kayumi Ijiri (Mie Prefecture); 2. Konami (Osaka); 3. Hanawadai (Ibaraki Prefecture); 4. Komuro Uedai (Chiba Prefecture); 5. Futamata (Aichi Prefecture); 6. Shakado (Yamanashi Prefecture); 7. Suginori (Iwate Prefecture); 8. Shiogamori (Iwate Prefecture); 9. Hakuza (Aomori Prefecture); 10. Tanabatake (Nagano Prefecture); 11. Imojiya (Yamanashi Prefecture); 12. Nishinomae (Yamagata Prefecture); 13. Sannai Maruyama (Aomori Prefecture); 14. Takibamuro (Saitama Prefecture); 15. Shiizuka (Ibaraki Prefecture); 16. Gohara (Gunma Prefecture); 17. Nomotai (Aomori Prefecture); 18. Babagawa (Osaka); 19. Surihagi (Miyagi Prefecture); 20. Kamegaoka (Aomori Prefecture) (modified and redrawn from Osaka Furitsu Yayoi Bunka Hakubutsu-kan 1998: 25)

as "straw men" to avoid epidemics and other disasters. Publications by Haruo Fujimura (1983; 1991) indicate that the breakage ratio of clay figurines, as well as that of stone "swords" (see pp. 151–155), at the Final Jomon Kunenbashi site in Iwate Prefecture is higher than breakage ratios of the other artifacts. However, Fujinuma (1997), Akihiko Kaneko (1999), and Ono (1999) argue that the seemingly high breakage ratio does not mean that the figurines were intentionally broken (see also Noto 1983).

The oldest Jomon clay figurine to date comes from the Incipient Jomon Kayumi Ijiri site in Mie Prefecture (fig. 5.2.1). The ample bosom seems to indicate that the figurine represents a female (Sugitani et al. 1998). Examples of clay figurines from the Initial and Early Jomon periods are not uncommon, but their total number is still relatively small. The representation of the human body in these figurines is usually quite abstract (fig. 5.1.2–5).

The number of clay figurines during and after the Middle Jomon period is much larger than in the previous periods. In particular, the Middle Jomon culture in the Chubu region is known for an abundance of finely made clay figurines (e.g., fig. 5.2.2). Scholars such as Fujimori (1963) believe that these Middle Jomon clay figurines are the representation of the earth goddess. In Fujimori's opinion, earth goddess worship is frequently associated with an agricultural society, and therefore the common presence of Middle Jomon clay figurines implies the presence of incipient plant cultivation. Other scholars believe that these clay figurines were the symbols of fertility in general. Middle Jomon clay figurines in the northern Tohoku region are mostly slab-shaped (e.g., fig. 5.1.13). At Sannai Maruyama, for example, a large number of slab-shaped clay figurines (fig. 5.3) have been recovered from Middle Jomon layers (Ogasawara and Katsuragi 1999).

Late and Final Jomon clay figurines are characterized by their wide stylistic variability. Clay figurines from these periods include the heart-shaped figurine (Late Jomon in Kanto; see fig. 5.1.16), the mountain-shaped-head clay figurine (named after the triangular shape of the head; Late Jomon in Kanto; see fig. 5.1.15), the "horned-owl" clay figurine (Late Jomon in Kanto; see fig. 5.1.14), the "sitting" clay figurine (Late Jomon in Tohoku; fig. 5.1.17, fig. 5.2.3), and the "slit-goggle" (shakoki) clay figurine (Final Jomon in Tohoku; see figs. 5.1.20, 5.2.4) (Yoneda 1984). Some of these clay figurines are elaborately made, while others were apparently less labor-intensive.

The relative abundance of clay figurines from Middle to Final Jomon sites compared to the previous Jomon subperiods can be seen easily by examining basic statistics. Table 5.1 lists the numbers of Jomon sites

Figure 5.2 Clay figurines from 1. Kayumi Ijiri (Incipient Jomon; Mie Prefecture); 2. Tanabatake (Middle Jomon; Nagano Prefecture); 3. Kazahari (Late Jomon; Aomori Prefecture); 4. Ebisuda (Final Jomon; Aomori Prefecture) (Sources: 1. Nihon Kokogaku Kyokai 1998: plate 17; permission for reproduction obtained from Mie-ken Maizo Bunkazai Center; 2. Nihon Kokogaku Kyokai 1989: plate 17; permission for reproduction obtained from Togariishi Koko-kan; 3. photograph by courtesy of Hachinohe-shi Jomon Gakushu-kan [Jomon Archaeological Museum of Hachinohe City]; 4. photograph by courtesy of Tokyo Kokuritsu Hakubutsu-kan [The Tokyo National Museum])

Figure 5.3   Middle Jomon slab-shaped clay figurines from the Sannai Maruyama site (photograph by courtesy of Aomori-ken Kyoiku-cho Bunka-ka)

associated with clay figurines in each region. Table 5.2 lists the numbers of clay figurines or figurine fragments reported from each region. Raw data for these tables were compiled by Kokuritsu Rekishi Minzoku Hakubutsu-kan (National Museum of Japanese History) in 1992. The tables clearly indicate that the majority of Jomon clay figurines were recovered from Middle, Late, and Final Jomon sites in Hokkaido, Tohoku, Kanto, and Chubu. These tables also show that the peak abundance of clay figurines occurred during different Jomon subperiods in different regions. In the Chubu region, an abundance of clay figurines is particularly noticeable during the Middle Jomon period. On the other hand, in the Kanto region, the peak occurred during the Late Jomon period. In Hokkaido, the peak was definitely in the Final Jomon period. According to tables 5.1 and 5.2, the peak in the Tohoku region also seems to have occurred in the Final Jomon period. It should be noted, however, that table 5.2 does not include the number of clay figurines from the Sannai Maruyama site (approximately 1,500; see fig. 5.3). This is because the exact number and time period of Sannai Maruyama figurines has yet to be reported in the final site report. Since almost all of the Sannai Maruyama figurines are from the Middle Jomon period, the total number of Middle Jomon figurines in the Tohoku region shown in the table (currently 533 pieces) should be much larger (approximately 2,000 pieces). This is approximately the same as the total number of Final Jomon figurines in the region (1,934 pieces). Thus, it seems more likely that in this region there were double peaks, both in the Middle and Final Jomon periods in terms of the total numbers of figurines. This also demonstrates how the numbers shown in table 5.2 can be strongly influenced by the discovery of a single Jomon site associated with a large number of figurines. In this regard, data shown in table 5.1 might be a better indicator of the overall regional and temporal variability.

As the case of Sannai Maruyama demonstrates, a mass of clay figurines is associated with a limited number of Middle, Late, and Final Jomon sites. According to Fujimura (2001), who examined the data published by Kokuritsu Rekishi Minzoku Hakubutsu-kan (1992), 31 Jomon sites are associated with more than 50 clay figurines. Some of these sites are also characterized by an abundance of other ritual artifacts or features. For example, at the Tateishi site in Iwate Prefecture, 302 Late Jomon clay figurines have been recovered along with nose- and ear-shaped clay artifacts (see the subsection "Clay masks" below) and seemingly ceremonial stone features (Oh-hazama-machi Kyoiku Iinkai 1979). At the Kunenbashi site (Final Jomon) in Iwate Prefecture (Kitakami-shi Kyoiku Iinkai 1977; 1978; 1979; 1980; 1984; 1985; 1986; 1987; 1988; 1991), a total of 641 Final Jomon clay figurines (Fujimura 2001) have been

Table 5.1 *Numbers of Jomon sites associated with clay figurines (percentages in parentheses)*

	Initial	Early	Middle	Late	Final	Unknown	Total[1]
Hokkaido	0 (0.0)	1 (1.4)	12 (16.2)	18 (24.3)	44 (59.5)	8 (10.8)	74 (100.0)
Tohoku	1 (0.4)	15 (5.5)	87 (31.8)	136 (49.6)	137 (50.0)	33 (12.0)	274 (100.0)
Kanto	16 (3.9)	10 (2.4)	119 (29.1)	229 (56.0)	132 (32.3)	25 (6.1)	409 (100.0)
Chubu	1 (0.3)	3 (0.8)	288 (77.4)	85 (22.8)	51 (13.7)	19 (5.1)	372 (100.0)
Hokuriku	1 (0.9)	2 (1.8)	65 (59.6)	52 (47.7)	31 (28.4)	3 (2.8)	109 (100.0)
Tokai	3 (4.6)	1 (1.5)	12 (18.5)	20 (30.8)	32 (49.2)	10 (15.4)	65 (100.0)
Kinki	2 (6.9)	1 (3.4)	1 (3.4)	14 (48.3)	19 (65.5)	0 (0.0)	29 (100.0)
Chugoku	0 (0.0)	0 (0.0)	0 (0.0)	7 (100.0)	2 (28.6)	0 (0.0)	7 (100.0)
Shikoku	0 (0.0)	0 (0.0)	0 (0.0)	2 (28.6)	1 (14.3)	4 (57.1)	7 (100.0)
Kyushu	0 (0.0)	0 (0.0)	0 (0.0)	15 (62.5)	12 (50.0)	5 (20.8)	24 (100.0)
Total	24 (1.8)	33 (2.4)	584 (42.6)	578 (42.2)	461 (33.6)	107 (7.8)	1,370 (100.0)

Note: [1] The total specimen number for each region may be less than the sum total of all the subperiod specimen numbers because, when the possible attribution of a specimen ranges over two or more subperiods, the specimen is entered under all the possible subperiods.

Sources: Compiled from Fujimura 2001: 144. Raw data for Fujimura's table were originally published by Kokuritsu Rekishi Minzoku Hakubutsu-kan 1992: 453–483.

Table 5.2 *Numbers of clay figurines (including fragments) recovered from Jomon sites (percentages in parentheses)*

	Initial	Early	Middle	Late	Final	Unknown	Total[1]
Hokkaido	0 (0.0)	2 (0.7)	39 (13.7)	48 (16.8)	193 (67.7)	11 (3.9)	285 (100.0)
Tohoku	1 (0.0)	97 (2.5)	533 (13.8)	1,388 (35.9)	1,934 (50.0)	46 (1.2)	3,865 (100.0)
Kanto	37 (1.5)	13 (0.5)	348 (13.7)	1,407 (55.2)	791 (31.1)	48 (1.9)	2,547 (100.0)
Chubu	1 (0.0)	13 (0.5)	2,190 (79.9)	354 (12.9)	153 (5.6)	44 (1.6)	2,741 (100.0)
Hokuriku	4 (0.7)	6 (1.1)	274 (51.0)	224 (41.7)	154 (28.7)	4 (0.7)	537 (100.0)
Tokai	4 (1.5)	3 (1.1)	20 (7.4)	79 (29.2)	157 (57.9)	11 (4.1)	271 (100.0)
Kinki	3 (1.2)	1 (0.4)	1 (0.4)	19 (7.3)	247 (95.4)	1 (0.4)	259 (100.0)
Chugoku	0 (0.0)	0 (0.0)	0 (0.0)	12 (100.0)	5 (41.7)	0 (0.0)	12 (100.0)
Shikoku	0 (0.0)	0 (0.0)	0 (0.0)	2 (18.2)	3 (27.3)	6 (54.5)	11 (100.0)
Kyushu	0 (0.0)	0 (0.0)	0 (0.0)	142 (91.6)	137 (88.4)	7 (4.5)	155 (100.0)
Total	50 (0.5)	135 (1.3)	3,405 (31.9)	3,675 (34.4)	3,774 (35.3)	178 (1.7)	10,683 (100.0)

Note: [1]The total specimen number for each region may be less than the sum total of all the subperiod specimen numbers, because, when the possible attribution of a specimen ranges over two or more subperiods, the specimen is entered under all the possible subperiods.

Source: Compiled from Kokuritsu Rekishi Minzoku Hakubutsu-kan 1992: 484.

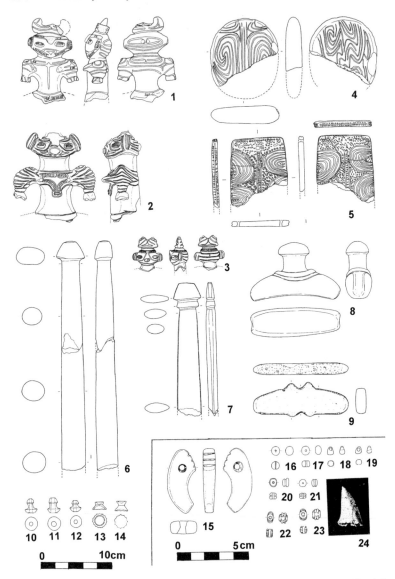

Figure 5.4 Ritual artifacts from the Kunenbashi site (Final Jomon; Iwate Prefecture): 1–3. clay figurines; 4. stone tablet; 5. clay tablet; 6. stone rod; 7. "stone sword"; 8. crown-shaped stone artifact; 9. *dokko*-shaped stone artifact, 10–14: clay earrings; 15. comma-shaped stone bead; 16–23. clay beads; 24. shark tooth (diagram by courtesy of Kitakami-shi Kyoiku Iinkai [Board of Education of Kitakami City])

recovered together with a large number of ritual artifacts (see fig. 5.4), such as "stone swords," stone and clay tablets, and clay earrings, as well as potsherds, stone tools, and bone fragments. Since the site is located in marshy lowlands, and since no residential features have been identified from the site, the function of the site is suggested to have been primarily ceremonial.

In addition to clay figurines, stone figurines, which are also considered to have been representations of females, were produced during the Jomon period (Y. Inano 1983; 1999). Examples of Jomon stone figurines include those associated with the Early Jomon Lower-Ento culture in Tohoku (fig. 5.5.1–6), and those with the Final Jomon Kamegaoka culture in Tohoku (fig. 5.5.7–12). According to Murakoshi (1974), Early Jomon clay and stone figurines share morphological characteristics, and their distribution areas within the sphere of the Lower-Ento culture (a mid–late Early Jomon culture in northern Tohoku) are mutually exclusive. This seems to indicate that Early Jomon clay and stone figurines had similar functions or symbolic meanings. On the other hand, regarding the Kamegaoka styles of stone figurines, Yusuke Inano (1983) notes that, while the stone and clay figurines share certain characteristics, the facial expression, depiction of clothing, and other characteristics are different. Based on these results, Inano suggests that the function of the Kamegaoka styles of stone figurines was different from that of clay figurines. These observations suggest that lumping clay and stone figurines into the same category of ritual artifact may blur the differences in their symbolic meanings. Although Inano (1983) has provided solid analysis to outline the differences, so far no scholars have provided convincing interpretations of the implications of these differences.

Stone rods and "stone swords" (phallic stones)

While clay and stone figurines are generally considered as representations of females, scholars suggest that stone rods (*sekibo*) represent male sexuality. Because the shape is reminiscent of male genitals, many scholars believe that, just like clay figurines, stone rods are essentially a symbol of fertility. Others (e.g., Mizuno 1963; 1999) suggest that stone rods were specifically related to hunting rituals conducted exclusively by men. Two types of stone rods, large ones and small ones, have been reported from Jomon sites. The large type (e.g., fig. 5.6), which measures approximately 5 to 20 centimeters in diameter, and is sometimes more than 1 meter long, is associated primarily with Middle and Late Jomon sites; they were often used as upright stones at the center of a stone feature or placed in a pit-dwelling (Yamamoto 1983).

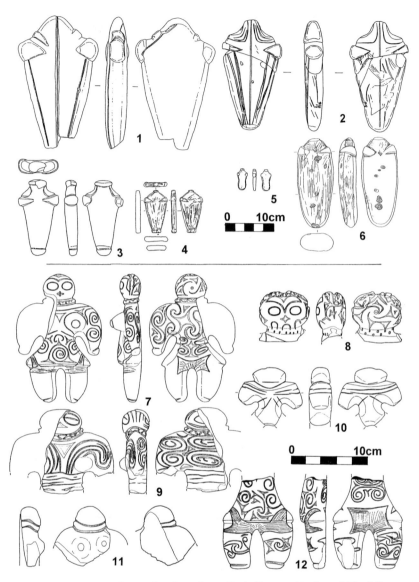

Figure 5.5   Stone figurines from Early Jomon (1–6) and Final Jomon
(7–12) sites: 1. Odai; 2. Kumanosawa; 3. Uchinotai; 4. Haginodai II;
5. Ganjadate; 6. Naganotai I; 7. Togoshinai; 8. Makumae; 9. Shinjo
Okamachi; 10. Nomotai; 11. Michimae; 12. Kanazawa Yashiki (1, 2, 7,
9, 10, 11: Aomori Prefecture; 3, 4, 6: Akita Prefecture; 5, 8, 12: Iwate
Prefecture) (compiled from Yusuke Inano 1983: 88–89; 1997: 408 409;
permission for reproduction obtained from Yusuke Inano)

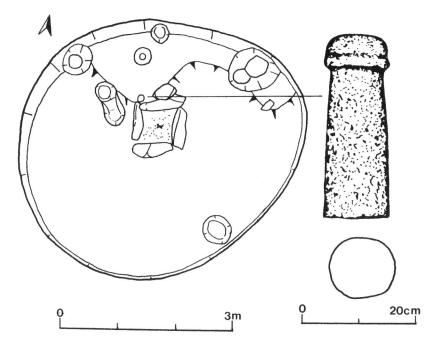

0 _____ 3m   0 _____ 20cm

Figure 5.6   Large stone rod recovered from a Middle Jomon pit-dwelling at the Sori site, Nagano Prefecture (redrawn from Muto and Kobayashi 1978, published in T. Yamamoto 1979: 669)

Smaller stone rods are primarily associated with Late and Final Jomon sites (fig. 5.7.1–5). Many of them are elaborately made (often carefully polished), and some of them have incised lines on the knobbed end(s) (Shinsuke Goto 1999) (see fig. 5.7.4–5). Late and Final Jomon sites are also associated with so-called "stone swords," or *sekken* (the double-edged sword; fig. 5.7.6–15) and *sekito* (the single-edged sword; fig. 5.7.16–27) (Nomura 1983). The primary difference between stone rods and "stone swords" is the shape of the cross-section: the cross-section of stone rods is circular, while "stone swords" are flatter. However, the boundary between these two categories of artifacts is not always clear. Many scholars believe that Late and Final Jomon small stone rods and "stone swords" developed directly from Middle Jomon large stone rods (e.g., Y. Kobayashi 1951; 1959; Yamamoto 1979; 1983). Others believe that the flat shape of "stone swords" indicates a different origin. Some scholars even suggest that the shape was influenced by early bronze tools of continental Asia (Esaka 1965; Nomura 1983; Kiyotaka Nakayama 1992). According to Nomura

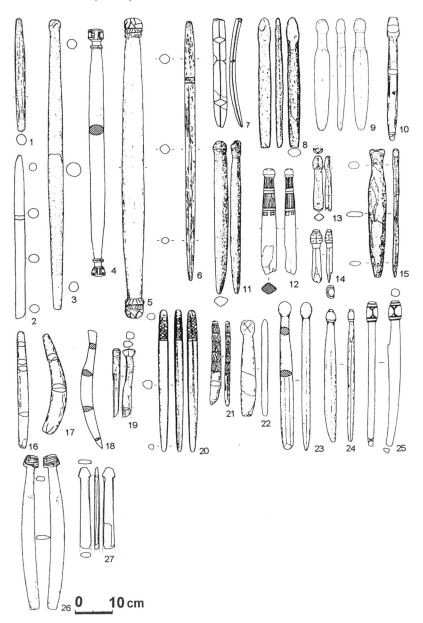

Figure 5.7   Stone rods and "swords": 1–5. stone rods; 6–15. *sekken* (double-edged stone "swords"); 16–27. *sekito* (single-edged stone "swords") (modified from Shinsuke Goto 1999: 75; permission for reproduction obtained from Shinsuke Goto)

(1983), an abundance of small stone rods and "swords" is particularly noticeable at sites of the Final Jomon Kamegaoka culture in the Tohoku region.

Because many large stone rods and small stone rods/"swords" are broken, several scholars have suggested that, just as in the case of clay figurines, intentional breakage was part of the stone rod and/or "sword" rituals (e.g., Mizuno 1999). As noted above, Fujimura (1991) reports a higher breakage ratio of "stone swords" from the Final Jomon Kunenbashi site than other types of artifacts. At the Late and Final Jomon Terano-higashi site in Tochigi Prefecture, all the "stone swords" (a total of fifty-eight) were broken, and many of them show burn marks (Tochigi-ken Kyoiku Iinkai et al. 1994).

Clay masks

Approximately thirty clay masks or mask fragments have been recovered from more than twenty Late and Final Jomon sites, primarily in the Tohoku region. In addition, nose-, mouth-, or ear-shaped clay artifacts (presumably parts of composite masks made of organic materials) have been recovered from four Late Jomon sites, including Hatten, Shidanai, and Tateishi in Iwate Prefecture (Kiyoshi Nakayama 1998). Ohtsuka (1988) classifies Jomon clay masks into seven different types: (1) realistic masks (Final Jomon; fig. 5.8.a), (2) curved-nose masks (the end of Late Jomon to Final Jomon; fig. 5.8.b), (3) mask-shaped clay artifacts (Final Jomon; fig. 5.8.c; the name comes from the fact that there are no holes for the eyes and mouths), (4) composite masks (Late Jomon; fig. 5.8.d), (5) "clown" masks (Late and Final Jomon; fig. 5.8.e), (6) "tattooed" masks (Late and Final Jomon: fig. 5.8.f), and (7) painted masks (Late and Final Jomon: fig. 5.8.g–h).

Figure 5.8 shows the locations of sites associated with clay masks and schematic drawings of the seven types of clay masks suggested by Ohtsuka (1988). Among these, there is only one example of the "realistic mask," from the Final Jomon Mamachi site in Hokkaido (Site no. 1 in the figure). Some of the other types, such as painted masks (from the Late Jomon Butsunami site in Osaka Prefecture and the Final Jomon Hotto site in Saitama Prefecture), are also limited in number. Recoveries of "tattooed" masks and mask-shaped clay artifacts are more common, and the examples have increased since Ohtsuka (1988) published his typology (Kiyoshi Nakayama 1998).

It should be noted that these clay masks appeared rather suddenly during the Late Jomon period and that their distribution is particularly dense in northern Tohoku. Citing ethnographic examples from northern Pacific

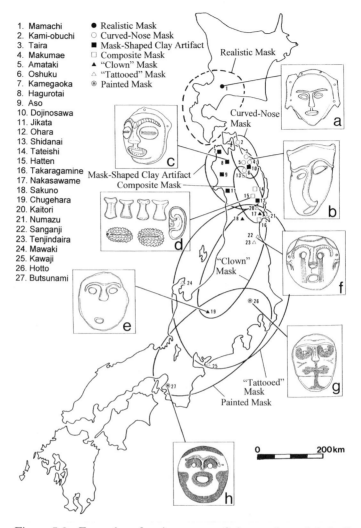

Figure 5.8   Examples of various types of clay masks and their distribution: a. realistic mask (Mamachi; Hokkaido); b. curved-nose mask (partially reconstructed; Makumae; Iwate Prefecture); c. mask-shaped clay artifact (Hagurotai, Aomori Prefecture); d. composite mask (Hatten; Iwate Prefecture); e. "clown" mask (Chugehara, Nagano Prefecture); f. "tattooed" mask (partially reconstructed; Sanganji; Fukushima Prefecture); g–h. painted masks (g: Hotto; Saitama Prefecture; h: Butsunami; Osaka prefecture, reconstructed from fragments) (modified from Kazuyoshi Ohtsuka 1988: 147; permission for reproduction obtained from Kazuyoshi Ohtsuka)

Rim areas, Ohtsuka (1988) suggests that at least the painted masks, "tattooed" masks, and composite masks must have been used at the time of initiation ceremonies. With the exception of the mask-shaped clay artifacts, which do not have holes for eyes and mouths, and the size of which is too small to be actually worn, most of these were probably worn by people. The presence of a fair number of clay figurines with masks also supports this idea (Ohtsuka 1988).

Other ritual artifacts and ornaments

Although clay/stone figurines, stone rods/"swords" and clay masks are the three most well-known categories of ritual artifacts from the Jomon period, various other kinds of ritual artifacts have also been reported. These include clay and stone tablets (A. Inano 1983; Isomae and Saito 1999; see fig. 5.4.4–5), triangular clay and stone tablets (T. Kaneko 1983; fig. 5.9.1–2), triangular-prism-shaped clay and stone artifacts (Kojima 1983a; fig. 5.9.3–4), ball-shaped clay artifacts (Kojima 1983b; fig. 5.9.5–6), *seiryuto*-shaped stone tools (Togashi 1983; fig. 5.9.8), crown-shaped stone and clay artifacts (E. Nakajima 1983; Takayuki Okamoto 1999a; fig. 5.9.7; see also fig. 5.4.8), *dokko*-shaped stone tools (Takayuki Okamoto 1999b; see fig. 5.4.9) and *gyobutsu* stone bars (Yoshiasa 1999; fig. 5.9.9). *Seiryuto* (the blue dragon sword) is a Japanese name for a long-handled Chinese sword with a blue-dragon decoration on the handle. Some scholars believe that *seiryuto*-shaped stone tools are copies of ancient Chinese bronzes, thus assuming active interaction with the continent during the Middle and Late Jomon periods. On the other hand, *dokko* means a tool used by Buddhist monks, and the name is based simply on the morphological similarity. Finally, *gyobutsu* means "imperial treasures." The name came from the fact that two of these Jomon stone tools found in Ishikawa Prefecture were designated as imperial treasures in 1877 (Takano 1979). While each item shows a different regional distribution, overall their distributions are particularly dense in northern Tohoku and/or part of Hokuriku (see the "Primary distribution areas" column in table 5.3).

   In addition to these ritual artifacts, various kinds of ornaments have been recovered from Jomon sites. These include stone and clay small beads (fig. 5.4.16–23; fig. 5.10.1), stone tubular beads (fig. 5.10.2), comma-shaped stone beads (fig. 5.4.15), stone slitted earrings (fig. 5.10.3–4), large jade beads (fig. 5.10.5–8), pulley-shaped clay earrings (fig. 5.10.9–14), shell bracelets (fig. 5.10.15–16), and deer antler waist pendants (fig. 5.10.17–18). Some of these are commonly recovered as

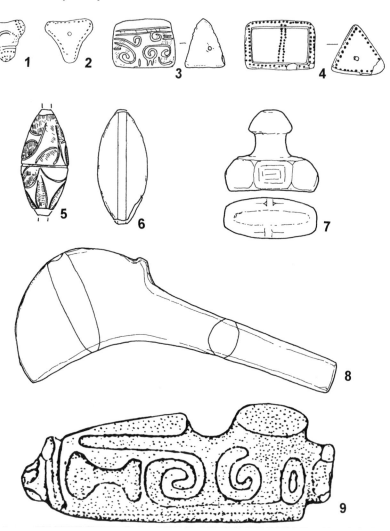

Figure 5.9   Various ritual artifacts: 1–2. triangular clay tablets; 3–4. triangular-prism-shaped clay artifacts; 5–6. ball-shaped clay artifacts; 7. crown-shaped stone artifact; 8. *seiryuto*-shaped stone tool; 9. *gyobutsu* stone bar (scale: approximately 1/3) (redrawn from T. Kaneko 1983: 117; Kojima 1983a: 132; 1983b: 143; E. Nakajima 1983: 151; Togashi 1983: 202; Yoshiasa 1999)

grave goods, while others are more frequently found in nonmortu-
ary contexts (see below).

Regional and temporal variability in ritual artifacts and ornaments

Table 5.3 summarizes the temporal and regional variability in various
types of ritual artifacts. The table demonstrates an overall increase in the
number of types through time: an abundance of ritual artifacts in the Late
and Final Jomon periods is evident. It also shows a relative abundance
of these artifacts in eastern Japan. With the exception of shell bracelets,
which are common in both eastern and western Japan, all the categories
listed in the table are more abundantly found in eastern Japan than in
western Japan.

Although the distribution areas of these artifacts do not completely overlap, several regions, including northern Tohoku, Chubu, and
Hokuriku, seem to have been the core areas of the distribution of at
least several of the categories. Examination of the "rise and fall" of these
artifacts in various regions provides complex pictures regarding changes
in Jomon ceremonial practices over time. These patterns are especially
interesting when examined in combination with changes in other aspects
of Jomon ceremonial practices, such as burials and monumental features.
In the following section, I will review the burial data.

Types of burial

A variety of burial types have been identified from Jomon sites. Both
primary and secondary burials exist, although the former outnumber the
latter.

Primary burials

Among primary burials from the Jomon period, the most common type
is the pit burial. A pit burial consists of a pit (usually circular, oval, or
oblong) that was used to inter one or more human bodies without cremation. Variations in pit burials include flask-shaped ones. Figure 5.11
shows an example of an Early Jomon flask-shaped pit burial recovered at
the Furuyashiki site, Aomori Prefecture. Many scholars believe that most
of these flask-shaped pits were originally constructed as storage pits (see
chapter 3), and later reused as burials.

While pit burials with skeletal remains are rich sources of information,
archaeologists are not always so fortunate as to find actual human remains

Table 5.3 *Period and distribution of ritual artifacts and ornaments*

	Incipient	Initial	Early	Middle	Late	Final	Primary distribution areas	References
Clay figurines	very rare	present	present	abundant	abundant	abundant	eastern Japan (Hokkaido, Tohoku, Kanto, Hokuriku, and Chubu) (tables 5.1 & 5.2)	Fujimura 2001; Kokuritsu Rekishi Minzoku Hakubutsu-kan 1992
Stone figurines			present			abundant	Tohoku	Y. Inano 1983; 1997; 1999
Large stone clubs				abundant	present	present	Kanto and Chubu	Yamamoto 1983
Small stone clubs and "stone swords"					fairly abundant	abundant	eastern Japan, esp. in Tohoku	Shinsuke Goto 1999; Nomura 1983
Clay masks					present	present	eastern Japan, esp. in Tohoku (fig. 5.8)	Nakayama 1998; Ohtsuka 1988
Clay and stone tablets						abundant	Tohoku	A. Inano 1983; Isomae and Saito 1999; Yoneda 1984
Seiryuto-shaped stone tools				present	present		southern Hokkaido and Tohoku	Togashi 1983
Triangular-prism-shaped clay and stone artifacts				present	present	present	Tohoku, Kanto, Chubu, and Hokuriku	Kojima 1983a
Triangular clay and stone tablets				abundant	present	present	Tohoku and Hokuriku (esp. Niigata Pref.)	T. Kaneko 1983
Ball-shaped clay artifacts					present	present	Kanto and Hokuriku	Kojima 1983b
Crown-shaped stone and clay artifacts						present	Chubu, Hokuriku, and part of Tohoku	E. Nakajima 1983; T. Okamoto 1999a

Dokko-shaped stone artifacts		present	present	Tohoku, Kanto, and Chubu (esp. Gifu Pref.)	T. Okamoto 1999b
Gyobutsu stone bars	present		present	Chubu	Yoshiasa 1999
Shell bracelets	present	abundant	abundant	eastern and western Japan	Kataoka 1983
Large jade beads	abundant	fairly abundant	present	Hokkaido, Tohoku, Kanto, Hokuriku, and Chubu (see chap. 6)	Ando 1982
Pulley-shaped clay earrings	present	abundant	abundant	Kanto	Shitara 1983

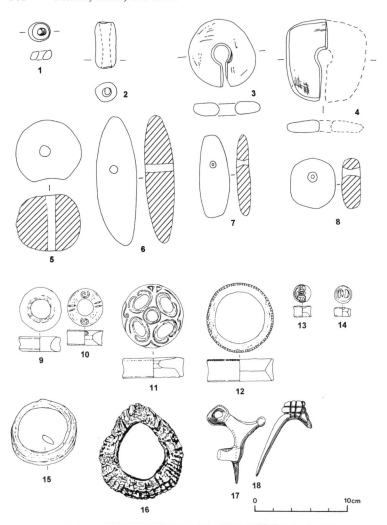

Figure 5.10   Ornaments: 1–2. clay beads; 3–4. slitted stone earrings; 5–8. large jade beads; 9–14. pulley-shaped clay earrings; 15–16. shell bracelets; 17–18. deer antler waist pendants (compiled and redrawn from Nagano-ken Chuodo Iseki Chosa-dan 1982: figures 240–241; Ando 1982: 223; Shitara 1983: 207; Kataoka 1983: 232; Harunari 1986: 302)

Figure 5.11 Early Jomon flask-shaped pit burial recovered from the Furuyashiki site, Aomori Prefecture (photograph by courtesy of Kamikita-machi Rekishi Minzoku Shiryo-kan [Historical Museum of Kamikita Town])

in burial pits. Because the soil in the Japanese archipelago is quite acidic, the condition of skeletal remains is generally poor. With the exception of burials associated with shell-middens, where calcium from the shells has helped preserve the bones, it is not common to find skeletal remains. Accordingly, over the past several decades, Japanese archaeologists have identified a number of circular, oval, or oblong pits as Jomon burials based on circumstantial evidence. In some cases, the presence of ornaments (such as stone and clay beads and earrings) and grave goods (such as a special type of pottery and stone tool) can be used as indicators to distinguish burial pits from other types of pits. In other cases, phosphate and lipid analyses provide supporting evidence for the identification of burials.

Intrasite settlement pattern analyses have revealed that these burial pits often form clusters or specific configurations, such as circles and rows, within a settlement. One of the well-known examples comes from the Middle Jomon Nishida site in Iwate Prefecture. As shown in fig. 5.12, burial pits are located at the center of the settlement in a radiating pattern. The spatial distribution of various features at this site seems to have been organized in concentric circles: the burial area, which is located at the center of the settlement, is surrounded by a circular arrangement of

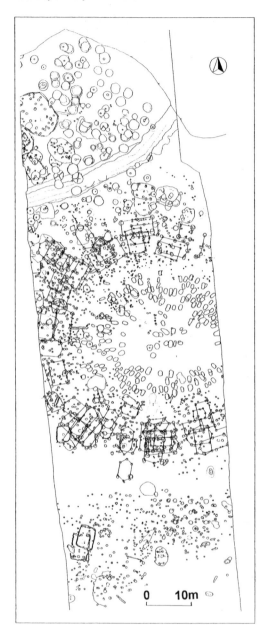

Figure 5.12   Feature distribution at the Middle Jomon Nishida site, Iwate Prefecture (modified from Masaru Sasaki 1994: 30; permission for reproduction obtained from Masaru Sasaki)

so-called "raised-floor" buildings (structures associated with post-holes). Located outside this zone are pit-dwellings and storage pits, which seem to form the outermost ring of the concentric patterns (K. Imamura 1996; T. Kobayashi 1992b).

Another good example of a cemetery at the center of a settlement comes from the Early Jomon Nanbori site in Kanagawa Prefecture. As discussed in chapter 4, the site was originally excavated by Wajima (1958) in the 1950s. While his original excavation did not reveal the presence of burial pits, reexcavation of the site from 1984 to 1989 (Takei 1990) revealed that a number of possible burial pits are located in the central "plaza" within the horseshoe-shaped configuration of pit-dwellings.

Unlike burial pits at Nishida and Nanbori, burial pits at Sannai Maruyama (see chapter 4) form rows along the tamped-down-earth path-ways. The 1992–1994 excavations of the site revealed two rows of burial pits on both sides of a 420-meter tamped-down-earth pathway stretch-ing from the central part of the Stadium Area to the eastern edge of the site (Aomori-ken Kyoiku-cho Bunka-ka 1996a; 1997a; 1998d). Recent excavations also revealed another set of burial rows extending from the western edge of the Stadium Area (Aomori-ken Kyoiku-cho Bunka-ka 2000a; 2001) toward the southeast (for the location of the Stadium Area within the site, see fig. 4.17). The latter set of rows may be connected to the two rows of burials identified in the West Parking Lot Area in the 1976 excavation (fig. 5.13; Aomori-ken Kyoiku Iinkai 1977; see also G. Abe 1983). Based on stratigraphic observations, the majority of the burial pits at Sannai Maruyama are tentatively dated to the middle of the Middle Jomon period. However, the absence of skeletal remains and the scarcity of associated artifacts make it difficult to date these features with precision.

Pit burials are sometimes associated with stone markers or alignments. At Sannai Maruyama, several burial pits were marked with circular stone arrangements. The excavators of the site call these features *kanjo haiseki-bo* or circular stone burials. A total of seven of them have been identified in Excavation Areas 13, 14, and 17 (Aomori-ken Kyoiku-cho Bunka-ka 1999; 2000a; 2001). Figure 5.14 shows an example of these circular stone burials. As shown in the figure, this feature is associated with three overlapping burial pits, but only the most recent one (Pit A) has been excavated. The pit is associated with shallow grooves along the walls, from which a fragment of a carbonized wooden board was identified. Based on this finding, the excavator suggests the possibility of the presence of a wood frame (Katsuragi 2000). Stratigraphic observations revealed that the feature is likely to have been from the middle to late phase of the Middle Jomon period.

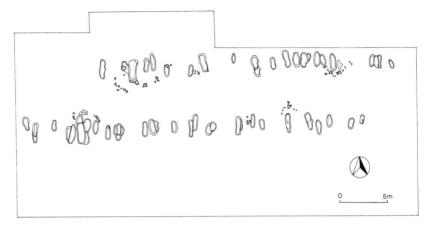

Figure 5.13   Two rows of Middle Jomon pit burials recovered from the Sannai Maruyama site, Aomori Prefecture (redrawn from Aomori-ken Kyoiku Iinkai 1977: 359)

Some of the burial pits are associated with stone slabs lining the inside of rectangular pits. They are called stone coffin burials (also called composite stone coffin burials) and are characteristic of the Late Jomon culture of the northern Tohoku region. Examples of stone coffin burials include those from the Yamanotoge and Horiai sites in Aomori Prefecture (fig. 5.15). Some scholars believe that some of these stone coffin burials are secondary rather than primary burials (see, e.g., Niitsu 1999).

Japanese scholars have also noticed that a distinct type of burial called *hai-oku-bo,* or abandoned-house burial, developed at Middle and Late Jomon sites in the western Kanto region (Doi 1990; Shitara 1999). These are multiple burials in a pit-dwelling, usually associated with a shell-midden. In some cases, skeletal remains were placed directly on the floor of a pit-dwelling, and were subsequently covered by shell layers. In other cases, burial pits were dug into the shell layers accumulated in an abandoned pit-dwelling. Early discoveries of this type of feature were interpreted as a result of mishaps such as food poisoning, but an increase in similar examples revealed that the bodies of the deceased were in most cases intentionally placed or buried (Y. Nishida 1996). Among the numerous examples of these abandoned-house burials are those at the Mukodai site in Chiba Prefecture (Shitara 1999), and the Kitagawa shell-midden in Kanagawa Prefecture (Takei 1990).

Finally, jar burials associated with infant skeletal remains have been reported from scores of Jomon sites. According to Kikuchi (1983), of the thirty-six examples of jar burials in good condition that have been

Figure 5.14   Circular Stone Burial no. 11 at Sannai Maruyama, Aomori
Prefecture (modified from Aomori-ken Kyoiku-cho Bunka-ka 2000a:
11; permission for reproduction obtained from Aomori-ken Kyoiku-cho
Bunka-ka)

reported up to 1983, twelve (33.3 percent) were associated with fetus
remains, and seventeen (47.2 percent) with babies younger than one year
old. Of the remaining seven examples, six (16.7 percent) were associated
with remains of babies or infants of one to six years old, and only one
example contains skeletal remains of a child older than six years old. In
other words, more than 80 percent of these jar burials are burials of fetuses
or babies younger than one year old. Kikuchi's study also indicates that
the majority of these jars were buried upright, and that the jars are often
bottomless, or have holes drilled in the bottom. Based on these examples,

Figure 5.15   Late Jomon stone coffin burials at the Horiai site, Aomori Prefecture (from Kasai and Takahashi 1981: photo 11; permission for reproduction obtained from Hiraka-machi Kyodo Shiryo-kan [History Museum of Hiraka Town])

Figure 5.16 Middle Jomon jar burial for an infant at Sannai Maruyama, Aomori Prefecture (photograph by courtesy of Aomori-ken Kyoiku-cho Bunka-ka)

archaeologists often identify a cluster of upright buried jars within a site as burials for babies or infants. At Sannai Maruyama, approximately 800 buried jars have been interpreted as burial jars for infants (Okada 1995a) (fig. 5.16).

Secondary burials

In comparison to primary burials, the number of secondary burials recovered from the Jomon period is small, but the number of examples has recently been increasing. Late and Final Jomon sites in the Kanto and Tohoku regions are sometimes associated with so-called "collective secondary burials" or *ta-itai saiso-bo*. This type of burial usually consists of a

Figure 5.17   Collective secondary burial at the Late Jomon Nakazuma
shell-midden, Ibaraki Prefecture (from Shinoda and Kanai 1999: 131;
permission for reproduction obtained from Toride-shi Maizo Bunkazai
Center [Archaeological Center of Toride City])

large circular or square pit, which measures approximately 1–2 meters in
diameter and 1–1.5 meters in depth. Dozens of to over a hundred skeletal
remains are associated with each of these burial pits. For example, at the
Nakazuma shell-midden in Ibaraki Prefecture (Shinoda and Kanai 1999),
skeletal remains of at least 105 individuals have been identified from a
circular pit (fig. 5.17). Many crania were placed near the wall of the
pit, suggesting that the bodies were probably reduced to skeletons by
the time of the reburial. However, some of the bones, such as sections of
the vertebrae, still retain anatomically natural positions, which may suggest that some parts of the soft tissues were still in existence at the time of
the reburial. Because the insides of some of the crania were not filled with
soil but remained hollow, Nishimoto (in T. Kobayashi et al. 1998: 93–94)
suggests that the method of reducing the corpses to skeletons prior to the
reburial was exposure to the air, not interment in the ground.

Other examples of collective secondary burials include the Gongen-
bara, Gionbara, Miyamoto-dai, and Kosaku sites in Chiba Prefecture,

and the Sanganji site in Fukushima Prefecture (all dated to Late Jomon) (R. Takahashi 1999). In the case of Miyamoto-dai, a small pit, possibly a postmold, was found at the center of the burial pit. If this was indeed a postmold, it may imply that the burial pit was covered by some kind of superstructure. Because of this evidence, Ryuzaburo Takahashi (1999) suggests that the burial pit remained open for a certain length of time and the skeletal remains of the newly deceased were added intermittently.

Another type of well-known secondary burial is the jar burial for an adult. Unlike jar burials for infants, in which skeletal remains retain their anatomically natural positioning, the positioning of adult human remains in burial jars often indicates artificial placement (i.e., secondary burials). Also, in most cases, each of these jars is too small to contain an adult body.

Examples of jar burials as secondary burials are commonly reported from Late Jomon sites in the Tohoku region. For example, at the Yakushi-mae site in Aomori Prefecture (Kuraishi-mura Kyoiku Iinkai 1997), three jar burials were placed in a circular pit (fig. 5.18). Of the three, Burial Jar no. 1 contained skeletal remains of an adult male, while Burial Jar no. 3 contained remains of an adult female. Although neither of the skeletal remains retained anatomically natural positioning, Morimoto and Kato (1997), who analyzed and described these remains, suggest that some of the bones in Burial Jar no. 3 (such as the first to sixth vertebrae) seem to have retained their anatomically natural positioning at the time of reburial. Thus, he suggests that the two individuals probably passed away at different times (the death of the individual in Burial Jar no. 3 being later), and that the conditions of the two corpses at the time of the reburial must have been different from each other. The poor preservation condition of the skeletal remains from Burial Jar no. 2 did not allow bioarchaeologists to determine the age and sex of the buried individual.

Similar types of jar burials have been recovered from approximately thirty Late Jomon sites in Aomori Prefecture (Kasai 1983). One such site is the Horiai site, where stone coffins were also identified (see fig. 5.15). Because jar burials and stone coffin burials were found side by side, the excavator of the site suggests that the corpses were first buried in the stone coffins, and were later reburied in the jars. The co-occurrence of these two types of burial in a single site has also been observed at several other Late Jomon sites in the Tohoku region (Kasai 1983).

Late and Final Jomon sites in the Tokai region are occasionally associated with a distinctive type of secondary burial called the square-shaped bone-pile burial (*banjo-shuseki-bo*). Figure 5.19 shows an example of this

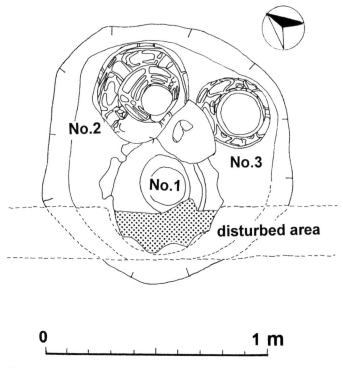

Figure 5.18   Late Jomon jar burials at the Yakushimae site, Aomori
Prefecture (modified and redrawn from Kuraishi-mura Kyoiku Iinkai
1997: 40)

type of burial recovered from the Final Jomon Motokariya shell-midden
in Aichi Prefecture. In this example, long bones, such as femurs, tibias,
ulnas, and humeri, were placed in a square shape, and broken fragments
of a cranium were placed at the corners and the center of the square
(Shitara 1999). Similar examples have been found from several other
Final Jomon sites in the same region. Because the pattern of the bone
placement is quite distinctive, archaeologists have suggested the presence of strict mortuary rules or ideology behind this practice (Y. Nishida
1996; Shitara 1999).

     Examples of secondary burials from western Japan are more common
than from eastern Japan (K. Nakamura 1999). In the Kyushu, Shikoku,
and Chugoku regions, some of the pit burials found from Initial and
Early Jomon cave sites are secondary burials. Examples of these sites
include Futsuka-ichi Cave (Initial Jomon), Kawarada Cave (Initial
Jomon), and Hegi Cave (Early Jomon) in Oita Prefecture, Kyushu. Many

Figure 5.19   Square-shaped bone-pile burial (*banjo-shuseki-bo*) at the
Final Jomon Motokariya shell-midden, Aichi Prefecture (photograph
by courtesy of Kariya-shi Kyoiku Iinkai [Board of Education of Kariya
City])

archaeologists also think that most of the Late and Final Jomon jar burials for adults, which are commonly found throughout western Japan, are
secondary burials (but see K. Nakamura 1991; 1999).

Finally, the presence of burnt human skeletal remains indicates that
cremation was occasionally practiced by the Jomon people. Among the
earliest examples of cremated skeletal remains are the three burnt crania recovered from the Early Jomon Hikozaki shell-midden in Okayama
Prefecture. Also, at the Early Jomon Funakura shell-midden in Okayama
Prefecture, burnt skeletal remains were recovered over a primary burial
with a flexed body (K. Nakamura 1999). Examples of burnt skeletal
remains from the Late and Final Jomon periods include those at Ikeda-
dera in Osaka Prefecture (Late Jomon), Miyataki in Nara Prefecture (Late
Jomon), and Onizuka in Osaka Prefecture (Final Jomon). Burnt skeletal
remains are also occasionally found in Late and Final Jomon jar burials
in Kyushu (K. Nakamura 1999).

Some of the burnt skeletal remains are associated with stone features
that are clearly ceremonial. At the Final Jomon Teraji site in Niigata

Prefecture, fragmented burnt skeletal remains of more than eleven individuals (ten adults and one juvenile), as well as a small quantity of burnt animal bone fragments, were recovered from a circular stone hearth in the center of a stone feature (G. Abe 1983; E. Nakajima and T. Watanabe 1994; Y. Nishida 1996). At the Nakamura Nakadaira site in Nagano Prefecture, a feature paved with flagstones, a pit with burnt human bones, and a stone feature associated with pottery containing burnt human bone were recovered. The total amount of burnt human bone recovered from these features weighs more than 30 kilograms. Since the weight of burnt bone from a single individual is estimated to be approximately 2 kilograms, there must have been the remains of approximately fifteen people (Y. Nishida 1996). These rather unusual examples suggest that the concept of cremation among the Jomon people may have been quite different from that of modern societies.

Regional and temporal variability in burials

It is evident from the above that the types of Jomon burial are quite diverse. Table 5.4 summarizes regional and temporal variability in the various types of burial described above. The two most common types of burials, pit burials and jar burials for infants, are found abundantly in both eastern and western Japan. Some other types, such as abandoned-house burials, collective secondary burials, and square-shaped bone-pile burials, are quite limited in their temporal and spatial distribution. Jar burials for adults are characteristic of Late Jomon burials in Tohoku, but are also commonly found in Kinki, Chugoku, Shikoku, and Kyushu throughout the Late and Final Jomon periods. Given the spatial discontinuity between the two regions, it is more likely that the two traditions originated separately. Finally, examples of cremation have been reported from both eastern and western Japan, but this practice is relatively infrequent throughout the Jomon period.

Data presented in table 5.4 also demonstrate that variability in Jomon burials began to increase during the Middle Jomon period, and that there was a variety of burial practices during the Late Jomon period. Since the table does not include Late and Final Jomon burials associated with monumental features such as stone circles and *kanjo-dori* (Late Jomon communal cemeteries in Hokkaido; see the section on "Construction of monumental structures" below, pp. 182–195), the actual variability is even more diverse. Accordingly, many Japanese archaeologists identify the end of the Middle Jomon and the beginning of the Late Jomon periods as the time of a major change in Jomon burial practice (e.g., Niitsu 1999).

Table 5.4 *Period and distribution of different types of burial*

	Incipient	Initial	Early	Middle	Late	Final	Primary distribution areas	References
Pit burials	present		abundant	abundant	abundant	abundant	eastern and western Japan	Nishimura 1965; O. Nakamura 1999
Circular stone burials				present	fairly common	present	Tohoku	Kodama 2003
"Stone coffin" burials					present		Tohoku, Kanto, Chubu, and Hokuriku	Kodama 2003; Niitsu 1999
"Abandoned-house" burials				present	present		Kanto	T. Doi 1990
Jar burials for infants			present	abundant	abundant	abundant	eastern and western Japan	Kikuchi 1983
Collective secondary burials					present		Kanto	R. Takahashi 1999
Jar burials for adults (primarily secondary burials?)				present	present	present	characteristic in Aomori Pref. in Late Jomon; fairly common in Kinki in Late and Final Jomon	Kasai 1983; Kikuchi 1983; O. Nakamura 1999
Square-shaped bone-pile burials						present	Tokai	Nishida 1996; Shitara 1999
Cremation burials		present	present	present	present	present	eastern and western Japan	Kikuchi 1983; Nishida 1996

Note: This table does not include burials associated with monumental features, such as stone circles and *kanjo-dori*. For summaries of these features, see pp. 182–191.

Burials and social inequality

This change in mortuary practices from the Middle to Late Jomon periods is particularly meaningful in light of recent discussions on the development of hunter-gatherer social inequality. As mentioned previously, traditionally Japanese archaeologists have viewed Jomon society as an egalitarian society. One of the few exceptions is Hitoshi Watanabe (1983; 1990), who suggested a model of the origins of social inequality among sedentary hunter-gatherers. Citing ethnographic examples from northern Pacific Rim hunter-gatherers including the Northwest Coast of North America and the Ainu of Hokkaido, Watanabe suggested that interfamilial occupational differentiation between hunter-fishers of large mammals (e.g., whales and bears) or fish (e.g., swordfish) and hunter-fishers of medium to small mammals or fish resulted in hereditary social stratification. He also suggested that these stratified hunter-gatherer societies are characterized by an abundance of prestige items and ceremonial practices as symbols of high social status.

Hitoshi Watanabe (1990) applied this model to the study of the Jomon culture. Based on the fact that large mammal and fish remains, such as bear and swordfish, have been recovered from several Jomon sites, Watanabe suggested that the Jomon society was stratified. Furthermore, he argued that finds of elaborately decorated pottery and various kinds of ornaments recovered from Middle through Final Jomon sites, as well as being evidence of complex ceremonial activities in these Jomon sub-periods, also support the argument that this was a stratified society characterized by a "prestige economy."

Because the archaeological examples that Watanabe (1990) cited came from only an extremely small number of sites excavated before 1960 (Sakatsume 1961), his work has been seen by most Japanese archaeologists as a presentation of a possible model rather than a convincing interpretation (for the evaluation of his work, see Habu 1993). However, recent analyses of Jomon burial data by Oki Nakamura (1999; 2000) indicate that a certain level of hereditary inequality may have existed at least in the Late and Final Jomon periods in the Tohoku region.

Oki Nakamura (2000) examines the kinds and numbers of grave goods (including ornaments probably worn by the deceased) recovered from Jomon burials in 373 sites. Despite large temporal and regional variability, he suggests that changes in grave goods throughout the Jomon period can be divided into three phases. The following is a summary of results of his analysis.

Phase I (Incipient to late Initial Jomon periods)   This phase is generally characterized by an abundance of everyday commodities such as deep jars and stone tools (including arrowheads, scrapers, and awls). These are the most basic grave goods not only in this phase but also throughout the rest of the Jomon period. Exquisite ornaments are rare in this phase, although a small number of pendants made with stones, shells, and shark teeth have been reported. No child burials have been identified from this phase. Since the total number of burials associated with grave goods is very small, no data are available regarding the differences in burial goods based on gender. Approximately 20 to 30 percent of burials were associated with one or more burial goods (statistics based on the data from only three sites: the Hokuto site in Hokkaido, and the Shinnaya and the Ienomae sites in Aomori Prefecture) (O. Nakamura 2000).

Phase II (the end of Initial to Middle Jomon periods)   During this phase, the presence of "exquisite" ornaments and pots became common. These include slitted stone earrings, tubular stone beads, shell bracelets, large jade beads, deer antler "waist pendants" (possibly men's knife handles), clay earrings, boar ivory pendants and bracelets, and amber ornaments. During this phase, lacquered shallow bowls (see the next chapter) and stone rods also appeared as grave goods for the first time. Deep jars and stone tools continued to be part of the grave good assemblages from this phase. Relative occurrences of burials with one or more grave goods vary from 10 to 30 percent. Relative occurrences of burials with exquisite grave goods range from 1 to 14 percent, with the majority of sites having less than 10 percent. Grave good differences based on gender can also be observed. Slitted stone earrings and clay earrings have been reported only with female skeletal remains, whereas "waist pendants" have been recovered only with male skeletal remains. A very small number of child burials associated with exquisite grave goods, such as those from the Ishiyama shell-midden in Shiga Prefecture (terminal phase of the Incipient Jomon period) and the Urayama Terazo site in Toyama Prefecture (Middle Jomon), have been reported from this phase (O. Nakamura 2000).

Phase III (Late and Final Jomon periods)   This phase is characterized by an increase in the numbers and kinds of grave goods as well as rapid temporal changes in exquisite grave goods. A variety of stone, clay, shell, and bone ornaments as well as lacquered wood artifacts have been reported from many Late and Final Jomon sites. Ritual artifacts, such as stone rods, "stone swords," clay figurines, and stone and clay tablets, are also reported. Pots as grave goods include not only deep and shallow

Table 5.5 *Percentages of child burials associated with grave goods (absolute numbers in parentheses)*

	Incipient–Middle Jomon	Late Jomon	Final Jomon
Hokkaido/Northern Tohoku	0.0 (0/8)	0.0 (0/8)	17.1 (6/35)
Southern Tohoku	0.0 (0/6)	8.3 (1/12)	25.0 (4/16)
Kanto/Chubu	2.6 (1/39)	4.5 (6/132)	0.0 (0/2)
Hokuriku	0.0 (0/2)	– (0/0)	– (0/0)
Tokai	– (0/0)	20.0 (1/5)	1.6 (2/124)
Kinki/Chugoku/Shikoku	11.1 (1/9)	10.7 (3/28)	8.3 (1/12)
Kyushu	0.0 (0/22)	0.0 (0/15)	50.0 (1/2)
Average	2.3 (2/86)	5.1 (10/195)	7.3 (14/191)

Source: O. Nakamura 1999.

bowls but also jars with narrow necks and spouted pots to contain liquid. The occurrence of burials with grave goods ranges between 10 and 30 percent, with the burials with exquisite grave goods being approximately 10 percent. The exceptions are several Late Jomon sites such as the Bibi no. 4 site and the Kashiwagi B *kanjo-dori* site (see below), where respectively 24 and 20 percent of burials were associated with exquisite grave goods. Differences based on sex observed in the previous phase are generally supported, although exceptions to the general rules are also observed. Occurrences of child burials with exquisite grave goods increased significantly relative to the previous phase. Among the twenty-six examples of Jomon child burials associated with exquisite grave goods, twenty-four (ten from Late Jomon and fourteen from Final Jomon) are from Phase III (see table 5.5). In particular, an increase in the relative occurrences in the Final Jomon in the Hokkaido and Tohoku regions is noticeable (17.1 percent in Hokkaido and northern Tohoku, and 25.0 percent in southern Tohoku). Differences in the number of exquisite grave goods between burials are also larger than in the previous phase, particularly in the Tohoku region and Hokkaido. This seems to indicate the appearance of a small number of individuals distinguished by special funeral treatment (O. Nakamura 2000).

On the basis of this analysis, Nakamura (2000) suggests that these changes reflect the process of the development of social inequality throughout the Jomon period. In particular, he interprets the increase in the number of child burials associated with exquisite grave goods as reflecting the emergence of hereditary social inequality in the Late and Final Jomon periods. Citing Morris (1987) and Hayden (1995), Nakamura also suggests that rapid temporal changes in the types of exquisite grave goods within this phase imply that these artifacts were controlled and manipulated as status symbols by a small number of elites; once the status symbol became accessible to a larger number of people, a new status symbol was created or defined by the elites. By suggesting this new model, Nakamura (2000) criticizes previous studies of Jomon burials, which assumed Jomon society to have been egalitarian.

Mortuary practices and cultural landscapes

Systematic examination of burial data in the context of past cultural landscapes is also critical to our understanding of Jomon mortuary practices. Traditionally, many Japanese archaeologists have suggested that the presence of collective burials or cemeteries associated with large settlements is an important indicator of long-term sedentism (e.g., Seido 1977). However, chronological studies of burials and pit-dwellings at several Jomon sites indicate that the presence of a cemetery does not imply automatically that the site was a long-term residence of fully sedentary people.

The Hazama-higashi site in Chiba Prefecture is the first case in point. Salvage excavation of the site revealed thirty pit-dwellings dating to the Early Jomon period (Funabashi-shi Kyoiku Iinkai 1975). Of these, twenty-six are dated to the Kurohama phase, which is the third of the five Early Jomon phases in the region (the Lower Hanazumi, Sekiyama, Kurohama, Moroiso, and Jusanbodai phases from the oldest to the youngest; the Moroiso phase is usually further divided into three subphases: Moroiso-a, -b, and -c). In addition to the twenty-six pit-dwellings from the Kurohama phase, two pit-dwellings are dated from the Moroiso-a subphase, which follows immediately after the Kurohama phase. The remaining two other pit-dwellings are dated to the subsequent Moroiso-b subphase. In other words, in terms of the size of the settlement, the Hazama-higashi site was at its peak during the Kurohama phase. The size of the settlement decreased significantly in the following Moroiso-a and Moroiso-b subphases.

However, burial data from this site indicate apparent differences in the intensity of site use from the Kurohama phase to the Moroiso phase. The site is associated with a cluster of oval pits, which are located in the northwestern part of the site. Because of the shape of these pits, and because of an abundance of "ceremonial" pottery in them (see small, shallow bowls in fig. 5.20), it is likely that the majority are burial pits (Funabashi-shi Kyoiku Iinkai 1975). Jade beads are also associated with some of these pits. Excavation of the Hazama-higashi site revealed a total of about 200 pits of this type. The majority of them are from the

Figure 5.20   Shallow bowls recovered from burial pits at the Hazama-higashi site, Chiba Prefecture (photographs by courtesy of Koku-ritsu Rekishi Minzoku Hakubutsu-kan [National Museum of Japanese History])

Moroiso-a and Moroiso-b subphases rather than the preceding Kuro-hama phase. In other words, archaeological data indicate that these burial pits are not contemporaneous with the majority of the pit-dwellings, which were constructed during the Kurohama phase. However, there is no evidence of burials at the site relating to that period. After the majority of the pit-dwellings were abandoned, the burials began to appear. By this time, the site was no longer a large settlement, but instead probably only one or two pit-dwellings were occupied. Therefore, the function of the site shifted over time from primarily a residential site to primarily a cemetery site.

The Hazama-higashi site is not an exception. A similar example can be found at the Akyu site in Nagano Prefecture in the Chubu region (Nagano-ken Chuodo Iseki Chosa-dan 1982; Nagano-ken Kyoiku Iinkai 1979). The site is known for the presence of many clusters of stones, the function of which does not seem to be practical in nature. The total number of these stone clusters is approximately 270, and, together with a large number of additional scattered stones, these stone clusters formed a large, circular configuration. The total number of stones found within this area is approximately 50,000 (Y. Mori 1999). Oval pits which look like burial pits have been recovered at the center of the circular stone feature. Some of these pits are associated with large, upright stone markers. Based on the styles of associated pottery, excavators dated the majority of stone clusters and burial pits to the Moroiso-a and Moroiso-b subphases.

In terms of the construction of pit-dwellings, however, the peak of the site occupation occurred not during the Moroiso phase, but during the preceding phases. Approximately fifty pit-dwellings have been identified from the Nakagoshi phase (contemporaneous with the Lower Hanazumi phase, the first phase of Early Jomon in the Kanto region), which is dated to the beginning of the Early Jomon period. After this phase, the site was abandoned for the following two phases (Kaminoki and Ario; contemporaneous with the Sekiyama phase, the second phase of the Early Jomon in Kanto), and then was reoccupied during the Kurohama phase and the Moroiso-a and Moroiso-b subphases. Nineteen pit-dwellings were constructed during the Kurohama phase. The total number of pit-dwellings from the Moroiso-a subphase decreases to eleven, and finally to two for the Moroiso-b subphase. Once again, there is a pattern in which the initial occupation was characterized by a large number of residential features (i.e., pit-dwellings). This was followed by a shift in site function whereby we now have only a small number of pit-dwellings but have substantial numbers of ceremonial and burial features.

A similar pattern can be found at the third example, the Kitagawa site in Kanagawa Prefecture. Salvage excavation of the site revealed the presence of five Moroiso-a pit-dwellings and nineteen Moroiso-b pit-dwellings. No pit-dwellings have been identified from the following Moroiso-c subphase. Oval burial pits have also been recovered at the site. Some of them were from the Moroiso-b subphase, whereas others were from the Moroiso-c subphase. The only burial pit associated with human skeletal remains was from the Moroiso-c subphase. A jade earring was found in association with this burial. It is evident in this case that the construction of burials continued following the major period of the use of the site as a residential base.

To summarize, in all three cases presented here, each site originally functioned as a large residential site. During this early phase of site occupation, there were no burials or ceremonial features. Later, when each site ceased to function as a large residential base, its function shifted from primarily residential to more ceremonial. Given the archaeological data described above, it is most likely that the people who used to live in the site, or their descendants, returned periodically to bury the dead or to perform ceremonial activities at these sites.

These case studies demonstrate that the relationship between large residential sites and associated burials may not be as straightforward as is generally believed. The presence of burials does not imply that a person's life cycle was confined to one single settlement. Rather, the presence of burials or ceremonial features at a site should be interpreted in the context of the overall settlement system.

Construction of ceremonial and monumental features

As is evident from the case of the Akyu site, some of the Jomon sites are associated with ceremonial features. The types of so-called ceremonial features from the Jomon period are quite diverse. Many of them consist of stones and/or earthworks, and are quite large. In many cases, the construction of these features must have required a significant amount of human labor and cooperation.

Stone circles and other stone features

The most common type of Jomon ceremonial feature is made of stones. Although the first appearance of ceremonial stone features goes back to the Initial Jomon period (Akimoto 1999: 173), the number remained small through the Initial to the first half of the Early Jomon period. During the second half of the Early Jomon period, however, elaborate stone features were constructed in at least several sites in the Chubu region. For example, at the Early Jomon Wappara site in Nagano Prefecture (I. Oba 1957a), elongated stones were recovered in a circular configuration. The excavators of the site suggested that these stones were originally placed upright (fig. 5.21). Since the site is at a high altitude (approximately 800 m ASL; Hirabayashi 1957), with a wonderful view of the mountains of the Northern Japanese Alps, Iwao Oba (1957b: 159), the principal investigator of the site, suggested that the feature must have been related

Figure 5.21 Reconstruction of the Early Jomon circular stone feature at the Wappara site, Nagano Prefecture (from K. Suzuki 1988: 114–115; photograph by courtesy of Kodansha)

to mountain worship. Other scholars (e.g., Ohtsuka 1988) have suggested that the site was a place where hunting rituals were performed. This is because a large number of arrowheads and stemmed scrapers (possibly used for butchering animals) were found at the site. The site is also associated with a large number of slitted stone earrings. Since many of the earrings are unfinished, scholars believe that the production of these earrings took place at the site (K. Mori 1988: 18). Because the stone features at both Akyu (see above, p. 181) and Wappara are dated to the Early Jomon Moroiso phase (see chapter 4), and because discoveries of similar features are less common in this region prior to this phase, scholars have suggested that a major change in Jomon cultural landscapes occurred at the end of the Early Jomon period.

The number of stone features from the Middle Jomon period is larger than that of the Early Jomon period (Kodama 2003). At the Kumori site in Gunma Prefecture, a circular stone arrangement, the diameter of which measures approximately 40 meters, has been identified. Similarly, at the Ushiishi site in Yamanashi Prefecture, a stone circle that consists of Inner and Outer Rings has been reported. The diameter of this stone circle measures approximately 50 meters. On the other hand, stone features found at several other sites, such as the Sengo site in Nagano Prefecture (Niitsu 1999) and the Goshono site in Iwate Prefecture (Ichinohe-machi Kyoiku Iinkai 1993), are less formally organized. For example, in the case of Goshono, small clusters of stones have been recovered together

Figure 5.22   "Sundial" type of stone cluster at Nonakado of the Oyu
site, Akita Prefecture (from K. Mori 1988: 29; photograph by courtesy
of Kodansha)

with a large number of scattered stones. The distribution area of these
stones covers approximately 80 meters (east–west) by 50 meters (north–
south). While some of the stone clusters seem to have functioned as
grave markers, it is likely that the entire area covered by both clustered
and scattered stones represents a place for ceremonial activities.

Recoveries of Late and Final Jomon stone features are numerous.
In particular, an abundance of large stone circles is characteristic
of Hokkaido and northern Tohoku. These Late Jomon stone circles
can be divided into two types. The first type consists of a larger
number of small stone clusters. For example, at the Oyu site in Akita
Prefecture, two large stone circles, each of which comprises a number
of small stone clusters, have been recovered. These two stone circles are
named Manza and Nonakado stone circles respectively. Some of the small
stone clusters found at the site are known as the "sundial" type, in which
elongated stones are placed in a radiating pattern, with a large upright
stone at the center (fig. 5.22). A series of test excavations recently conducted by the Board of Education of Kazuno City revealed that pit burials

are located under most of the small stone clusters, including "sundials." Association of burial pits with "sundials" and other types of small stone clusters have been confirmed at other Late Jomon stone circles such as Otoe and Nishizakiyama in Hokkaido (Kodama 2003).

The other type of Late Jomon stone circle consists primarily of circular or square alignments of stones. For example, at the Late Jomon Komakino site in Aomori Prefecture, a large stone circle made of three concentric rings (the Center, Inner, and Outer Rings) was excavated (fig. 5.23). The Outer Ring measures approximately 35 meters in diameter. While the stones of the three concentric rings are not burial markers, the stone circle is associated with eleven smaller stone clusters (Stone Features nos. 1–11), three burial jars, and eight circular stone burials (nos. 1–8). Also, approximately fifty "flask-shaped" pit burials have been recovered from outside the stone circle, on the eastern side of the site.

According to Kodama (2003), the construction of the Komakino stone circle must have required not only carrying approximately 2,400 stone boulders from the riverbed of the nearby Arakawa River (70 m above sea level, or ASL) to the site (140–150 m ASL), but also leveling the ground to make a flat area of approximately 500 square meters on a hillside. Also, in Kodama's estimate, about 315 cubic meters of soil have been moved from the upper side of the site to the lower side.

The construction of these large stone circles in the Tohoku region seems to have occurred in a fairly limited time period within a restricted area. It is particularly worth noting that, in the Tohoku region, the construction of stone circles was *not* characteristic of the Middle Jomon period when large settlements such as Sannai Maruyama were commonly constructed, but of the Late Jomon period when very few large settlements were constructed.

Stone circles represent only a small proportion of ceremonial stone features from the Late Jomon period. For example, at the Monzen site in Iwate Prefecture (Sato and Kumagai 1995), a Late Jomon arrow-shaped stone feature that consists of approximately 1,350 stones was recovered (fig. 5.24). In addition, approximately 15,000 stones were densely scattered in an area about 10 by 30 meters on the eastern side of the arrow-shaped feature. Many of these are granite beach gravels and thus must have been brought into the site from the nearby beach, which was at least 1 kilometer away. The site is also associated with a Middle and Late Jomon shell-midden.

Discoveries of ceremonial stone features from the Final Jomon period are also common, particularly in the Kanto, Chubu, and Hokuriku regions. For example, at the Teraji site, where a large hearth associated with a large quantity of burnt skeletal remains was recovered (see above,

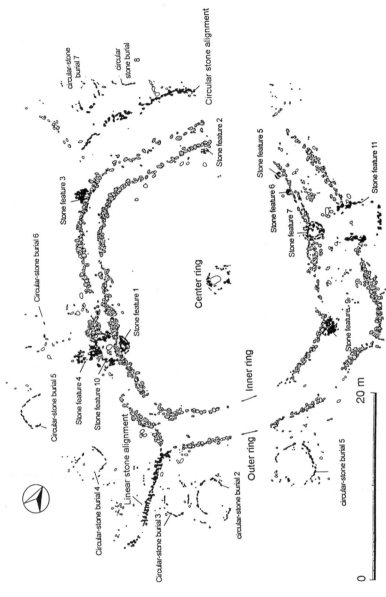

Figure 5.23 Late Jomon stone circle at the Komakino site, Aomori Prefecture (from Kodama 2003: 245; permission for reproduction obtained from Daisei Kodama)

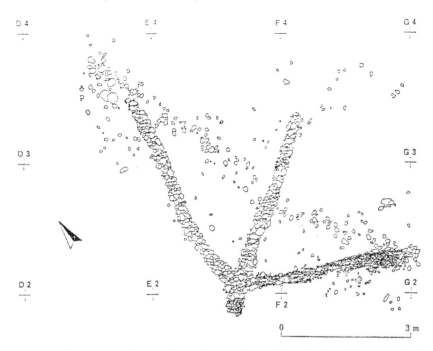

Figure 5.24   Arrow-shaped stone feature from the Late Jomon period at the Monzen site, Iwate Prefecture (from Sato and Kumagai 1995: 78; permission for reproduction obtained from Rikuzen-takada-shi Kyoiku Iinkai [Board of Education of Rikuzen-takada City])

pp. 173–174), a composite stone feature complex that includes two oval stone wall features, a square stone wall feature with four wooden posts, and arc-shaped stone walls was excavated. Other sites associated with Final Jomon stone features include the Kinsei site in Yamanashi Prefecture (Yamanashi-ken Maizo Bunkazai Chosa Center 1989) and the Yaze site in Gunma Prefecture (A. Miyake 1994).

Kanjo dori

The Late Jomon culture in Hokkaido is characterized by the presence of not only stone circles but also *kanjo dori*, i.e., burials with a circular embankment. *Kanjo dori* is a form of mortuary complex that appeared in some parts of Hokkaido during the end of the Late Jomon period (Ikawa-Smith 1992; Otani 1983). Figure 5.25 shows a schematic plan of *kanjo dori* (Otani 1983). As shown in this figure, it consists of a large circular pit, an embankment that surrounds the circular pit, and grave pits constructed in the circular area. In this figure, the central grave pit is

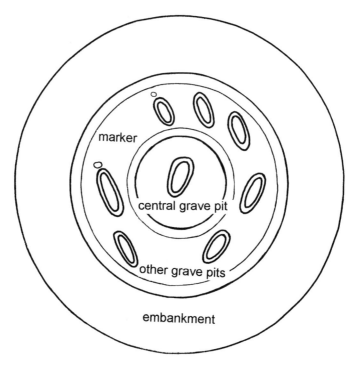

Figure 5.25   Schematic plan of *kanjo dori* (modified and redrawn from Otani 1983: 47)

distinguished from the others, although this is not always the case (Otani 1983). The number of grave pits within each *kanjo dori* varies between one and twenty-one (Ikawa-Smith 1992). In other words, while *kanjo dori* are known as collective burials, in some cases there is only a single grave pit. The embankment was apparently made of the back dirt from the large circular pit (Otani 1983). The distribution of *kanjo dori* is primarily clustered in the Ishikari Plain of western Hokkaido (the Kashiwagi B, Kiusu, Suehiro, Bibi 4, and Misawa 1 sites), although four other sites (Otoe Minami, Ashibetsu Nokanan, Ichani, and Shuen Kurisawa) have been identified in central and eastern Hokkaido (fig. 5.26).

The most well-known *kanjo dori* site is the Kiusu site. Located near downtown Chitose, the site is associated with fourteen *kanjo dori*. Figure 5.27 shows the major *kanjo dori* found at the site. As shown in the figure, the size of these *kanjo dori* is not uniform, their diameters ranging between 30 and 75 meters, and the height of the embankments between 0.5 and 5.4 meters. Some of them share part of their embankment.

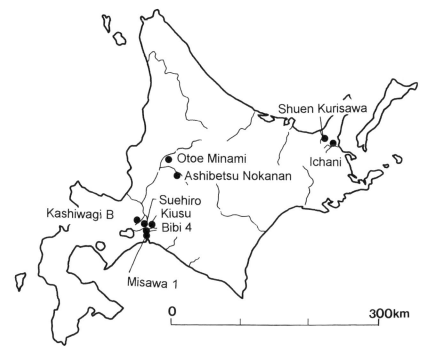

Figure 5.26 Distribution of *kanjo dori* (modified and redrawn from Otani 1983: 47)

The amount of soil moved to construct the largest one (*Kanjo Dori* no. 2) is estimated to have been 3,080 ± 300 square meters (Otani 1983: 48). Assuming that one person moved about 1 square meter of soil per day, it would have taken 123 days for 25 people to construct this feature (Otani 1983).

According to Otani (1983), grave goods found in burial pits in *kanjo dori* are nothing special. They include pottery, stone tools such as arrowheads and stone axes, ornaments such as beads and shell bracelets, and the small type of stone rods. Because of the fairly common presence of stone rods, Otani suggests that the people buried in these graves were shamans who were in charge of ceremonial activities, but not distinguished by a higher social status. However, Oki Nakamura (2000) notes that the occurrences of burials associated with exquisite grave goods at two *kanjo dori* sites, Bibi 4 and Kashiwagi B, are 24 percent and 20 percent respectively. Considering that the average occurrences in this period is about 10 percent, these numbers are much higher. This may suggest that a society associated with *kanjo dori* was characterized by some kind of social stratification.

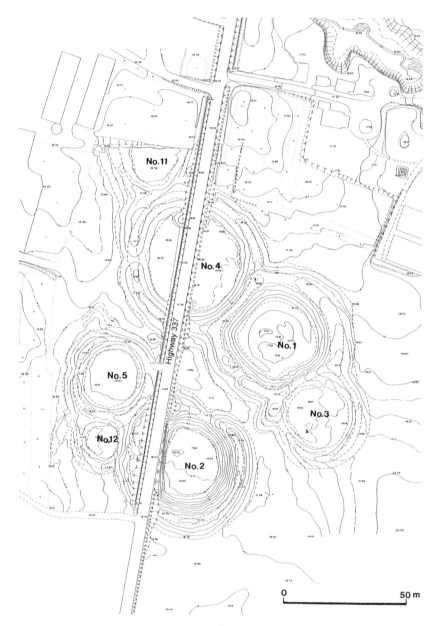

Figure 5.27 *Kanjo dori* at the Kiusu site, Hokkaido (diagram by courtesy of Chitose-shi Kyoiku Iinkai [Board of Education of Chitose City])

Kanjo dori were constructed in a limited time period, and Jomon people ceased to construct them after several hundred years. It is also worth noting that, just as in the case of Late Jomon stone circles in Hokkaido and Tohoku, most *kanjo dori* sites are associated with only a small number of pit-dwellings or other types of substantial residential features for winter occupation. Ikawa-Smith (1992) emphasizes the fact that the construction of *kanjo dori* occurred after the Late Jomon people in this area had ceased to form large settlements with a number of pit-dwellings (presumably winter settlements); i.e., the appearance of *kanjo dori* coincided with the disappearance of what appeared to be winter aggregation sites. She suggests that *kanjo dori* sites may have represented places where people came together during the warm season for communal hunting and fishing activities, marriage transactions, and other ritual activities (Ikawa-Smith 1992: 86), and that this change may have been caused by an environmental crisis as a result of cooling temperatures.

Earthen mounds

In addition to *kanjo dori*, discoveries of earthen mounds at several Jomon sites provide another line of evidence that Jomon people constructed large-scale earthworks. At the Terano-higashi site in Tochigi Prefecture, a ring-shaped earthen mound dated to the Late and Final Jomon periods was identified. Figure 5.28 shows a schematic diagram of the site. While the eastern half of the mound was destroyed by river improvement work during the Edo period, the other half was well preserved. The diameter of the outside of the ring-shaped mound measures approximately 165 meters, and the width of the embankment ranges between 15 and 30 meters. The elevation of the inside of the ring shape (the "plaza") is lower than the ground surface of the outside, and the difference in elevation between the mound top and the lowest part of the inside measures 4.4 meters. Apparently the Jomon people dug or scraped the ground surface of the inside and piled up the soil around the dug area (Tochigi-ken Kyoiku Iinkai et al. 1994).

Stratigraphic observations of the mound, as well as the examination of associated artifacts, indicate that it was formed continuously from the middle of the Late Jomon period to the middle of the Final Jomon period. Because many layers of the mound include burnt soil and a large number of charcoal fragments, the excavators of the site suggest that rituals associated with fire must have been performed repeatedly inside the ring, and the back dirt accumulated intermittently on the outside of the "plaza," which eventually formed the embankment. Whether the

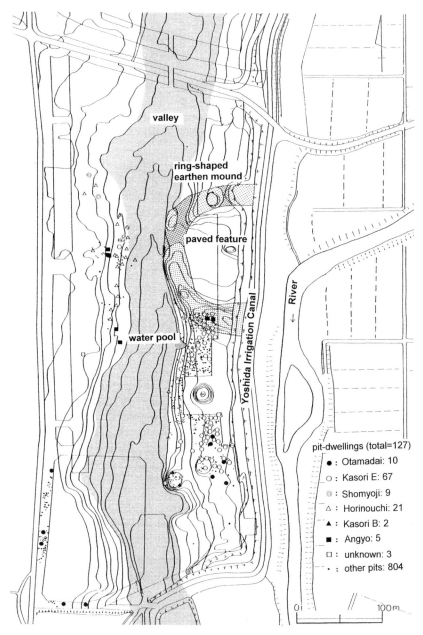

Figure 5.28   Ring-shaped earthen mound (Late and Final Jomon) at
the Terano-higashi site, Tochigi Prefecture (modified and redrawn from
Tochigi-ken Kyoiku Iinkai and Oyama-shi Kyoiku Iinkai 1994: 12)

construction of the mound was intentional or not is a topic of debate. Many scholars suggest that it was intentionally formed to construct the embankment as a monumental feature. Others believe that, just as in the case of Jomon shell-middens, long-term accumulation of garbage resulted in the formation of the mound. In either case, the recovery of a large number of ritual artifacts, such as clay figurines, stone rods and "swords," clay earrings, and stone beads, from both the mound itself and the "plaza" area, indicates that the formation of the mound was related to ceremonial activities (Tochigi-ken Kyoiku Iinkai et al. 1994).

It is interesting to note that the majority of the pit-dwellings recovered from the Terano-higashi site are dated prior to the construction of the mound. As shown in fig. 5.29, most pit-dwellings at the site are either from the Middle Jomon period (the Otamadai and Kasori-E phases) or from the beginning of the Late Jomon period (the Shomyoji phase), i.e., before the construction of the mound began in the Horinouchi phase (Tochigi-ken Kyoiku Iinkai *et al.* 1994). Thus, just as in the case of several of the burial/ceremonial sites described above, it is likely that the function of the site shifted primarily from residential to ceremonial over time. Similar ring-shaped earthen mounds have been identified from several other Late and Final Jomon sites in the Kanto region, including the Minoh site in Chiba Prefecture (Chiba-ken Bunkazai Center 2000).

Features associated with large wooden posts

Finally, features associated with large wooden posts have been reported from several Jomon sites (Hashimoto 1994). At the Chikamori site (Minami 1994) in Ishikawa Prefecture, the bottoms of approximately 350 wooden posts were recovered in waterlogged conditions. Many of these were half-moon-shaped (i.e., vertically split to approximately half), and were grooved at the bottom. Since some of the wooden posts had vines around the grooves, the excavators suggest that the function of the grooves was to facilitate transportation. All the wooden posts were identified as chestnut.

Among the findings at Chikamori is the discovery of eight circular features associated with ten (or sometimes eight) large, half-split wooden posts. Figure 5.30 shows one of these features. As shown in the figure, the diameter of each post measures approximately 60 to 80 centimeters. The feature is also associated with a pair of crescent-shaped wooden posts, which were interpreted as the entrance. The locations of the ten posts are on an almost perfect circle, and the five pairs of posts were placed symmetrically on both sides of the central axis that goes through the "entrance."

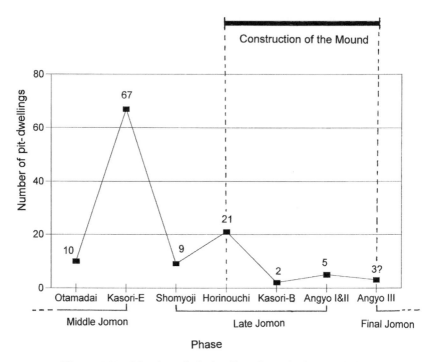

Figure 5.29   Number of pit-dwellings in each phase and the construction period of the earthen mound at Terano-higashi (data taken from Tochigi-ken Kyoiku Iinkai and Oyama-shi Kyoiku Iinkai 1994)

This suggests that the builders of these features had some knowledge of basic geometry. Because of the extremely large size of the posts, the features were reconstructed as ceremonial "wood circles," although some scholars, including Minami (1994), the principal investigator of the site, believe that they were actually remains of buildings. In either case, cutting these large posts and constructing the feature would have required a significant amount of labor. The excavation of the site also revealed the presence of several square and rectangular features associated with either four or six large wooden posts. Unlike the circular features, the wooden posts of the square and rectangular features were not half-split but were complete trunks.

Circular features associated with half-split wooden posts have also been reported from Final Jomon layers of the Mawaki site in Ishikawa Prefecture (Noto-machi Kyoiku Iinkai 1986; 1992; Kato 1994) (fig. 5.31), the Yonaizumi site in Ishikawa Prefecture (Nishino 1994), and the Teraji site in Niigata Prefecture (E. Nakajima and T. Watanabe 1994). Also,

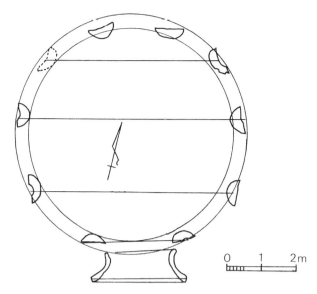

Figure 5.30   Circular feature associated with large wooden posts recovered from the Chikamori site, Ishikawa Prefecture (modified and redrawn from Kanazawa-shi Kyoiku Iinkai [Board of Education of Kanazawa City] cited in Minami 1994: 28)

at the Final Jomon Yaze site in Gunma Prefecture, six half-split posts, the diameter of each of which measures approximately 45 centimeters, were recovered in a rectangular plan (A. Miyake 1994). Together with the six large chestnut posts of the Sannai Maruyama site (see chapter 4), these examples demonstrate the range of corporate work conducted by the Jomon people.

Discussion

What emerges from the above description of mortuary and ceremonial practices is an extremely complex mosaic of sociocultural elements. Each element (i.e., each type of ritual artifact, burial, and ceremonial feature) has its own temporal duration and spatial distribution, and varies in its abundance quantity. Although the amount of currently available data are still limited, they nevertheless show some interesting patterns.

First, these data indicate that variability in Jomon mortuary and ceremonial practices increased significantly through time. The increase can be observed in all three categories of data analyzed here (i.e., ritual artifacts, burial, and ceremonial features). In particular, the transitions from the

Figure 5.31   Circular feature associated with large wooden posts recovered from the Mawaki site (from Noto-machi Kyoiku Iinkai 1992: photo 6; permission for reproduction obtained from Noto-machi Kyoiku Iinkai)

Early to the Middle Jomon, and from the Middle to the Late through to the Final Jomon seem to have been the two critical periods during which a number of new elements appeared. If we assume that variability in mortuary and ceremonial practices reflects the degree of social complexity (for the definition of social complexity used in this book, see chapter 1), then these results indicate that the degree of Jomon social complexity increased significantly through time. Furthermore, if, as Oki Nakamura (2000) suggests, hereditary social stratification developed through the Late and Final Jomon periods in eastern Japan, then it is quite likely that some of the elements that appeared during or after the Late Jomon period, such as the elaboration of ceremonial artifacts, were directly related to the emergence of a certain level of social stratification among the Jomon people. On the other hand, other elements, particularly those that can be commonly found in the Early and Middle Jomon periods, are less likely to be reflections of status differentiation.

It should also be emphasized that, although data presented by Oki Nakamura (2000) show a certain trend toward increasing social inequality by birth (a possible indication of incipient ascribed status) in the Late and Final Jomon periods, overall the degree of vertical differentiation in these periods seems to have been relatively small. Among the cultural elements that characterize social stratification among hunter-gatherer groups on the Northwest Coast of North America and in California (e.g., Ames and Maschner 1999), some elements, such as warfare and differentiation by house size, are missing in the Jomon data. Furthermore, differences in the quality and/or quantity of burial goods between adult burials are not nearly as evident as in the case of well-known stratified societies (e.g., Peebles and Kus 1977). No evidence for the development of complex political structure is available either.

Equally interesting is the fact that the increase over time in variability in mortuary and ceremonial practices does not necessarily seem to have been associated with subsistence intensification, increasing sedentism, and higher population density. As discussed in chapter 2, Koyama's (1978; 1984) estimates of Jomon population indicate that the population increased steadily during the Initial and Early Jomon periods, reached its maximum during the Middle Jomon period, and then declined through the Late and Final Jomon periods. Furthermore, as discussed in the previous chapter, many of the well-known large Jomon settlements are from the Middle Jomon period, not from the Late and Final Jomon periods. While Late Jomon large settlements are common in certain areas of eastern Japan, such as the shell-midden concentration area of eastern Kanto (especially Chiba Prefecture; see chapter 3), an overall decline in average site size and density from the Middle to Late and Final Jomon periods is apparent.

As discussed in the first chapter, the presence of large settlements is characteristic of a collector system (either fully sedentary or only seasonally sedentary), under which intensive exploitation of temporally or spatially aggregated resources takes place. Large settlements are very rarely associated with forager systems. Thus, it is very unlikely that the organizational complexity of Jomon subsistence–settlement systems increased from the Middle to the Late and Final Jomon periods. On the other hand, various lines of evidence discussed in this chapter demonstrate an overall increase in the complexity of mortuary and ceremonial practices from Middle to Late and Final Jomon periods, some of which are likely to be reflections of a certain level of social inequality.

These results would suggest that the development of Jomon cultural complexity followed quite a different trajectory from that of other well-known complex hunter-gatherers, including those on the Northwest Coast of North America, where evolutionary developments in subsistence, settlement, and social systems can be generally identified. Put another way, examination of the development of Jomon social inequality leads to the question of whether complex hunter-gatherer cultures in various parts of the world all developed through similar stages. This is an important issue, and it will be discussed in more depth in chapter 7.

Second, the overall increase through time in the complexity of mortuary and ceremonial practices does not imply that more fine-grained analyses of these data are unnecessary. On the contrary, large regional variability observed in the data presented in this chapter indicates that the processes of the refinement of mortuary and ceremonial practices, which may have been closely related to the emergence of social inequality, took various forms in different regions, and that the timing of these developments varied. Thus, in order to understand the processes, it is necessary not only to conduct analysis of mortuary and ceremonial data from a specific region but also to study subsistence and settlement in the region so that we can examine these different lines of evidence in the context of changes in cultural landscapes as a whole.

Third, mortuary and ceremonial practices can also shed light on the study of Jomon settlement patterns. Traditionally, Japanese archaeologists have assumed that the presence of a cemetery in a prehistoric settlement is an important indicator of full sedentism (e.g., Seido 1977; H. Watanabe 1986). However, examination of Jomon burial data indicates that the construction of burials and the occupation of pit-dwellings at each site did not necessarily occur at the same time (see pp. 179–182). This implies that cultural landscapes of the Jomon people included previously occupied settlements, and their overall land use is likely to have been much more complex than has previously been assumed. Adding mortuary and ceremonial behaviors as components of the settlement systems of Jomon collectors and/or foragers may allow us to explain certain archaeological patterns that are not explicable from strictly ecological or economic perspectives.

Finally, the presence of monumental features and their relative abundance in the Late and Final Jomon periods in comparison to the preceding periods may offer insights into the role of corporative work in the possible development of Jomon social complexity. As mentioned previously, Feinman (1995) suggests dual pathways, corporate-based and network-based strategies, toward the development of social inequality. In this regard, examination of the timing of the appearance of monumental features (i.e., evidence of corporate work) in relation to the development of social inequality in Jomon societies can contribute to theories of the emergence of social inequality among hunter-gatherers.

The possible importance of the other pathway toward social inequality suggested by Feinman (1995), the one based on network strategies, can be examined through the analysis of exchange and trade. In the next chapter, I will discuss these issues along with two other related topics, crafts and long-distance transportation.

6   Crafts and exchange networks

As in the case of Jomon mortuary and ritual analyses, studies of Jomon crafts and exchange/trade networks have been underrepresented in the English-language literature. While the sophistication of Jomon material culture, particularly that of pottery, has long attracted the attention of Anglo-American scholars, the extremely detailed typological chronology of Jomon pottery and other artifacts drove off most non-Japanese-speaking scholars from serious engagement in the analysis of these materials.

From the perspective of recent Anglo-American archaeology, however, examination of crafts and exchange networks is an essential step in understanding the development of hunter-gatherer cultural complexity (e.g., Ames and Maschner 1999; Arnold 1992). In particular, over the past couple of decades, archaeologists in English-speaking countries have presented various models of how craft specialization, which often occurred in the course of the sophistication of material culture, and long-distance exchange/trade were linked with the development of hereditary social inequality (i.e., differences in social status ascribed at birth) and political organizations (e.g., Brumfiel and Earle 1987a; Costin 1991; Earle and Ericson 1977; Renfrew and Shennan 1982; Torrence 1986).

During the 1970s and the early 1980s, when processual archaeology was influential, the development of production specialization and exchange/trade networks was typically seen from the perspective of the "adaptationist model" (Brumfiel and Earle 1987b: 2). The model assumed that production specialization and exchange, which were organized by "system-serving" political elites, facilitated the development of more effective subsistence economies. Processual archaeologists also typically assumed that political systems evolve in direct proportion to their access to, and control over, resources (Hirth 1996). Thus, the development of production specialization and exchange was seen from the perspective of unilinear cultural evolution.

With the advent of postprocessual archaeology, the "adaptationist model" gave way to the "political model" (Brumfiel and Earle 1987b: 3), in which political leaders are seen as "self-serving" (e.g., Hayden 1995) rather than "system-serving." This paradigm shift can be seen as part of the general shift toward greater emphasis on human agency and historical contingency rather than regularity in archaeological explanations of the past. However, the other tenet inherited from the processual archaeology era, the idea of unilinear cultural evolution, is still quite influential. While more researchers (e.g., Hirth 1996) suggest the necessity of critically reexamining the unilinear model by focusing on variability in cultural trajectories (i.e., the long-term development of, and changes in, individual cultures), the majority of the models dealing with production specialization and exchange still assume cultural evolution from simple to complex.

The examination of Jomon crafts and exchange/trade can shed new light on our understanding of the role of these cultural elements in the development of, and changes in, hunter-gatherer cultural complexity. This is because the Jomon evidence for the sophistication of crafts and exchange/trade networks seems to indicate complex patterns that may not necessarily fit into the conventional model of unilinear cultural evolution.

Despite an abundance of case studies examining long-distance movements of exotic materials in the Jomon period, very few of these studies have focused on long-term changes in such practices. Similarly, relatively few scholars have systematically examined the possibility of production specialization in the context of Jomon cultural developments. Given the situation, the primary objective of this chapter is to present an overview of currently available data, rather than a new synthesis, of Jomon crafts and exchange/trade. The first and second sections of this chapter provide outlines of the current status of the study of Jomon pottery, and analyses of Jomon wood-working and lacquerware, basketry, and textiles respectively. Following these sections, the third section examines issues of exchange/trade of exotic materials, including obsidian, jade, asphalt, and salt, as well as some nonexotic materials. The fourth section reviews archaeological evidence of Jomon dugout canoes as a means of transportation. Finally, the concluding section discusses the implications of these studies, the limitations of currently available data, and suggestions for future research.

Studies of Jomon pottery

Unlike the material culture of many other hunter-gatherer groups, the artifact assemblage of the Jomon people is characterized by numerous ceramic vessels, some of which are intricately decorated. The artistic sophistication of these pots in terms of both decorative motifs and vessel form has attracted the attention of archaeologists as well as many art historians.

As discussed in chapter 2, the study of Jomon pottery has a long history, but research foci in this field have been placed primarily on typological chronology. Originally presented by Yamanouchi (1932a; 1932b; 1932c; 1937; 1964a; 1964b) and refined by numerous Japanese archaeologists, Jomon pottery chronology has provided Japanese researchers with finely meshed temporal and spatial scales with which to interpret Jomon data.

BOX 6: *Typological and stylistic analyses of Jomon pottery*

The core component of Yamanouchi's pottery typology is *keishiki*, which is the translation of the word "type." The concept was originally introduced from the West to Japanese archaeology through the writing of Montelius (1932; translated into Japanese by Kosaku Hamada), but was substantially modified by Yamanouchi (1932a; 1932b; 1932c; 1937; 1964a; 1964b) and his followers. As a result of the modification, the concept of "*keishiki*" used in contemporary Jomon archaeology became quite unique.

According to Yamanouchi (1937), *keishiki* is the basic unit for measuring temporal and spatial variability of Jomon pottery. Many *keishiki* defined by Yamanouchi were named after an assemblage from a specific layer or area of a single Jomon site. For example, the Middle Jomon Kasori-E-*shiki* (*shiki* is the abbreviation of *keishiki*) in the Kanto region was named after the pottery assemblage excavated from Area E of the Kasori shell-midden in Chiba Prefecture.

Because Yamanouchi's definition of *keishiki* is an explicitly time-sensitive unit, each *keishiki* of pottery may include a variety of forms and decorations. For instance, if a Late or Final Jomon site is excavated, it is common to find both finely and coarsely made pots from a single site within a single cultural layer. In this case, a single *keishiki* name is assigned to the whole assemblage that includes both finely and coarsely made pots. The finely made pots would also include a variety of forms, such as deep bowls, shallow bowls, and vessels with spouts. The majority of coarsely made pots are usually deep bowls. Thus, one of the most important criteria that Yamanouchi used to define each *keishiki* is co-occurrence (on the basis of stratigraphy). Stylistic seriation is another important criterion used to define each *keishiki* of Jomon pottery, although this can be pursued only within a group of pots of similar form or with similar decorative motifs. By combining these two criteria, Jomon archaeologists have tried to identify numerous pottery *keishiki* as the smallest temporal and spatial units that one can define.

Because the concept of *keishiki* defined by Yamanouchi is a holistic unit, many scholars have interpreted the concept as closer to that of "style" rather than "type" in Anglo-American archaeology, and have translated the word accordingly. Following this tradition, I have been using the word "style" in this book (e.g., the Moroiso style), and will continue to do so throughout the rest of the book (for more discussions on the concept of *keishiki*, see Hudson and Yamagata 1992).

Rather than describing the details of Yamanouchi and his followers' work, the following discussion will focus on three issues that are directly relevant to the examination of the long-term changes in Jomon pottery production and circulation. These include (1) changes in vessel form, including diversification between finely made and coarsely made pots, (2) the development and convergence of style zones, and (3) the movement of pottery seen from petrological and chemical analyses.

Diversification of vessel form and the appearance of coarsely made pottery

The classification of Jomon pottery forms is rather arbitrary. Many Japanese scholars (e.g., Fujimura 1983; Kono 1953; Sahara 1979) have divided Jomon pottery into four basic forms of pots: (1) deep bowls or jars (*fukabachi*; deep vessels with wide mouths, including those with slightly contracted necks; fig. 6.1.1; see also the cover photo), (2) shallow bowls (*asabachi*) (fig. 6.1.2), (3) vessels with narrow mouths, often with long necks (*tsubo*; fig. 6.1.3), and (4) vessels with spouts (*chuko*; fig. 6.1.4). Some scholars define bowls of medium depth as an independent subcategory (*hachi*) between deep and shallow bowls. Extremely shallow bowls are sometimes called plates (*sara*). In addition to the four basic forms, other forms of pots, such as lamp-shaped pottery (fig. 6.2), are also present, although the total number is much smaller.

The most common form of Jomon pottery is the deep bowl. Having appeared at the beginning of the Jomon period, the deep bowl remained the most dominant form of pottery through the rest of the Jomon period. Researchers suggest that the majority of Incipient Jomon deep bowls had round bottoms, although some of the early Incipient Jomon pots may have had a unique shape characterized by a square mouth and flat bottom (T. Kobayashi 1979; 1994; 1996a). Round and pointed bottoms dominated the pottery assemblage of the Initial Jomon period, but flat bottoms became the norm during and after the Early Jomon.

Toward the end of the Early Jomon period, shallow bowls appeared for the first time as part of the pottery assemblage. For example, assemblages of Early Jomon Moroiso-style pottery in the Kanto and Chubu regions include a fair number of shallow bowls (see fig. 5.20). Because many of the shallow bowls were recovered from burial pits, scholars assume that they were either used at the time of funeral ceremonies or made specifically as grave goods (see chapter 5).

The appearance of shallow bowls in the Early Jomon, however, did not trigger the immediate diversification in vessel form. While the following Middle Jomon period is known for an abundance of heavily decorated pots, such as the "fire-flame" pottery (see the cover photo) in the Hokuriku region, deep bowls remained dominant through the Middle

Figure 6.1   Four basic forms of Jomon pottery: 1. deep bowl; 2. shallow bowl; 3. vessel with spout; 4. vessel with narrow neck (Korekawa Nakai, Aomori Prefecture; photographs provided by courtesy of Hachinohe-shi Jomon Gakushu-kan)

Jomon period. Nevertheless, several new forms of pottery such as the lamp shape appeared for the first time during the Middle Jomon period.

It was in the Late and Final Jomon periods when various forms of vessels finally flourished in Jomon pottery assemblages. During these subperiods, there was an increase in the proportion of shallow bowls to deep bowls (Fujimura 1983). In addition, a variety of forms, including jars and vessels with spouts, are more commonly reported from these two Jomon subperiods. As an example, fig. 6.3 shows variability in vessel form in the Final Jomon pottery assemblage at the Kunenbashi site, Iwate Prefecture.

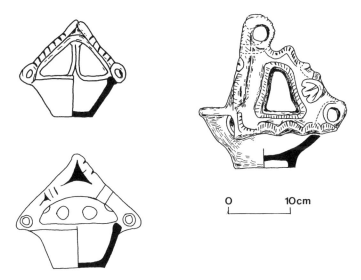

Figure 6.2   Lamp-shaped pottery from the Middle Jomon Sori site, Nagano Prefecture (compiled and redrawn from Fujimori 1965c: 95, 100)

Late and Final Jomon pottery assemblages are also characterized by the common presence of coarsely made pots. While some of the Early and Middle Jomon styles do include less decorated pots (usually pots with only cord marks) as part of the assemblages, clear differentiation of coarsely made pots from finely made pots is a characteristic of only the Late and Final Jomon periods. According to Fujimura (1983), coarsely made pots typically comprise 40–70 percent of the Late and Final Jomon pottery assemblages in eastern Japan. This implies that finely made pots, which we commonly see in catalogs of Jomon pottery exhibitions, are only a small proportion of Jomon pottery assemblages, at least for the Late and Final Jomon periods (Sahara 1979).

Figure 6.4 shows the composition of a Late Jomon pottery assemblage from the Ishigami shell-midden in Saitama Prefecture (Sahara 1979). Among various categories of vessels shown in the figure, coarsely made deep bowls account for 65.0 percent of the assemblage. Of the rest, 29.4 percent are finely made deep bowls. Other forms of vessels (shallow bowls and vessels with spouts) account for only 5.6 percent.

According to Sahara (1979), coarsely made deep bowls typically show heavy usewear, such as soot and scorching marks, while finely made vessels are less damaged. In Sahara's opinion, this indicates that these coarsely made deep bowls were primarily used for everyday

Figure 6.3   Various forms of pottery excavated from the Final Jomon Kunenbashi site, Iwate Prefecture (photograph by courtesy of Akiko Inano, Iroha Photo Studio)

vessel category	number (%)
deep bowls (coarsely made) 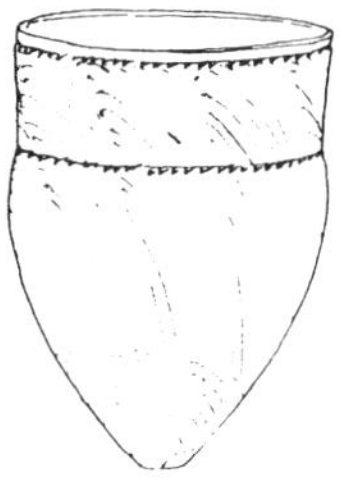	321 (65.0)
deep bowls (finely made) 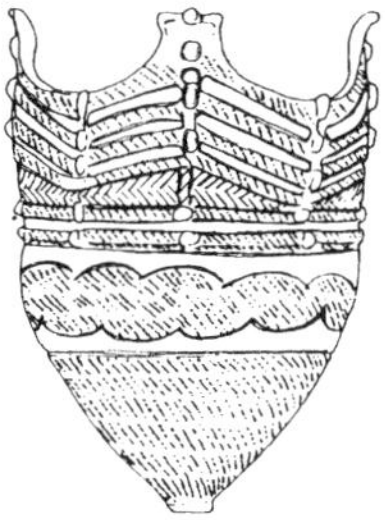	145 (29.4)
shallow bowls (finely made) 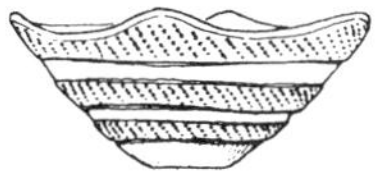	26 (5.3)
spouted vessels (finely made) 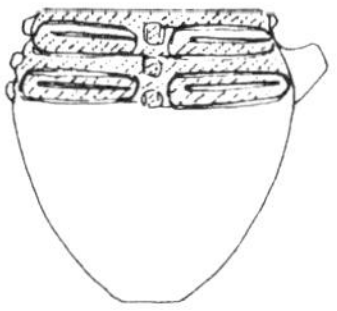	2 (0.3)
total	494 (100.0)

Figure 6.4 Pottery assemblage at the Ishigami site (compiled from Sahara 1979: 54). The category of shallow bowls includes pedestaled ones.

cooking, while finely made vessels functioned more in ritual contexts. Japanese scholars have also suggested that the common presence of vessels with spouts from these periods, despite their low percentages in the overall assemblage, can be seen as circumstantial evidence for the brewing of alcoholic beverages in ritual contexts.

In summary, previous studies of Jomon pottery indicate that there were two major changes in pottery assemblages. The first change occurred at the end of the Early Jomon period, when shallow bowls appeared for the first time as part of the Jomon pottery assemblage. Since many of the shallow bowls have been recovered from ritual contexts, it is likely that the shallow bowls represent nonutilitarian pots. This is in sharp contrast with pottery assemblages from the preceding periods, in which deep bowls as vessels for cooking and storage were practically the only vessel form. The second major change occurred in the Late Jomon period, when a variety of vessel forms became part of the assemblage. At the same time, there was clear differentiation between finely made and coarsely made pottery. Given the timing, it is very likely that these changes in pottery assemblages were closely related to the development of ritual practices in the Late and Final Jomon periods discussed in chapter 5.

The diversification in vessel form and the appearance of coarsely made pottery in the Late and Final Jomon periods are particularly noticeable in eastern Japan, where the developments seem essentially to have been indigenous. On the other hand, changes in Late and Final Jomon pottery assemblages in western Japan seem to have been under the influence of changes in pottery production techniques in the Korean peninsula. According to Naoko Matsumoto (1996a; 1996b), throughout western Japan (the Kinki, Chugoku, Shikoku, and Kyushu regions) there was a tendency to simplify pottery decoration from the Late to Final Jomon periods. This tendency, which occurred shortly after the transition from the Chulmun (comb-patterned) to Mumun (plain) pottery in the Korean peninsula at around 1300 BC, ultimately led to the dominance of plain, or nearly plain, pottery in Final Jomon assemblages in western Japan. This is especially noticeable in Kyushu where, by the beginning of the Final Jomon period, cord marks and most other decorations disappeared from all the forms of pots. This was accompanied by the clear separation of unburnished pottery from burnished pottery (Naoko Matsumoto 1996b). The former category primarily consists of deep bowls whereas the majority of the latter category of pots are shallow bowls. At about the same time, in the Kinki, Chugoku, and Shikoku regions, deep bowls became plain, but shallow bowls remained decorated (fig. 6.5). Thus, throughout western Japan, the dichotomy between coarsely made deep bowls, which were primarily used for cooking, and finely made shallow bowls, which are likely to have been either ceremonial or

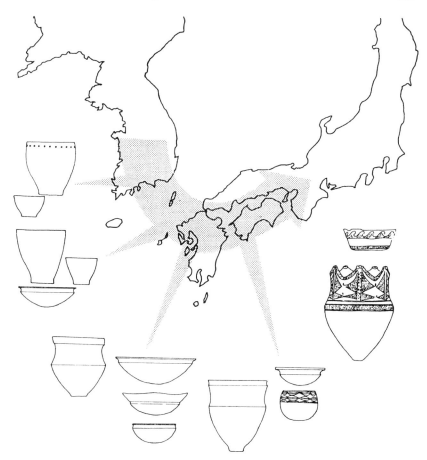

Figure 6.5   Influence of Mumun pottery from the Korean peninsula and the disappearance of pottery decoration in western Japan in the Late and Final Jomon periods (from Matsumoto 1996a; permission for reproduction obtained from Naoko Matsumoto)

serving vessels, became the norm by the middle of the Final Jomon period (Naoko Matsumoto 1996a: 256–259). Such a change made Final Jomon pottery in western Japan closer in terms of appearance to Yayoi pottery than to earlier Jomon pottery.

Regional variability in interaction spheres reflected in pottery styles

Changes over time in Jomon pottery are also evident through analyses of pottery style zones. As discussed above, typological classification of pottery not only provides a detailed chronological ordering, but it also divides the area of study into regional style zones.

As shown in fig. 2.5 (p. 39), throughout the Incipient Jomon period regional diversity in ceramic styles is not discernible. For example, linear-relief pottery has been reported from Honshu, Shikoku, and Kyushu, i.e., three of the four large islands of the Japanese archipelago. Regional variability in stylistic characteristics of Jomon pottery began to develop during the Initial Jomon period. Two major style zones during this period, the shell-incised (*chinsen-mon*) pottery zone in the east and the dowel-impressed (*oshigata-mon*) pottery zone in the west, are frequently cited by Japanese archaeologists as a reflection of this emergent regional variability (e.g., Kamaki 1965; see also fig. 2.5).

By the time of the Early Jomon period, the general zoning based on regional variability in pottery was more or less established. According to Kamaki (1965); six distinctive regional zones can be distinguished from each other, based on differences in stylistic characteristics of Early Jomon pottery. These are: (I) eastern Hokkaido; (II) southwestern Hokkaido and northern Tohoku; (III) southern Tohoku; (IV) Kanto, Chubu, Hokuriku, and Tokai; (V) Kinki, Chugoku, and Shikoku; and (VI) Kyushu (fig. 6.6.1; it should be noted that some of these six zones can be further divided into two or more subzones, which are nevertheless closely similar to each other. Researchers do not therefore necessarily agree regarding the exact number of style zones from this period). While the total number of style zones, as well as the size of the style zones, waxed and waned through time, most scholars agree that the general pattern of regional zoning remained quite consistent over the Middle Jomon period (fig. 6.6.2) to the beginning of the Late Jomon period (Kamaki 1965: 20–23; see also fig. 2.5 for the durations and distribution ranges of various styles in each region).

By the middle of the Late Jomon period, pottery in the eastern half of Honshu began to be more stylistically homogeneous (Zone III in fig. 6.6.3). Eventually, regional zones in the Japanese archipelago converged into two large regional groups in the Final Jomon period: one group in eastern Japan (Hokkaido, Tohoku, Kanto, Chubu, and Hokuriku), and the other in western Japan (Tokai, Kinki, Chugoku, Shikoku, and Kyushu). Kamaki (1965) states that, although the eastern Japan group can be divided into three smaller style zones (Zones I, II, and III in fig. 6.6.4), similarities between the pottery within these three zones are much closer than with the pottery in Zone IV (cf. Hayashi 1986; Yane 1996). Many scholars interpret this phenomenon as a reflection of the formation of intensive interactive spheres in eastern and western Japan respectively. In particular, Hayashi (1986) indicates that the interaction

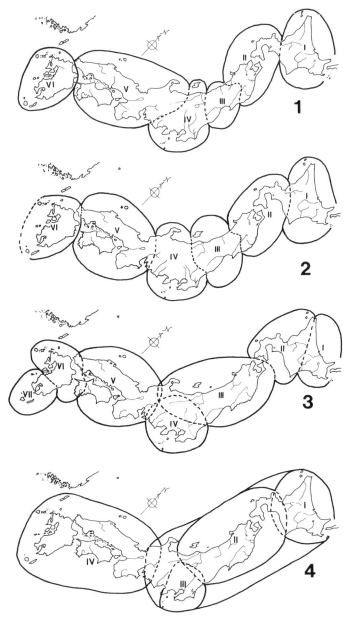

Figure 6.6   Changes in regional zones based on variability in pottery: 1. Early Jomon; 2. Middle Jomon; 3. Late Jomon; 4. Final Jomon (redrawn from Kamaki 1965: 21–24)

sphere in western Japan overlaps in general with the Ongagawa style of pottery, which was chronologically the first style of Yayoi pottery. He suggests that this interaction sphere formed the foundation for accepting the continental cultural complex at the beginning of the Yayoi period. Forms and decoration of Final Jomon pottery in eastern Japan, on the other hand, show strong influences from the Kamegaoka (also called Obora) style of pottery, which is primarily found in the Tohoku region (Zone II in fig. 6.6.4) but also sporadically throughout eastern Japan. Scholars such as Kamaki (1965) and Hayashi (1986) suggest that the presence of intensive interaction networks was characteristic of the Final Jomon culture in this region.

To summarize, through the analysis of pottery styles, Japanese archaeologists have suggested that regionally distinct groups were formed by the Early Jomon period and that they continued to exist until the beginning of the Late Jomon period. For the latter half of the Late Jomon and Final Jomon periods, an increase in the number of larger interactive spheres is assumed. Behind these interpretations is a long history of archaeologists' assumptions that the adoption of the same style (*keishiki*) is a reflection of a certain level of group identity (e.g., T. Kobayashi 1992a; Mukosaka 1958; I. Okamoto 1959; Mamoru Takahashi 1958). While the nature of this "group identity" has been subject to further scrutiny (for discussions of stylistic characteristics and people's identity, see also Hardin 1991; Hodder 1981; 1991), the fact that the convergence of regional style zones into two large zones occurred in the Late Jomon period, when the characteristics of both Jomon pottery assemblages and ritual practices went through significant changes, seems to indicate that this expansion of "interaction spheres" was closely related to the development of Jomon social complexity over time (discussed in chapter 5).

Movement of pottery seen from chemical and petrological analyses

Petrological and chemical analyses can shed new light on Jomon pottery production and circulation, although the amount of currently available data is still quite limited. Habu and Hall's (1999; 2001) X-ray fluorescence (XRF) analyses of Early Jomon Moroiso-style pottery excavated from five sites in the Kanto and Chubu regions suggest that approximately 80–90 percent of Moroiso-style pottery at each site is likely to have been locally made. Kojo's (1981) petrological analyses of inclusions of Moroiso-style pottery also indicate that 70–80 percent of Moroiso-style pottery from seventeen sites in the Kanto region was locally made. Similar results have been obtained through XRF analysis of Middle Jomon pottery from four sites in the Tohoku region, including the Sannai Maruyama site (Habu et al. 2003). These results seem to indicate that the majority of Early and Middle Jomon pots were locally made, while a certain percentage of Early and Middle Jomon pots may have been circulated within a style zone, either as exchange items or as containers of exchange items.

Results of chemical analyses of Late and Final Jomon pottery show rather different patterns. Hall's (n.d.) XRF analyses of Late Jomon samples (Kasori-B-style pottery) in the Chiba Prefecture of the Kanto region indicate that locally produced pottery was not necessarily dominant in Late Jomon sites. This may imply changes in the mode of pottery production and circulation from the Early/Middle to Late Jomon. Because Late and Final Jomon pots, especially finely made ones, tend to be thinner and seem to have been fired to higher temperatures than Incipient to Middle Jomon pots, the possibility of specialized production at a limited number of sites needs to be taken into consideration. While the amount of available information is inadequate to make any conclusive statement, systematic chemical and petrological analyses will be critical for examining this issue further.

BOX 7: *Cognitive approach and usewear analysis*

In addition to stylistic and fabric analyses of pottery, several scholars have adopted alternative approaches to examining different aspects of Jomon pottery production, circulation, and use. One promising approach to the study of Jomon pottery is represented by Naoko Matsumoto's (1996b) work. Using a cognitive approach (e.g., Renfrew and Zubrow 1994), Matsumoto analyzed the color and thickness of Late and Final Jomon pottery in western Japan. Traditionally, neither of these attributes has been used as a major criterion in defining Jomon pottery styles. Her analysis indicates that (1) spatial variation in color is different from that in thickness, and (2) the spatial cline of color changed significantly from the Late to the Final Jomon periods. Regarding the latter result, she suggests that the change must have been strongly influenced by the transition from Chulmun to Mumun pottery in the Korean peninsula: in other words, the Jomon people in northwestern Kyushu, who lived closest to the Korean peninsula and thus had a better chance actually to see Mumun pottery, first introduced the new, reddish color of Mumun pottery into the production of their own pottery. According to her interpretation, this occurred because of the nature of this particular attribute (color); since color is a visual attribute, it was easily imitated even through limited contact. On the other hand, the thickness of the vessels did not change significantly when the new color was adopted by the Jomon people, because thickness is less easily transmitted through visual observation alone. She also indicates that, because thickness is an attribute that can be accurately transmitted only through careful observation and/or direct information exchange between potters, it may be a better index than color of the degree of direct

BOX 7: (*cont.*)

interaction between potters. She concludes that various factors, such as the degree of visibility, possibility of verbal expression, and related knowledge and technologies, must have affected the spatial and temporal differences in these two attributes. By decomposing the concept of style into attributes and focusing on attributes that had been largely neglected by other Japanese archaeologists, Matsumoto was able to demonstrate that archaeologists can effectively approach a cognitive aspect of Jomon pottery production.

Usewear analysis by Masashi Kobayashi (1997) also shows promising results. Kobayashi, who conducted ethnoarchaeological research into Kalinga pottery in the Philippines (M. Kobayashi 1994; see also Longacre and Skibo 1994), applied an ethnoarchaeological model of cooking marks to prehistoric Japanese data. His results indicate that Final Jomon deep bowls in eastern Japan tend to have interior carbon deposits near or at the bottom of vessels. According to his model, this is an indication that food inside the vessel was boiled and cooked until the water had completely evaporated, and that the food was only in the bottom of the vessel. Soot-remain patterns on the vessel exterior are also consistent with this interpretation. On the other hand, Yayoi pottery shows more diverse cooking marks: large cooking pots with slightly contracted necks have very few interior carbon deposits, which indicates that these were probably used to make a kind of stew. Kobayashi suggests that this type of cooking mark probably came from cooking meat and vegetables. Medium-sized and small cooking pots have interior carbon deposits in the middle to the lower half of the vessel, suggesting that food was cooked until the water had completely evaporated, but the content was filling more than half of the depth of the vessel. By comparing these results with his own ethnographic observations, Kobayashi suggests that this second type of cooking mark on Yayoi pottery was typically a result of rice cooking. On the basis of these results, Kobayashi suggests that the differentiation between the main meal (rice) and accompanying dish (meat and vegetables), which is the standard way for modern Japanese people to conceptualize a proper meal, occurred after the transition from the Jomon to the Yayoi period.

These alternative approaches are all relatively new in the field of Jomon archaeology, and the results available to date are still limited. Nevertheless, they show promising patterns, which provide quite different perspectives from the traditional approaches described above. These new approaches can provide new lines of evidence to discuss such issues as individual actions and human agency, which are increasingly attracting the attention of contemporary Anglo-American archaeologists.

Technological achievements reflected in perishables: wood-working, lacquerware, basketry and textiles

Unlike potsherds and stone tools, artifacts made of organic materials, such as wood and fiber, are not commonly preserved in Jomon sites. Recovery of wooden artifacts, baskets, cordage, and textiles from a limited number of waterlogged sites, however, indicates that these perishables must have been an important part of Jomon artifact assemblages. In particular, the role of the production of lacquered wood artifacts (lacquerware) in Jomon society is a focus of researchers' attention.

The early study of Jomon lacquerware goes back to the 1920s (Kazuhiko Kobayashi 1995; K. Suzuki 1992). The 1926 excavation of the waterlogged Korekawa Nakai site in Aomori Prefecture revealed the presence of a large number of wooden artifacts covered with lacquer. These included lacquered wood bracelets, combs, and a sword-shaped artifact (Hachinohe-shi Hakubutsu-kan 1988; fig. 6.7.2–4). Lacquered baskets (fig. 6.7.1) and pots were also found. These findings were unexpected, since the production of lacquered artifacts of such high quality would have required extremely complex processes. The processes include extracting sap from the lacquer tree (*Rhus verniciflua*; a species of poison oak called *urushi*), refining the sap, and adding color (K. Suzuki 1988). According to Kimio Suzuki (1992), Jomon people used both iron oxide (Fe_2O_3) and cinnabar (HgS) for red, and minute carbon particles (probably soot) for black.

Excavations of several other waterlogged sites from the 1940s through the 1970s, such as the Kamo site in Chiba Prefecture (Nobuhiro Matsumoto et al. 1952), revealed that the production of lacquerware goes back at least to the Early Jomon period. The excavation of the Torihama shell-midden in Fukui Prefecture in the 1970s (Aikens and Higuchi 1982: 127–130; Fukui-ken Kyoiku Iinkai 1979; Morikawa and Hashimoto 1994) also provided ample examples of lacquerware from the Early Jomon period.

In contrast to the long history of the study of Jomon lacquerware, the study of other Jomon perishables, such as textiles and cordage, was an underdeveloped field until more recently. Until the 1960s, most archaeologists had assumed that the Jomon people were wearing animal-based clothing, such as hide and fur (e.g., Shuichi Goto 1956). Subsequently, a small number of Jomon potsherds with textile impressions, as well as fragments of textiles, made researchers realize that the Jomon people were producing plant-based textiles (N. Ito 1966; Y. Ogasawara 1970; Tsunoyama 1971; I. Yoshida 1965).

Examples of actual fabric remains found from Jomon sites have increased significantly over the past several decades (see, e.g., Y. Ogasawara 1983). According to Ozeki (1996) the majority of both textile impressions and pieces of textiles show a similar structure: fabrics made of twisted warp (fig. 6.8.1). Figure 6.9 shows three pieces of this type of fabric excavated from the Final Jomon Sanno-gakoi site in Miyagi Prefecture (A. Oba 2001). Ethnographically, similar kinds of fabric are still made in Niigata Prefecture and are called *angin*, which means knitted fabric. *Angin* was traditionally made with the fibers of false nettle (*Boehmeria*), which can be woven with a simple warp-weighted loom. Ozeki (1996) reports that the raw materials of textile fragments

Figure 6.7 Lacquered artifacts excavated from the Korekawa Nakai site: 1. basket (8.5 cm in height); 2. wooden comb handles (left: 4.4 cm in width); 3. wooden bracelets (left: 7.7 cm in diameter); 4. sword-shaped wooden artifact (67 cm in length) (photographs by courtesy of Hachinohe-shi Jomon Gakushu-kan)

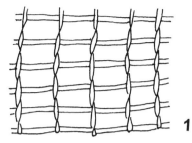

Figure 6.8 Schematic models showing (1) the general structure of Jomon fabric made of twisted warp, and (2) the structure of plain-woven fabric excavated from the Torihama shell-midden, Fukui Prefecture (Early Jomon) (redrawn from Ozeki 1996: 57, 63)

Figure 6.9 Three fragments of fabric made of twisted warp, the Sanno-gakoi site, Miyagi Prefecture (photograph by courtesy of Ichihasama-machi Kyoiku Iinkai [Board of Education of Ichihasama Town])

found from Jomon sites include two species of false nettles *(Boehmeria nivea,* and *B. tricuspis)* as well as cut-leaved elm *(Ulmus laciniata)*.

In addition to fabrics made of twisted warp, Ozeki (1996) reports four examples of plain weaves and variations of them from Jomon sites:

Torihama (Early Jomon), Sannai Maruyama (Early Jomon), Heijo in Ehime Prefecture (Late Jomon), and Ishigo in Aomori Prefecture (Final Jomon). Figure 6.8.2 shows the structure of a variation of plain-woven fabric excavated from the Torihama site reported by Ozeki (1996: 63). Her experimental studies indicate that the warp-weighted loom, which she used to produce the *angin* type of fabric, can be used to produce similar plain weaves.

BOX 8: *Perishables excavated from Sakuramachi and Sannai Maruyama*

Recent excavations of several waterlogged Jomon sites have revealed the relative importance of plant-based artifacts in general in the Jomon material culture. A good example of this is the excavation of the Middle Jomon Sakuramachi site in Toyama Prefecture (R. Ito 2001; Oyabe-shi Kyoiku Iinkai 1998). At Sakuramachi, a large number of wooden artifacts, baskets (fig. 6.10), cordage, and lacquerware have been reported along with more than 100 wooden beams, crosspieces, and posts. Many of these architectural materials have holes and grooves suggesting a high level of architectural technology at that time. Architects who have studied these remains suggest that most of them were part of raised-floor buildings. The Sakuramachi site was also associated with a large quantity of food remains, including chestnuts, buckeyes, and walnuts. Actual remains of buckeye tree roots were also found. Ryuzo Ito (2001), the chief excavator of the site, suggests that Sakuramachi was a nut-processing special-purpose site. He also suggests that features associated with wooden frames found at the site are related to buckeye processing (see similar features described in chapter 3).

Excavation of the Sannai Maruyama site (see chapter 4) in Aomori Prefecture is another example from which rich information on the use and production of perishable artifacts was obtained. Because the site area included several waterlogged middens from the Early Jomon period, a large number of organic remains, including baskets, bracelets, cordage, and textiles have been recovered. As described above, a piece of plain-woven fabric from this site has been reported by Ozeki (1996). Preliminary results of macrofloral remains analysis (Kim 2001) from these middens indicate that the relative abundance of several herbaceous plants, including *Boehmeria* (false nettle), increased significantly through the Early Jomon period. As discussed previously, *Boehmeria* is considered to have been one of the raw materials favored by the Jomon people for cordage and textile production. Accordingly, changes in human–plant relationships at and near the site, including the development of secondary vegetation and even the possibility of plant management, should be taken into account when the acquisition of raw materials for producing these artifacts is being discussed.

Recent discoveries indicate that Jomon lacquer technique was applied not only to wooden artifacts and baskets but also to textiles. At the Kakinoshima B site in Hokkaido, fabric with twisted warp covered with red lacquer was recovered (Asahi Shinbun-sha 2000). Because potsherds dated to the end of the Initial Jomon period were recovered near the burial pit, excavators of the site date the burial to the same period. The

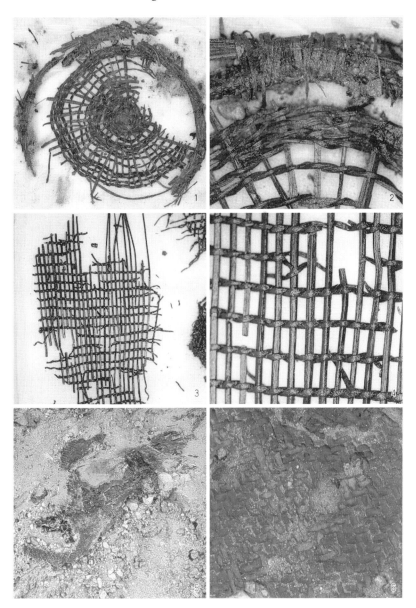

Figure 6.10 Baskets excavated from the Sakuramachi site: 1. basket bottom; 2. close-up photograph of 1; 3. basket fragment; 4. close-up photograph of 3; 5. field photograph of a basket; 6. close-up of 5 (from Oyabe-shi Kyoiku Iinkai 1998: 29; permission for reproduction obtained from Oyabe-shi Kyoiku Iinkai)

excavators also suggest that the lacquered fabric represents part of the clothing worn by the deceased. At the Early Jomon Daibu site in Niigata Prefecture, twisted plant-based threads were covered with two layers of lacquer (Asahi Shinbun-sha 2000). Finally, at the Final Jomon Aota site in Niigata Prefecture (Arakawa 2001), twenty-five lacquered bundles of plant-based threads were recovered.

From these new findings, and from the previous findings of lacquered wooden artifacts and baskets, it seems that the development of Jomon lacquer technique was closely related to the production of wooden artifacts, baskets, cordage, and textiles. The presence of lacquered pots, such as those at the Early Jomon Ondashi site in Yamagata Prefecture (Harada 1996; Y. Sasaki 1996; Takeda 1996), may indicate that pottery production was also part of this technological complex.

Since refining *urushi* (poison oak) sap to produce lacquer is very time-consuming and highly specialized work (Kenjo 1983), it is likely that the production of lacquered artifacts required the presence of specialists (K. Suzuki 1988; 1992). It should also be noted that the production of lacquered artifacts requires a certain degree of sedentism (not necessarily full sedentism but at least seasonal sedentism). Since the processes required to refine raw *urushi* sap and produce lacquered artifacts of high quality take several months, it is unlikely that the production of Jomon lacquered artifacts was conducted under an extremely mobile type of settlement system (i.e., the forager end of the settlement system spectrum).

The issue of possible specialization of lacquer–wood–basket–textile production should be discussed in relation to the possible development of gender-based division of labor and social inequality. While currently available archaeological evidence is still limited, systematic examination of the archaeological contexts of perishable artifacts can provide us with extremely useful information regarding these aspects of Jomon society. In particular, a recent increase in the number of burials associated with perishable grave goods may shed light on the study of gender- or age-specific use of these perishable artifacts. For example, at the Late Jomon Karinba no. 3 site in Eniwa City, Hokkaido, a large number of lacquered artifacts were recovered from several burial pits (Kamiya 2000). If the majority of burial goods were in fact perishable artifacts, such as lacquered wooden combs and bracelets, lack of clear evidence of status differentiation in stone and pottery burial goods may not necessarily imply the absence of social inequality.

Chronologically, examples of lacquer use seem to go back as early as the Initial Jomon period (e.g., Kakinoshima B; see p. 218). Abundant examples of lacquered artifacts from the Early Jomon period, including those from the Torihama shell-midden (see p. 215), the Kamo site (see

p. 215) and the Ondashi site in Yamagata Prefecture (Harada 1996; Y. Sasaki 1996; Takeda 1996), indicate that lacquer technology had become an established component of the Jomon cultural complex by this time. Furthermore, the artistic sophistication of lacquered objects from Late and Final Jomon sites, such as the Late Jomon Juno site in Saitama Prefecture (Saitama-ken Kyoiku Iinkai 1984) and the Final Jomon Korekawa Nakai site (see p. 215), has been noted by many researchers. From these examples, it seems that the Initial/Early Jomon and Late/Final Jomon periods were the two crucial transitional periods in the development of Jomon lacquer technology. Whether this interpretation is valid or not needs to be substantiated by a larger number of examples.

Exchange networks of exotic and nonexotic goods

Along with the sophistication of pottery and perishable artifacts described above, many archaeologists have considered long-distance exchange/trade of raw materials to be a salient characteristic of the Jomon culture. Scholars have particularly been interested in the long-distance movement of obsidian, jade, asphalt, and salt during the Jomon period.

Obsidian

Obsidian is volcanic glass that is formed by rapid cooling of molten, high-silica lava. Because obsidian is ideally suited for the production of stone tools that require sharp edges such as projectile points, arrowheads, and scrapers, it was extensively used for stone tool production throughout the Jomon period.

According to Oda (1982), forty locations within the Japanese archipelago are known as major sources of obsidian. As shown in fig. 6.11, many of these sources are clustered in Hokkaido, central Japan, and Kyushu. More recently, Warashina (2001) lists as many as eighty sources. Sources of obsidian specimens can be identified through various scientific methods, such as XRF analysis (Hall and Kimura 2002; Higashimura 1986; Warashina 1999; 2001; Warashina and Higashimura 1983) and neutron activation analysis (Ninomiya 1983; Ninomiya et al. 1985; 1987). Using these analyses, Japanese scholars have attempted to understand the circulation of obsidian during the Palaeolithic and Jomon periods (e.g., Kanayama 1998; Oda 1982; S. Saito 1985). Fission track and obsidian hydration analyses have also been used to date obsidian samples from many Jomon sites (Masao Suzuki 1969; 1970a; 1970b; 1973; 1974b). Results of recent excavations of several Jomon obsidian quarries (excavation pits for obsidian nodules) in Nagano Prefecture (K. Miyasaka

Figure 6.11   Locations of major obsidian sources: 1. Shirataki; 2.
Oketo; 3. Tokachi; 4. Akaigawa; 5. Shimoyukawa; 6. Fukaura; 7. Odate;
8. Toga; 9. Wakimoto; 10. Gassan; 11. Itayama; 12. Oshirakawa; 13.
Kogenyama; 14. Omachi; 15. Asama; 16. Wada Pass; 17. Kirigamine;
18–22. Hakone; 23. Amagi; 24–25. Kozu Island; 26–27. Oki Island; 28.
Hime Island; 29. Koshidake; 30. Iki Island; 31. Muta; 32. Furusato; 33.
Yodohime; 34–37. Aso; 38. Izumi; 39. Mifune; 40. Ibusuki (redrawn
from Oda 1982: 170)

1998; Otake 1998; 2000) indicate that systematic mining and circulation systems of obsidian may go back as early as the Incipient Jomon period.

Among obsidian tools and debris recovered from Jomon sites, those found in present-day Tokyo and its vicinity (Kanagawa, Saitama, and Chiba Prefectures) have been most extensively analyzed (S. Saito 1985). The majority of obsidian artifacts found in these prefectures have been identified as materials from three groups of obsidian sources: (1) Wada Pass, Kirigamine, and other sources in Nagano Prefecture (see nos. 16 and 17 in fig. 6.11; these sources are often collectively referred to as "Shinshu," an ancient name for the Nagano Prefecture area), (2) Hakone (nos. 18–22; a group of volcanoes on the boundary between Kanagawa and Shizuoka Prefectures), and (3) Kozu Island (nos. 24 and 25).

According to Sachie Saito (1985), during the Initial and Early Jomon periods, the relative occurrence of obsidian at each site in the southern Kanto region (Kanagawa, Tokyo, Saitama, and Chiba Prefectures) corresponds roughly with the distance from the obsidian sources: that is, obsidian was most frequently used at sites in Kanagawa (the closest prefecture to all the three major sources), less frequently in Tokyo, rarely in Saitama, and extremely rarely in Chiba (the farthest away from the sources). This seems to imply that obsidian exchange during these periods did not involve any major "trade centers" (see fig. 6.12 left). Her analysis, however, suggests that such a pattern had disappeared by the Middle Jomon period, when the overall occurrence of obsidian in all the four prefectures increased significantly. Similarly, both Takura Izumi (1996b) and Kanayama (1998) suggest that, by the end of the Early Jomon period obsidian exchange/trade networks were established, in which obsidian as a raw material was imported to a limited number of large settlements that functioned as trade or redistribution centers (fig. 6.12 right). In particular, Kanayama (1998) interprets this as a change from egalitarian to nonegalitarian societies. Citing Polanyi (1980), Kanayama suggests that this change in the distribution system of obsidian reflects the appearance of political chiefs, who were in charge of the redistribution of obsidian and other exotic goods such as jade.

To examine these lines of evidence further, the establishment of systematic sourcing methods for obsidian will be critical. So far, the majority of the XRF analyses of Jomon obsidian have generated X-ray intensity ratios between major, minor, and trace elements (e.g., Warashina 1999; 2001). Neutron activation analysis (e.g., Ninomiya 1983; Ninomiya et al. 1987) has yielded quantitative chemical data. Given the fact that obsidian sourcing in North America is primarily based on quantitative chemical analyses, and not on intensity ratios, it is difficult to evaluate the results between the various research

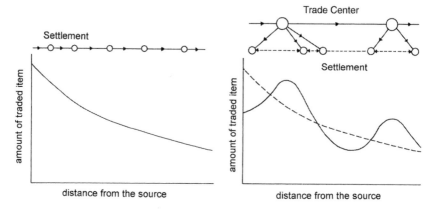

Figure 6.12   Two alternative models of prehistoric trade networks: left: trade networks lacking trade centers; right: trade networks based on trade centers (modified and redrawn from T. Izumi 1996b: 130)

groups. The presence of a large number of obsidian sources within the Japanese archipelago also makes sourcing difficult.

Jade

Jade (jadeite) is another item that shows evidence of long-distance exchange/trade by the Jomon people. Unlike obsidian, sources of jade within the Japanese archipelago are extremely limited in number. The most well-known source is located along the Kotaki River, a tributary of Hime River, in Itoigawa City, Niigata Prefecture (Ando 1982). Another source in this area has been identified along the Oumi River, which is less than 10 kilometers away from the former source (Ando 1982). These two sources are often collectively referred to as "Itoigawa" (the large solid triangle in fig. 6.14). While several other sources are known, chemical analyses indicate that the majority of Jomon jade artifacts were made of raw materials from Itoigawa (Warashina 1999).

The oldest Jomon jade artifact known to date is a large bead recovered from an Early Jomon grave pit at the Tenjin site, Yamanashi Prefecture (Yamanashi-ken Kyoiku Iinkai 1994). The source has been identified by XRF analysis as Itoigawa (Warashina 1999). The following Middle Jomon period is the time from which a large number of jade artifacts have been reported. Figure 6.13 shows jade beads recovered from the Sannai Maruyama site (see chapter 4). Although various shapes of jade beads were produced, large, oval beads (see fig. 5.10.6–7) are most commonly found.

Figure 6.13   Large jade beads recovered from the Sannai Maruyama
site (photograph by courtesy of Aomori-ken kyoku-cho Bunka-ka)

Some of the Middle Jomon sites associated with jade artifacts are
production sites where a large number of beads were produced. It is
known that jade bead production sites from the Middle Jomon period
are all located in close proximity to the jade sources in Itoigawa (within
an approximately 40 kilometer radius from the sources) (Ando 1982).
Examples of these include the Chojagahara and Teraji sites in Niigata
Prefecture, and the Sakai A site in Toyama Prefecture. At the Sakai A
site, for example, more than 10,000 pieces of jade (either in the form
of unworked nodules, preforms, or finished beads), weighing more than
650 kilograms in total, have been recovered. Jade-working tools such as
hammer stones, anvils, and whetstones were recovered from all of the
production sites (Kurishima 1985).

Smaller numbers of jade beads and preforms have been widely reported
from Middle Jomon sites outside the Itoigawa area and its vicinity, but
none of them seems to have been a large-scale production site (Ando
1982). The distribution of these "consumer" sites is dense not only in
the Hokuriku region, in which the Itoigawa area is located, but also in
certain parts of the Chubu and Kanto regions (fig. 6.14). Many of these
sites are large settlements, and jade beads are often associated with burials
(T. Izumi 1996b). Kurishima (1985) points out that the areas where sites
with jade are densely distributed overlap with the areas where the Middle

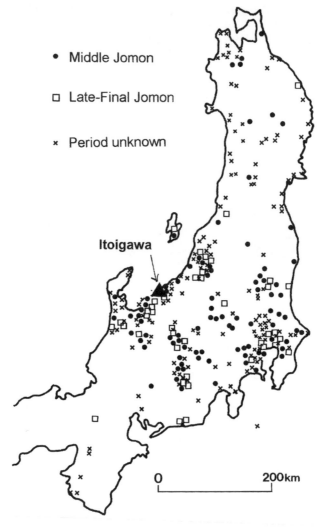

Figure 6.14   Distribution of Jomon sites associated with jade artifacts
(modified and redrawn from Kurishima 1985: 40)

Jomon culture was most prosperous judging by site size and the artistic
sophistication of pottery. He also suggests that such a distribution pattern
of jade indicates the existence of a Middle Jomon exchange/trade network
of jade between a limited number of large settlements that functioned as
"trade centers." Thus, he suggests that Middle Jomon jade artifacts were

first exported to a limited number of trade centers, and were subsequently redistributed to smaller settlements.

The overall number of jade artifacts found in Late Jomon sites is much smaller than that found in Middle Jomon sites. Ando (1982) interprets this decrease as a reflection of a decline in the socioeconomic power of the people in the Itoigawa area and its vicinity. The production of jade beads became prevalent again in the Final Jomon period, when bead production sites appeared not only in Itoigawa and its vicinity but also throughout eastern Japan (Ando 1982). In many cases, the source of the jade found in these production sites seems to be Itoigawa (T. Izumi 1996b; Warashina 1999). Takura Izumi (1996b) suggests that, unlike the Middle Jomon jade distribution system, which was based on the export of jade beads and preforms from the Itoigawa area to the others, the jade distribution systems of the Final Jomon must have been based on the long-distance exchange/trade of unworked jade nodules. Thus, he suggests that the function of jade "trade centers" away from the original source became more important in the Final Jomon period.

In summary, there was long-distance trade of jade in both the Middle and Final Jomon periods, but the exchange patterns of these two periods have different characteristics. Given the timing, it is likely that the former is related to the development of organizational complexity in the Middle Jomon period, whereas the latter could be a reflection of emergent social inequality as discussed in chapter 5.

Asphalt

Since the late nineteenth century, archaeologists have recognized traces of asphalt on various kinds of Jomon artifacts (Abiko 1982). As a type of waterproof adhesive that can be easily dissolved with heat, Middle through Final Jomon people of eastern Japan used natural asphalt extensively to haft stone and bone tools as well as to repair broken pottery and other types of ceramic artifacts (Abiko 1982). Examples of Jomon artifacts with asphalt are shown in fig. 6.15.

Asphalt has been recovered from Jomon sites both in the form of solid lumps (e.g., the Late Jomon Akasakata site in Iwate Prefecture [T. Izumi 1996b] and the Late Jomon Mako B site in Hokkaido [C. Abe 2000]) and in a pot (the Middle Jomon Kaihata site in Iwate Prefecture [T. Izumi 1996b] and the Late Jomon Toyozaki B site in Hokkaido [C. Abe 2000]). These are likely to have been the two forms of asphalt transportation.

Natural asphalt, which can be obtained in petroleum deposit areas, is available only in the coastal part of present-day Akita, and Niigata Prefectures and part of southern Hokkaido (shaded areas in fig. 6.16).

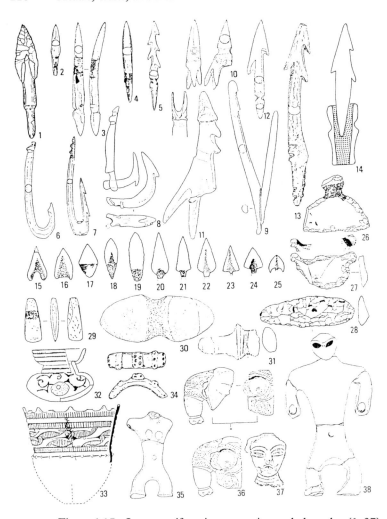

Figure 6.15   Jomon artifacts incorporating asphalt as glue (1–37) and as eye pieces of figurine (38): 1. stone arrowhead with attached bone tang; 2–5. bone spears; 6–7. bone fishhooks; 8–9. bone composite fishhooks; 10–11. bone composite harpoon heads; 12–13. bone harpoon heads; 14. reconstruction of harpoon head hafting suggested by M. Kusumoto (shaded area indicates the use of asphalt); 15–25. stone arrowheads; 26–27. stone stemmed scrapers; 28. stone sickle; 29. polished stone axe; 30–31. *dokko*-shaped stone artifacts; 32. spout repaired with asphalt; 33. pottery cracks repaired with asphalt; 34. clay object; 35–37. clay figurines repaired with asphalt; 38. eye pieces of clay figurine (from Abiko 1982: 211; permission for reproduction obtained from Shoji Abiko)

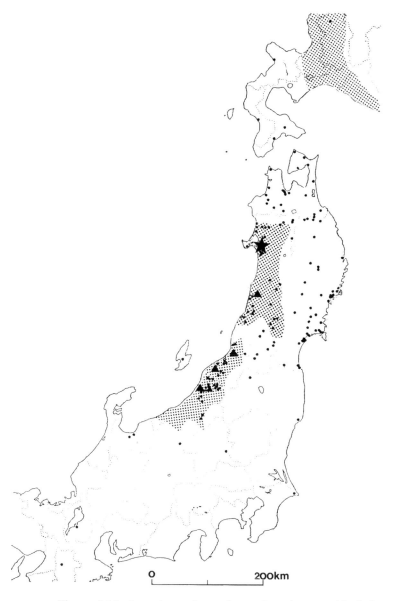

Figure 6.16 Locations of petroleum deposit areas (shaded areas),
asphalt sources (▲), an asphalt quarry (⋆), and Jomon sites from which
artifacts with asphalt have been reported (●) (modified and redrawn
from Abiko 1982: 208)

Archaeologists (e.g., Abiko 1982; T. Izumi 1996b) suggest that at least one Jomon site, the Tsukigi site in Akita Prefecture (the large solid star in fig. 6.16), represents an asphalt quarry. Located in the northern part of the petroleum deposit in Honshu, the site yielded Middle, and possibly Final, Jomon pottery together with the deposit of natural asphalt. As late as the early twentieth century, local farmers near the site were collecting asphalt by digging through rice paddy fields during their agricultural off-season (Abiko 1982). Other possible quarries in the Jomon period include several natural outputs of petroleum in Niigata and Yamagata Prefectures (▲ in fig. 6.16). Ethnographic and historical records list various locations called *kusouzu* (smelly water), where local people used to collect both petroleum and asphalt (Abiko 1982: 211–212).

Consumer sites of asphalt are abundant. Abiko (1982) reports that a total of 145 Jomon sites, as well as 3 Yayoi sites, are associated with artifacts showing traces of asphalt use (● in fig. 6.16). Approximately half (70 sites; 48.3 percent) of the 145 sites are located in Akita, Yamagata, and Niigata Prefectures, which correspond to the petroleum deposit areas in northern Honshu. The majority (60 sites) of the rest (75 sites) are in 3 other northern Honshu prefectures, Aomori (24 sites), Iwate (18 sites) and Miyagi (18 sites). Although the absolute number of sites with asphalt must have increased significantly since Abiko (1982) compiled these data, the regional distribution pattern of these sites indicated by Abiko seems reasonably reliable. Judging from his data, the distribution of these sites on the Pacific side of northern Tohoku is almost as dense as on the Japan Sea side (see fig. 6.16). Sourcing of Jomon asphalt from consumer sites has been attempted by archaeometrists (e.g., Asano et al. 1999), but the results are still preliminary.

Chronologically, the use of asphalt started as early as the beginning of the Middle Jomon period. The majority of Middle Jomon artifacts with asphalt are arrowheads. During this initial phase of asphalt use, the amount of circulated asphalt seems to have been quite limited. The use of asphalt became more common during the Late Jomon period, when it was also used to haft bone tools, such as harpoon heads and fish spears, and to repair ceramic artifacts (Abiko 1985). Experimental archaeological studies by Kusumoto (1976) indicate that the use of asphalt for hafting must have played a critical role in the development of the composite type of harpoon heads in Tohoku.

The use of asphalt was most prevalent in the Final Jomon period, during which it was used not only for hafting and repairing but also as a base coat for producing lacquered baskets, and sometimes also for lacquered pottery (Abiko 1985). Given the fact that the amount of asphalt required

Figure 6.17 Evaporation pots excavated from the Satohama shell-midden, Miyagi Prefecture (from M. Okamura 1992; permission for reproduction obtained from Tohoku Rekishi Hakubutsu-kan [Museum of Tohoku History])

to cover a complete basket or a pot is significantly larger than the amount to haft a tool, and given the fact that asphalt as an exotic item must have been quite valuable, Abiko (1985) suggests that its use with lacquer must have reinforced the luxurious nature of lacquered artifacts.

Salt

The possible importance of salt exchange in the Late and Final Jomon periods has been suggested by some scholars. So-called "evaporation pots" for salt production have been reported from several Late and Final Jomon sites in the Kanto and Tohoku regions. Unlike other Late and Final Jomon pots from these regions, so-called evaporation pots (usually deep bowls) are extremely thin (approximately 2–4 millimeters), and their bases are usually either round or tapered. When the base is flat, the diameter is extremely small (fig. 6.17). The surface of the walls of these pots typically shows evidence of repeated heating. Usually there was no decoration on these pots, and the outer surface was roughly smoothed with a wooden or bamboo tool (Kawasaki 1983).

Evaporation pots for salt making were first identified in the 1960s by Yoshiro Kondo (1984) at the Hirohata shell-midden site in Ibaraki

Prefecture. At the site, he found a large number of extremely thin pot-sherds together with layers of ash. Many of these potsherds were covered with whitish-grey residue, which consists primarily of calcium carbon-ate ($CaCO_3$). Since similar residue had been recovered on evaporation pots for salt making from later periods, Kondo identified the Hirohata examples as pots for salt production (Y. Kondo 1984; see also Terakado 1983). Excavations of similar potsherds and ash layers in the 1960s at two Late Jomon lowland sites in Ibaraki Prefecture, Hodo and Maeura, confirmed the common presence of this type of site in northern Kanto. At the Hodo site, where approximately 70 percent of excavated potsherds consists of evaporation pots, three pits with ash layers were identified as possible hearths for salt production (Mitsuru Takahashi 1996). Large hearths associated with evaporation pots and ash layers have also been reported from other Late and Final Jomon sites in Ibaraki Prefecture, such as Kamitakatsu and Koyamadai (Masahiro Suzuki 1993). These sites are all considered to have been "salt production sites." Similar sites have also been reported from the Tohoku region, especially in the Matsushima Bay area of Miyagi Prefecture. Examples of these sites include the Final Jomon Nigade shell-midden and the Satohama shell-midden (Terakado 1983).

The recovery of evaporation pots is not confined to these possible "salt production sites." In the Kanto region, evaporation pots have been reported from approximately 100 Late and Final Jomon sites (Mitsuru Takahashi 1996). Some of these are shell-middens, which are not too far away from "salt production sites." However, most of these shell-midden sites are not associated with ash layers or hearths for salt production. Other sites with evaporation pots are located further inland, sometimes more than 100 kilometers away from the nearest coast. The number of recovered evaporation pots in these inland sites is usually extremely small. Mitsuru Takahashi (1996) suggests that the ocean water was first boiled at the limited number of production sites to make thick salty water, and was then brought into the shell-midden sites for the later stages of salt pro-duction. Others believe that the shell-midden sites represent consumer sites. Both groups of researchers suggest that recovery of evaporation pots in inland sites represents long-distance exchange of salt or salted food (T. Izumi 1996b; Masahiro Suzuki 1993; Mitsuru Takahashi 1996; Terakado 1983).

Because salt production sites and evaporation pots are the only lines of evidence for the exchange or trade of salt or salted food, we know rela-tively little about the nature and scale of salt production and circulation. Many scholars (e.g., Horikoshi 1999; Kawasaki 1983; Masahiro Suzuki 1993) suggest that salt was used to preserve seafood, such as fish. In their opinions, subsistence specialization of each local group in the Late Jomon period in Kanto resulted in the necessity to preserve marine food as an important trade item. While this is an attractive hypothesis, further studies are required to test its validity.

Other items obtained from restricted sources

In addition to obsidian, jade, asphalt, and salt, various other items that were available only at restricted sources have been reported. These include amber, cinnabar, and marine shells. Amber, which is yellowish or brownish fossilized resin, has been recovered from a small number of Jomon sites in Hokkaido and northern Tohoku (Matsushita 1982). Many of the examples, including those recovered from the Middle Jomon layers of the Sannai Maruyama site in Aomori Prefecture (Okada 1995a), are small unworked amber fragments. In addition, amber beads have been reported from Late to Final Jomon sites in Hokkaido, including Bibi 4 (Matsushita 1982) and Takisato 33 (Asahi Shinbun-sha 1992). The most well-known source of amber is Kuji in Iwate Prefecture, but there are also sources in Hokkaido. Identification of amber sources using infrared absorption spectrometry has been attempted by Japanese archaeometrists (M. Sato et al. 1999).

Cinnabar (mercury sulfide) is another item with restricted sources utilized by the Jomon people. Chemical analyses of red lacquer applied to Jomon artifacts indicate that both iron oxide (colcothar) and cinnabar were used as red pigment for lacquerware production (T. Izumi 1996b). Unlike iron oxide, which can be obtained at many locations, sources of cinnabar are quite limited. Evidence of cinnabar processing in the Jomon period is reported from the Morizoe site in Mie Prefecture, where cinnabar residues were identified on grinding stones, stone mortars, and pottery. The site is located near a cinnabar mine of a later historical period, and it is likely that the residents of the site utilized the same source (T. Izumi 1996b).

Finally, various exotic shells, such as Conidae (*imogai* in the Japanese common name; cone shells), *Patella flexuosa optima* (*oh-tsutanoha gai*; limpet), and Cypraeidae (*takaragai*; cowrie), have been recovered from Jomon sites that are far removed from their original sources (M. Okamura 1996). The original habitat of these shellfish must have been the subtropical ocean near the Ryukyu Islands or even further south. Nevertheless, these shells are reported from Jomon sites as far north as Hokkaido. At the Late Jomon Toi shell-midden in Hokkaido (Toi-machi Kyoiku Iinkai 1993), for example, beads and pendants made of these southern shells have been excavated (M. Okamura 1996). Recovery of shark teeth from inland Jomon sites also indicates that certain marine products were valued by the Jomon people as exchange items.

Items made of more common materials

Evidence of specialized production and wide-range circulation is not limited to the artifacts made of materials from restricted sources. Japanese archaeologists suggest that tools made of more common materials, such as polished stone axes/adzes and chipped stone "axes," may also have been produced at a limited number of sites. For example, scholars have identified the Middle Jomon Ozaki site, which is located in the Tanzawa Mountains of Kanagawa Prefecture (Kanagawa-ken Kyoiku Iinkai 1973), as a production site of polished stone axes/adzes. From this site, a large number of both finished and unfinished polished stone axes/adzes were recovered. The majority of them were made of tuff, a type of raw material available at the riverside approximately 40 meters away from the site. The site is also associated with a large number of whetstones and hammer stones, both of which were essential tools for the manufacture of polished stone axes/adzes (J. Suzuki 1985). As a result of the relative abundance of these three categories of stone tools (i.e., polished stone axes/adzes, whetstones and hammer stones), the lithic assemblage at the Ozaki site is very different from those of other Middle Jomon sites in the region. Since polished stone axes/adzes typically account for only a small portion of the lithic assemblage at Middle Jomon sites, and since unfinished polished stone axes/adzes are seldom found at most other sites, it is reasonable to call the Ozaki site a production site. However, the common availability of tuff and other raw materials suitable for manufacturing polished stone axes/adzes throughout the Tanzawa Mountain area makes the sourcing of polished stone axes/adzes found at "consumer" sites difficult (J. Suzuki 1985). Evidence for production specialization of polished stone axes/adzes has also been reported from the Terasaka site in Saitama Prefecture and the Sakai A site in Toyama Prefecture. The majority of axes/adzes at Terasaka were made of greenstone, whereas those at Sakai A were made of serpentine (T. Izumi 1996b; J. Suzuki 1985).

In the case of chipped stone "axes," which probably functioned primarily as digging tools (see chapter 4), the availability of raw materials such as basalt, hornfels, sandstone, and clayslate (J. Suzuki 1983) is even less restricted than is the case for polished stone axes/adzes. Nevertheless, evidence of intensive production and circulation of chipped stone axes is reported from several Jomon sites such as Futagoyama in Kumamoto Prefecture (T. Izumi 1996b). Jiro Suzuki (1985) suggests that the recovery of more than 100 chipped stone axes from a single pit-dwelling at the Nukui-Minami site (Koganei-shi Kyoiku Iinkai 1974) in Tokyo also indicates specialized production for wide circulation.

Evidence of specialized production is also available for stone rods. The Kinsei Jinja site in Gifu Prefecture, for example, has been identified as a production site for stone rods (for a description of stone rods, see chapter 5) (Miyano 1998). The site is located near the outcrops of welded pyroclastic rocks, a type of stone that can be easily split into elongated shapes. Approximately 800 finished and unfinished stone rods as well as a large number of hammer stones and whetstones, most of which are probably dated to the Late Jomon period, have been recovered from the site (Miyano 1998). While welded pyroclastic rocks must have been a convenient type of raw material with which to manufacture long stone rods, they could easily have been made with other types of stone unless mass-production was intended. Evidence of intensive stone rod production is also reported from the Middle Jomon Onga site in Gunma Prefecture. Finally, at the Late and Final Jomon Fujioka Jinja site in Tochigi Prefecture, approximately 1,100 pulley-shaped clay earrings, both complete and broken, have been excavated (Iwabuchi 2000). The number is too large for consumption within the site only, and thus seems to indicate specialized production for wider circulation, even though clay apparently was not an item from restricted sources. Since the site is associated with various other types of ritual artifacts, such as stone rods, *dokko*-shaped stone tools, clay tablets, and stone pendants, it is possible that the production of clay earrings was closely related to ritual activity conducted by the site occupants as a whole.

Finally, some waterlogged sites show evidence of intensive woodworking, some of which may indicate production specialization. At the Early Jomon Torihama site (Morikawa and Hashimoto 1994), a large number of both preforms and finished forms of wooden axe/adze handles were excavated. An abundance of preforms is a strong indication of intensive production of these artifacts at the site. At the waterlogged Final Jomon On'ido site in Niigata Prefecture, preforms of wooden containers have been recovered. All of them are similar in size and form (oblong bowl with a spout and a handle), suggesting the possibility of mass production (T. Izumi 1996b). Evidence of intensive Jomon wood-working is also reported from such waterlogged sites as Late Jomon Akayama Jin'ya-ato (Kanabako 1996; Kawaguchi-shi Iseki Chosakai 1989) and Middle to Late Jomon Juno (Saitama-ken Kyoiku Iinkai 1984) in Saitama Prefecture, Final Jomon Shigasato (Shiga-ken Kyoiku Iinkai 1973) in Shiga Prefecture, and Sakuramachi (see above) in Toyama Prefecture. Morikawa and Hashimoto (1994), T. Izumi (1996b), and M. Yamada (1983) all suggest that soaking wood in water may have been a necessary step toward making wood-carving easy, thus suggesting the advantage of lowland sites near a lake or marsh for specialized wood-working.

Transportation

Long-distance movements of exotic and nonexotic items required the presence of effective transportation methods. Scholars suggest that both overland and water routes were actively used by the Jomon people. In particular, the recovery of dugout canoes from waterlogged Jomon sites indicates that the use of canoes was a critical component. So far, about fifty examples of dugout canoes have been reported from Early to Final Jomon sites (Asahi Shinbun-sha 1998).

Currently the oldest excavated canoe is that from the Early Jomon layer of the Torihama shell-midden in Fukui Prefecture (Morikawa and Hashimoto 1994). The canoe is over 6 meters long, and approximately 60 centimeters wide. It was made by hollowing out the half-split trunk of a Japanese cedar tree (*Criptomeria japonica*). Morikawa and Hashimoto (1994) suggest that the primary tools used to manufacture the canoe were stone adzes and/or axes. Burn marks on the canoe indicate that burning was used to make the hollowing out easier. In the final stage of canoe manufacture, the surface was carefully polished. Paddles made of Japanese cedar have also been recovered from the Early Jomon layers at the same site. Another dugout canoe dating to the Late Jomon period was also found at the site (Morikawa and Hashimoto 1994).

Examples of dugout canoes and/or paddles are also reported from such Jomon sites as Kamo (Early Jomon; Chiba Prefecture) (Nobuhiro Matsumoto et al. 1952), Nakazato (Tokyo; Middle Jomon, fig. 6.18) (Hayakawa 1985; Kita-ku Kyoiku Iinkai 1997), and Yuri (Fukui Prefecture; Late and Final Jomon) (Morikawa and Hashimoto 1994). In addition to Japanese cedar, other species such as *Aphananthe aspera* (*mukunoki* is the Japanese common name), *Torreya nucifera* (*kaya*; Japanese nutmeg), *Cephalotaxus harringtonia* (*inugaya*), and *Cinnamonium camphora* (*kusunoki*; camphor) were used to make these canoes (Morikawa and Hashimoto 1994). Some of the recovered canoes are larger than the Early Jomon example from Torihama. For example, the dugout canoe recovered from the Early Jomon Uranyu site in Kyoto Prefecture is approximately 1 meter wide. Although the bow and stern were not preserved, the estimated length of the canoe is approximately 10 meters (Asahi Shinbun-sha 1998). Like the Early Jomon canoe found at Torihama, this canoe was made of Japanese cedar, and many burn marks were observed inside.

Figure 6.18   Early Jomon dugout canoe recovered from the Nakazato
site, Tokyo (from Kita-ku Kyoiku Iinkai 1997: photo 7; permission for
reproduction obtained from Kita-ku Kyoiku Iinkai)

Discussion

It is clear from the above that changes in Jomon crafts, including pottery
and various perishables, and the development of exchange systems were
complex. Two major changes in pottery assemblages took place, the first
at the end of the Early Jomon, and the second during the Late Jomon.
Furthermore, regional style zones were established by the Early Jomon
period, and these eventually converged to become two large regional
groups through the Late to the Final Jomon. The presence of lacquerware
and other perishable artifacts indicates a relatively high level of technological achievement by the Early Jomon, culminating in the Late and
Final Jomon. Finally, there is considerable evidence for the systematic
acquisition and long-distance exchange of exotic items, as well as of certain everyday commodities, although the timing of the development of
these exchange networks varies. It is important to note that the patterns
of development of these exchange systems do not always show increasing
complexity through time.

Two important questions arise from the examination of this general picture. The first is the question of the relationship between the development of exchange networks and that of social complexity. The case studies discussed above suggest that the timing of the development of long-distance exchange networks of certain items paralleled an increase in organizational complexity in subsistence and settlement from the Early to the Middle Jomon, as discussed in chapter 4. These developments include reorganization of obsidian exchange systems at the end of the Early Jomon, and specialized production and the development of corresponding trade networks of jade beads during the Middle Jomon. Other developments are likely to have been more closely tied to the increase in social complexity during the Late and Final Jomon periods. They include an increase in the use of asphalt through the Late to Final Jomon, and the production and distribution of salt during the Late and Final Jomon. Given the possible emergence of hereditary social inequality during the Late and Final Jomon periods discussed in chapter 5, it is possible that certain aspects of the latter developments functioned either as conditions, causes, or consequences of the development of Jomon social inequality. From these lines of evidence, it is reasonable to suggest that the development of various production specializations and exchange networks resulted in an increase in both horizontal differentiation (from the end of the Early Jomon to Middle Jomon) and vertical differentiation (the Late and Final Jomon), which in turn contributed to an overall increase in Jomon social complexity.

The second question is the effect of the development of craft and exchange/trade networks on Jomon subsistence-settlement systems. As discussed in chapter 1, the collector–forager model is based on the premise that subsistence and settlement systems of hunter-gatherers are strongly dependent on the distribution of critical resources. If the exchange of resources, especially that of food, was practiced, the structure of the model may need to be substantially modified, since the trade or exchange of resources was not a factor that was incorporated in the original model. In other words, if the exchange of critical resources was extensively practiced, it is likely that adjustments were made to the system to accommodate the exchange networks.

The development of Middle and Late Jomon sites in the east Tokyo Bay area (present-day Chiba Prefecture) may be a case in point. As discussed in chapter 3, this area is notable for an abundance of Middle and Late Jomon shell-middens, many of which are associated with large settlements. Unlike other parts of the Kanto region, where site density and the average settlement size decreased significantly from the Middle to the Late Jomon, this area apparently remained densely occupied during the Late Jomon period (e.g., Horikoshi 1972). Kazuhito Goto (1982) suggests that this area is notable for the scarcity of raw materials suitable for the production of stone tools (see also Kidder 1993). Because the majority of the stone tools found at these sites are made from non-local materials, Goto proposes that the residents of these shell-midden sites imported various kinds of stone in exchange for dried shellfish. With no substantial archaeological evidence to support the possibility of exporting shellfish, this hypothesis remains highly controversial. Nevertheless, the common presence of stone tools made of nonlocal materials indicates that long-distance exchange was an integral part of the whole system. Thus, the unusual high density of Late Jomon sites in this region needs to be further examined in this context.

In summary, the sophistication of Jomon crafts, the development of exchange networks, and certain levels of production specialization are all likely to be closely related to various aspects of Jomon social complexity, including both horizontal and vertical differentiation. It should also be kept in mind that craft and exchange systems were part of the Jomon cultural landscape as a whole. In order to propose a model of cause and effect relationships between craft, exchange, and social stratification, it is necessary to understand how each craft and exchange system operated in relation to other aspects of Jomon society. While very few systematic studies have been conducted along this line, I believe that the amount of data available from Jomon sites is sufficiently large to warrant such a project.

Part IV

Discussion and conclusion

7   Discussion and conclusion

Having discussed four aspects of the Jomon culture (subsistence, settlement, mortuary/ceremonial practices, and crafts/exchange), the next step is to present a model of long-term change in Jomon cultural complexity. Traditionally, Japanese archaeologists have approached this issue under the direct or indirect influence of classical Marxist theories (see chapter 4). For example, scholars such as Ken Amakasu (1986) and Isamu Okamoto (1975; 1986) have identified the Jomon period as an egalitarian society that preceded a class society. These scholars interpreted the prosperity of the Jomon culture as the result of the growth of "forces of production" caused by population increases. They also regarded the transition to the following Yayoi period as the inevitable consequence of the contradiction encompassed in the non-food-producing economy, in which the growth of the "forces of production" eventually exceeded the reproduction rate of the natural environment (Amakasu 1986: 8). Thus, long-term changes from the Incipient through to the Middle Jomon periods were interpreted as progressive, with an increasing degree of sedentism. These scholars also suggested that a decrease in the number of sites from the Middle to the Late/Final Jomon was a result of the imbalance between the growth of "forces of production" and the limitations of the environment.

Amakasu also saw the nature of Jomon economy as primarily self-sufficient, with the exchange of exotic items reflecting the existence of a small surplus. Other scholars, such as Kiyotari Tsuboi (1962), who did not explicitly adopt a Marxist approach, also saw the Jomon people as sedentary and egalitarian. The fact that most Japanese scholars viewed the Jomon as a Neolithic culture also contributed to the conventional picture of an affluent and sedentary hunter-gatherer society.

Aspects of the Jomon culture reviewed in the previous chapters, however, indicate that regional and temporal variability in Jomon subsistence, settlement, and social complexity was more diverse than has been previously assumed. For example, the assumption of Jomon sedentism during and after the Early Jomon period needs to be reappraised, as does the assumption of Jomon egalitarianism. Most of all, the discrepancy between the long-term change in organizational complexity in subsistence and settlement, which reached its maximum extent in the Middle Jomon in eastern Japan, and the seemingly progressive development in social complexity, which culminated in the Final Jomon, requires further explanation.

A number of questions can be raised concerning these two seemingly contradictory patterns. Why did the decline in organizational complexity in subsistence and settlement occur at the end of the Middle Jomon, and not before or after then, even if one accepts the classical Marxist theory of the limitations of a non-food-producing economy? Why did the Jomon as a complex hunter-gatherer culture eventually follow a different pathway from other well-known examples of complex hunter-gatherers, such as those in California and the Northwest Coast of North America, in which increasing complexity in subsistence–settlement and social inequality went essentially hand in hand (Koyama and Thomas 1981)? To answer these questions, conditions, causes, and consequences of long-term changes through the Jomon period need to be identified.

In this concluding chapter, I present a preliminary model of long-term change in Jomon subsistence, settlement, and society. The collector–forager model introduced in chapter 1 provides the basic guideline in the following discussion: the model is used as the framework within which to sort various types of data from each of the six Jomon subperiods.

It should be noted that Binford (1978; 1980; 1982) originally developed the collector–forager model to explain synchronic diversity in subsistence–settlement systems, not to deal with diachronic changes (for more discussion on this issue, see Fitzhugh and Habu 2002b; Habu and Fitzhugh 2002). In particular, the primary focus of Binford's 1980 article was on examining system variability under different natural environments. Using ethnographic examples (Murdock 1967), the latter half of the article attempted to find correlations between effective temperature (ET; measured by both the total amount and yearly distribution of solar radiation characteristic of a given place) and subsistence–settlement type. The results of his analysis indicate a strong correlation between ET and subsistence–settlement type; hunter-gatherers in the high ET areas (those who live in an equatorial or semitropical environment) tend to be mobile foragers, whereas many hunter-gatherer groups in the areas of lower ET are closer to the collector end of the continuum. An exception to this rule would be hunter-gatherers in some fully Arctic settings (e.g., Canadian Arctic Inuit), where the percentage of mobile groups is significantly higher than that in a temperate or boreal environment. Binford (1980: 17) suggests that many of these examples can be identified as what he calls *serial specialists* or *serial foragers*, who are primarily relying on foraging strategies (i.e., characterized by low logistical mobility), but who change their primary target resources seasonally.

The fact that the primary focus of the original model was on synchronic dynamics, however, does not deny the applicability of the model to the examination of long-term changes. As case studies in the Fitzhugh and Habu (2002a) volume indicate, the model can be operationalized in various ways to provide explanations for long-term system change. Long-term changes in the types of available resources and their spatial distribution would result in changes in subsistence–settlement systems. In addition, various nonenvironmental factors could also be causes or conditions of long-term hunter-gatherer system change. These include (1) technological developments, (2) an increase or decrease in population density or pressure, (3) the adoption of plant cultivation and other types of environmental management, (4) trade/exchange of critical resources, and (5) changes in social relations, including the development of social alliances or warfare.

In the following, I outline major changes in archaeological data in each of the six Jomon subperiods, and explain these changes in the context of the collector–forager model. The effects of long-term environmental fluctuations, including the warming trends from the Late Pleistocene to Mid-Holocene, on Jomon subsistence, settlement, and society are discussed in the context of the model. I also argue that the model can help explain the cultural development from the Incipient to Early Jomon by reference to the concept of serial foraging. Interpretations of the changes in the latter half of the Jomon period seem to demand the active incorporation of factors other than subsistence and settlement, some of which are listed above. Accordingly, the effects of these factors on the overall systems are also considered in the following discussion.

Development of Jomon cultural complexity

From Late Palaeolithic to Incipient Jomon: emergence of Jomon foragers

The transition from the Palaeolithic to the Jomon period has generally been discussed in the context of rapidly changing climate in the terminal Pleistocene (Harunari 1998; Ikawa-Smith 2000; Tsutsumi 1998). Scholars have suggested that changes in flora and resulting changes in fauna triggered a series of reorganizations of people's subsistence strategies (e.g., Inada 1986; I. Okamoto 1986; Tsuji 1997b). In particular, a significant decrease in and eventual extinction of large terrestrial mammals, such as Naumann's elephant (*Palaeoloxodon naumanni*), Yabe's giant deer (*Sinomegaceros yabei*), and bison (*Bison priscus*), after 17,000 bp (ca. 20,000 cal BP) seem to have played a critical role in these subsistence reorganizations (Inada 1986). It is possible that changes in fauna during this period were also accelerated by overkills. Many scholars suggest that the disappearance of large terrestrial mammals resulted in a shift in hunting targets from large to middle-sized terrestrial mammals, namely to sika deer (*Cervus nippon*) and wild boar (*Sus scrofa*).

Because the presence of middle-sized deer (both sika deer and its ancestor *Cervus praenipponic*) on the Japanese archipelago goes back as far as 40,000 bp (Inada 1986), Harunari (1998) questions whether Late Palaeolithic people were really large mammal hunters. However, the presence of middle-sized terrestrial animals itself does not automatically disqualify the hypothesis of Late Palaeolithic people being large-mammal hunters. What matters is the relative ranking of these resources among all the available resources on the basis of both economic (i.e., labor investment vs. return) and social/ideological criteria. In other words, even if middle-sized deer were relatively abundant throughout the Late Palaeolithic period, it is likely that their overall dietary importance increased significantly as the number and kinds of large terrestrial mammals decreased.

A series of changes in lithic assemblages in the terminal Palaeolithic through to the beginning of the Incipient Jomon period seems to have corresponded to the shift in prey species and resulting changes in hunting methods. According to Inada (1986; 2001), hunting tools in the transition from the Late Palaeolithic to the Jomon period went through the following five sequential stages in terms of characteristic tools: (1) small bifacial points (approximately 5 centimeters in length or smaller) and so-called knife-shaped tools (also likely to have been used as projectile points), (2) composite tools made of microblades, (3) Mikoshiba projectile points (large bifaces), (4) tanged bifacial points, and (5) arrowheads. As discussed in chapter 2, at the Odai Yamamoto I site, lithics of the third stage are associated with radiocarbon dates of ca. 13,800–12,700 bp (ca. 16,500–15,100 cal BP) along with plain pottery, thus making this third stage the beginning of the Jomon period. Tanged bifacial points that characterize the fourth stage are typically associated with sites of the linear-relief pottery phase, such as Kamikuroiwa (12,165 ± 320 bp; I-944) (1σ: 15,350–13,450 cal BP) and Tazawa. However, regional variability is also noticeable. Namely, in Kyushu and Hokkaido, microblades remained in use later than in the other areas. For example, linear-relief pottery from Fukui Cave (12,700 ± 500 bp; GaK-950) (1σ: 15,850–14,250 cal BP) is associated with microblades, thus suggesting that the use of microblades was later in this region.

Given these contexts, the transition from the Late Palaeolithic to the Jomon period should be seen as part of these continuous changes, rather than as an epoch-making event. It should also be noted that the use of arrowheads did not become prevalent until the fifth stage, which corresponds to the latter half of the Incipient Jomon period. However, if the two triangular points recovered from the Odai Yamamoto I site (fig. 2.2; lower) were in fact used as arrowheads (see chapter 2), then the bow-and-arrow technology was either invented during or before the third stage, or introduced from continental Asia together with pottery production. Shiraishi (2000) also reports the presence of arrowheads associated with plain pottery at the Yoshioka site complex in Kanagawa Prefecture.

It is likely that the subsistence strategy of this transitional period was primarily that of the forager end of the collector–forager continuum. The majority of the sites associated with plain pottery and linear-relief pottery in Honshu and Shikoku (in terms of lithics, the Mikoshiba phase to the tanged bifacial point phase) are either open sites or cave sites, associated with no, or very few, features, suggesting relatively mobile settlement systems. Evidence for plant food collecting and processing is also relatively scarce, although some scholars (e.g., Inada 2001; Miyashita 1980) believe that the appearance of pottery on the Japanese archipelago was closely related to an increase in the reliance on plant food. In any case, the amount of plain or linear-relief pottery in these sites is usually relatively small.

Other scholars suggest that changes in subsistence strategies during this transitional period may have included the utilization of marine and/or freshwater fish. According to Hiroyuki Sato (1992), for example, some of the terminal Palaeolithic sites such as Araya (Niigata Prefecture), which are associated with microblades and so-called Araya-style burins, represent resource extraction locations for exploiting anadromous fish. This is because these sites tend to be located near large rivers, and the lithic assemblages share similarities with Early Neolithic fishing sites in northeast Asia. Recovery of salmon remains from the Maedakochi site (Incipient Jomon) indicates that at least some Incipient Jomon groups were fishing salmon (Matsui 1995; K. Imamura 1996). However, the scarcity of faunal remains from other sites in the Late Palaeolithic/Incipient Jomon periods makes the evaluation of the importance of fishing during this transitional period difficult.

Unlike Incipient Jomon data in Honshu and Shikoku, data from Incipient Jomon sites in southern Kyushu and Tanegashima (an island south of Kyushu) show clearer evidence of plant food use. At the Yokoi Takenoyama site in Kagoshima Prefecture, which is associated with plain pottery and microblades (i.e., the beginning of the Incipient Jomon period), grinding stones and possible stone mortars have been reported together with a small number of arrowheads (Kagoshima-shi Kyoiku Iinkai 1990). At the Sojiyama site in Kagoshima Prefecture (middle Incipient Jomon), two pit-dwellings, one fire pit with a ventilation shaft (see chapter 3), and several hearths were identified (Kagoshima-shi Kyoiku Iinkai 1992). Lithic assemblages from Sojiyama and several other contemporaneous sites, such as Kakoinohara in Kagoshima (Kaseda-shi Kyoiku Iinkai 1998) and Okunonita in Tanegashima (Nishino'omote-shi Kyoiku Iinkai 1995), show not only an increase in plant food processing tools such as grinding stones, but also marked diversity (Miyata 2000). This may suggest possible differentiation in site function and occupational seasonality, perhaps related to the earlier emergence there of a collector type of subsistence–settlement system than in the rest of the Japanese archipelago. Miyata (2000) suggests repeated use of these three sites (Sojiyama, Kakoinohara, and Okunonita), a characteristic that also fits into the picture of a collector system.

Initial Jomon: expansion of target resources

With the exception of southern Kyushu, where an emergent type of collector system may be detected among some Incipient Jomon sites, residentially mobile forager systems seem to have characterized the Incipient Jomon culture of the rest of the Japanese archipelago. For most Incipient Jomon sites, evidence for the systematic exploitation of clumped resources is scarce, and only a small number of pit-dwellings have been reported.

These characteristics began to change during the Initial Jomon period (ca. 9500–6000 bp, or 11,000–6900 cal BP). One of the new developments during this period is the appearance of shell-middens. A good example is the Natsushima shell-midden in Kanagawa Prefecture (Sugihara and Serizawa 1957) dated to the Yoriito-mon phase (the first phase of the Initial Jomon period) through to the end of the Initial Jomon. An oyster shell collected from the bottom layer of the shell-midden (associated with Yoriito-mon-style pottery) is dated to 9450 ± 400 bp (M-769) (1σ: 10,850–9550 cal BP). Located on the Miura peninsula of the western Tokyo Bay area, the shell layer measured as much as 1.5 meters in thickness, and consisted primarily of oyster (*Crassostrea gigas*) and granular ark shell (*Tegillarca granosa*). Faunal remains reported from the site include both fish, such as tuna (*Thunnus thynnus*), mullet (*Mugil cephalus*), black porgy (*Acanthopagrus schlegeli*), sea bass (*Lateolabrax japonicus*), and flathead (*Platycephalus indicus*) (K. Imamura 1996), and terrestrial mammals, such as wild boar, raccoon dog, and hare. Hunting tools (e.g., arrowheads), fishing tools (e.g., bone fishhooks and needles), and plant food processing tools (e.g., pebble tools, grinding stones, and stone mortars) have also been reported. These lines of evidence indicate the rapid expansion of target resources toward so-called *r*-selected species (smaller mammals, plants, fish, and shellfish).

The radiocarbon date for the Natsushima shell-midden places the Jomon as one of the earliest examples of prehistoric hunter-gatherers who systematically exploited marine resources. Clear evidence of maritime adaptation in the Early Holocene from the other parts of the Pacific Rim region include On Your Knees Cave (ca. 10,000 cal BP) of Prince of Wales Island in southeastern Alaska, the Anangula site (ca. 8500 cal BP) in the Aleutian Islands, and the Hidden Falls site (ca. 8200 cal BP) (Fitzhugh 2002). However, unlike these examples, where the residents seem to have been heavily reliant on marine resources, the contribution of marine food to the Initial Jomon diet in Honshu seem to have been significantly less. This is because the number of shell-middens is relatively small in comparison to the number of inland settlements and open sites. With the possible exception of Late Jomon shell-midden sites in the eastern Tokyo Bay area (see pp. 238–239), there is little evidence elsewhere in Honshu that marine resources were the staple food of the Jomon people. Thus, characterizing the Honshu Jomon people as maritime foragers is inadequate in most instances (see also chapter 3).

Despite the signs of the increasing exploitation of *r*-selected species, I suggest that the majority of Initial Jomon people in Honshu remained residentially mobile foragers. The majority of settlements during this period are small, associated with only three to five pit-dwellings (I. Okamoto 1975). Most Initial Jomon sites are located on narrow ridges on hills, not suitable for constructing larger villages. Lack of storage pits indicates that food storage was not yet an important component of Incipient Jomon subsistence strategies.

In many regards, Initial Jomon people seem to have resembled what Binford (1980) referred to as "serial specialists," or "serial foragers." Like typical foragers, serial foragers are characterized by high residential mobility, low logistical mobility, and lack of storage. However, unlike typical foragers, who are adapted to spatially and seasonally homogeneous environments, serial specialists occur in environments where seasonal variability of critical resources is quite large. Binford (1980: 17) states that serial specialists "execute residential mobility so as to position the group with respect to particular food species that are temporally phased in their availability through a seasonal cycle." Although most of the ethnographically known serial foragers are located in cold climates (Binford 1980: 16), some early exploiters of *r*-selected species in temperate zones may also have adopted similar strategies.

The expansion of target resources is likely to have been caused or conditioned by multiple factors. Initial Jomon sites are generally associated with a much larger amount of pottery than Incipient Jomon sites. This seems to indicate that the ability to process and cook efficiently r-selected species (namely plant food and shellfish) resulted in heavier reliance on these types of food. Also, the continuing warming trend resulted in the expansion of various kinds of oak trees in central/western Honshu (including the Kanto region), Shikoku, and Kyushu (Tsuji 1997b). The warming trend also resulted in higher sea levels, which must have significantly affected the quality and quantity of available seafood.

While most of the Initial Jomon settlements in Honshu are relatively small, some examples in Hokkaido from the same period have different characteristics. For example, at the Nakano B site in Hakodate, Hokkaido, 546 Initial Jomon pit-dwellings have been reported (Izumita 1996). Many of the dwellings overlap one another, suggesting repeated occupations of the place. A large number of burial pits and flask-shaped storage pits, both of which are considered to be markers of sedentary collectors, were also discovered. The site is associated with more than 20,000 stone net sinkers, suggesting the possibility that intensive fishing was the subsistence basis of the site residents.

In southern Kyushu, where a collector type of system may have developed as early as the Incipient Jomon period (see pp. 247–248), a continuing pattern of unique developments can be observed. At the early Initial Jomon Uenohara no. 4 site (Kagoshima Prefecture), forty-six pit-dwellings, fifteen fire-pits with ventilation shafts, and other features were recovered. The site was covered by the volcanic ash layer dated to ca. 9500 bp (ca. 11,000 cal BP).

The early development of organizational complexity in subsistence and settlement seems to have formed the foundation for the development of sophisticated ceremonial practices. By the latter half of the Initial Jomon period, clay figurines, pulley-shaped clay and stone ear spools, jars with necks, and other seemingly ceremonial artifacts and features appeared in this region. The Uenohara no. 3 site provides a good example of an artifact assemblage from this period (Kagoshima-ken Kyoiku Iinkai 1997). Some Japanese archaeologists equate the level of sophistication of ceremonial artifacts evidenced at Uenohara no. 3 with that of the Late Jomon in Kanto and Tohoku. This unique development, however, was subsequently terminated by a volcanic eruption of the Kikai Caldera (a submarine volcano located south of Yakushima Island) dated to approximately 6400 bp (ca. 7300 cal BP) (Shinto 1997).

Early Jomon: development of collector systems and organizational complexity in subsistence and settlement

The emergence of serial foraging strategies during the Initial Jomon period opened the pathway to the development of more logistically organized systems. Unlike typical foragers, who tend to be more generalists (see chapter 3: p. 63), serial foragers are specialists who focus on the bulk exploitation of a limited number of critical resources. Without systematic food storage, however, the Initial Jomon system remained residentially mobile.

The development of storage techniques at the beginning of the Early Jomon period seems to have triggered the development of less residentially mobile systems in various parts of the Japanese archipelago. As discussed in chapter 3, excavations of storage pits are primarily from the Early Jomon and subsequent periods, with the exception of southern Kyushu. Together with the appearance of storage pits, other characteristics that are typical of collecting systems are commonly reported from Early Jomon sites. These characteristics include the presence of large settlements and the functional differentiation of sites. Some of the large settlements are associated with cemeteries and/or large ceremonial stone features, even though they were not necessarily contemporaneous (see chapter 5). Also, the number of ceremonial or religious artifacts, such as clay and stone figurines, talc earrings and beads, shows an increase over time.

Of these, the common presence of large settlements is diagnostic of the Early Jomon culture throughout eastern Japan. A number of settlements associated with dozens of pit-dwellings are reported from the beginning of the Early Jomon period on. Some of these settlement sites are characterized by a circular or horseshoe-shaped configuration of pit-dwellings such as those of the Nanbori site (see chapter 4). Other settlements show more clustered or linear configurations (e.g., Okada 2003).

Because many of these pit-dwellings are overlapping, it is clear that not all of them were simultaneously occupied. Examination of the pottery associated with them also confirms this interpretation. Based on these observations, Tatsuo Kobayashi (1986) suggests that the maximum number of simultaneously occupied dwellings must have been only five or six. Some of the Early Jomon villages, such as the Early Jomon component of the Sannai Maruyama site (see chapter 5), may have been larger. Regardless of the number of simultaneously occupied pit-dwellings, most of these large settlement sites seem to have been repeatedly occupied; a trait that is characteristic of collectors because of the necessity to exploit efficiently spatially and seasonally clumped resources.

Results of Case Study 1 presented in chapter 4 indicate that at least some Early Jomon systems associated with large settlements were those of seasonally sedentary collectors, not fully sedentary ones. The results also show the relatively fluid nature of these systems, including the possible presence of forager systems at the end of the Early Jomon. They indicate that organizational complexity in Jomon subsistence and settlement neither evolved from simple to complex, nor was it universal.

Despite the fluid nature of subsistence–settlement systems, the implication of the common appearance of collector systems during the Early Jomon period seems quite profound. In particular, the fact that various new developments in both mortuary/ceremonial practices and crafts/exchange systems occurred for the first time during this period indicate emergent social complexity (not necessarily hierarchical, but with more differentiation between individuals as well as between settlements) in accordance with the development of collector systems (for details, see chapters 5 and 6).

The shift toward the collector type of system is particularly noticeable in eastern Japan, notably in the Chubu, Kanto, and Tohoku regions. In western Japan, discoveries of large settlements from this period are less common. Population estimates by Koyama (1984) also suggest only a small increase in western regions (see chapter 2). Given these lines of evidence, it is likely that western Japan in general was associated with less specialized systems (i.e., closer to foragers) than those in the Chubu, Kanto, and Tohoku regions.

Middle Jomon: intensification of plant use, and its collapse

The Middle Jomon period, especially that of the Chubu, Kanto, and Tohoku regions, is known for its relative abundance of large settlements, heavily decorated pottery (see chapter 6), and ceremonial artifacts such as clay figurines and stone rods (see chapter 5). High site density and ample evidence for long-distance trade of exotic materials, such as jade (see chapter 6), also characterize this period. An abundance of so-called chipped stone axes in the southwestern Kanto and Chubu Mountain regions has also been noted by many archaeologists. As discussed in chapters 3 and 4, several scholars (e.g., Fujimori 1950) have suggested that these chipped stone axes were used as hoes for plant cultivation, while others believe their abundance reflects the practice of intensive plant root collecting (see also Habu 2001). In either case, a high level of subsistence intensification and specialization on particular types of plant food can be assumed. Fujimori (1950) also noted that, in the Chubu Mountain region, hunting tools such as arrowheads are extremely scarce during the Middle Jomon period. This also supports the hypothesis of a high level of plant food specialization. In short, Middle Jomon people in these regions seem to have been on the collector end of the forager–collector continuum.

Because of the large size of many settlements and the rich material culture, the development in the Chubu and Kanto regions described above has attracted many researchers' attention. As a result, the system associated with chipped stone axes is frequently regarded as the most representative case of Middle Jomon prosperity. This development of a so-called "Middle Jomon type" of system has been attributed to the progressive development of the Jomon culture in general, or the development of the "forces of production" in particular when discussed within the framework of classical Marxism. However, results from Case Study 1 in chapter 4 indicate that the development of this new system in the Chubu Mountain region may have been originally triggered by a system change in the Kanto region. Thus, the importance of historically unique situations, in this case a shift from collecting to foraging systems in one region and the resulting population movement to a neighboring region, needs to be seriously considered to understand the change from the Early to Middle Jomon in these regions (see chapter 4).

As discussed in chapter 3, Keiji Imamura (1996) notes that the northeastern Kanto region is characterized by an abundance of storage pits. He suggests that this reflects a heavy reliance on nuts. If this was the case, it implies the presence of another highly specialized collector system. An abundance of storage pits is also noticeable in some Middle Jomon sites in Tohoku, although their regional distribution patterns have yet to be analyzed.

In the northern Tohoku region, extremely large settlements appeared in the latter half of the Middle Jomon period, notably during the Upper Ento-d, -e, Enokibayashi, and Saibana phases. These include the Sannai Maruyama site (see Case Study 2 in chapter 4) and the Tominosawa site (Aomori-ken Maizo Bunkazai Chosa Center 1989; 1991a; 1991b; 1991c; 1992a; 1992b). While the function and occupational seasonality of these sites need to be further investigated (see chapter 4), there is little doubt that they were associated with a high level of organizational complexity in subsistence and settlement.

The cause for this development is currently unidentified. However, it is worth noting that, in Aomori Prefecture, the preceding subphases (Upper-Ento-a to -c phases in the beginning of the Middle Jomon) are characterized by a significant decline in the number of sites. This may imply the existence of a forager system prior to the development of a complex collector system, a situation that resembles the case in the Kanto and Chubu regions (see Case Study 1 of chapter 4). Given this situation, an examination of system dynamics at the interregional scale, including the possibility of population movement from one region to another, is required.

Although the Middle Jomon culture is characterized by the presence of a large number of ceremonial artifacts and features, evidence for vertical social inequality is scarce. As Oki Nakamura's (2000) work (see chapter 5) indicates, Middle Jomon graves are not much different from those in the previous period in terms of variability in grave goods. Nevertheless, a significant increase in certain types of ceremonial artifacts and long-distance exchange from the Early to the Middle Jomon can be observed (see chapters 5 and 6). This seems to indicate that, despite the lack of clear evidence of vertical social differentiation, Middle Jomon society as a whole was much more complex than Early Jomon society, if we follow the wider definition of social complexity outlined in chapter 1.

At the end of the Middle Jomon period, the prosperity of these systems reached an abrupt end throughout the Chubu, Kanto, and Tohoku regions. On the basis of his analysis of the number of excavated pit-dwellings, Keiji Imamura (1996: 156) indicates that populations in the Kanto and Chubu regions increased by as much as 50 to 150 times and then went down close to the original level within 600 to 700 years. Although no similar statistics are available from the Tohoku region, a rapid disappearance of most large settlements in the end of the Middle Jomon is reported by both Okada (2003) and Kodama (2003).

It is also worth noting that, according to Keiji Imamura (1996: 93), 70 percent of all excavated pit-dwellings in the Chubu and Kanto regions belong to the Middle Jomon period, and 50 percent of all excavated pit-dwellings in these districts belong to the latter half of the Middle Jomon. This clearly demonstrates the unusual nature of the subsistence–settlement systems of this period in these regions, which may lie outside the range of hunting-gathering practice. In this regard, reexamination of the Middle Jomon "plant cultivation hypothesis" (e.g., Fujimori 1950), as well as the possibility of environmental management (see, e.g., Y. Sato et al. 2003), will be critical.

The mechanism of this sudden decline of the highly specialized systems has yet to be investigated. In the past, many Japanese archaeologists have attributed this dramatic change in the Chubu, Kanto, and Tohoku regions to the cooling climate at the end of the Middle Jomon (e.g., Okada 2003; Kodama 2003; Yasuda 1995). While the wide occurrence of this phenomenon makes this hypothesis seemingly convincing, no scholars have attempted to explain *how* the cooling climate actually caused the rapid change of these systems. The relative scarcity of reliable radiocarbon dates from the Middle Jomon period, with the exception of those from the Sannai Maruyama site (see chapter 4), also makes the evaluation of the cooling climate hypothesis difficult. Other scholars interpret this change as a result of epidemics, but no archaeological evidence to support this hypothesis is currently available.

As an alternative hypothesis, I suggest the possibility that the extremely specialized subsistence strategies associated with these systems were capable of supporting much larger populations, but at the same time were more susceptible to minor environmental fluctuations or other external disruptions. In other words, Middle Jomon people in these regions may have gone too far toward specialization.

Although the majority of large Middle Jomon settlements are associated with evidence of intensive plant food exploitation, shell-midden sites in the east Tokyo Bay area are exceptions. As discussed in chapter 3, in this area, ring- or horseshoe-shaped shell-middens associated with a large number of pit-dwellings began to be constructed during this period. Whether this implies a heavy reliance on marine food or simply reflects seasonally intensive exploitation of marine food remains to be further investigated (see chapter 3).

The rapid development and disappearance of extremely specialized systems can be observed only in eastern Japan. Change from the Early to Middle Jomon in western Japan seems to have been more gradual, and not necessarily directional. Population estimates by Koyama (1984) show only minor increases, if not decreases, in Kinki, Chugoku, Shikoku, and Kyushu (see chapter 2). Overall, Middle Jomon hunter-gatherers in western Japan seem to have remained further from the collector end of the forager–collector continuum than their counterparts in eastern Japan.

Late Jomon: further development of social complexity

The shift from the Middle to Late Jomon period in the Tohoku, Kanto, and Chubu regions is generally characterized by decreasing organizational complexity in subsistence and settlement, but increasing social complexity. The number of extremely large settlements dated to the Late Jomon is much smaller than that of the Middle Jomon. A significant decrease in site density is also apparent (Koyama 1984). However, this does not imply that the people in these regions were on the forager end of the forager–collector scale. In most cases, subsistence-settlement systems in these regions can be understood within the range of collector systems. In the Kanto and Chubu regions, the level of organizational complexity in subsistence and settlement, which is reflected in site density and site size variability, seems to be roughly equivalent to that of the Early Jomon (with the exception of the east Tokyo Bay area; see below). In Tohoku, the average size of settlements seems smaller than in the Early Jomon. The development of ceremonial sites away from settlements in this region (Kodama 2003) may be related to this small settlement size.

An indication of the emergence of hereditary social stratification can be seen in child burials. As suggested by Oki Nakamura (2000), an increase in the relative occurrences of child burials with grave goods can be observed in eastern Japan (see table 5.5). This trend started in the Late Jomon period, and continued through to the Final Jomon period.

In terms of possible archaeological correlates of social complexity, there are three major lines of evidence. First, there was an increase in the number and kinds of ceremonial artifacts and features (see table 5.3). In particular, there was a sudden increase in large stone circles at the beginning of the Late Jomon in northern Tohoku and Hokkaido. Second, long-distance movement of items obtained from restricted sources, including asphalt and salt, becomes more conspicuous. Third, specialized production of finely made pottery, lacquerware, and other perishable artifacts seems to have occurred during and after the Late Jomon. As discussed in chapters 5 and 6, these three lines are all possible pathways toward vertical social hierarchy.

To identify which factor or factors were utilized by emergent elites to establish their position and power, it is necessary to determine the chronological order of the occurrence of these events in each region. While such data are not presented in this book, fine-grained excavation reports of Jomon sites would allow us to compile a database of this kind. It is quite possible that emergent leaders in different regions adopted different strategies to obtain their power.

Despite a slight increase in the number and percentage of child burials with grave goods, the degree of vertical social differentiation during the Late Jomon seems to have been relatively small. Evidence for hereditary social stratification other than from child burials is limited, and differences in grave goods between adult burials are not significant. Elaboration of burial customs seems to be more closely related to the development of communal burials (e.g., *kanjo dori*) rather than vertical differentiation between individuals.

I suggest that the development of vertical differentiation was limited by the reduced organizational complexity in subsistence and settlement. Because continuity in ceremonial practices can be observed from the Middle to Late Jomon (Kodama 2003; Okada 2003), the seed for the development of Late Jomon social complexity must have been sown

during the Middle Jomon period. Complex site structure and the construction of large monuments observed among large Middle Jomon sites,
such as those at Sannai Maruyama, indicate that Middle Jomon society
was highly complex. However, because evidence for vertical stratification from the Middle Jomon is virtually absent, it is more likely that the
nature of this social complexity was based more on horizontal differentiation. For the construction of large monuments, the presence of leaders
must have been critical, but their positions may not have been hereditary.

I also hypothesize that the disappearance of highly specialized collector
systems at the end of the Middle Jomon period triggered the emergence
of vertical differentiation in the following Late Jomon period. Under the
rapid collapse of the existing system, the role of group leaders must have
become more important, thus providing the opportunity for the existing horizontal differentiation to become more vertical. However, with
the decline of intensive subsistence strategies, the amount of surplus
available to be manipulated by the leaders may have been relatively
small. While monument construction and elaborate ceremonial practice,
long-distance trade, and craft specialization could be used to manipulate
power, ultimately the elites had to have access to a food surplus. Individuals working as monument builders, traders, or craft specialists would
have needed to be fed. Elaboration of trade networks and craft specialization may have supplemented the subsistence base, but not to the point
of establishing complex political organizations.

Although most parts of eastern Japan experienced a significant decline
in the number and size of sites from the Middle to Late Jomon, the
east Tokyo Bay area was an exception. Large shell-middens associated
with many pit-dwellings, such as Kasori and Kainohana in Chiba Prefecture, were present from the Middle through to the Late Jomon periods.
Because of their high density, Horikoshi (1972: 22) suggests that the
territory of each settlement associated with a shell-midden was possibly
only 2–3 kilometers in radius. This is extremely small when compared to
the average size of hunter-gatherer territory suggested by Vita-Finzi and
Higgs (1970) (i.e., approximately 10 kilometers in radius). If this was the
case, and if these sites indeed represent residential bases, it is possible
that overcrowding in this region resulted in the restriction of the occupants' residential mobility (cf. Rosenberg 1998). Alternatively, it is also
possible that the apparent overcrowding may simply reflect the repeated
use of these sites as special-purpose camps for the seasonally intensive
exploitation of marine food.

Unlike in eastern Japan, data from western Japan (the Kinki, Chugoku,
Shikoku, and Kyushu regions) indicate that site density increased steadily
from the Middle to Late Jomon (see table 2.5). Although the density is

much lower than in eastern Japan, no decrease in site size and site density is observed. This may imply that, because subsistence–settlement systems in western Japan were less specialized, they were not as vulnerable to environmental fluctuations and other risks as the systems in eastern Japan. It is also worth noting that influences from continental Asia began to be noticed on various aspects of material culture, including pottery production technology (see chapter 5). In sum, the diverging paths between eastern and western Japan, the former continuing to follow its unique development of Jomon social complexity, and the latter gradually accepting external influences, began to be apparent during this period.

Final Jomon: the transition to Yayoi

By the Final Jomon period, continuing influences from the Mumun culture (ca. 3300–1300 cal BP) of the Korean peninsula began to alter various aspects of the Jomon culture in western Japan. Material culture, including stylistic characteristics of pottery, shows strong influences from the Mumun culture. In the latter half of the Final Jomon period, rice paddy fields and dolmens (megalithic tombs), both of which are hallmarks of the Mumun culture, appeared in northern Kyushu.

Whether this transitional phase in northern Kyushu should be regarded as the terminal phase of the Jomon period or should be classified as the Initial Yayoi period has been a topic of debate. Traditionally, it has been classified as the latter half of the Final Jomon period. However, scholars such as Sahara (1987) argue that, because evidence of rice cultivation has been found, the cultures of northern Kyushu in this phase should be labeled as belonging to the Initial Yayoi period (note this chronological division is applied only to northern Kyushu).

In traditional chronologies, this transitional phase was dated to ca. 500–300 bp, and these dates were roughly equated with the calendrical dates 500–300 BC. The rest of the Yayoi period has been divided into three subperiods: Early (ca. 300–100 BC), Middle (ca. 100 BC–AD 100), and Late (ca. AD 100–300). Because the Yayoi culture spread from northern Kyushu to the east, the Early Yayoi period is present only in western Japan. As a result, the end of the Final Jomon period in eastern Japan is estimated to have been approximately 100 BC. However, if, as Harunari et al. (2003) suggest, the beginning of the transitional period in northern Kyushu goes back as early as 1000–900 BC, then absolute dates for the Final Jomon and the Yayoi periods need to be substantially modified.

The cause of the shift from hunting-gathering to a food-producing economy at the end of the Final Jomon warrants further discussion. While diffusion may describe what happened during this transition, it does not explain *why* the change occurred. Looking at the population estimates by Koyama (1984), the estimates for western Japan show a slight decrease (4,400 to 2,100 in Kinki, 2,400 to 2,000 in Chugoku, 2,700 to 500 in Shikoku, and 10,100 to 6,300 in Kyushu). This may reflect a system change in these regions, which may have triggered the adoption of new cultural elements from the continent. Systematic analyses of regional settlement patterns are required to investigate the issue further.

The number of immigrants who came to the Japanese archipelago from the Korean peninsula is another topic of debate. Scholars such as Hanihara (1987) and Hudson (1999) indicate that the transition to the Yayoi period entailed a large-scale migration from the Korean peninsula. While the dual structure model for the population history of the Japanese (see chapter 2) is generally well accepted, the actual number of immigrants at the transition from Jomon to Yayoi is still hotly debated. If in fact a large-scale migration occurred, then the reason why a large number of the Mumun people moved into the Japanese archipelago needs to be investigated. In this regard, external conditions may be as important as internal changes in order to explain this major shift (see also Habu 2002b).

In eastern Japan, archaeological data that would allow us to infer Final Jomon subsistence–settlement systems are relatively scarce. In the Kanto and Chubu regions, the number of sites and site density show a dramatic decrease. Koyama's (1984) population estimates for the Kanto region decreased from 51,600 (Late Jomon) to 7,700 (Final Jomon). For the Chubu region, the decrease is from 22,000 to 6,000 (see chapter 2; table 2.5). Furthermore, most of these sites are not associated with any pit-dwellings or other residential features, making any kind of analysis on settlement systems difficult. In the Tohoku region, the decrease in the number of sites is not as dramatic (from 43,800 to 39,500) as in Kanto and Chubu, but the recovery of large settlements is still uncommon. Many of the well-known Final Jomon sites are either ceremonial sites or waterlogged sites associated with artifact concentrations (possibly also ceremonial).

Compared to the extreme scarcity of subsistence and settlement data, recoveries of ceremonial sites are more commonly reported. Examples of these sites include the Teraji site (Niigata Prefecture), the Kinsei site (Yamanashi Prefecture), and the Yaze site (Gunma Prefecture) (see chapter 6). Recovery of waterlogged sites associated with a large number of pottery and ceremonial artifacts is also common, particularly from the Tohoku region. These sites include the Korekawa Nakai site (Aomori Prefecture), the Kamegaoka site (Aomori Prefecture), and the Kunenbashi site (Iwate Prefecture) (see chapter 5).

It should be noted that many scholars have pointed out a strong continuity in pottery decoration in eastern Japan from the terminal Final Jomon to Yayoi. Thus, the rapid decline in the number of sites in eastern Japan does not imply that people in this region eventually died out.

Three possible hypotheses can be suggested to explain the small number of sites and low estimated population for the Final Jomon period. First, it is possible that Final Jomon people were not living in pit-dwellings but constructed non-semisubterranean structures that are difficult to identify archaeologically (e.g., tents or surface dwellings with no post-molds). However, while this would explain the scarcity of pit-dwellings, it would not explain the scarcity of sites.

Second, the location of Final Jomon sites may be very different from the other Jomon sites, making the recovery rates of Final Jomon sites much lower. The lowland areas and hills of the Japanese archipelago have been relatively thoroughly surveyed as a result of large-scale land development since the 1960s, but the recovery rate of sites in mountainous areas is much lower. It should also be kept in mind that the site recovery rates vary between regions. Thus, the numbers of sites in relatively underdeveloped areas, such as the Tohoku region, may be significantly underestimated.

Third, the duration of the Final Jomon period in eastern Japan may have been shorter than is currently assumed. Conventional chronology places the Final Jomon from ca. 3000 to 2100 bp, which calibrates to ca. 3300–2100 cal BP. However, reliable radiocarbon dates from the terminal Late Jomon through to the Final Jomon are scarce. If the duration of the Final Jomon period was shorter than the traditional estimate, then the population estimates for each region would be larger.

For the moment, we know relatively little about the Final Jomon subsistence–settlement system in eastern Japan. The fact that very few large sites associated with pit-dwellings have been reported seems to support the possibility of residentially mobile foragers. On the other hand, it should be noted that the production of lacquerware and other lacquered artifacts would require a certain level of sedentism, the necessity to stay in one place for at least several months. Because Final Jomon culture in the Tohoku region is characterized by the presence of exquisitely made lacquerware (i.e., lacquered wood containers), lacquered baskets, and lacquered pottery, it is likely that at least some groups in this region maintained seasonally, if not fully, sedentary lifeways.

Hypothetically speaking, several factors may have caused these changes. The cooling climate in the first millennium BC in the northern hemisphere has been noted by several scholars (Endo 1999; see also Karabanov et al. 2000). Such a change may have caused a decrease in one or more critical resources that formed part of the Late Jomon subsistence base. As discussed in Case Study 1 in chapter 4, a minor change in environmental conditions could lead to a major system change. It is also very likely that external influences from continental Asia affected these regions. Unlike in western Japan, where strong influences from the continent can be observed on various aspects of material culture, clear evidence of direct influence is scarce in eastern Japan. But it is quite possible that the growing cultural differences between the east and the west triggered a major system reorganization in these regions.

Concluding remarks

As discussed above, long-term changes in the Jomon culture can be explained as the accumulation of numerous changes at both the local and regional levels. These changes were caused or conditioned by multiple factors. Some can be explained by either environmental changes or technological developments. Other changes seem have been more closely related to social and ideological factors, including rituals, craft specialization, and long-distance trade. The constellation of these numerous changes over the 10,000-year span of the Jomon culture resulted in the unique historical trajectory of this prehistoric hunter-gatherer culture. As a whole, the historical trajectory proposed here does not fit into the conventional picture of unilinear evolution. The mechanism of each change, however, can be adequately explained by using ecological or social models that assume the validity of general laws.

The degree of residential mobility/sedentism is the key that links subsistence and settlement practices with the social practices of the Jomon people. As many ecological models suggest, the degree of residential mobility is inseparably tied to environmental conditions and resulting subsistence strategies. At the same time, the degree to which the Jomon people moved their residential bases would have significantly affected both their cultural landscapes and annual/long-term cycles of their social life. Thus, understanding the degree of residential mobility is a first step toward understanding the Jomon society as a whole.

The model presented in this chapter still has many missing parts. Through a series of case studies, similar to those presented in chapter 4, these gaps can be filled in. And the extremely rich Jomon database allows us to conduct numerous new projects on the Jomon, both at the macro scale (e.g., regional settlement pattern analysis) and the micro scale (e.g., household archaeology).

Throughout this book, I have attempted to show the range of temporal and spatial variability within the Jomon culture, and to explain the reasons for and implications of the variability. Although the archaeological data examined here are coming from the Japanese archipelago, methodological and theoretical issues discussed in this book can be shared by archaeologists working elsewhere in the world. In this regard, I hope that the publication of this book will help enhance active interactions between Japanese archaeology and world archaeology, especially in the field of hunter-gatherer archaeology.

References

Abe, Chiharu. 2000. Jomon jidai no asphalt riyo [Use of asphalt during the Jomon period]. *Shiroi Kuni no Uta [Essays on Northern Land]* 524: 22–25 (in Japanese).

Abe, Gihei. 1983. Haiseki [Ceremonial features with stone arrangements]. In *Jomon Bunka no Kenkyu IX: Jomon-jin no Seishin Bunka [Studies of the Jomon Culture, vol. IX: Mortuary and Ceremonial Practices]*, ed. Shinpei Kato, Tatsuo Kobayashi, and Tsuyoshi Fujimoto, pp. 32–45. Tokyo: Yuzankaku (in Japanese).

Abe, Yoshiro. 2000. Jomon jidai no seigyo to Nakazato kaizuka no keisei [Jomon subsistence and the accumulation of the Nakazato shell-midden]. In *Nakazato Kaizuka [The Nakazato Shell-Midden]*, ed. Kita-ku Kyoiku Iinkai [Board of Education of Kita Ward], pp. 243–259. Tokyo: Kita-ku Kyoiku Iinkai (in Japanese).

Abiko, Shoji. 1978. Jomon shiki doki no keishiki to hennen [Jomon pottery typology and chronology]. In *Nihon Kokogaku o Manabu I: Nihon Kokogaku no Kiso [Studying Japanese Archaeology, vol. I: Foundations of Japanese Archaeology]*, ed. Hatsushige Otsuka, Mitsunori Tozawa, and Makoto Sahara, pp. 170–188. Tokyo: Yuzankaku (in Japanese).

1982. Asphalt. In *Jomon Bunka no Kenkyu VIII: Shakai, Bunka [Studies of the Jomon Culture, vol. VIII: Society and Culture]*, ed. Shinpei Kato, Tatsuo Kobayashi, and Tsuyoshi Fujimoto, pp. 205–222. Tokyo: Yuzankaku (in Japanese).

1985. Asphalt no ryutsu to Tohoku no chiiki-ken [Regional interactive spheres and the circulation of asphalt in the Tohoku region]. *Kikan Kokogaku [Archaeology Quarterly]* 12: 43–46 (in Japanese).

Adams, Robert McCormick. 1965. *Land behind Baghdad: A History of Settlement on the Diyala Plains.* Chicago: University of Chicago Press.

Aida, Kaoru, and Satoshi Koike. 1986. Dai II bunka-so [The second cultural layer]. In *Tsukimino Iseki-gun Kamino Iseki Dai Ichi Chiten [Location 1 of the Kamino Site of the Tsukimino Site Complex]*. Yamato: Yamato-shi Kyoiku Iinkai [Board of Education of Yamato City] (in Japanese).

Aikens, C. M. 1981. The last 10,000 years in Japan and eastern North America: parallels in environment, economic adaptation, growth of social complexity, and the adoption of agriculture. In *Affluent Foragers: Pacific Coasts East and West*, ed. Shuzo Koyama and David H. Thomas, pp. 261–273. Senri Ethnological Studies, No. 9. Osaka: National Museum of Ethnology.

1995. First in the world: the Jomon pottery of Japan. In *The Emergence of Pottery: Technology and Innovation in Ancient Societies*, ed. William K. Barnett and John W. Hoopes, pp. 11–22. Washington, D.C.: Smithsonian Institution Press.

Aikens, C. Melvin, Kenneth M. Ames, and David Sanger. 1986. Affluent collectors at the edges of Eurasia and North America: some comparisons and observations on the evolution of society among north-temperate coastal hunter-gatherers. In *Prehistoric Hunter-Gatherers in Japan*, ed. Takeru Akazawa and C. Melvin Aikens, pp. 3–26. The University Museum, The University of Tokyo, Bulletin No. 27. Tokyo: University of Tokyo Press.

Aikens, C. M., and Don E. Dumond. 1986. Convergence and common heritage: some parallels in the archaeology of Japan and western North America. In *Windows on the Japanese Past: Studies in Archaeology and Prehistory*, ed. Richard J. Pearson, Gina L. Barnes, and Karl L. Hutterer, pp. 163–178. Ann Arbor: Center for Japanese Studies, University of Michigan.

Aikens, C. Melvin, and Takayasu Higuchi. 1982. *Prehistory of Japan*. San Diego: Academic Press.

Aikens, C. Melvin, and Song Nai Rhee, eds. 1992. *Pacific Northeast Asia in Prehistory: Hunter-Fisher-Gatherers, Farmers, and Sociopolitical Elites*. Pullman: Washington State University Press.

Akayama, Yozo. 1982. Tateana jukyo [Pit-dwellings]. In *Jomon Bunka no Kenkyu VIII: Shakai, Bunka [Studies of the Jomon Culture*, vol. VIII: *Society and Culture]*, ed. Shinpei Kato, Tatsuo Kobayashi, and Tsuyoshi Fujimoto, pp. 110–121. Tokyo: Yuzankaku (in Japanese).

Akazawa, Takeru. 1969. Jomon kaizuka-san gyorui no taicho sosei narabi ni sono senshi gyorogaku-teki imi [Body size comparison of the fish from the Jomon shellmound people]. *Jinruigaku Zasshi [Journal of the Anthropological Society of Nippon]* 77(4): 154–178 (in Japanese with English title and summary).

1980. Fishing adaptation of prehistoric hunter-gatherers at the Nittano site, Japan. *Journal of Archaeological Science* 7: 325–344.

1981. Maritime adaptation of prehistoric hunter-gatherers and their transition to agriculture in Japan. In *Affluent Foragers: Pacific Coasts East and West*, ed. Shuzo Koyama and David H. Thomas, pp. 213–258. Osaka: National Museum of Ethnology.

1982a. Jomon people's subsistence and settlements: discriminatory analysis of the Later Jomon settlements. *Jinruigaku Zasshi [Journal of the Anthropological Society of Nippon]* 90 (Supplement): 55–76.

1982b. Cultural change in prehistoric Japan: receptivity to rice agriculture in the Japanese archipelago. In *Advances in World Archaeology 1*, ed. Fred Wendorf and Angela E. Close, pp. 151–211. New York: Academic Press.

1986a. Regional variation in procurement systems of Jomon hunter-gatherers. In *Prehistoric Hunter-Gatherers in Japan*, ed. Takeru Akazawa and C. Melvin Aikens, pp. 73–92. Tokyo: University of Tokyo Press.

1986b. Hunter-gatherer adaptations and the transition to food production in Japan. In *Hunters in Transition*, ed. Marek Zvelebil, pp. 151–166. Cambridge: Cambridge University Press.

1986c. Regional diversity in Jomon subsistence and its relation to the racial history of the Japanese. In *Traditional Fishing in the Pacific*, ed. Atholl Anderson, pp. 199–213. Honolulu: Pacific Anthropological Records.

1987. Variability in the types of fishing adaptation of the Later Jomon people, ca. 2500 to 300 B.C. In *The Archaeology of Prehistoric Coastlines*, ed. G. Bailey and J. Parkington, pp. 78–92. Cambridge: Cambridge University Press.

Akazawa, Takeru, and C. Melvin Aikens, eds. 1986. *Prehistoric Hunter-Gatherers in Japan*. Tokyo: University Museum, University of Tokyo Press.

Akazawa, Takeru, and Kiyoaki Maeyama. 1986. Discriminant function analysis of Later Jomon settlements. In *Windows on the Japanese Past: Studies in Archaeology and Prehistory*, ed. Richard J. Pearson, Gina L. Barnes, and Karl L. Hutterer, pp. 279–292. Ann Arbor: Center for Japanese Studies, University of Michigan.

Akimoto, Nobuo. 1999. Kanjo resseki [Stone circles]. *Jomon Jidai [Journal of Jomon Period Studies]* 10(3): 167–176 (in Japanese with English title).

Akita-ken Kokogaku Kyokai [Archaeological Association of Akita Prefecture]. 1979. *Nashinokizuka Iseki Hakkutsu Chosa Hokoku-sho [Excavation Report of the Nashinokizuka Site]*. Akita: Akita-ken Kokogaku Kyokai (in Japanese).

Akita-ken Maizo Bunkazai Center [Archaeological Center of Akita Prefecture]. 1999. *Ikenai Iseki [The Ikenai Site]*. Akita: Akita-ken Maizo Bunkazai Center (in Japanese).

Amakasu, Ken. 1986. Soron: seisan-ryoku hatten no shodankai [Stages of the development of forces of production]. In *Iwanami Koza Nihon Kokogaku III: Seisan to Ryutsu [Iwanami Lectures in Japanese Archaeology*, vol. III: *Production and Circulation]*, ed. Yoshiro Kondo and Koichi Yokoyama, pp. 1–31. Tokyo: Iwanami Shoten (in Japanese).

Ames, Kenneth M. 1985. Hierarchies, stress and logistical strategies among hunter-gatherers in northwestern North America. In *Prehistoric Hunter-Gatherers: The Emergence of Cultural Complexity*, ed. T. Douglas Price and James A. Brown, pp. 155–180. Orlando: Academic Press.

Ames, Kenneth M., and Herbert D. G. Maschner. 1999. *Peoples of the Northwest Coast: Their Archaeology and Prehistory*. London: Thames and Hudson.

Amino, Yoshihiko. 1997. *Nihon Shakai no Rekishi [History of the Japanese Society]*. Tokyo: Iwanami Shoten (in Japanese).

Anazawa, Wako. 1985. "Kokogaku" to shite no "jinrui-gaku: process kokogaku (new archaeology) to sono genkai" ["Anthropology" as "archaeology": processual archaeology (new archaeology) and its limitation]. *Kodai Bunka [Cultura Antiqua]* 37(4): 143–152, 37(5): 189–206, 37(6): 237–249, 37(7): 285–297 (in Japanese with English title).

Anderson, Atholl J. 1988. Coastal subsistence economies in prehistoric southern New Zealand. In *The Archaeology of Prehistoric Coastlines*, ed. Geoff Bailey and John Parkington, pp. 93–101. Cambridge: Cambridge University Press.

Ando, Norikazu. 1982. Hisui [Jade]. In *Jomon Bunka no Kenkyu VIII: Shakai, Bunka [Studies of the Jomon Culture*, vol. VIII: *Society and Culture]*, ed. Shinpei Kato, Tatsuo Kobayashi, and Tsuyoshi Fujimoto, pp. 180–192. Tokyo: Yuzankaku (in Japanese).

Annaka-shi Kyoiku Iinkai [Board of Education of Annaka City]. 1996. Nakanoya Matsubara. Annaka: Annaka-shi Kyoiku Iinkai (in Japanese).

Anonymous. 2000. Tokushu, Jomon no sekai [Special section: the Jomon world]. *Mitsui Graph [Mitsui Illustrated]* 119: 3–15 (in Japanese).

Aomori-ken Kyoiku Iinkai [Board of Education of Aomori Prefecture], ed. 1977. *Sannai Maruyama (2) Iseki, Chikano Iseki III [The Sannai Maruyama (2) Site, The Chikano Site, Part III]*. Aomori: Aomori-ken Kyoiku Iinkai (in Japanese).

Aomori-ken Kyoiku-cho Bunka-ka [Cultural Affairs Section of the Agency of Education of Aomori Prefecture], ed. 1996a. *Sannai Maruyama Iseki V [The Sannai Maruyama Site, vol. V]*. Aomori: Aomori-ken Kyoiku Iinkai [Board of Education of Aomori Prefecture] (in Japanese).

——— ed. 1996b. *Sannai Maruyama Iseki VI [The Sannai Maruyama Site, vol. VI: Summary of Previous Excavations]*. Aomori: Aomori-ken Kyoiku Iinkai [Board of Education of Aomori Prefecture] (in Japanese).

——— ed. 1997a. *Sannai Maruyama Iseki VII [The Sannai Maruyama Site, vol. VII]*. Aomori: Aomori-ken Kyoiku Iinkai [Board of Education of Aomori Prefecture] (in Japanese).

——— ed. 1997b. *Sannai Maruyama Iseki VIII [The Sannai Maruyama Site, vol. VIII]*. Aomori: Aomori-ken Kyoiku Iinkai [Board of Education of Aomori Prefecture] (in Japanese).

——— ed. 1998a. *Sannai Maruyama Iseki IX [The Sannai Maruyama Site, vol. IX]*. Aomori: Aomori-ken Kyoiku Iinkai [Board of Education of Aomori Prefecture] (in Japanese).

——— ed. 1998b. *Sannai Maruyama Iseki X [The Sannai Maruyama Site, vol. X]*. Aomori: Aomori-ken Kyoiku Iinkai [Board of Education of Aomori Prefecture] (in Japanese).

——— ed. 1998c. *Sannai Maruyama Iseki XI [The Sannai Maruyama Site, vol. XI]*. Aomori: Aomori-ken Kyoiku Iinkai [Board of Education of Aomori Prefecture] (in Japanese).

——— ed. 1998d. *Sannai Maruyama Iseki XII [The Sannai Maruyama Site, vol. XII]*. Aomori: Aomori-ken Kyoiku Iinkai [Board of Education of Aomori Prefecture] (in Japanese).

——— ed. 1999. *Sannai Maruyama Iseki XIII [The Sannai Maruyama Site, vol. XIII]*. Aomori: Aomori-ken Kyoiku Iinkai [Board of Education of Aomori Prefecture] (in Japanese).

——— ed. 2000a. *Sannai Maruyama Iseki XIV [The Sannai Maruyama Site, vol. XIV]*. Aomori: Aomori-ken Kyoiku Iinkai [Board of Education of Aomori Prefecture] (in Japanese).

——— ed. 2000b. *Sannai Maruyama Iseki XV [The Sannai Maruyama Site, vol. XV]*. Aomori: Aomori-ken Kyoiku Iinkai [Board of Education of Aomori Prefecture] (in Japanese).

——— ed. 2000c. *Sannai Maruyama Iseki XVI [The Sannai Maruyama Site, vol. XVI]*. Aomori: Aomori-ken Kyoiku Iinkai [Board of Education of Aomori Prefecture] (in Japanese).

——— ed. 2000d. *Sannai Maruyama Iseki XVII [The Sannai Maruyama Site, vol. XVII]*. Aomori: Aomori-ken Kyoiku Iinkai [Board of Education of Aomori Prefecture] (in Japanese).

ed. 2001. *Sannai Maruyama Iseki XVIII [The Sannai Maruyama Site,* vol. XVIII]. Aomori: Aomori-ken Kyoiku Iinkai [Board of Education of Aomori Prefecture] (in Japanese).

ed. 2002a. *Sannai Maruyama Iseki XIX [The Sannai Maruyama Site,* vol. XIX]. Aomori: Aomori-ken Kyoiku Iinkai [Board of Education of Aomori Prefecture] (in Japanese).

ed. 2002b. *Sannai Maruyama Iseki XX [The Sannai Maruyama Site,* vol. XX]. Aomori: Aomori-ken Kyoiku Iinkai [Board of Education of Aomori Prefecture] (in Japanese).

Aomori-ken Maizo Bunkazai Chosa Center [Archaeological Center of Aomori Prefecture], ed. 1989. *Tominosawa (1), (2) Iseki [The Tominosawa Nos. 1 and 2 Sites].* Aomori: Aomori-ken Kyoiku Iinkai: Aomori [Board of Education of Aomori Prefecture] (in Japanese).

ed. 1991a. *Tominosawa (1), (2) Iseki II [The Tominosawa Nos. 1 and 2 Sites,* vol. II]. Aomori: Aomori-ken Kyoiku Iinkai: Aomori [Board of Education of Aomori Prefecture] (in Japanese).

ed. 1991b. *Tominosawa (1), (2) Iseki III [The Tominosawa Nos. 1 and 2 Sites,* vol. III]. Aomori: Aomori-ken Kyoiku Iinkai: Aomori [Board of Education of Aomori Prefecture] (in Japanese).

ed. 1991c. *Tominosawa (1), (2) Iseki IV [The Tominosawa Nos. 1 and 2 Sites,* vol. IV]. Aomori: Aomori-ken Kyoiku Iinkai: Aomori [Board of Education of Aomori Prefecture] (in Japanese).

ed. 1992a. *Tominosawa (1), (2) Iseki V [The Tominosawa Nos. 1 and 2 Sites,* vol. V]. Aomori: Aomori-ken Kyoiku Iinkai: Aomori [Board of Education of Aomori Prefecture] (in Japanese).

ed. 1992b. *Tominosawa (1), (2) Iseki VI [The Tominosawa Nos. 1 and 2 Sites,* vol. VI]. Aomori: Aomori-ken Kyoiku Iinkai: Aomori [Board of Education of Aomori Prefecture] (in Japanese).

ed. 1994a. *Sannai Maruyama (2) Iseki II [The Sannai Maruyama (2) Site,* vol. II]. Aomori: Aomori-ken Kyoiku Iinkai [Board of Education of Aomori Prefecture] (in Japanese).

ed. 1994b. *Sannai Maruyama (2) Iseki III [The Sannai Maruyama (2) Site,* vol. III]. Aomori: Aomori-ken Kyoiku Iinkai [Board of Education of Aomori Prefecture] (in Japanese).

ed. 1995. *Sannai Maruyama (2) Iseki IV [The Sannai Maruyama (2) Site,* vol. IV]. Aomori: Aomori-ken Kyoiku Iinkai [Board of Education of Aomori Prefecture] (in Japanese).

Aomori-shi Kyoiku Iinkai [Board of Education of Aomori City], ed. 1994. *Sannai Maruyama (2) Iseki. Kosannai Iseki Hakkutsu Chosa Hokoku-sho [Excavation Report of the Sannai Maruyama (2) Site and the Kosannai Site].* Aomori: Aomori-shi Kyoiku Iinkai (in Japanese).

ed. 1996. *Sannai Maruyama (2) Iseki Hakkutsu Chosa Hokoku-sho [Excavation Report of the Sannai Maruyama (2) Site].* Aomori: Aomori-shi Kyoiku Iinkai (in Japanese).

Arakawa, Takashi. 2001. Niigata-ken Aota iseki no chosa [Archaeological investigation of the Aota site, Niigata Prefecture]. In *Nihon Kokogaku Kyokai 2001 Nendo Taikai Kenkyu Happyo Yoshi [Abstracts of Papers Presented at the Fall 2001 Meeting of the Japanese Archaeological Association],* pp. 25–27.

Tokyo: Nihon Kokogaku Kyokai [Japanese Archaeological Association] (in Japanese).

Arnold, Jeanne. E. 1992. Complex hunter-gatherer-fishers of prehistoric California: chiefs, specialists, and maritime adaptations of the Channel Islands. *American Antiquity* 57(1): 60–84.

1995. Social inequality, marginalization, and economic process. In *Foundations of Social Inequality*, ed. T. Douglas Price and Gary M. Feinman, pp. 87–104. New York: Plenum.

1996a. Archaeology of complex hunter-gatherers. *Journal of Archaeological Method and Theory* 3(2): 77–126.

1996b. Understanding the evolution of intermediate societies. In *Emergent Complexity: The Evolution of Intermediate Societies*, ed. Jeanne E. Arnold, pp. 1–12. Ann Arbor: International Monographs in Prehistory.

Asahi Shinbun-sha. 1992. *'92 Kodaishi Hakkutsu Somakuri [Summary of Archaeological Excavations: 1992]*. Tokyo: Asahi Shinbun-sha (in Japanese).

1998. *'98 Kodaishi Hakkutsu Somakuri [Summary of Archaeological Excavations: 1998]*. Tokyo: Asahi Shinbun-sha (in Japanese).

2000. *2000 Kodaishi Hakkutsu Somakuri [Summary of New Archaeological Excavations: 2000]*. Tokyo: Asahi Shinbun-sha (in Japanese).

Asano, Katsuhiko, Jun Ito, and Tada'aki Ogasawara. 1999. Kita-Tohoku no "Asphalt no michi" no kaimei [Examination of the "Asphalt Road" in northern Tohoku]. In *Nihon Bunkazai Kagaku-kai dai 16 kai Taikai Kenkyu Happyo Yoshi [Abstracts of the Papers Presented at the 16th Annual Meeting of the Japanese Society for Scientific Studies on Cultural Properties]*, pp. 34–35. Nara: Nihon Bunkazai Kagaku-kai (in Japanese).

Aso, Masaru. 1960. Jomon jidai Koki no shuraku [Late Jomon settlements]. *Kokogaku Kenkyu [Quarterly of Archaeological Studies]* 7(2): 9–16 (in Japanese).

ed. 1985. *Senpukuji Doketsu no Hakkutsu Kiroku [Record of the Excavations of Senpukuji Cave]*. Tokyo: Tsukiji Shokan (in Japanese).

Baba, Hisao. 1990. Ainu, Ryukyu-jin wa Jomon-jin no chokkei shison ka [Are the Ainu and Ryukyu people the direct descendants of the Jomon people?]. In *Soten Nihon no Rekishi, I: Genshi-hen [Controversies in Japanese History, vol. I: Prehistoric Periods]*, ed. Kimio Suzuki, pp. 106–123. Tokyo: Shinjinbutsu Orai-sha (in Japanese).

Baoding Diqu Wenwu Guanlisuo, Xushui Xian Wenwu Guanlisuo, Beijing Daxue Kaoguxi, Hebei Daxue Lishixi [Baoding Prefectural Administration of the Preservation of Ancient Monuments, Xushui County Administration of the Preservation of Ancient Monuments, Archaeology Department of Beijing University, and History Department of Hebei University]. 1992. Hebei Xushuixian Nanzhuangtou yizhi shijue jianbao [Trial digging at the Nanzhuangtou site in Xushui County, Hebei Province]. *Kaogu [Archaeology]* 11: 961–970 (in Chinese with English title).

Barnes, Gina L. 1993. *China, Korea and Japan: The Rise of Civilization in East Asia*. London: Thames and Hudson.

Barnes, Gina L., and Masaaki Okita. 1999. Japanese archaeology in the 1990's. *Journal of Archaeological Research* 7(4): 349–395.

Baumhoff, Martin A. 1963. Resource intensification among hunter-gatherers: acorn economies in prehistoric California. *University of California Publications in Archaeology and Ethnology* 49: 155–236.

Binford, Lewis R. 1978. *Nunamiut Ethnoarchaeology.* New York: Academic Press.

1980. Willow smoke and dogs' tails. *American Antiquity* 45(1): 4–20.

1982. The archaeology of place. *Journal of Anthropological Archaeology* 1(1): 5–31.

1983. Long-term land-use patterning: some implications for archaeology. In *Working at Archaeology*, ed. Lewis R. Binford, pp. 379–386. New York: Academic Press.

1990. Mobility, housing and environment: a comparative study. *Journal of Anthropological Research* 46(2): 119–152.

Bleed, Peter. 1989. Foreign archaeologists in Japan: strategies for exploitation. *Archaeological Review from Cambridge* 8(1): 19–27.

1992. Ready for anything: technological adaptation to ecological diversity at Yagi, an Early Jomon community in southwestern Hokkaido, Japan. In *Pacific Northeast Asia in Prehistory: Hunter-Fisher-Gatherers, Farmers, and Sociopolitical Elites*, ed. C. Melvin Aikens and Song Nai Rhee, pp. 47–52. Pullman: Washington State University Press.

Bleed, Peter, and Ann Bleed. 1981. *Animal Resources of the Yagi Community: A Theoretical Reconstruction of Early Jomon Hunting Patterns.* Technical Report, No. 81–06, Lincoln: Division of Archaeological Research, Department of Anthropology, University of Nebraska-Lincoln.

Bleed, Peter, Carl Falk, Ann Bleed, and Akira Matsui. 1989. Between the mountains and the sea: optimal hunting patterns and faunal remains at Yagi, an Early Jomon community in southwestern Hokkaido. *Arctic Anthropology* 26(2): 107–126.

Bowman, Sheridan. 1990. *Radiocarbon Dating.* Berkeley: University of California Press.

Brumfiel, Elizabeth, and Timothy K. Earle, eds. 1987a. *Specialization, Exchange and Complex Societies.* Cambridge: Cambridge University Press.

1987b. Specialization, exchange and complex societies: an introduction. In *Specialization, Exchange and Complex Societies*, ed. Elizabeth M. Brumfiel and Timothy K. Earle, pp. 1–9. Cambridge: Cambridge University Press.

Bunka-cho Bunkazai Hogo-bu Kinenbutsu-ka [Monuments and Sites Division, Japanese Agency for Cultural Affairs]. 1996. *Maizo Bunkazai Kankei Tokei Shiryo [Statistics Related to Cultural Resource Management in Japan].* Tokyo: Bunkacho Bunkazai Hogo-bu Kinenbutsu-ka.

Campbell, J. M. 1968. Territoriality among ancient hunters: interpretations from ethnography and nature. In *Anthropological Archaeology in the Americas*, ed. Betty J. Meggers, pp. 1–21. Washington, D.C.: The Anthropological Society of Washington.

Cannon, Aubrey. 1998. Contingency and agency in the growth of Northwest Coast maritime economies. *Arctic Anthropology* 35(1): 57–67.

Chang, Kwang-chih, ed. 1968. *Settlement Archaeology.* Palo Alto: National Press Books.

Chard, Chester S. 1974. *Northeast Asia in Prehistory*. Madison: University of Wisconsin Press.

Chiba-ken Bunkazai Center [Archaeological Center of Chiba Prefecture]. 2000. *Kimitsu-shi Minoh kaizuka genchi setsumei-kai shiryo [Open-House Handout, Excavation of the Minoh Shell-Midden, Kimitsu City]*. Chiba: Chiba-ken Maizo Bunkazai Center.

Chisholm, Brian S. 1985. Kodai-jin wa nani o tabete ita ka: jinkotsu no tanso doitai-hi ni yoru bunseki-ho [What did ancient people eat: stable carbon isotope analysis of human bones]. *Kagaku Asahi [Asahi Journal of Science]* November: 126–130 (in Japanese).

Chisholm, Brian S., and Hiroko Koike. 1988. Stable carbon isotopes and pale-odiet in Japan. In *Showa 63 Nendo Nihon Bunkazai Kagaku-kai Taikai Kenkyu Happyo Yoshi-shu [Abstracts of the Papers Presented at the 1988 Meeting of the Japanese Society for Scientific Studies on Cultural Properties]*, pp. 64–65. Tokyo: Nihon Bunkazai Kagaku-kai (in Japanese).

Chisholm, Brian S., Hiroko Koike, and Nobuyuki Nakai. 1988. Tanso antei doitaihi-ho ni yoru kodai shokusei no kenkyu [A study of paleodiet using stable carbon isotope analysis]. *Kokogaku to Shizen Kagaku [Archaeology and Natural Science]* 20: 7–16 (in Japanese).

1992. Carbon isotopic determination of paleodiet in Japan: marine versus ter-restrial resources. In *Pacific Northeast Asia in Prehistory*, ed. C. Melvin Aikens and Song Nai Rhee, pp. 69–73. Pullman: Washington State University Press.

Cohen, Mark N. 1981. Pacific Coast foragers: affluent or overcrowded? In *Afflu-ent Foragers: Pacific Coasts East and West*, ed. Shuzo Koyama and David H. Thomas, pp. 275–295. Senri Ethnological Studies No. 9. Osaka: National Museum of Ethnology.

Costin, Cathy L. 1991. Craft specialization: issues in defining, documenting, and explaining the organization of production. In *Archaeological Method and The-ory 3*, ed. Michael B. Schiffer, pp. 1–56. Tucson: University of Arizona Press.

Crawford, Gary W. 1983. *Paleoethnobotany of the Kameda Peninsula Jomon*. Anthropological Papers, No. 73. Ann Arbor: Museum of Anthropology, Uni-versity of Michigan.

1992a. Prehistoric plant domestication in East Asia. In *The Origins of Agricul-ture: An International Perspective*, ed. C. Wesley Cowan and Patty Jo Watson, pp. 7–38. Washington, D.C.: Smithsonian Institution Press.

1992b. The transitions to agriculture in Japan. In *Transitions to Agriculture in Prehistory*, ed. Anne Birgitte Gebauer and T. Douglas Price, pp. 117–132. Madison: Prehistory Press.

1997. Anthropogenesis in prehistoric northeastern Japan. In *People, Plants and Landscapes: Studies in Paleoethnobotany*, ed. Kristen J. Germillion, pp. 86–103. Tuscaloosa: University of Alabama Press.

Crawford, Gary W., William M. Hurley, and Masakazu Yoshizaki. 1978. Impli-cations of plant remains from the Early Jomon Hamanasuno site. *Asian Per-spectives* 19: 144–155.

D'Andrea, Catheryn A., Gary W. Crawford, Masakazu Yoshizaki, and Takehisa Kudo. 1995. Late Jomon cultigens in northeastern Japan. *Antiquity* 69: 146–152.

Doi, Takashi. 1990. Haka ni arawareta Jomon shakai no tokushitsu wa nanika [Major characteristics of the Jomon society seen from mortuary analyses]. In *Soten Nihon no Rekishi, I: Genshi-hen [Controversies in Japanese History*, vol. I: *Prehistoric Periods]*, ed. Kimio Suzuki, pp. 169–185. Tokyo: Shinjinbutsu Orai-sha (in Japanese).

Doi, Yoshio. 1985. Jomon jidai shuraku-ron no gensoku-teki mondai: shuraku iseki no futatsu no arikata ni tsuite [Fundamental problems concerning settlement theories for the Jomon period: two settlement types]. *Tokyo Koko [Tokyo Archaeology]* 3: 1–12 (in Japanese with English title).

Earle, Timothy K., and Jonathon E. Ericson. 1977. *Exchange Systems in Prehistory.* New York: Academic Press.

Emori, Susumu. 2000. Kaitaku to Ainu minzoku [Land development and the Ainu people]. *Shiroi Kuni no Uta [Essays on Northern Land]* 528: 4–13 (in Japanese).

Endo, K. 1999. Linkage in Holocene and Latest Pleistocene environmental changes. *Bulletin of the National Museum of Japanese History* 81: 143–153.

Erlandson, Jon M. 1988. Role of shellfish in prehistoric economies: a protein perspective. *American Antiquity* 53(1): 102–109.

Esaka, Teruya. 1965. Seiryuto-gata sekki ko [A study of stone objects in the shape of Chinese broadswords]. *Shigaku [Historical Studies]* 38(1): 75–102 (in Japanese with English title and summary).

Esaka, Teruya, Kenji Okamoto, and Sakae Nishida. 1967. Ehime-ken Kamikuroiwa Iwakage [Kamikuroiwa Rockshelter, Ehime Prefecture]. In *Nihon no Doketsu Iseki [Cave Sites in Japan]*, ed. Nihon Kokogaku Kyokai Doketsu Chosa Iinkai [JAA Committee on the Study of Cave Sites], pp. 224–236. Tokyo: Heibon-sha (in Japanese).

Fawcett, Clare. 1990. A study of the socio-political context of Japanese archaeology. Ph.D. Dissertation, McGill University, Montreal.

1995. Nationalism and postwar Japanese archaeology. In *Nationalism, Politics, and the Practice of Archaeology*, ed. P. L. Kohl and C. Fawcett, pp. 232–246. Cambridge: Cambridge University Press.

Feinman, Gary M. 1995. The emergence of inequality: a focus on strategies and processes. In *Foundations of Social Inequality*, ed. T. Douglas Price and Gary M. Feinman, pp. 255–279. New York: Plenum.

Fitzhugh, Ben. 2002. The origins of maritime hunter-gatherers in the North Pacific Rim: a view from Kodiak Island. In *New Perspectives on the Study of Prehistoric Hunter-Gatherer Cultures*, ed. Shiro Sasaki, pp. 49–82. Senri Ethnological Reports 33. Osaka: National Museum of Ethnology (translated into Japanese by Shiro Sasaki).

2003. The evolution of complex hunter-gatherers on the Kodiak Archipelago. In *Hunter-Gatherers of the North Pacific Rim*, ed. Junko Habu, James M. Savelle, Shuzo Koyama, and Hitomi Hongo, pp. 13–48. Senri Ethnological Studies 63. Osaka: National Museum of Ethnology.

Fitzhugh, Ben, and Junko Habu, eds. 2002a. *Beyond Foraging and Collecting: Evolutionary Change in Hunter-Gatherer Settlement Systems.* New York: Kluwer-Plenum Publishing Corporation.

2002b. Introduction to Part I: regional scale processes of settlement pattern change. In *Beyond Foraging and Collecting: Evolutionary Change in*

Hunter-Gatherer Settlement Systems, ed. Ben Fitzhugh and Junko Habu, pp. 15–17. New York: Kluwer-Plenum Publishing Corporation.

Fitzhugh, William W., and Chisato O. Dubreuil, eds. 1999. *Ainu: Spirit of a Northern People*. Washington, D. C.: Arctic Studies Center, National Museum of Natural History, Smithsonian Institution in association with the University of Washington Press.

Flannery, Kent V. 1976. *The Early Mesoamerican Village*. New York: Academic Press.

Fuji, Norio. 1984. *Koko Kafun-gaku [Archaeo-palynology]*. Tokyo: Yuzankaku (in Japanese).

Fujimori, Eiichi. 1949. Genshi yakihata rikuko no sho-mondai [On primitive swidden agriculture]. In *Yukan Shinshu [Shinshu Evening Newspaper]*. November 20, Nagano (in Japanese).

1950. Nihon genshi rikuko no sho-mondai [On primitive dry field cultivation in Japan]. *Rekishi Hyoron [Critiques in History]* 4(4): 41–46 (in Japanese).

1963. Jomon jidai noko-ron to sono tenkai [The development of hypotheses on Jomon agriculture]. *Kokogaku Kenkyu [Quarterly of Archaeological Studies]* 10(2): 21–33 (in Japanese).

1965a. Chuki Jomon bunka-ron: atarashii Jomon Chuki noko-ron no kanosei ni tsuite [A study of the Middle Jomon culture: the possibility of a new approach to Middle Jomon agriculture]. In *Idojiri [The Idojiri Site]*, ed. Eiichi Fujimori, pp. 157–160. Tokyo: Chuo Koron Bijutsu Shuppan (in Japanese with English summary).

1965b. Jomon Chuki noko kotei-ron no gen-dankai [The present stage in the development of the Middle Jomon agriculture hypothesis]. *Kodai Bunka [Cultura Antiqua]* 15(5): 111–116 (in Japanese).

ed. 1965c. *Idojiri [The Idojiri Site]*. Tokyo: Chuo Koron Bijutsu Shuppan (in Japanese with English summary).

1966. Genshi kodai shuraku no kokogaku-teki kenkyu ni tsuite [Archaeological studies of prehistoric and protohistoric settlements]. *Rekishi Kyoiku [Historical Education]* 14(3): 1–11 (in Japanese).

1970. Jomon Chuki shokubutsu saibai no kigen [The origins of Middle Jomon plant cultivation]. In *Jomon Noko [Jomon Agriculture]*, ed. Eiichi Fujimori, pp. 207–214. Tokyo: Gakusei-sha (in Japanese).

Fujimura, Haruo. 1983. Jomon doki sosei-ron [On Jomon pottery assemblages]. In *Jomon Bunka no Kenkyu V: Jomon Doki III [Studies of the Jomon Culture, vol. V: Jomon Pottery, Part III]*, ed. Shinpei Kato, Tatsuo Kobayashi, and Tsuyoshi Fujimoto, pp. 237–250. Tokyo: Yuzankaku (in Japanese).

1991. Iwate-ken Kunenbashi Iseki shutsudo dogu zanzon-bu mokuroku [Catalog of clay figurine parts recovered from the Kunenbashi site, Iwate Prefecture]. *Moegi [Journal of Keio Girls' High School]* 26 (in Japanese).

2001. Ibutsu kenkyu ni totte no shutsudo kotai-su no riyo kachi [The importance of quantitative studies in artifact analyses]. *Jomon Jidai [Journal of Jomon Period Studies]* 12: 141–150 (in Japanese).

Fujinuma, Kunihiko. 1997. *Jomon no Dogu [Jomon Clay Figurines]*. Tokyo: Kodansha (in Japanese).

Fujisawa, Sohei, and Shigeki Hayashi. 1961. Mikoshiba Iseki: dai 1 ji hakkutsu chosa gaiho [The Mikoshiba site: preliminary report of the first excavation]. *Kodaigaku [Ancient Studies]* 9(3) (in Japanese).

Fujiwara, Hiroshi. 1998. *Inasaku no Kigen o Saguru [In Pursuit of the Origin of Agriculture]*. Tokyo: Iwanami Shoten (in Japanese).

Fukui-ken Kyoiku Iinkai [Board of Education of Fukui Prefecture]. 1979. *Torihama Kaizuka: Jomon Zenki o Shu to Suru Teishicchi Iseki no Chosa I [The Torihama Shell-Midden: The Excavation of a Waterlogged Early Jomon Site*, vol. I]. Fukui: Fukui-ken Kyoiku Iinkai (in Japanese).

———. 1985. *Torihama Kaizuka: Jomon Zenki o Shu to Suru Teishicchi Iseko no Chosa V [The Torihama Shell-Midden: The Excavation of a Waterlogged Early Jomon Site*, vol. V]. Fukui: Fukui-ken Kyoiku Iinkai (in Japanese).

Funabashi-shi Kyoiku Iinkai [Board of Education of Funabashi City]. 1975. *Hazama-higashi Iseki [The Hazama-higashi Site]*. Funabashi: Funabashi-shi Kyoiku Iinkai (in Japanese).

Fureiku Dojinkai ["Flake" Association]. 1971. Mizuno Masayoshi Shi no Jomon jidai shuraku-ron hihan [Criticisms of the settlement study by Masayoshi Mizuno]. *Fureiku [Flake]* 1: 1–37 (in Japanese).

Gero, Joan, and Margaret Conkey, eds. 1991. *Engendering Archaeology*. Oxford: Basil Blackwell.

Goto, Kazuhito. 1970. Genshi shuraku kenkyu no hoho-ron josetsu [Introduction to the methodology of studies on prehistoric settlements]. *Sundai Shigaku [Sundai Journal of History]* 27: 63–124 (in Japanese).

———. 1982. Jomon shuraku no gainen [On the concept of Jomon settlements]. In *Jomon Bunka no Kenkyu VIII: Shakai, Bunka [Studies of the Jomon Culture*, vol. VIII: *Society and Culture]*, ed. Shinpei Kato, Tatsuo Kobayashi, and Tsuyoshi Fujimoto, pp. 20–48. Tokyo: Yuzankaku (in Japanese).

Goto, Shinsuke. 1999. Sekibo, sekken, sekito [Stone "clubs," stone "daggers" and stone "swords"]. *Jomon Jidai [Journal of Jomon Period Studies]* 10(4): 71–82 (in Japanese with English title).

Goto, Shuichi. 1956. Jomon jidai no seikatsu: i, shoku, ju [Life of the Jomon people: clothes, food, and houses]. In *Nihon Kokogaku Koza III [Lectures in Japanese Archaeology*, vol. III], pp. 247–288. Tokyo: Kawade Shobo (in Japanese).

Groot, Gerard J. 1951. *The Prehistory of Japan*. New York: Columbia University.

Grootes, P. M., M. Stuiver, J. W. C. White, C. Johnsen, and J. Jouzel. 1993. Comparison of oxygen isotope records from the GISP 2 and GRIP Greenland ice core. *Nature* 366: 552–554.

Habu, Junko. 1988. Numbers of pit-dwellings in Early Jomon Moroiso stage sites. *Jinruigaku Zasshi [Journal of Anthropological Society of Nippon]* 96(2): 147–165.

———. 1989a. Contemporary Japanese archaeology and society. *Archaeological Review from Cambridge* 8(1): 36–45.

———. 1989b. Jukyoshi-su kara mita iseki no kibo: Jomon jidai zenki Moroiso-shiki-ki no shiryo o mochiite [Site size and total numbers of pit-dwellings in Early Jomon Moroiso phase sites]. In *Kokogaku no Sekai [The World of Archaeology]*, ed. Keio Gijuku Daigaku Minzokugaku

Kokogaku Kenkyushitsu [Department of Ethnology and Archaeology, Keio University], pp. 71–92. Tokyo: Shin-Jinbutsu Orai Sha (in Japanese).

1993. Jomon bunka no kenkyu ni minzoku-shi wa do yakudatsu ka [Ethnographic analogy in the study of the Jomon culture]. In *Shin-shiten Nihon no Rekishi I [New Perspectives in Japanese History, vol. I]*, ed. Kimio Suzuki and Hideshi Ishikawa, pp. 140–147. Tokyo: Shin-jinbutsu Orai-sha (in Japanese).

1996. Jomon sedentism and intersite variability: collectors of the Early Jomon Moroiso phase in Japan. *Arctic Anthropology* 33(2): 38–49.

1999. Book review: Keiji Imamura (1996), *Prehistoric Japan: New Perspectives on Insular East Asia. Anthropological Science* 107(2): 195–198.

2000. Jomon-jin no teiju-do [Residential mobility of the Jomon people]. *Kodai Bunka [Cultura Antiqua]* 52(2): 29–38, 52(4): 18–29 (in Japanese with English title and summary).

2001. *Subsistence-Settlement Systems and Intersite Variability in the Moroiso Phase of the Early Jomon Period in Japan*. Ann Arbor: International Monographs in Prehistory.

2002a. Book review: M. J. Hudson (1999), *Ruins of Identity: Ethnogenesis in the Japanese Islands. Journal of East Asian Archaeology* 3(3–4): 255–258.

2002b. Jomon collectors and foragers: regional interactions and long-term changes in settlement systems among prehistoric hunter-gatherers in Japan. In *Beyond Foraging and Collecting: Evolutionary Change in Hunter-Gatherer Settlement Systems*, ed. Ben Fitzhugh and Junko Habu, pp. 53–72. New York: Kluwer-Plenum Publishing Corporation.

2002c. A life-history of the Sannai Maruyama site: changes in site function, residential mobility and cultural landscape [Sannai Maruyama iseki no life-history: iseki no kino, teijudo, bunka keikan no hensen]. In *New Perspectives on the Study of Prehistoric Hunter-Gatherer Cultures* [Senshi Shuryo-Saishu Bunka Kenkyu no Atarashii Shiya], ed. S. Sasaki, pp. 161–183. Senri Ethnological Reports 33. National Museum of Ethnology, Osaka (in Japanese).

Habu, Junko, and Clare Fawcett. 1990. Education and archaeology in Japan. In *Excluded Past: Archaeology in Education*, ed. Peter Stone and Robert MacKenzie, pp. 217–230. London: Unwin Hyman.

1999. Jomon archaeology and the representation of Japanese origins. *Antiquity* 73: 587–593.

Habu, Junko, and Ben Fitzhugh. 2002. Introduction. In *Beyond Foraging and Collecting: Evolutionary Change in Hunter-Gatherer Settlement Systems*, ed. Ben Fitzhugh and Junko Habu, pp. 1–11. New York: Kluwer-Plenum Publishing Corporation.

Habu, Junko, and Mark E. Hall. 1999. Jomon pottery production in central Japan. *Asian Perspectives* 38(1): 90–110.

2001. Jomon pottery production at Honmura-cho and Isarago sites: insights from geochemistry. *Anthropological Science* 109(2): 141–166.

Habu, Junko, Mark E. Hall, and Tadayuki Ogasawara. 2003. Pottery production and circulation at the Sannai Maruyama site, northern Japan: chemical evidence from early middle Jomon pottery. In *Hunter-Gatherers of the North Pacific Rim*, ed. Junko Habu, James M. Savelle, Shuzo Koyama, and Hitomi Hongo, pp. 199 220. Senri Ethnological Studies 63. Osaka: National Museum of Ethnology.

Habu, Junko, Minkoo Kim, Mio Katayama, and Hajime Komiya. 2001. Jomon subsistence-settlement systems at the Sannai Maruyama site. *Bulletin of the Indo-Pacific Prehistory Association* 21: 9–21.

Hachinohe-shi Hakubutsu-kan [Hachinohe City Museum]. 1988. *Jomon no Bi: Korekawa Nakai Iseki Shutsudo-hin Zuroku dai II shu [Jomon Art: Artifacts Excavated from the Korekawa Nakai Site,* vol. II*]*. Hachinohe: Hachinohe-shi Hakubutsu-kan [Hachinohe City Museum] (in Japanese).

Hall, Mark E. n.d. Pottery production during the Late Jomon period: insights from the chemical analyses of Kasori-B pottery. *Journal of Archaeological Science* (in press).

Hall, Mark E., and Hideaki Kimura. 2002. Quantitative EDXRF studies of obsidian in northern Hokkaido. *Journal of Archaeological Science* 29: 259–267.

Hanihara, Kazuro. 1986. The origin of the Japanese in relation to other ethnic groups in East Asia. In *Windows on the Japanese Past: Studies in Archaeology and Prehistory,* ed. Richard J. Pearson, Gina L. Barnes, and Karl L. Hutterer, pp. 75–84. Ann Arbor: Center for Japanese Studies, University of Michigan.

1987. Estimation of the number of early migrants to Japan: a simulative study. *Journal of the Anthropological Society of Nippon* 95(3): 391–403.

1991. Dual structure model for the population history of the Japanese. *Japan Review* 2: 1–33.

Hara, Shuzaburo. 1972. Nihon ni okeru kagaku-teki genshi, kodaishi kenkyu no seiritsu to tenkai [Establishment and development of scientific studies of prehistoric and protohistoric Japan]. In *Rekishi Kagaku Taikei I [Historical Science,* vol. I*]*, ed. Shuzaburo Hara, pp. 343–409. Tokyo: Azekura Shobo (in Japanese).

Harada, Masayuki. 1996. Ondashi iseki shutsudo-hin no imi suru mono [Implications of archaeological materials excavated from the Ondashi site]. In *Ondashi Iseki [The Ondashi Site],* ed. Yamagata Kenritsu Ukitamu Fudoki no Oka Koko Shiryo-kan [Archaeological Museum of Yamagata Prefecture], pp. 34–39. Yamagata: Yamagata Kenritsu Ukitamu Fudoki no Oka Koko Shiryo-kan (in Japanese).

Hardin, Margaret Ann. 1991. Sources of ceramic variability at Zuni Pueblo. In *Ceramic Ethnoarchaeology,* ed. William A. Longacre, pp. 40–70. Tucson: University of Arizona Press.

Harunari, Hideji. 1973. Basshi no igi (1) [The significance of tooth extraction, Part 1]. *Kokogaku Kenkyu [Quarterly of Archaeological Studies]* 20(2): 25–48 (in Japanese).

1974. Basshi no igi (2) [The significance of tooth extraction, Part 2]. *Kokogaku Kenkyu [Quarterly of Archaeological Studies]* 20(3): 41–58 (in Japanese).

1979. Jomon Banki no kongo kyoju kitei [Rules of postmarital residence in the Latest Jomon period]. *Okayama Daigaku Hobungakubu Gakujutsu Kiyo: Shigaku Hen [Transactions of the Faculty of Law and Literature, University of Okayama: History Section]* 40: 25–63 (in Japanese).

1982. Jomon Shakai Ron [On the Jomon society]. In *Jomon Bunka no Kenkyu VIII: Shakai, Bunka [Studies of the Jomon Culture*, vol. VIII: *Society and Culture and the Surrounding Environment]*, ed. Shinpei Kato, Tatsuo Kobayashi, and Tsuyoshi Fujimoto, pp. 223–252. Tokyo: Yuzankaku (in Japanese).

1986. Rules of residence in the Jomon period, based on the analysis of tooth extraction. In *Windows on the Japanese Past: Studies in Archaeology and Prehistory*, ed. Richard J. Pearson, Gina Lee Barnes, and Karl L. Hutterer, pp. 293–310. Ann Arbor: Center for Japanese Studies, University of Michigan.

1998. Mammal and human relationships at the Pleistocene–Holocene transition in Japan. In *Abstracts of Papers Presented at the Symposium on the Comparative Archaeology of the Pleistocene–Holocene Transition*, ed. Akira Ono, pp. 19–22. Sakura: National Museum of Japanese History (in English and Japanese).

2000. Kyusekki Jidai kara Jomon Jidai e [From Palaeolithic to Jomon]. In *Nihon Bunkazai Kagaku kai Dai 17-kai Taikai Kenkyu Happyo Yoshi-shu [Abstracts of the Papers Presented at the 17th Annual Meeting of the Japanese Society for Scientific Studies on Cultural Properties]*, pp. 2–3. Sakura: Nihon Bunkazai Kagaku-kai (in Japanese).

Harunari, Hideji, Shin'ichiro Fujio, Mineo Imamura, and Minoru Sakamoto. 2003. Yayoi Jidai no kaishi nendai: ^{14}C nendai no sokutei kekka ni tsuite [The beginning of the Yayoi period: results of radiocarbon dating]. In *Nihon Kokogaku Kyokai dai 68 kai Sokai Kenkyu Happyo Yoshi [Proceedings of the 68th Annual Meeting of the Japanese Archaeological Association]*, pp. 65–68. Tokyo: Nihon Kokogaku Kyokai [Japanese Archaeological Association] (in Japanese).

Hashimoto, Sumio. 1994. Kanjo mokuchuretsu to hansaichu no hakken [Discovery of wooden circles]. *Kokogaku Journal [Journal of Archaeology]* 377: 2–6 (in Japanese).

Hata, Kojiro. 1998. Sannai Maruyama iseki chosa hokoku [The 1998 excavation of Sannai Maruyama]. Paper presented at Kokusai Shuryo-saishu-min Kaigi Dai 8 kai [8th International Conference on Hunting and Gathering Societies (CHAGS 8)], Aomori (in Japanese).

Hayakawa, Izumi. 1985. Jomon jidai no marukibune [Dugout canoes from the Jomon period]. *Kikan Kokogaku [Archaeology Quarterly]* 12: 12 (in Japanese).

Hayashi, Kensaku. 1965. Jomon bunka no hatten to chiiki-sei 2: Tohoku [Development and regional diversity of the Jomon culture, Section 2: The Tohoku Region]. In *Nihon no Kokogaku II: Jomon Jidai [Japanese Archaeology*, vol. II: *The Jomon Period]*, ed. Yoshimasa Kamaki, pp. 64–96. Tokyo: Kawade Shobo (in Japanese).

1974. Jomon-ki no shudan ryoiki [Group territory during the Jomon period]. *Kokogaku Kenkyu [Quarterly of Archaeological Studies]* 20(4): 12–19 (in Japanese).

1975. Jomon-ki no shudan ryoiki: horon [Further discussion on group territory during the Jomon period]. *Kokogaku Kenkyu [Quarterly of Archaeological Studies]* 21(3): 33–40 (in Japanese).

1980. Kainohana kaizuka no shika, inoshishi itai [Reexamination of the deer and wild pig remains from the Kainohana shell mound]. *Hoppo Bunka*

Kenkyu [Bulletin of the Institute for the Study of North Eurasian Cultures, Hokkaido University] 13: 75–134 (in Japanese with English title and summary).

1986. Kamegaoka to Ongagawa [The Kamegaoka and Ongagawa cultures]. In *Iwanami Koza Nihon Kokogaku V: Bunka to Chiiki-sei [Iwanami Lectures in Japanese Archaeology, vol. V: Cultures and Regional Variability]* ed. Yoshiro Kondo and Koichi Yokoyama, pp. 93–124. Tokyo: Iwanami Shoten (in Japanese).

Hayden, Brian. 1981. Research and development in the Stone Age: technological transitions among hunter-gatherers. *Current Anthropology* 22(5): 519–548.

1990. Nimrods, piscators, pluckers, and planters: the emergence of food production. *Journal of Anthropological Archaeology* 9(1): 31–69.

1995. Pathways to power: principles for creating socioeconomic inequalities. In *Foundations of Social Inequality*, ed. T. Douglas Price and Gary M. Feinman, pp. 15–86. New York: Plenum.

Higashimura, Takenobu. 1986. *Sekki Sanchi Suitei-ho [Sourcing of Stone Tools]*. Tokyo: New Science-sha (in Japanese).

Hirabayashi, Teruo. 1957. Wappara iseki no chigaku narabini gansekigaku teki kosatsu [Geological and petrological investigation of the Wappara site]. In *Wappara Iseki [The Wappara Site]*, ed. Iwao Oba, pp. 195–212. Nagano: Nagano ken Bunkazai Hogo Kyokai (in Japanese).

Hirth, Kenneth G. 1996. Political economy and archaeology: perspectives on exchange and production. *Journal of Archaeological Research* 4(3): 203–239.

Hodder, Ian. 1981. Society, economy and culture: an ethnographic case study amongst the Lozi. In *Patterns of the Past: Studies in Honour of David Clarke*, ed. Ian Hodder, Glynn Isaac, and Norman Hammond, pp. 67–95. Cambridge: Cambridge University Press.

1991. The decoration of containers: an ethnographic and historical study. In *Ceramic Ethnoarchaeology*, ed. William A. Longacre, pp. 71–94. Tucson: University of Arizona Press.

1999. *The Archaeological Process: An Introduction*. Oxford: Blackwell Publishers.

Horiguchi, M. 1983. Saitama-ken Juno deitanso iseki no gaikyo to shizen kankyo ni kansuru 2, 3 no mondai [Summary of Juno peaty site and some problems of its natural environment]. *Daiyonki Kenkyu [Quaternary Research]* 22(3): 231 244 (in Japanese with English title and summary).

Horikoshi, Masayuki. 1972. Jomon jidai no shuraku to kyodo soshiki: Tokyo-wan engan chiiki o rei to shite [Settlements and social organization during the Jomon period, with special reference to the coastal area of Tokyo Bay]. *Sundai Shigaku [Sundai Journal of History]* 31: 1–29 (in Japanese).

1999. Jomon jidai no seien [Salt production of the Jomon period]. *Shiroi Kuni no Uta [Essays on Northern Land]* 518: 24–27 (in Japanese).

Hudson, Mark J. 1999. *Ruins of Identity: Ethnogenesis in the Japanese Islands*. Honolulu: University of Hawai'i Press.

2003. Foragers as fetish in modern Japan. In *Hunter-Gatherers of the North Pacific Rim*, ed. Junko Habu, James M. Savelle, Shuzo Koyama, and Hitomi Hongo, pp. 263–274. Senri Ethnological Studies 63. Osaka: National Museum of Ethnology.

Hudson, Mark J., and Mariko Yamagata. 1992. Introduction to Kobayashi Tatsuo's "Regional organization in the Jomon period." *Arctic Anthropology* 29(1): 82–85.

Iba, Isao, and Takahiro Iwahashi. 1992. Shiga-ken Otsu-shi Awazu-Kotei iseki [The Awazu lake-bottom site in Otsu City, Shiga Prefecture]. *Nihon Kokogaku Nenpo [Archaeologia Japonica] 43 (Annual Report of the Japanese Archaeological Studies and Excavations: Fiscal Year 1990):* 520–523 (in Japanese with English title and summary).

Iba, Isao, Akira Matsui, and Tsuneo Nakajima. 1999. The Awazu shell midden. In *Ancient Lakes: Their Cultural and Biological Diversity,* ed. G. Kawanabe, W. Coulter, and A. C. Rosevelt, pp. 135–145. Ghent, Belgium: Kenobi Productions.

Ichihara, Hisafumi. 1959. Jomon jidai no kyodotai o megutte [On the community during the Jomon period]. *Kokogaku Kenkyu [Quarterly of Archaeological Studies]* 6(1): 8–20 (in Japanese).

————— 1984. Wajima Seiichi ron [Contributions of Wajima Seiichi]. In *Jomon Bunka no Kenkyu X: Jomon Jidai Kenkyu-shi [Studies of the Jomon Culture, vol. X: History of Jomon Archaeology],* ed. Shinpei Kato, Tatsuo Kobayashi, and Tsuyoshi Fujimoto, pp. 241–252. Tokyo: Yuzankaku (in Japanese).

Ichinohe-machi Kyoiku Iinkai [Board of Education of Ichinohe Town]. 1993. *Goshono Iseki, I [The Goshono Site, vol. I].* Ichinohe: Ichinohe-machi Kyoiku Iinkai (in Japanese).

Ikawa-Smith, Fumiko. 1980. Current issues in Japanese archaeology. *American Scientist* 68: 134–145.

————— 1986. Late Pleistocene and Early Holocene technologies. In *Windows on the Japanese Past: Studies in Archaeology and Prehistory,* ed. Richard J. Pearson, Gina L. Barnes, and Karl L. Hutterer, pp. 199–218. Ann Arbor: Center for Japanese Studies, University of Michigan.

————— 1992. Kanjo dori: communal cemeteries of the Late Jomon in Hokkaido. In *Pacific Northeast Asia in Prehistory: Hunter-Fisher-Gatherers, Farmers, and Sociopolitical Elites,* ed. C. Melvin Aikens and Song Nai Rhee, pp. 83–89. Pullman: Washington State University Press.

————— 1995. The Jomon, the Ainu, and the Okinawans. In *Communicating with Japan,* ed. D. J. Dicks, pp. 43–55. Montreal: Concordia University.

————— 2000. Younger Dryas, radiocarbon calibration, and the beginning and adoption of pottery use in Eastern Asia. Paper presented at the Frywell Symposium, 65th Annual Meeting of the Society for American Archaeology, Philadelphia, April 8.

————— 2002. Gender in Japanese archaeology. In *Pursuit of Gender: Worldwide Archaeological Approaches,* ed. Sarah M. Nelson and Myriam Rosen-Ayalon, pp. 323–354. Walnut Creek: Altamira Press.

Imamura, Keiji. 1992. Jomon Zenki matsu no Kanto ni okeru jinko gensho to sore ni kanren suru shogensho [Population decrease and associated phenomena at the end of the Early Jomon period in the Kanto Region]. In *Musashino no Kokogaku: Yoshida Itaru Sensei Koki Kinen Ronbunshu [Essays in Honor of Dr. I. Yoshida's Seventieth Birthday],* edited and published by Yoshida Itaru Sensei Koki Kinen Ronbunshu Kanko kai [Editorial Committee of Essays in Honor of Dr. Yoshida's Seventieth Birthday], pp. 85–115, Tokyo (in Japanese).

1996. *Prehistoric Japan: New Perspectives on Insular East Asia.* Honolulu: University of Hawai'i Press.

Imamura, Mineo. 1999. Koseido ^{14}C nendai sokutei to kokogaku: hoho to kadai [High precision ^{14}C dating and archaeology: methods and problems]. *Gekkan Chikyu Special Issue* 26: 23–31 (in Japanese).

Imamura, Mineo, Seiichiro Tsuji, Hideji Harunari, Toyohiro Nishimoto, and Minoru Sakamoto. 1999. Jomon Jidai no koseido hennen o mezashite II: sojo o riyo shita nendai no seimitsu-ka [Towards the establishment of a Jomon chronological framework with high precision dating, part 2: the use of stratigraphic information]. In *Nihon Bunkazai Kagaku-kai dai 16 kai Taikai Kenkyu Happyo Yoshi [Abstracts of the Papers Presented at the16th Annual Meeting of the Japanese Society for Scientific Studies on Cultural Properties],* pp. 88–89. Nara: Nihon Bunkazai Kagaku-kai (in Japanese).

Inada, Takashi. 1986. Jomon bunka no keisei [The beginning of the Jomon culture]. In *Iwanami Koza Nihon Kokogaku VI: Henka to Kakki [Iwanami Lectures in Japanese Archaeology,* vol. VI: *Changes and Innovations],* ed. Yoshiro Kondo and Koichi Yokoyama, pp. 65–117. Tokyo: Iwanami Shoten (in Japanese).

2001. *Yudo suru Kyusekki-jin [Mobile Palaeolithic People].* Tokyo: Iwanami Shoten (in Japanese).

Inano, Akiko. 1983. Ganban [Stone tablets]. In *Jomon Bunka no Kenkyu IX: Jomon-jin no Seishin Bunka [Studies of the Jomon Culture,* vol. IX: *Mortuary and Ceremonial Practices],* ed. Shinpei Kato, Tatsuo Kobayashi, and Tsuyoshi Fujimoto, pp. 102–113. Tokyo: Yuzankaku (in Japanese).

Inano, Yusuke. 1983. Gangu [Stone figurines]. In *Jomon Bunka no Kenkyu IX: Jomon-jin no Seishin Bunka [Studies of the Jomon Culture,* vol. IX: *Mortuary and Ceremonial Practices],* ed. Shinpei Kato, Tatsuo Kobayashi, and Tsuyoshi Fujimoto, pp. 86–94. Tokyo: Yuzankaku (in Japanese).

1997. Ento doki ni tomonau gangu 2 [Stone figurines associated with Ento pottery, Part 2]. In *Dogu Kenkyu no Chihei: "Dogu to sono Joho" Kenkyu Ronshu (1) [New Directions in the Study of Clay Figurines: Clay Figurines and Related Information],* ed. Junki Yaegashi, pp. 401–409. Tokyo: Benseisha (in Japanese).

1999. Gangu [Stone figurines]. *Jomon Jidai [Journal of Jomon Period Studies]* 10(4): 139–146 (in Japanese with English title).

Inumaru, Yoshikazu. 1976. Watanabe Yoshimichi. In *Nihon no Rekishika [Historians of Japan],* ed. Keiji Nagahara and Masanao Shikano, pp. 275–283. Tokyo: Nihon Hyoron Sha (in Japanese).

Isarago Kaizuka Iseki Chosa-dan [Excavation Team of the Isarago Shell-Midden Site], ed. 1981. *Isarago Kaizuka Iseki [The Isarago Shell-Midden Site].* Tokyo: Isarago Kaizuka Iseki Chosa-kai [Committee for the Excavation of the Isarago Shell-Midden Site] (in Japanese).

Ishii, Hiroshi. 1977. Jomon shakai ni okeru shudan ido to shakai soshiki [Group migration and social organization in Jomon society]. In *Chosa Kenkyu Shuroku [Excavation and Research Results],* ed. Kohoku New Town Maizo

Bunkazai Chosadan [Excavation Team of Archaeological Sites in Kohoku New Town], pp. 1–42. Yokohama: Kohoku New Town Maizo Bunkazai Chosadan (in Japanese).

———. 1982. Shuraku no keizoku to ido [Settlement continuity and movement]. In *Jomon Bunka no Kenkyu VIII [Studies of the Jomon Culture VIII]*, ed. Shinpei Kato, Tatsuo Kobayashi, and Tsuyoshi Fujimoto, pp. 49–59. Tokyo: Yuzankaku (in Japanese).

Isomae, Jun'ichi, and Kazuko Saito. 1999. Ibutsu kenkyu: Ganban, doban [Stone and clay tablets]. *Jomon Jidai [Journal of Jomon Period Studies]* 10 (4): 147–155 (in Japanese with English title).

Ito, Nobuo. 1966. Jomon jidai no nuno [Textiles from the Jomon period]. *Bunka [Culture]* 30(1): 1–20 (in Japanese).

Ito, Ryuzo. 2001. Kodo ni hattatsu shita ki no Jomon bunka [Highly developed Jomon wood technology]. *Shiroi Kuni no Uta [Essays on Northern Land]* 536: 22–25 (in Japanese).

Iwabuchi, Kazuo. 2000. Yomigaeru Jomon-jin no kurashi: Tochigi-ken Fujioka Jinja iseki [Reconstructing the life of the Jomon people: excavation of the Fujioka Jinja site, Tochigi Prefecture]. *Shiroi Kuni no Uta [Essays on Northern Land]* 527: 22–25 (in Japanese).

Izawa, Kohei. 1951. Kuri tai bunka-ken [The chestnut culture zone]. In *Shinano Mainichi Shinbun (Suwa ban) [Shinano Mainichi Newspaper (Suwa Edition)]* December 12, pp. 4. Suwa (in Japanese).

Izeki, Hirotaro. 1977. Kanshinsei no kaimen hendo [Holocene sea level changes]. In *Nihon no Daiyonki Kenkyu [The Quaternary Period: Recent Studies in Japan]*, ed. Yoko Ota, Yoshiro Kato, Ryuichi Tsuchi, Kenzo Hatori, Tokihiko Matsuda, and Nobuyuki Yonekura, pp. 89–97. Tokyo: Tokyo Daigaku Shuppankai [University of Tokyo Press] (in Japanese).

Izumi, Seiichi. 1962. Genshi kyodotai-ron [The theory of primitive communities]. *Kodaishi Koza [Lectures in Ancient History]* 2: 209–239 (in Japanese).

Izumi, Takura. 1996a. Jomon doki no naritachi [Development of Jomon pottery]. In *Rekishi Hakkutsu II: Jomon Doki Shutsugen [Excavation of the Past, vol. II: Emergence of Jomon Pottery]*, ed. Takura Izumi, pp. 49–73. Tokyo: Kodansha (in Japanese).

———. 1996b. Jomon doki, bunka no tayosei [Diversity in Jomon pottery and Jomon culture]. In *Rekishi Hakkutsu II: Jomon Doki Shutsugen [Excavation of the Past, vol. II: Emergence of Jomon Pottery]*, ed. Takura Izumi, pp. 110–130. Tokyo: Kodansha (in Japanese).

Izumita, Takeshi. 1996. Nakano B iseki no kyoi [Archaeological discoveries at the Nakano B site]. In *Rekishi Hakkutsu II: Jomon Doki Shutsugen [Excavation of the Past, vol. II: Emergence of Jomon Pottery]*, ed. Takura Izumi, pp. 69–71. Tokyo: Kodansha (in Japanese).

Jiangxi Bowuguan [Kiangsi Provincial Museum]. 1976. Jiangxi Wannian Dayuan Xianrendong dongxue yizhi dierci fajue baogao [Excavation (second excavation season) of the Neolithic site of Hsien-jên-tung (Fairly Cave) at Ta-yüan in Wan-nien, Kiangsi Province]. *Wenwu [Cultural Relics]* 12: 23–35 (in Chinese with English title).

Jiangxi Sheng Wenwu Guanli Weiyuanhui [CPAM, Kiangsi Province]. 1963. Jiangxi Wannian Dayuan Xianrendong Dongxue yizhi shijue [Trial diggings at the Neolithic site of Hsien Jên Tung, Ta Yuan, Wan Nien, Kiangsi Province]. *Kaogu Xuebao [Acta Archaeologica Sinica]* 1: 1–16 (in Chinese with English title).

Jochim, Michael A., ed. 1979. *Breaking Down the System: Recent Ecological Approaches in Archaeology*. New York: Academic Press.

Jomon Mahoroba-haku Jikko Iinkai [The Jomon World '96 Committee]. 1996. *Jomon no Tobira [A Door to the Jomon Period]*. Tokyo: NHK Shuppan (in Japanese).

Kagoshima-ken Kyoiku Iinkai [Board of Education of Kagoshima Prefecture]. 1997. *Kakoinohara Iseki [The Kakoinohara Site]*. Kagoshima-ken Kyoiku Iinkai (in Japanese).

Kagoshima-shi Kyoiku Iinkai [Board of Education of Kagoshima City]. 1990. *Yokoi Takenoyama Iseki [The Yokoi Takenoyama Site]*. Kagoshima: Kagoshima-shi Kyoiku Iinkai (in Japanese).

1992. *Sojiyama Iseki [The Sojiyama Site]*. Kagoshima: Kagoshima-shi Kyoiku Iinkai (in Japanese).

Kajiwara, Hiroshi. 1995. *Kokusai Symposium Higashi Asia-Kyokuto no Doki no Kigen, Yokoshu [International Symposium on the Origins of Pottery in Eastern Asia and the Far East, Summaries]*. Sendai: Tohoku Fukushi University (in Japanese).

1998. The transitional period of Pleistocene–Holocene in Siberia and the Russian Far East in terms of the origin of pottery. In *Abstracts of Papers Presented at the Symposium on the Comparative Archaeology of the Pleistocene–Holocene Transition*, ed. Akira Ono, pp. 23–31. Sakura: National Museum of Japanese History (in English and Japanese).

Kamaki, Yoshimasa. 1965. Jomon bunka no gaikan [Overview of the Jomon culture]. In *Nihon no Kokogaku II: Jomon Jidai [Japanese Archaeology, vol. II: The Jomon Period]*, ed. Yoshimasa Kamaki, pp. 2–28. Tokyo: Kawade Shobo (in Japanese).

Kamaki, Yoshimasa, and Chosuke Serizawa. 1965. Nagasaki-ken Fukui Iwakage [Fukui Rockshelter in Nagasaki Prefecture]. *Kokogaku Shukan [Anthology of Archaeology]* 3(1): 1–14 (in Japanese).

1967. Nagasaki-ken Fukui Doketsu [Fukui Cave in Nagasaki Prefecture]. In *Nihon no Doketsu Iseki [Cave Sites in Japan]*, ed. Nihon Kokogaku Kyokai Doketsu Chosa Iinkai [JAA Special Committee for the Study of Cave Sites], pp. 254–265. Tokyo: Heibon-sha (in Japanese).

Kamikawana, A. 1970. Sites in Yamanashi Prefecture and Middle Jomon agriculture. *Asian Perspectives* 11: 53–68.

Kamiya, Shinichi. 2000. Karinba 3 [The Karinba No. 3 site]. In *Hakkutsu sareta Nihon Retto 2000 [Excavations on the Japanese Archipelago, 2000: Reports on New Archaeological Discoveries]*, ed. Bunkacho [Agency of Cultural Affairs], pp. 28–29. Tokyo: Asahi Shinbun-sha (in Japanese).

Kanabako, Fumio. 1996. Saitama-ken Akayama Jin'ya-ato iseki [The Akayama Jin'ya-ato site, Saitama Prefecture]. *Kikan Kokogaku [Archaeology Quarterly]* 55: 66–71 (in Japanese).

Kanagawa-ken Kyoiku Iinkai [Board of Education of Kanagawa Prefecture]. 1973. *Ozaki Iseki [The Ozaki Site]*. Yokohama: Kanagawa-ken Bunkazai Kyokai (in Japanese).

Kanayama, Yoshiaki. 1998. Shuraku-kan no koryu to koeki [Interaction and exchange between settlements]. *Kikan Kokogaku [Archaeology Quarterly]* 64: 59–63 (in Japanese).

Kaneko, Akihito. 1999. Ibutsu kenkyu: dogu (Tohoku Ko-Banki no dogu) [Late and Latest Jomon clay figurines of Tohoku Region]. *Jomon Jidai [Journal of Jomon Period Studies]* 10 (4): 127–132 (in Japanese with English title).

Kaneko, Hiromasa. 1965. Kaizuka to shokuryo shigen [Shell-middens and food resources]. In *Nihon no Kokogaku II: Jomon Jidai [Japanese Archaeology, vol. II: The Jomon Period]*, ed. Yoshimasa Kamaki, pp. 372–398. Tokyo: Kawade Shobo (in Japanese).

1967. Doketsu iseki shutsudo no dobutsu izontai [Faunal remains excavated from cave sites]. In *Nihon Doketsu Iseki [Cave Sites in Japan]*, ed. Nihon Kokogaku Kyokai Doketsu Iseki Chosakai Tokubetsu Iinkai [JAA Special Committee for the Study of Cave Sites], pp. 372–398. Tokyo: Heibon-sha (in Japanese).

1969. Tori to Jomon-jin no seikatsu [Birds in the lives of the Jomon people]. *Kokogaku Journal [Journal of Archaeology]* 28: 5–9 (in Japanese).

1976. Jomon iseki shutsudo no dobutsu izontai [Faunal remains excavated from Jomon sites]. *Kokogaku Note [Archaeology Notes]* 6: 1–19 (in Japanese).

1979. Jomon jidai no shuryo, gyoro [Hunting and fishing during the Jomon period]. *Rekishi Koron [History Magazine]* 39: 67–71 (in Japanese).

1982. Jomon-jin no seikatsu to dobutsu [Animals in the lives of the Jomon people]. In *Nihon no Bijutsu, No. 190: Jomon Jidai II (Chuki) [Japanese Art, No. 190: The Jomon Period, Part II (Middle Jomon)]*, ed. Takashi Doi, pp. 87–98. Tokyo: Shibundo (in Japanese).

Kaneko, Takuo. 1983. Sankaku-kei doban, Sankaku-kei sekiban [Triangular clay and stone tablets]. In *Jomon Bunka no Kenkyu IX: Jomon-jin no Seishin Bunka [Studies of the Jomon Culture, vol. IX: Mortuary and Ceremonial Practices]*, ed. Shinpei Kato, Tatsuo Kobayashi, and Tsuyoshi Fujimoto, pp. 114–127. Tokyo: Yuzankaku (in Japanese).

Karabanov, E., A. Prokopenko, D. Williams, and G. Khursevich. 2000. A new record of Holocene climate change from the bottom sediments of Lake Baikal. *Palaeogeography, Palaeoclimatology, Palaeoecology* 156(3–4): 211–224.

Kasai, Tsutomu. 1983. Tohoku hokubu ni okeru Jomon jidai no kaiso-bo [Secondary burials from the Jomon period in northern Tohoku]. *Kikan Kokogaku [Archaeology Quarterly]* 2: 5 (in Japanese).

Kasai, Tsutomu, and Jun Takahashi, eds. 1981. *Hiraka-machi Horiai I-go Iseki Hakkutsu chosa Hokoku-sho [Excavation Report of the Horiai I Site, Hiraka Town]*. Hiraka: Hiraka-machi Kyoiku Iinkai [Board of Education of Hiraka Town] (in Japanese).

Kaseda-shi Kyoiku Iinkai [Board of Education of Kaseda City]. 1998. *Kakoino-hara Iseki: Dai I Bunsatsu (Kyusekki Jidai, Jomon Jidai Sosoki) [The Kakoino-hara Site, vol. I: The Palaeolithic and Jomon Periods]*. Kaseda: Kaseda-shi Kyoiku Iinkai (in Japanese).

Kataoka, Yumi. 1983. Kaiwa [Shell bracelets]. In *Jomon Bunka no Kenkyu IX: Jomon-jin no Seishin Bunka [Studies of the Jomon Culture*, vol. IX: *Mortuary and Ceremonial Practices]*, ed. Shinpei Kato, Tatsuo Kobayashi, and Tsuyoshi Fujimoto, pp. 231–241. Tokyo: Yuzankaku (in Japanese).

Kato, Michio. 1994. Ishikawa-ken Noto-machi Mawaki iseki [The Mawaki site, Noto town, Ishikawa Prefecture]. *Kokogaku Journal [Journal of Archaeology]* 377: 18–24 (in Japanese).

Katsuragi, Kazuho. 2000. Kanjo haiseki-bo [Circular stone burials]. In *Sannai Maruyama Iseki XIV [The Sannai Maruyama Site*, vol. XIV], ed. Aomori-ken Kyoiku-cho Bunka-ka [Cultural Affairs Section of the Agency of Education of Aomori Prefecture], p. 9. Aomori: Aomori-ken Kyoiku Iinkai [Board of Education of Aomori Prefecture] (in Japanese).

Kawaguchi, Sadanori. 1982. Jomon Sosoki no chozoketsu: Kagoshima-ken Higashi-kurotsuchida Iseki [Incipient Jomon storage pit recovered from the Higashi-kurotsuchida site, Kagoshima Prefecture]. *Kikan Kokogaku [Archaeology Quarterly]* 1: 63 (in Japanese).

Kawaguchi-shi Iseki Chosakai [Excavation Team of Kawaguchi City]. 1989. *Akayama [The Akayama Site].* Kawaguchi: Kawaguchi-shi Kyoiku Iinkai [Board of Education of Kawaguchi City] (in Japanese).

Kawasaki, Suminori. 1983. Seien [Salt production]. *Kikan Kokogaku [Archaeology Quarterly]* 1: 44–46 (in Japanese).

Keally, Charles T. 1971. Setorumento akeoroji [Settlement archaeology]. *Shinano* 23(2): 200–209 (in Japanese).

Keally, Charles T., and Yasuhiro Muto. 1982. Jomon jidai no nendai [Dating of the Jomon period]. In *Jomon Bunka no Kenkyu I: Jomon-jin to sono Kankyo [Studies of the Jomon Culture*, vol. I: *The Jomon People and the Surrounding Environment]*, ed. Shinpei Kato, Tatsuo Kobayashi, and Tsuyoshi Fujimoto, pp. 246–275. Tokyo: Yuzankaku (in Japanese).

Kelly, Robert L. 1983. Hunter-gatherer mobility strategies. *Journal of Anthropological Research* 39(3): 277–306.

Kenjo, Toshiko. 1983. Shikko [Lacquerware technology]. In *Jomon Bunka no Kenkyu VII: Dogu to Gijutsu [Studies of the Jomon Culture*, vol. VII: *Tools and Technology]*, ed. Shinpei Kato, Tatsuo Kobayashi, and Tsuyoshi Fujimoto, pp. 285–292. Tokyo: Yuzankaku (in Japanese).

Kidder, Edward J. 1968. *Prehistoric Japanese Arts: Jomon Pottery.* Palo Alto: Kodansha International.

1993. The earliest societies in Japan. In *Cambridge History of Japan*, vol. I: *Ancient Japan*, ed. Delmer Brown, pp. 48–107. Cambridge: Cambridge University Press.

Kikuchi, Minoru. 1983. Kamekan-so [Jar burials]. In *Jomon Bunka no Kenkyu IX: Jomon-jin no Seishin Bunka [Studies of the Jomon Culture*, vol. IX: *Mortuary and Ceremonial Practices]*, ed. Shinpei Kato, Tatsuo Kobayashi, and Tsuyoshi Fujimoto, pp. 57–71. Tokyo: Yuzankaku (in Japanese).

Kim, Minkoo. 2001. Making sense of small seeds: cultural complexity of Jomon hunter-gatherers and changes in plant exploitation at Sannai Maruyama. Unpublished manuscript submitted to the Department of Anthropology, University of California at Berkeley. Berkeley.

Kimura, Moto'o. 1968. Evolutionary rate at the molecular level. *Nature* 217: 624–626.

Kishinoue, K. 1911. Prehistoric fishing in Japan. *Tokyo Teikoku Daigaku Noka Kiyo [Journal of College of Agriculture]* 2(7): 327–382.

Kitakami-shi Kyoiku Iinkai [Board of Education of Kitakami City]. 1977. *Kunenbashi Iseki Dai 3-ji Chosa Hokoku-sho [Report of the 3rd Excavation of the Kunenbashi Site]*. Kitakami: Kitakami-shi Kyoiku Iinkai (in Japanese).

——— 1978. *Kunenbashi Iseki Dai 4-ji Chosa Hokoku-sho [Report of the 4th Excavation of the Kunenbashi Site]*. Kitakami: Kitakami-shi Kyoiku Iinkai (in Japanese).

——— 1979. *Kunenbashi Iseki Dai 5-ji Chosa Hokoku-sho [Report of the 5th Excavation of the Kunenbashi Site]*. Kitakami: Kitakami-shi Kyoiku Iinkai (in Japanese).

——— 1980. *Kunenbashi Iseki Dai 6-ji Chosa Hokoku-sho [Report of the 6th Excavation of the Kunenbashi Site]*. Kitakami: Kitakami-shi Kyoiku Iinkai (in Japanese).

——— 1984. *Kunenbashi Iseki Dai 7-ji Chosa Hokoku-sho [Report of the 7th Excavation of the Kunenbashi Site]*. Kitakami: Kitakami-shi Kyoiku Iinkai (in Japanese).

——— 1985. *Kunenbashi Iseki Dai 8-ji Chosa Hokoku-sho [Report of the 8th Excavation of the Kunenbashi Site]*. Kitakami: Kitakami-shi Kyoiku Iinkai (in Japanese).

——— 1986. *Kunenbashi Iseki Dai 9-ji Chosa Hokoku-sho [Report of the 9th Excavation of the Kunenbashi Site]*. Kitakami: Kitakami-shi Kyoiku Iinkai (in Japanese).

——— 1987. *Kunenbashi Iseki Dai 10-ji Chosa Hokoku-sho [Report of the 10th Excavation of the Kunenbashi Site]*. Kitakami: Kitakami-shi Kyoiku Iinkai (in Japanese).

——— 1988. *Kunenbashi Iseki Dai 11-ji Chosa Hokoku-sho [Report of the 11th Excavation of the Kunenbashi Site]*. Kitakami: Kitakami-shi Kyoiku Iinkai (in Japanese).

——— 1991. *Kunenbashi Iseki Dai 10-ji Chosa Hokoku-sho (Hoi) [Report of the 10th Excavation of the Kunenbashi Site (Supplement)]*. Kitakami: Kitakami-shi Kyoiku Iinkai (in Japanese).

Kita-ku Kyoiku Iinkai [Board of Education of Kitakami City]. 1997. *Nakazato Kaizuka: Hakkutsu Chosa Gaiho [The Nakazato Shell-Midden: Preliminary Excavation Report]*. Tokyo: Kita-ku Kyoiku Iinkai (in Japanese).

——— 2000. *Nakazato Kaizuka [The Nakazato Shell-Midden]*. Tokyo: Kita-ku Kyoiku Iinkai (in Japanese).

Kiyokawa, Shigeto. 2000. Sannai Maruyama iseki kara shutsudo shita kurumi no idenshi kogaku-teki kenkyu [Analysis of walnut remains excavated from the Sannai Maruyama site from a perspective of genetic engineering]. In *Heisei 11 nendo Sannai Maruyama Iseki Hakkutsu Chosa Hokokukai, oyobi Tokubetsu Kenkyu Suishin Jigyo Hokoku-kai [Reports of Excavations of the Sannai Maruyama Site and Results of Studies on Sannai Maruyama Funded by the Prefectural Government, Fiscal Year 1999]*, pp. 5–8. Aomori Prefecture: Aomori-ken Kyoiku Iinkai [Board of Education of Aomori Prefecture] (in Japanese).

Kiyono, Kenji. 1949. *Kodai Jinkotsu no Kenkyu ni motozuku Nihon Jinshu Ron [A Theory on Japanese Race Based on Analysis of Skeletal Remains]*. Tokyo: Iwanami Shoten (in Japanese).

Kobayashi, Kazuhiko. 1995. Jomon jidai no shikko [Jomon lacquer technology]. *Kikan Kokogaku [Archaeology Quarterly]* 50: 31–36 (in Japanese).

Kobayashi, Ken'ichi, Mineo Imamura, Toyohiro Nishimoto, and Minoru Sakamoto. 2003. AMS ^{14}C nendai ni yoru Jomon Chuki doki, shuraku kenkyu [Studies of Middle Jomon pottery and settlements using AMS ^{14}C dates]. In *Nihon Kokogaku Kyokai dai 68 kai Sokai Kenkyu Happyo*

Yoshi [Proceedings of the 68th Annual Meeting of the Japanese Archaeological Association], pp. 49–52. Tokyo: Nihon Kokogaku Kyokai [Japanese Archaeological Association] (in Japanese).

Kobayashi, Masashi. 1994. Use-alteration analysis of Kalinga pottery: interior carbon deposits of cooking pots. In *Kalinga Ethnoarchaeology*, ed. William A. Longacre and James M. Skibo, pp. 127–168. Washington, D.C.: Smithsonian Institution.

——— 1997. Senshi jidai, Kodai ni okeru doki ni yoru nitaki hoho [Prehistoric and protohistoric cooking methods using pottery]. *Gekkan Bunkazai [Monthly Journal of Cultural Property]* October: 39–45 (in Japanese).

Kobayashi, Tatsuo. 1973. Tama New Town no senju-sha: shu to shite Jomon jidai no settlement system ni tsuite [Previous inhabitants of the Tama New Town area: settlement systems during the Jomon period]. *Gekkan Bunkazai [Monthly Journal of Cultural Property]* 112: 20–26 (in Japanese).

——— 1977a. Jomon sekai no shakai to bunka [Jomon society and culture]. In *Nihon Genshi Bijutsu Taikei [Archaeological Treasures of Japan: Jomon Pottery]*, by Tatsuo Kobayashi, pp. 156–159. Tokyo: Kodansha (in Japanese).

——— 1977b. *Nihon Genshi Bijutsu Taikei [Archaeological Treasures of Japan: Jomon Pottery]*. Tokyo: Kodansha (in Japanese).

——— 1977c. *Nihon Toji Zenshu III: Dogu, Haniwa [Japanese Ceramics, vol. III: Clay Figurines and Haniwa]*. Tokyo: Kodansha (in Japanese).

——— 1979. Jomon doki [Jomon pottery]. In *Nihon no Genshi Bijutsu I: Jomon Doki I [Ancient Art of Japan, vol. I: Jomon Pottery I]*. Tokyo: Kodansha (in Japanese).

——— 1980. Jomon jidai no shuraku [Settlements during the Jomon period]. *Kokushigaku [Japanese History]* 110: 1–17 (in Japanese).

——— 1986. Genshi shuraku [Prehistoric settlements]. In *Iwanami Koza Nihon no Kokogaku IV: Shuraku to Saishi [Iwanami Lectures in Japanese History, vol. IV: Settlements and Religion]*, ed. Yoshiro Kondo and K. Yokoyama, pp. 37–75. Tokyo: Iwanami Shoten (in Japanese).

——— 1992a. Regional organization in the Jomon period. *Arctic Anthropology* 29(1): 82–95.

——— 1992b. Patterns and levels of social complexity in Jomon Japan. In *Pacific Northeast Asia in Prehistory: Hunter-Fisher-Gatherers, Farmers, and Sociopolitical Elites*, ed. C. Melvin Aikens and Song Nai Rhee, pp. 91–96. Pullman: Washington State University Press.

——— 1994. *Jomon Doki no Kenkyu [A Study of Jomon Pottery]*. Tokyo: Shogaku-kan (in Japanese).

——— 1996a. *Jomon-jin no Sekai [The World of the Jomon People]*. Tokyo: Asahi Shinbun-sha (in Japanese).

——— 1996b. Nishida. In *Ancient Japan*, ed. Richard J. Pearson, pp. 89–91. Washington, D.C.: M. Sackler Gallery, Smithsonian Institution.

——— 2000. *Jomon-jin Tsuiseki [In Pursuit of the Jomon People]*. Tokyo: Nihon Keizai Shinbun-sha (in Japanese).

Kobayashi, Tatsuo, Masaru Aso, Tozo Okamoto, Shinpei Kato, Koichi Nagamine, and Kensaku Hayashi. 1980. Zadankai Jomon doki no kigen [Discussion: the origin of Jomon pottery]. *Kokugakuin Zasshi [Journal of Kokugakuin University]* 81(1): 19–63 (in Japanese).

Kobayashi, Tatsuo, Fujio Fujita, Yasutoki Togashi, Toyohiro Nishimoto, Hideji Harunari, Akira Matsui, and Masahisa Yamada. 1998. *Symposium Nihon no Kokogaku II: Jomon Jidai no Kokogaku [Symposium on Japanese Archaeology,* vol. II: *Jomon Archaeology]*. Tokyo: Gakusei-sha (in Japanese).

Kobayashi, Yukio. 1951. *Nihon Kokogaku Gaisetsu [Overview of Japanese Archaeology]*. Tokyo: Tokyo Sogensha (in Japanese).

——— 1959. Gyobutsu Sekki [*Gyobutsu*-stone bars]. In *Zukai Kokogaku Jiten [Illustrated Dictionary of Japanese Archaeology]*, p. 245. Tokyo: Tokyo Sogensha (in Japanese).

Kodama, Daisei. 2003. Komakino stone circle and its significance for the study of Jomon social structure. In *Hunter-Gatherers of the North Pacific Rim*, ed. Junko Habu, James M. Savelle, Shuzo Koyama, and Hitomi Hongo, pp. 235–261. Senri Ethnological Studies 63. Osaka: National Museum of Ethnology.

Koganei-shi Kyoiku Iinkai [Board of Education of Koganei City]. 1974. *Nukui-minami [The Nikui-minami Site]*. Koganei: Koganei-shi Kyoiku Iinkai (in Japanese).

Kohl, Philip L., and Clare Fawcett. 1995a. Archaeology in the service of the state: theoretical considerations. In *Nationalism, Politics, and the Practice of Archaeology*, ed. Philip L. Kohl and Clare Fawcett, pp. 3–18. Cambridge: Cambridge University Press.

——— eds. 1995b. *Nationalism, Politics, and the Practice of Archaeology*. Cambridge: Cambridge University Press.

Kohoku New Town Maizo Bunkazai Chosa-dan [Excavation Team of the Kohoku New Town Area], ed. 1985. *Sannomaru Iseki Chosa Gaiho [Preliminary Report of the Sannomaru Site]*. Yokohama: Yokohama-shi Maizo Bunkazai Chosa Iinkai [Archaeological Committee of Yokohama City] (in Japanese).

——— ed. 1986. *Kodai no Yokohama [Ancient Yokohama]*. Yokohama: Yokohama-shi Kyoiku Iinkai [Board of Education of Yokohama City] (in Japanese).

Koike, Hiroko. 1973. Daily growth lines of the clam, *Meretrix lusoria*. *Jinruigaku Zasshi [Journal of the Anthropological Society of Nippon]* 81(2): 122–138.

——— 1979. Kanto chiho no kaizuka iseki ni okeru kairui saishu no kisetsu-sei to kaiso no taiseki sokudo [Seasonality of shell collecting activity and accumulation speed of shell-midden sites in Kanto, Japan]. *Daiyonki Kenkyu [Quaternary Research]* 17(4): 267–278 (in Japanese with English title and summary).

——— 1980. *Seasonal Dating by Growth-line Counting of the Clam*, Meretrix lusoria: *Toward a Reconstruction of Prehistoric Shell-Collecting Activities in Japan*. Tokyo: University of Tokyo Press.

——— 1981. Kairui no bunseki [Analysis of shellfish remains]. In *Isarago Kaizuka Iseki [The Isarago Shell-Midden Site]*, ed. Minato-ku Isarago Kaizuka Iseki Chosa-dan [Excavation Team of the Isarago Shell-Midden Site], pp. 607–615. Tokyo: Minato-ku Isarago Kaizuka Iseki Chosa-kai [Committee for the Excavation of the Isarago Shell-Midden Site] (in Japanese).

——— 1983. Kairui bunseki [Analysis of shellfish remains]. In *Jomon bunka no Kenkyu II: Seigyo [Studies of the Jomon Culture, vol. II: Subsistence]*, ed. Shinpei Kato, Tatsuo Kobayashi, and Tsuyoshi Fujimoto, pp. 221–237. Tokyo: Yuzankaku (in Japanese).

——— 1986a. Jomon shell mounds and growth-line analysis of molluscan shells. In *Windows on the Japanese Past: Studies in Archaeology and Prehistory*, ed. R. J.

Pearson, G. L. Barnes, and K. L. Hutterer, pp. 267–278. Ann Arbor: Center for Japanese Studies, University of Michigan.

1986b. Prehistoric hunting pressure and paleobiomass: an environmental reconstruction and archaeozoological analysis of a Jomon shellmidden area. In *Prehistoric Hunter-Gatherers in Japan*, ed. Takeru Akazawa and C. Melvin Aikens, pp. 27–53. Tokyo: University of Tokyo Press.

1992. Exploitation dynamics during the Jomon period. In *Pacific Northeast Asia in Prehistory Hunter-Fisher-Gatherers, Farmers, and Sociopolitical Elites*, ed. C. Melvin Aikens and Song Nai Rhee, pp. 53–67. Pullman: Washington State University Press.

Koike, Hiroko, and Brian S. Chisholm. 1988. Tanso antei doitai-ho ni yoru Nihon-san honyu dobutsu no shokusei bunseki-ho no kento [An application of stable-carbon isotopic ratios for the diet analysis of wild mammals]. *Saitama Daigaku Kiyo (Sogo-hen) [The Bulletin of the University of Saitama]* 6: 107–115 (in Japanese with English title and summary).

Koizumi, Kiyotaka. 1985. Kojinko-ron [Palaeodemography]. In *Iwanami Koza Nihon no Kokogaku, II: Ningen to Kankyo [Iwanami Lectures in Japanese Archaeology*, vol. II: *People and Natural Environment]*, ed. Yoshiro Kondo and Koichi Yokoyama, pp. 213–245. Tokyo: Iwanami Shoten (in Japanese).

Kojima, Toshiaki. 1983a. Sankaku-to-gata doseihin [Triangular-prism-shaped clay artifacts]. In *Jomon Bunka no Kenkyu IX: Jomon-jin no Seishin Bunka [Studies of the Jomon Culture*, vol. IX: *Mortuary and Ceremonial Practices]*, ed. Shinpei Kato, Tatsuo Kobayashi, and Tsuyoshi Fujimoto, pp. 128–140. Tokyo: Yuzankaku (in Japanese).

1983b. Yuko kyujo doseihin [Ball-shaped and perforated clay artifacts]. In *Jomon Bunka no Kenkyu IX: Jomon-jin no Seishin Bunka [Studies of the Jomon Culture*, vol. IX: *Mortuary and Ceremonial Practices]*, ed. Shinpei Kato, Tatsuo Kobayashi, and Tsuyoshi Fujimoto, pp. 141–148. Tokyo: Yuzankaku (in Japanese).

Kojo, Yasushi. 1981. Inter-site pottery movements in the Jomon period. *Journal of the Anthropological Society of Nippon* 89: 85–97.

Kokuritsu Rekishi Minzoku Hakubutsu-kan [National Museum of Japanese History]. 1992. *Dogu to Sono Joho [Clay Figurines ("Dogu") and Related Information]*. Kokuritsu Rekishi Minzoku Hakubutsu-kan Kenkyu Hokoku [Bulletin of the National Museum of Japanese History], vol. 37. Sakura: Kokuritsu Rekishi Minzoku Hakubutsu-kan (in Japanese with English title).

Komiya, Hajime. 1976. Yokohama-shi Kikuna kaizuka saishu no gyokairui izontai [Fish remains from the Kikuna shell-midden site, Yokohama, Japan]. *Shigaku [Historical Studies]* 47(4): 335–357 (in Japanese with English title).

1980. Tsuchiura-shi Kamitakatsu kaizuka sanshutsu gyokairui no dotei to kosatsu [Identification and consideration of shells and fish remains from Kamitakatsu shell mound, Tsuchiura City]. *Daiyonki Kenkyu [Quaternary Research]* 19(4): 281–227 (in Japanese with English title and summary).

1981. Kaizuka-san gyokairui no kaiseki to kadai [Analysis of fish and shellfish remains from shell-middens and its future research directions]. *Chiba-ken Bunkazai Center Kenkyu Kiyo [Bulletin of the Archaeological Center of Chiba Prefecture]* 6: 215–227 (in Japanese).

1983. Gyorui [Fish]. In *Jomon Bunka no Kenkyu II: Seigyo [Studies of the Jomon Culture*, vol. II: *Subsistence]*, ed. Shinpei Kato, Tatsuo Kobayashi, and Tsuyoshi Fujimoto, pp. 194–210. Tokyo: Yuzankaku (in Japanese).

Komiya, Hajime, and Kimio Suzuki. 1977. Kaizuka-san gyorui no taicho sosei fukugen ni okeru hyohon saishu ho no eikyo ni tsuite: toku ni kurodai no taicho sosei ni tsuite [The influence of sampling method on the restoration of body size comparison of prehistoric shell-midden fish; with the special reference to *Acanthopagrus schlegeli* (black sea bream)]. *Daiyonki Kenkyu [Quaternary Research]* 16(2): 71–75 (in Japanese with English title and summary).

Kondo, Naoyoshi, *et al.* 1992. Shimomouchi Iseki I, II bunka-so no hennen-teki ichi ni kakawaru sho-mondai [Chronological placement of cultural layers I and II at the Shimomouchi site]. In *Joshin'etsu Jidosha-do Maizo Bunkazai Hakkutsu Chosa Hokoku-sho I: Shimomouchi (Simomouti) Iseki [Excavation of Archaeological Sites prior to the Construction of Joshin'etsu Expressway*, vol. I: *The Shimomouchi Site]*, ed. Naoyoshi Kondo and Hideyuki Kobayashi, pp. 235–241. Nagano: Nagano-ken Kyoiku Iinkai [Board of Education of Nagano Prefecture] (in Japanese).

Kondo, Yoshiro. 1984. *Doki Seien no Kenkyu [A Study of Salt Production Method Using Pottery]*. Tokyo: Aoki Shoten (in Japanese with English title and summary).

Kono, Isamu. 1929. *Mikai-jin no shintai soshoku [Body Decoration among Native People]*. Tokyo: Shizengakkai Pamphlet (in Japanese).

1953. *Jomon Doki no Hanashi [A Study of Jomon Pottery]*. Tokyo: Sekai-sha (in Japanese).

Kotani, Yoshinobu. 1972a. Economic bases during the Later Jomon periods in Kyushu, Japan: a reconsideration. Ph.D. dissertation, University of Wisconsin.

1972b. Jomon jidai Banki no shokubutsu riyo no kenkyu: Uenoharu iseki no shokubutsu-sei ibutsu ni tsuite [A study of plant utilization during the Final Jomon period: plant remains from the Uenoharu site]. *Minzokugaku Kenkyu [Japanese Journal of Ethnology]* 36(4): 312–313 (in Japanese).

1972c. Implications of cereal grains from Uenoharu, Kumamoto. *Jinruigaku Zasshi [Journal of the Anthropological Society of Nippon]* 80(2): 159–162.

1981. Evidence of plant cultivation in Jomon Japan: some implications. In *Affluent Foragers, Pacific Coasts East and West*, ed. Shuzo Koyama and David H. Thomas, pp. 201–212. Osaka: National Museum of Ethnology.

Koyama, Shuzo. 1978. Jomon subsistence and population. *Senri Ethnological Studies* 2: 1–65.

1984. *Jomon Jidai [The Jomon Period]*. Tokyo: Chuo Koron-sha (in Japanese).

1995. Hanayaka narishi "Kita no Taikoku" [Flourish of a sophisticated northern culture]. In *Jomon Bunmei no Hakken: Kyoi no Sannai Maruyama Iseki [Discovery of the Jomon Civilization: New Findings at the Sannai Maruyama Site]*, ed. Takeshi Umehara and Yoshinori Yasuda, pp. 50–77. Tokyo: PHP Kenkyu-jo (in Japanese).

Koyama, Shuzo, and Yasuhiro Okada, eds. 1996. *Jomon Teidan: Sannai Maruyama no Sekai [Discussion on the Jomon Period: The World of the Sannai Maruyama]*. Yamakawa Shuppan, Tokyo (in Japanese).

Koyama, Shuzo and David H. Thomas, eds. 1981. *Affluent Foragers: Pacific Coasts East and West.* Senri Ethnological Studies No. 9. Osaka: National Museum of Ethnology.

Kuraishi-Mura Kyoiku Iinkai [Board of Education of Kuraishi Village]. 1997. *Yakushimae Iseki [The Yakushimae Site].* Aomori: Kuraishi-Mura Kyoiku Iinkai (in Japanese).

Kurishima, Yoshiaki. 1985. Kogyoku-sei taiju no kodai na bunpu-ken [Wide distribution area of large jade pendants]. *Kikan Kokogaku [Archaeology Quarterly]* 12: 39–42 (in Japanese).

Kuro'o, Kazuhisa. 1988. Jomon jidai Chuki no kyoju keitai [Settlement system during the Middle Jomon period]. *Rekishi Hyoron [Critiques in History]* 454: 9–21 (in Japanese).

Kusumoto, Masasuke. 1976. *Jomon-jin no Chie ni Idomu [Jomon Experimental Archaeology].* Tokyo: Chikuma Shobo (in Japanese).

Kuzmin, Yaroslav V., A. J. T. Jull, Zoya S. Lapshina, and Vitaly E. Medvedev. 1997. Radiocarbon AMS dating of the ancient sites with earliest pottery from the Russian Far East. *Nuclear Instruments and Methods in Physics Research B* 123: 496–497.

Kuzmin, Yaroslav V., and Charles T. Keally. 2001. Radiocarbon chronology of the earliest Neolithic sites in East Asia. *Radiocarbon* 43(2B): 1121–1128.

Lightfoot, Kent. 1993. Long-term developments in complex hunter-gatherer societies: recent perspectives from the Pacific Coast of North America. *Journal of Archaeological Research* 1(3): 167–201.

Longacre, William A., and James M. Skibo, eds. 1994. *Kalinga Ethnoarchaeology.* Washington: Smithsonian Institution Press.

McGuire, Randall H. 1983. Breaking down cultural complexity: inequality and heterogeneity. In *Advances in Archaeological Method and Theory*, vol. 8, ed. M. B. Schiffer, pp. 91–142. New York: Academic Press.

1992. *Death, Society, and Ideology in a Hohokam Community.* Boulder: Westview Press.

Mathiassen, Therkel. 1927. *Archaeology of the Central Eskimos.* Copenhagen: Gyldendal.

Matsui, Akira. 1985. "Sake/masu" ron no hyoka to kongo no tenbo [Controversy over salmon fishing: future perspectives]. *Kokogaku Kenkyu [Quarterly of Archaeological Studies]* 31(4): 39–67 (in Japanese).

1992. Wetland sites in Japan. In *The Wetland Revolution in Prehistory*, ed. Bryony Coles, pp. 5–14. WARP (Wet Land Archaeology Research Project) Occasional Paper 6. Exeter: WARP and the Prehistoric Society.

1995. Postglacial hunter-gatherers in the Japanese Archipelago: maritime adaptations. In *Man and Sea in the Mesolithic: Coastal Settlement above and below Present Sea Level*, ed. Anders Fischer, pp. 327–334. Oxford: Oxbow Books.

1996. Archaeological investigations of anadromous salmonoid fishing in Japan. *World Archaeology* 27(3): 444–460.

Matsumoto, Naoko. 1996a. Shuryo, gyoro to saishu no seikatsu: Jomon jidai [Hunting, fishing and gathering way of life: the Jomon period]. In *Ogo'ori shishi I [History of Ogo'ori City]*, vol. 1], pp. 193–267. Ogo'ori: Ogo'ori-shi [Ogo'ori City] (in Japanese).

1996b. Ninchi kokogaku-teki shiten kara mita doki yoshiki no kukan-teki hen'i: Jomon jidai banki kokushoku maken doki yoshiki o sozai to shite [A spatial variation in the color and thickness of prehistoric Jomon pottery of Japan: a case study of cognitive archaeology]. *Kokogaku Kenkyu [Quarterly of Archaeological Studies]* 42(4): 61–84 (in Japanese with English title).

Matsumoto, Nobuhiro, Ryosaku Fujita, Junzo Shimizu, and Teruya Esaka. 1952. *Kamo Iseki [Kamo: A Study of the Neolithic Site and a Neolithic Dug-out Canoe Discovered in Kamo, Chiba Prefecture, Japan].* Tokyo: Mita Shigakukai [Mita Historical Association] (in Japanese with English title and summary).

Matsushima, Yoshiaki. 1979. Minami Kanto ni okeru Jomon kaishin ni tomonau kairui gunshu no hensen [Littoral molluscan assemblages during the postglacial Jomon transgression in the southern Kanto, Japan]. *Daiyonki Kenkyu [Quaternary Research]* 17(4): 243–265 (in Japanese with English title and summary).

Matsushima, Yoshiaki, and Hiroko Koike. 1979. Shizen kaiso ni yoru naiwan no kankyo fukugen to Jomon jidai no iseki [Reconstruction of the littoral environment using the result of natural shell deposit analysis, with special reference to the distribution of Jomon sites]. *Kaizuka [Shell-Midden]* 22: 1–9 (in Japanese).

Matsushita, Wataru. 1982. Kohaku [Amber]. In *Jomon Bunka no Kenkyu VIII: Shakai, Bunka [Studies of the Jomon Culture, vol. VIII: Society and Culture],* ed. Shinpei Kato, Tatsuo Kobayashi, and Tsuyoshi Fujimoto, pp. 193–204. Tokyo: Yuzankaku (in Japanese).

Matsutani, Akiko. 1981a. Kaizo to tankazo ni yoru Jomon jidai no sakumotsu saibai no tankyu [A study of Jomon plant cultivation using spodographic and charcoal analysis]. *Kokogaku Journal [Journal of Archaeology]* 192: 18–21 (in Japanese).

1981b. Nagano-ken Suwa-gun Hara-mura Oishi iseki de shutsudo no tar jo tanka shushi no dotei ni tsuite [The identification of tar-like carbonized seeds excavated from the Oishi site in Hara Village, Suwa County, Nagano Prefecture]. In *Nagano-ken Chuodo Maizo Bunkazai Hozochi Hakkutsu Chosa Hokoku-sho: Hara-mura, sono 1 [Excavation Report of Chuo Highway Corridor Sites in Nagano Prefecture: Hara Village, Part 1],* pp. 141–143. Nagano: Nagano-ken Kyoiku Iinkai [Board of Education of Nagano Prefecture] (in Japanese).

1983. Egoma, shiso [Egoma and shiso mint]. In *Jomon Bunka no Kenkyu II: Seigyo [Studies of the Jomon Culture, vol. II: Subsistence],* ed. Shinpei Kato, Tatsuo Kobayashi, and Tsuyoshi Fujimoto, pp. 50–52. Tokyo: Yuzankaku (in Japanese).

1984. Sosa denken zo ni yoru tanka shushi no shikibetsu [Identification of carbonized seeds using SEM]. In *Kobunkazai no Shizen Kagaku-teki Kenkyu [Scientific Approaches to the Study of Cultural Property],* ed. Kobunkazai Henshu Iinkai [Editorial Committee of "Kobunkazai"], pp. 630–637. Tokyo: Nihon Gakujutsu Shinko-kai [Japan Society for the Promotion of Science] (in Japanese).

1988. Denshi kenbikyo de miru Jomon jidai no saibai shokubutsu [Cultivated plants from the Jomon period examined with a scanning electron microscope]. In *Hatasaku Bunka no Tanjo: Jomon Noko-ron e no Approach [Origins of Dry Field Cultivation: Approaches to Jomon Agriculture]*, ed. Komei Sasaki and Toshio Matsuyama, pp. 91–117. Tokyo: Nihon Hoso Shuppan Kyokai (in Japanese).

Medvedev, Vitaly E. 1994. Gasya iseki to Russia no Asia chiku tobu ni okeru doki shutsugen no mondai ni tsuite [The Gasya site and the appearance of pottery in the Russian Far East]. In *Kan-Nihon-kai Chiiki no Doki Shutugen-ki no Yoso [The Appearance of Pottery in the Circum Japan Sea Region]*, ed. Akira Ono and Toshinari Suzuki, pp. 9–20. Yuzankaku: Tokyo (translated into Japanese by Hiroshi Kajiwara).

Meese, D., R. Alley, T. Gow, P. M. Grootes, P. Mayewski, M. Ram, K. Taylor, E. Waddington, and G. Zielinski. 1994. *Preliminary Depth–Age Scale of the GISP Ice Core*. CRREL Special Report 94–1. Hanover, N. H.: Cold Regions Research and Engineering Laboratory.

Minagawa, Masao, and Takeru Akazawa. 1988. Jomon-jin no shokuryo sesshu [Jomon people's diet]. *Iden [Heredity]* 42(10): 15–23 (in Japanese).

   1992. Dietary patterns of Japanese Jomon hunter-gatherers: stable nitrogen and carbon isotope analyses of human bones. In *Pacific Northeast Asia in Prehistory: Hunter-Fisher-Gatherers, Farmers, and Sociopolitical Elites*, ed. C. Melvin Aikens and Song Nai Rhee, pp. 59–67. Pullman: Washington State University Press.

Minaki, Mutsuhiko. 1995. Noko wa okonawarete ita ka? Sannai Maruyama iseki no "saibai shokubutsu" [Was there agriculture? "Cultigens" from the Sannai Maruyama site]. In *Jomon Bunmei no Hakken: Kyoi no Sannai Maruyama Iseki [Discovery of the Jomon Civilization: New Findings at the Sannai Maruyama Site]*, ed. Takeshi Umehara and Yoshinori Yasuda, pp. 223–233. Tokyo: PHP Kenkyu-jo (in Japanese).

Minaki, Mutsuhiko, Yumiko Saito, and Seiichiro Tsuji. 1998. Sannai Maruyama Iseki dai 6 tetto standard column no ogata shokubutsu kaseki gun [Macro floral remains recovered from the standard column of the Sixth Transmission Tower Area of the Sannai Maruyama site]. In *Sannai Maruyama Iseki, IX, dai 2 bunsatsu [The Sannai Maruyama Site, vol. IX, Part 2]*, ed. Aomori-ken Kyoiku-cho Bunka-ka [Cultural Affairs Section of the Agency of Education of Aomori Prefecture], pp. 15–17. Aomori: Aomori-ken Kyoiku Iinkai [Board of Education of Aomori Prefecture] (in Japanese).

Minaki, Mutsuhiko, Seiichiro Tsuji, and Masakazu Sumita. 1998. Sannai Maruyama iseki dai 6 tetto Chiku VIa, VIb so kara sanshutsu shita ogata shokubutsu itai (kaseki) [Macro floral remains recovered from Layers VIa and VIb of the Sixth Transmission Tower Area of the Sannai Maruyama site]. In *Sannai Maruyama Iseki, IX, dai 2 bunsatsu [The Sannai Maruyama Site, vol. IX, Part 2]*, ed. Aomori-ken Kyoiku-cho Bunka-ka [Cultural Affairs Section of the Agency of Education of Aomori Prefecture], pp. 35–51. Aomori: Aomori-ken Kyoiku Iinkai [Board of Education of Aomori Prefecture] (in Japanese).

Minami, Hisakazu. 1994. Chikamori iseki no kyodai na mokuchu [Large wooden pots found at the Chikamori site]. *Kokogaku Journal [Journal of Archaeology]* 377: 25–30 (in Japanese).

Misawa, Akira (Wajima Seiichi). 1936. Kinzoku bunka no yunyu to seisan keizai no hattatsu [Introduction of metal culture and the development of food production]. In *Nihon Rekishi Kyotei dai 1 satsu- Genshi Shakai no Hokai made [Textbook of Japanese History, Part 1: Up to the Collapse of the Primitive Society]*, ed. Yoshimichi Watabe, Akira Misawa, Kimio Izu, and Jiro Hayakawa, pp. 142–202. Tokyo: Hakuyosha (in Japanese).

Miyake, Atsuki. 1994. Gunma-ken Tsukiyono-cho Yaze iseki no mokuchu iko [Features associated with wood posts found at the Yaze site, Tsukiyono Town, Gunma Prefecture]. *Kokogaku Journal [Journal of Archaeology]* 377: 7–12 (in Japanese).

Miyake, Tetsuya. 1977. Odai Yamamoto I Iseki [The Odai Yamoto I site]. *Nihon Kokogaku Nenpo [Archaeologia Japonica]* 28 *(Annual Report of the Japanese Archaeological Studies and Excavations: Fiscal Year 1975)*: 95 (in Japanese with English title).

——— ed. 1979. *Odai Yamamoto I Iseki Hakkutsu Chosa Hokoku [Report of the Excavation Research at the Odai-Yamamoto I Site]*. Aomori: Aomori Kenritsu Kyodo-kan [Aomori Prefectural Museum of History] (in Japanese).

Miyamoto, Chojiro.1994. Sannai Maruyama iseki no shuraku to kenchiku no kozo o saguru [Architectural studies of the Sannai Maruyama settlement]. *Asahi Graph* 3780 (Special Issue: Sannai Maruyama Site): 80–83 (in Japanese).

——— 1995. Kyobokuchu iko no shotai: Sannai Maruyama iseki no takayuka kenchiku [The function of the feature associated with large wooden posts: raised-floor buildings at Sannai Maruyama]. In *Jomon Bunmei no Hakken: Kyoi no Sannai Maruyama Iseki [Discovery of the Jomon Civilization: New Findings at the Sannai Maruyama Site]*, ed. Takeshi Umehara and Yoshinori Yasuda, pp. 214–222. Tokyo: PHP Kenkyu-jo (in Japanese).

Miyano, Jun'ichi. 1998. Shizen to tanjo e no ikei [Ceremonial practices related to nature and birth]. In *Heisei 10 nen Shunki Tokubetsu-ten: Jomon no Inori Yayoi no Kokoro [Special Exhibition in Spring 1998: Ceremonial Practices of the Jomon People; The Spirit of the Yayoi People]*, ed. Osaka Furitsu Yayoi Bunka Hakubutsu-kan [Museum of Yayoi Culture], pp. 36–43. Izumi: Osaka Furitsu Yayoi Bunka Hakubutsu-kan (in Japanese).

Miyasaka, Fusakazu. 1946. Togariishi senshi shurakushi no kenkyu [A study of the prehistoric settlement site of Togariishi]. *Suwa Shidankai Kaiho [Newsletter of Suwa Association of History]* 3: 16–25 (in Japanese).

Miyasaka, Kiyoshi. 1998. Wada Toge, Kirigamine no kokuyoseki gensanchi to iseki-gun [Obsidian sources and archaeological sites at Wada Pass and Kirigamine]. In *Dai 10 kai Nagano-ken Kyuseki Bunka Kenkyu Koryu-kai Happyo Yoshi [Proceedings of the 10th Workshop on Palaeolithic Studies in Nagano Prefecture]*, ed. Takashi Tsutsumi, pp. 15–28. Suwa: Nagano-ken Kyusekki Bunka Kenkyu Koryukai [Palaeolithic Studies Group in Nagano Prefecture] (in Japanese).

Miyashita, Kenji. 1980. Doki no shutsugen to Jomon bunka no kigen (shiron): shizen kankyo no fukugen to doki no kino o chushin ni shite [Appearance of pottery and the origin of the Jomon culture: a model, with special reference to the reconstruction of natural environment and function of pottery]. *Shinano* 32(4): 411–447 (in Japanese).

Miyata, Eiji. 2000. Minami Kyushu no Jomon Jidai Sosoki [Incipient Jomon cultures in southern Kyushu]. In *Symposium: Kyusekki kara Jomon e: Iko to Kukan Riyo: Happyo Yoshi [Papers of Millennium Symposia at Kagoshima by the Japanese Archaeological Association: From Palaeolithic Age to Jomon Period – Structural Remains and Space-Utilization]*, ed. Nihon Kokogaku Kyokai 2000 nendo Kagoshima Taikai Jikko Iinkai [Executive Committee of the Convention at Kagoshima, the Japanese Archaeological Association, October 2000], pp. 36–51. Kagoshima: Nihon Kokogaku Kyokai 2000 nendo Kagoshima Taikai Jikko Iinkai, Kagoshima (in Japanese with English title).

Mizoguchi, Koji. 2002. *Archaeological History of Japan: 30000 B.C. to A.D. 700.* Philadelphia: University of Pennsylvania Press.

Mizuno, Masayoshi. 1963. Jomon bunka ki ni okeru shuraku kozo to shukyo kozo [Settlement organization and religious structure during the Jomon period]. In *Nihon Kokogaku Kyokai Dai 29 kai Sokai Kenkyu Happyo Yoshi [Abstracts of the Papers Presented at the 29th General Conference of the Japanese Archaeological Association]*, pp. 11–12. Tokyo: Nihon Kokogaku Kyokai [Japanese Archaeological Association] (in Japanese).

1968. Kanjo kumiishi-bo-gun no imi suru mono [Circular stone burials]. *Shinano* 20(4): 255–263 (in Japanese).

1969a. Jomon jidai shuraku fukugen e no kiso-teki sosa [Towards the reconstruction of Jomon settlements]. *Kodai Bunka [Cultura Antiqua]* 21(4): 1–21 (in Japanese).

1969b. Genshi shakai I: Jomon no shakai [Prehistoric society, Part 1: Jomon society]. In *Nihon Bunka no Rekishi I: Daichi to Jujutsu [A History of Japanese Culture, vol. I: The Earth and Magic]*, ed. Naokazu Kokubu and Taro Okamoto, pp. 199–202. Tokyo: Gakushu Kenkyu-sha (in Japanese).

1970. Naze Jomon jidai shuraku-ron wa hitsuyo nano ka [Why is Jomon settlement archaeology necessary?]. *Rekishi Kyoiku [Education in History]* 18(3): 15–24 (in Japanese).

1979. *Nihon no Genshi Bijutsu V: Dogu [Ancient Art of Japan, vol. V: Clay Figurines]*. Tokyo: Kodansha (in Japanese).

1999. Kami o matsuru sumai to hiroba [Ceremonial use of space]. In *Jomon Sekai no Ichiman Nen [Ten Thousand Years of Jomon]*, ed. Takura Izumi and Yasutami Nishida, pp. 66–69. Tokyo: Shueisha (in Japanese).

Montelius, Oscar. 1932. *Kokogaku Kenkyu-ho [Die älteren Kulturperioden im Orient und in Europa]*. Tokyo: Oka Shoin (translated by Kosaku Hamada, in Japanese).

Mori, Koichi, ed. 1988. *Sekai no Dai Iseki 11: Nihon Bunka no Kaika [Great Monuments of the Ancient World 11: Japan]*. Tokyo: Kodansha (in Japanese).

Mori, Yuichi. 1998a. Sannai Maruyama iseki dai 6 tetto standard column kara sanshutsu shita konchu kaseki [Insect remains recovered from the standard column of the Sixth Transmission Tower Area of the Sannai Maruyama site]. In *Sannai Maruyama Iseki, IX, dai 2 bunsatsu [The Sannai Maruyama Site, vol. IX, Part 2]*, ed. Aomori-ken Kyoiku-cho Bunka-ka [Cultural Affairs Section of the Agency of Education of Aomori Prefecture], pp. 19–25. Aomori: Aomori-ken Kyoiku Iinkai [Board of Education of Aomori Prefecture] (in Japanese).

1998b. Sannai Maruyama iseki dai 6 tetto chiku dai VIa, VIb so kara erareta konchu kaseki [Insect remains recovered from Layers VIa and VIb of the Sixth Transmission Tower Area of the Sannai Maruyama site]. In *Sannai Maruyama Iseki, IX, dai 2 bunsatsu [The Sannai Maruyama Site*, vol. IX, Part 2*]*, ed. Aomori-ken Kyoiku-cho Bunka-ka [Cultural Affairs Section of the Agency of Education of Aomori Prefecture], pp. 151–162. Aomori: Aomori-ken Kyoiku Iinkai [Board of Education Aomori Prefecture] (in Japanese).

1999. Konchu kaiseki de daishuraku o saguru [Examining the large settlement through the analysis of insect remains]. *Kagaku [Science]* 54(9): 34–38 (in Japanese).

Morikawa, Masakazu, and Sumio Hashimoto. 1994. *Torihama Kaizuka [The Torihama Shell-Midden]*. Tokyo: Yomiuri Shinbun-sha (in Japanese).

Morimoto, Iwataro, and Katsutomo Kato. 1997. Yakushimae Iseki shutsudo no kamekan-nai kaiso jinkotsu ni tsuite [Human skeletal remains from jar burials excavated from the Yakushimae site]. In *Yakushimae Iseki [The Yakushimae Site]*, ed. Kuraishi-mura Kyoiku Iinkai [Board of Education of Kuraishi Village], pp. 52–66. Aomori: Kuraishi-mura Kyoiku Iinkai (in Japanese).

Morris, Ian. 1987. *Burial and Ancient Society: The Rise of the Greek City-State*. Cambridge: Cambridge University Press.

Mukosaka, Koji. 1958. Doki keishiki no bunpu-ken [Distribution areas of pottery styles]. *Kokogaku Techo [Archaeology Notes]* 2: 1–2 (in Japanese).

1970. Genshi jidai kyodo no seikatsu-ken [Group territory during the prehistoric period]. In *Kyodoshi Kenkyu Koza I: Kyodoshi Kenkyu to Kokogaku [Lectures in the Study of Local History*, vol. I: *Studies of Local History and Archaeology]*, ed. Toshio Kojima, Taro Wakamori, and Motoi Kimura, pp. 257–299. Tokyo: Asakura Shoten (in Japanese).

Murakoshi, Kiyoshi. 1974. *Ento Doki Bunka [Ento Pottery Culture]*. Tokyo: Yuzankaku (in Japanese).

1998. *Aomori Daigaku Kokogaku Kenkyu-jo Kenkyu Kiyo 1: Aomori-kennai ni okeru Jomon Jidai no Jukyo-ato Shutaisei (1) [Bulletin of the Archaeological Institute of Aomori University, No. 1: Catalog of Jomon Pit-Dwellings in Aomori Prefecture, Part 1]*. Aomori (in Japanese).

Murasaki, Kyoko. 2000. Karafuto Ainu no Hitobito [Sakhalin Ainu people]. *Shiroi Kuni no Uta [Essays on Northern Land]* 521: 4–13 (in Japanese).

Murata, Fumio. 1974. Kawasaki-shi Shiomidai iseki no Jomon Chuki shuraku fukugen e no ichi shiron [A reconstruction of the Middle Jomon village at the Shiomidai site, Kawasaki City]. *Kodai Bunka [Cultura Antiqua]* 26: 1–31 (in Japanese).

Murdock, G. P. 1967. *Ethnographic Atlas*. Pittsburgh: University of Pittsburgh Press.

Muto, Yasuhiro. 1999. Kanjo shuraku to hi-kanjo shuraku (Circular shaped settlements and non-circular settlements). *Kikan Kokogaku [Archaeology Quarterly]* 69: 6–7 (in Japanese).

Muto, Yuroku, and Kimiaki Kobayashi. 1978. *Sori: Dai 3, 4, 5-ji Hakkutsu Chosa Hokoku-sho [The Sori Site: Reports of the Third, Fourth and Fifth Excavations]*. Fujimi: Fujimi-machi Kyoiku Iinkai [Board of Education of Fujimi Town] (in Japanese).

Nagahara, Kciji.1974. Marx shugi rekishi-gaku ni tsuite [On Marxist history]. In *Marx Shugi Kenkyu Nyumon [Introduction to Marxist History]*, ed. Keiji Nagahara, pp. 3–13. Tokyo: Aoki Shoten (in Japanese).

Nagamine, Mitsukazu. 1977. *Nihon Genshi Bijutsu Taikei III [Ancient Japanese Art*, vol. III*]*. Tokyo: Kodansha (in Japanese).

——— 1986. Clay figurines and Jomon society. In *Windows on the Japanese Past: Studies in Archaeology and Prehistory*, ed. Richard J. Pearson, Gina Lee Barnes, and Karl L. Hutterer, pp. 255–265. Ann Arbor: Center for Japanese Studies, University of Michigan.

Nagano-ken Chuodo Iseki Chosa-dan [Excavation Team of Chuo Freeway Corridor Sites in Nagano Prefecture]. 1982. *Nagano-ken Chuodo Maizo Bunkazai Hozochi Hakkutsu Chosa Hokoku-sho: Hara-mura, sono 5 [Excavation Report of Chuo Freeway: Hara Village, Part 5]*. Nagano: Nagano-ken Kyoiku Iinkai [Board of Education of Nagano Prefecture] (in Japanese).

Nagano-ken Kyoiku Iinkai [Board of Education of Nagano Prefecture]. 1979. *Nagano-ken Chuodo Maizo Bunkazai Hozochi Hakkutsu Chosa Hokoku-sho: Chino-shi, Hara-mura sono 2 [Excavation Report of Chuo Freeway: Chino City and Hara Village, Part 2]*. Nagano: Nagano-ken Kyoiku Iinkai [Board of Education of Nagano Prefecture] (in Japanese).

Nagasaki, Motohiro. 1973. Yatsugatake seinan-roku no Jomon Chuki shuraku ni okeru kyodo saishiki no arikata to sono igi [Communal ceremonies of the Middle Jomon settlements in the southwestern foothills of Mt. Yatsugatake]. *Shinano* 25(4): 292–313, 25(5): 446–463 (in Japanese).

——— 1977. Chubu chiho no Jomon jidai shuraku [Jomon settlements in the Chubu region]. *Kokogaku Kenkyu [Quarterly of Archaeological Studies]* 23(4): 1–8 (in Japanese).

Nakajima, Eiichi. 1983. Sekkan, dokkan [Crown-shaped stone and clay artifacts]. In *Jomon Bunka no Kenkyu IX: Jomon-jin no Seishin Bunka [Studies of the Jomon Culture*, vol. IX: *Mortuary and Ceremonial Practices]*, ed. Shinpei Kato, Tatsuo Kobayashi, and Tsuyoshi Fujimoto, pp. 197–205. Tokyo: Yuzankaku (in Japanese).

Nakajima, Eiichi, and Tomokazu Watanabe. 1994. Niigata kennai no kyochu iko [Features associated with large wooden posts found in Niigata Prefecture]. *Kokogaku Journal [Journal of Archaeology]* 377: 13–17 (in Japanese).

Nakajima, Hiroaki. 2000. Toshin ni nemuru Jomon bunka no saihakken: Tokyo-to Nakazato kaizuka [Rediscovery of a Jomon site in Tokyo metropolis: the Nakazato shell-midden, Tokyo]. *Shiroi Kuni no Uta [Essays on Northern Land]* 528: 22–25 (in Japanese).

Nakajima, Hiroaki, and Taichi Hosaka. 1998. Tokyo-to Kita-ku Nakazato kaizuka [The Nakazato shell-midden in Kita Ward, Tokyo]. *Nihon Kokogaku Nenpo [Archaeologia Japonica] 49 (Annual Report of the Japanese Archaeological Studies and Excavations: Fiscal Year 1996)*: 489–492 (in Japanese with English title and summary).

Nakamura, Kenji. 1991. Kinki Chiho ni okeru Jomon banki no bosei ni tsuite [A study on the tomb system of the Late Jomon period in Kinki District]. *Kodai Bunka [Cultura Antiqua]* 43(1): 17–31 (in Japanese with English title).

1999. Haka to bochi kozo: Nishi-nihon [Burials and cemetery structures: western Japan]. *Kikan Kokogaku [Archaeology Quarterly]* 69: 60–64 (in Japanese).

Nakamura, Oki. 1999. Bosei kara yomu Jomon shakai no kaisoka [Social stratification in Jomon society on the basis of burial analysis]. In *Jomon-gaku no Sekai [The World of Jomon Archaeology]*, ed. Tatsuo Kobayashi, pp. 48–60. Tokyo: Asahi Shinbun-sha (in Japanese).

2000. Saishu shuryo-min no fukuso koi [Mortuary goods associated with hunter-gatherer burials]. *Kikan Kokogaku [Archaeology Quarterly]* 70: 19–23 (in Japanese).

Nakamura, Toshio, Masayo Minami, and Hiroki Oda. 2000. Kasoku-ki shitsuryo bunseki ni yoru koseido ^{14}C nendai sokutei: sokutei saido kara no gimon to teian [High precision ^{14}C dating using accelerator mass spectrometer: questions and suggestions from laboratory scientists]. In *Nihon Bunkazai Kagaku kai Dai 17 kai Taikai Kenkyu Happyo Yoshi-shu [Abstracts of the Papers Presented at the 17th Annual Meeting of the Japanese Society for Scientific Studies on Cultural Properties]*, pp. 4–5. Sakura: Nihon Bunkazai Kagaku-kai (in Japanese).

Nakamura, Toshio, and Seiichiro Tsuji. 1999. Aomori-ken Higashi-tsugaru-gun Kanita-machi Odai Yamamoto I Iseki shutsudo no doki hahen hyomen ni fuchaku shita biryo tanka-butsu no kasokuki ^{14}C nendai [AMS ^{14}C dates of carbon samples collected from the surface of potsherds recovered at the Odai Yamamoto I site at Kanita Town, Higashi-Tsugaru County, Aomori Prefecture]. In *Odai Yamamoto I Iseki no Kokogaku Chosa [Archaeological Research at the Odai Yamamoto I Site]*, ed. Odai Yamamoto I Iseki Hakkutsu Chosa-dan [Odai Yamamoto I Site Excavation Team], pp. 107–111. Tokyo: Odai Yamamoto I Iseki Hakkutsu Chosa-dan (in Japanese).

Nakayama, Kiyoshi. 1998. Keshin no matsuri [Jomon rituals with masks]. In *Heisei 10 nen Shunki Tokubetsu-ten: Jomon no Inori, Yayoi no Kokoro [Special Exhibition in Spring 1998: Ceremonial Practices of the Jomon People; The Spirit of the Yayoi People]*, ed. Osaka Furitsu Yayoi Bunka Hakubutsu-kan [Museum of Yayoi Culture], pp. 48–51. Izumi: Osaka Furitsu Yayoi Bunka Hakubutsu-kan (in Japanese).

Nakayama, Kiyotaka. 1992. Jommon bunka to tairiku-kei bunbutsu [The Jomon culture and artifacts introduced from the continent]. *Kikan Kokogaku [Archaeology Quarterly]*, 38:48–52 (in Japanese).

Naora, Nobuo. 1938. Shizen Nihon-jin no shokuryo bunka [The dietary culture of the prehistoric Japanese]. In *Jinruigaku Senshi-gaku Koza [Lectures in Anthropology and Prehistory]*, pp. 1–133. Tokyo: Yuzankaku (in Japanese).

1941–42. Shizen iseki shutsudo no jukotsu [Faunal remains found in prehistoric sites]. *Kodai Bunka [Cultura Antiqua]* 12(9): 504–506, 12(10): 566–569, 12(11): 628–630, 12(12): 684–687, 13(1): 64–66; 13(2): 117–122, 13(3): 178–182, 13(4): 231–242, 13(5): 291–300, 13(6): 351–356, 13(7): 410–416, 13(8): 463–471, 13(12): 651–660, 14(1): 56 (in Japanese).

Nara Bunkazai Kenkyu-jo Maizo Bunkazai Center [Center for Archaeological Operations of Nara National Research Institute for Cultural Properties]. 2002. 2000 nen-do maizo bunkazai kankei tokei shiryo [Statistical data on rescue excavations and cultural resource management in Japan, 2000]. *Maizo Bunkazai News [CAO News]* 107: 1–7 (in Japanese).

2003. 2001 nen-do maizo bunkazai kankei tokei shiryo [Statistical data on rescue excavations and cultural resource management in Japan, 2001]. *Maizo Bunkazai News [CAO News]* 112: 1–7 (in Japanese).

Nihon Kokogaku Kyokai [Japanese Archaeological Association]. ed. 1984. *Symposium: Jomon Jidai Shuraku no Hensen [Symposium on Changes in Jomon Settlements]*. Nihon Kokogaku Kyokai Showa 59 nendo Taikai Shiryo [Conference Proceedings of the 1984 Fall Meeting of the Japanese Archaeological Association]. Tokyo and Yamanashi: Nihon Kokogaku Kyokai (in Japanese).

ed. 1989. *Nihon Kokogaku Nenpo [Archaeologia Japonica]* 40. Annual Report of the Japanese Archaeological Studies and Excavations: Fiscal Year 1987. Tokyo: Nihon Kokogaku Kyokai (in Japanese with English summary).

ed. 1998. *Nihon Kokogaku Nenpo [Archaeologia Japonica]* 49. Annual Report of the Japanese Archaeological Studies and Excavations: Fiscal Year 1996. Tokyo: Nihon Kokogaku Kyokai (in Japanese with English title and summary).

Niimi, Michiko. 1991. Nenrei oyobi shibo jiki satei ni tsuite [Estimates of age and season of death of wild boar excavated from the Ikawazu site, Aichi Prefecture]. *Kokuritsu Rekishi Minzoku Hakubutsu-kan Kenkyu Hokoku [Bulletin of the National Museum of Japanese History]* 29: 123–143 (in Japanese).

Niitsu, Takeshi. 1999. Haiseki-bo [Burials marked by circular stone arrangements]. *Jomon Jidai [Journal of Jomon Period Studies]* 10(3): 80–92 (in Japanese with English title).

Ninomiya, Shuji. 1983. Kokuyoseki no sanchi dotei [Identification of sources and hydration dating of the obsidian specimens from the Hakeue site]. In *Hakeue Iseki [The Hakeue Site]*, pp. 121–127. Tokyo: ICU Archaeology Research Center, International Christian University (in Japanese with English title and summary).

Ninomiya, Shuji, Mamoru Aboshi, and Masumi Osawa. 1985. Mukainohara iseki shutsudo kokuyoseki sekki no sanchi suitei [Identification of sources of obsidian tools recovered from the Mukainohara site]. In *Mukainohara Iseki [The Mukainohara Site]*, ed. Yutaka Sumiyoshi and Yukiko Nakatsu, pp. 112–118. Tokyo: ICU Archaeology Research Center, International Christian University (in Japanese).

Ninomiya, Shuji, Takashi Tamura, and Hiroshi Sawano. 1987. Kokuyoseki, kokushoku chimitsu-shitsu anzan-gan, meno no kiki chuseishi hoshaka bunseki ni yoru gensanchi suitei [Identification of sources of obsidian, fine-grained black andesite, and agate using instrumental neutron activation analysis]. *Chiba-ken Bunkazai Center Kenkyu Kiyo [Bulletin of the Archaeological Center of Chiba Prefecture]* 11: 57–73 (in Japanese).

Nishida, Masaki. 1977. Saibai shushi: Torihama kaizuka [Cultigen seeds excavated from the Torihama shell-midden]. *Kikan Dolmen [Dolmen Quarterly]* 13: 85–89 (in Japanese).

1981. Jomon jidai no shokuryo shigen to seigyo katsudo: Torihama kaizuka no shizen ibutsu o chushin to shite [Food resources and subsistence activities during the Jomon period, with special reference to faunal and floral remains from Torihama shell-midden]. *Kikan Jinruigaku [Anthropology Quarterly]* 2(2): 3–83 (in Japanese).

1983. The emergence of food production in Neolithic Japan. *Journal of Anthropological Archaeology.* 2: 305–322.

1986. *Teiju Kakumei: Yudo to Teiju no Jinrui-shi [The Sedentism Revolution: Human History of Migration and Sedentism].* Tokyo: Shin'yo-sha (in Japanese).

Nishida, Yasutami. 1996. Shi to Jomon doki [Death and Jomon pottery]. In *Rekishi Hakkutsu II: Jomon Doki Shutsugen [Excavation of the Past,* vol. II: *Emergence of Jomon Pottery],* ed. Takura Izumi, pp. 94–109. Tokyo: Kodansha (in Japanese).

Nishimoto, Toyohiro. 1995. Sakana to tori no nikushoku seikatsu: Sannai Maruyama iseki no dobutsu-shitsu shokuryo no mondai [Fish and birds as primary protein sources: animal food of the residents of Sannai Maruyama]. In *Jomon Bunmei no Hakken: Kyoi no Sannai Maruyama Iseki [Discovery of the Jomon Civilization: New Findings at the Sannai Maruyama Site],* ed. Takeshi Umehara and Yoshinori Yasuda, pp. 207–213. Tokyo: PHP Kenkyu-jo (in Japanese).

1998. Sannai Maruyama iseki dai 6 tetto chiku shutsudo no cho-rui, honyurui itai [Bird and mammal remains recovered from the Sixth Transmission Tower Area of the Sannai Maruyama site]. In *Sannai Maruyama Iseki, IX, dai 2 bunsatsu [The Sannai Maruyama Site,* vol. IX, Part 2], ed. Aomori-ken Kyoiku-cho Bunka-ka [Cultural Affairs Section of the Agency of Education of Aomori Prefecture], pp. 53–60. Aomori: Aomori-ken Kyoiku Iinkai [Board of Education of Aomori Prefecture] (in Japanese).

Nishimura, Masae. 1965. Maiso [Mortuary practices]. In *Nihon no Kokogaku, II: Jomon Jidai [Japanese Archaeology,* vol. II: *The Jomon Period],* ed. Yoshimasa Kamaki, pp. 335–352. Tokyo: Kawade Shobo (in Japanese).

Nishino, Hidekazu. 1994. Kanazawa-shi Yonaizumi iseki no kanjo mokuchuretsu [Wood circle found at the Yonaizumi site, Kanazawa City]. *Kokogaku Journal [Journal of Archaeology]* 377: 31–37 (in Japanese).

Nishino'omote-shi Kyoiku Iinkai [Board of Education of Nishino'omote City]. 1995. *Okunonita Iseki, Oku-arashi Iseki [The Okunonita and Oku-arashi Sites].* Nishino'omote: Kagoshima (in Japanese).

Niwa, Yuichi. 1978. Jomon jidai Chuki ni okeru shuraku no kukan kosei to shudan no sho-kankei [Relations between the spatial structure of settlements and human groups during the Middle Jomon period]. *Shirin* 61(2): 274–312 (in Japanese).

1982. Jomon jidai no shudan kozo [Group structure during the Jomon period]. In *Kokogaku Ronko: Kobayashi Yukio Hakushi Koki Kinen Ronbunshu [Archaeological Discussions: Essays in Honor of Dr. Yukio Kobayashi's Seventieth Birthday],* ed. Kobayashi Yukio Hakushi Koki Kinen Ronbunshu Kanko Iinkai [Editorial Committee of Essays in Honor of Dr. Yukio Kobayashi's Seventieth Birthday], pp. 41–74. Tokyo: Heibon-sha (in Japanese).

Nomura, Takashi. 1983. Sekken, sekito [Stone swords]. In *Jomon Bunka no Kenkyu IX: Jomon-jin no Seishin Bunka [Studies of the Jomon Culture,* vol. IX: *Mortuary and Ceremonial Practices],* ed. Shinpei Kato, Tatsuo Kobayashi, and Tsuyoshi Fujimoto, pp. 181–196. Tokyo: Yuzankaku (in Japanese).

Noto, Ken. 1983. Dai ni no dougu: dogu [Secondary tools: clay figurines]. In *Jomon Bunka no Kenkyu IX: Jomon-jin no Seishin Bunka [Studies of the Jomon Culture, vol. IX: Mortuary and Ceremonial Practices]*, ed. Shinpei Kato, Tatsuo Kobayashi, and Tsuyoshi Fujimoto, pp. 74–85. Tokyo: Yuzankaku (in Japanese).

Noto-machi Kyoiku Iinkai [Board of Education of Noto Town]. 1986. *Ishikawa-ken Noto-machi Mawaki Iseki [The Mawaki Site, Noto Town, Ishikawa Prefecture]*. Noto: Noto-machi Kyoiku Iinkai (in Japanese).

1992. *Zusetsu Mawaki Iseki [Illustrated Guide to the Mawaki Site]*. Noto: Noto-machi Kyoiku Iinkai (in Japanese).

Oba, Aya. 2001. Jomon banki no taimu-kapuseru: Miyagi-ken Sanno-gakoi iseki [A time capsule from the Final Jomon period: the Sanno-gakoi site, Miyagi Prefecture]. *Shiroi Kuni no Uta [Essays on Northern Land]* 535: 22–25 (in Japanese).

Oba, Iwao, ed. 1957a. *Wappara Iseki [The Wappara Site]*. Matsumoto: Nagano-ken Bunkazai Hogo Kyokai [Committee for the Preservation of Cultural Properties in Nagano Prefecture] (in Japanese).

1957b. Wappara iseki no kokogaku-teki kosatsu [Archaeological investigation of the Wappara site]. In *Wappara Iseki [The Wappara Site]*, pp. 117–156. Matsumoto: Nagano-ken Bunkazai Hogo Kyokai [Committee for the Preservation of Cultural Properties in Nagano Prefecture] (in Japanese).

Obayashi, Taryo. 1971. Jomon jidai no shakai soshiki [Social organization during the Jomon period]. *Kikan Jinruigaku [Anthropology Quarterly]* 2(2): 3–83 (in Japanese).

Obayashi, Taryo, Chojiro Miyamoto, Takashi Nomura, Fujio Fujita, Yasuhiro Okada, and Koichi Mori. 1994. Zentai toron [General discussion]. *Asahi Graph* 3780 (Special Issue: Sannai Maruyama Site): 97–117 (in Japanese).

Oda, Shizuo. 1982. Kokuyoseki [Obsidian]. In *Jomon Bunka no Kenkyu VIII: Shakai, Bunka [Studies of the Jomon Culture, vol. VIII: Society and Culture]*, ed. Shinpei Kato, Tatsuo Kobayashi, and Tsuyoshi Fujimoto, pp. 168–179. Tokyo: Yuzankaku (in Japanese).

Odai Yamamoto I Iseki Hakkutsu Chosa-dan [Odai Yamamoto I Site Excavation Team], ed. 1999. *Odai Yamamoto I Iseki no Kokogaku Chosa [Archaeological Research at the Odai Yamamoto I Site]*. Tokyo: Odai Yamamoto I Iseki Hakkutsu Chosa-dan (in Japanese).

Ogasawara, Tadayuki, and Kazuho Katsuragi. 1999. Sannai Maruyama shutsudo no dogu no kenkyu [Analysis of clay figurines excavated from Sannai Maruyama]. In *1998 Nendo Sannai Maruyama Iseki Tokubetsu Kenkyu (Shakai) [Report of the 1998 Grant of Sannai Maruyama Special Studies (Society)]*. Aomori: Aomori-ken Kyoiku Iinkai [Board of Education of Aomori Prefecture] (in Japanese).

Ogasawara, Yoshihiko. 1970. Jomon, Yayoi shiki jidai no nuno [Textiles from the Jomon and Yayoi periods]. *Kokogaku Kenkyu [Quarterly of Archaeological Studies]* 17(3): 29–49 (in Japanese).

1983. Amimono, Nuno [Textiles and fabrics]. In *Jomon Bunka no Kenkyu VII: Dogu to Gijutsu [Studies of the Jomon Culture, vol. VII: Tools and Technology]*, ed. Shinpei Kato, Tatsuo Kobayashi, and Tsuyoshi Fujimoto, pp. 293–304. Tokyo: Yuzankaku (in Japanese).

Ogiwara, Masako. 1987. Ainu [Ainu]. In *Bunka Jinruigaku Jiten [Encyclopedia of Cultural Anthropology]*, ed. Eikichi Ishikawa, Tadao Umesao, Taryo Obayashi, Masao Gamo, Komei Sasaki, and Takao Sofue, pp. 4–5. Tokyo: Kobundo (in Japanese).

Oh-hazama-machi Kyoiku Iinkai [Board of Education of Oh-hazama Town]. 1979. *Tateishi Iseki [The Tateishi Site]*. Oh-hazama: Oh-hazama-machi Kyoiku Iinkai (in Japanese).

Ohtsuka, Kazuyoshi. 1967. Jomon jidai no sosei: maiso keitai ni yoru bunseki [Jomon mortuary practices: analysis based on burial types]. *Shien [Journal of Rikkyo Daigaku Shigakkai]* 27(3) (in Japanese).

——— 1988. Jomon no matsuri [Jomon rituals]. In *Kodaishi Fukugen II: Jomon-jin no Seikatsu to Bunka [Reconstruction of Ancient History, vol. II: Lifeways and Culture of the Jomon People]*, pp. 113–148. Tokyo: Kodansha (in Japanese).

Okada, Yasuhiro. 1995a. Ento doki bunka no kyodai shuraku [A large settlement from the Ento Pottery culture: the Sannai Maruyama site in Aomori Prefecture]. *Kikan Kokogaku [Archaeology Quarterly]* 50: 25–30 (in Japanese).

——— 1995b. Nihon saidai no Jomon shuraku "Sannai Maruyama iseki" [The largest Jomon site in Japan, the "Sannai Maruyama site"]. In *Jomon Bunmei no Hakken: Kyoi no Sannai Maruyama Iseki [Discovery of the Jomon Civilization: New Findings at the Sannai Maruyama site]*, ed. Takeshi Umehara and Yoshinori Yasuda, pp. 12–30. Tokyo: PHP Kenkyu-jo (in Japanese).

——— 1997. Sannai Maruyama iseki kara no hokoku [A report from the Sannai Maruyama site]. In *Jomon Toshi o Horu [Excavating a Jomon City]*, ed. Yasuhiro Okada and NHK [Nihon Hoso Kyokai] Aomori, pp. 9–33. Tokyo: Nihon Hoso Kyokai [Japanese Broadcasting Corporation] (in Japanese).

——— 1998a. Sannai Maruyama iseki no shuraku hensen [Long-term change in the Sannai Maruyama settlement]. In *Kokusai Shuryo-saishu-min Kaigi Aomori Symposium [International Conference on Hunting and Gathering Societies (CHAGS): Aomori Symposium]*, pp. 10–12, 29–31. Aomori: Committee for CHAGS Aomori Symposium (in Japanese).

——— 1998b. Higashi Nihon no Jomon bunka [Jomon culture in eastern Japan]. *Kikan Kokogaku [Archaeology Quarterly]* 64: 31–35 (in Japanese).

——— 2003. Jomon culture of northeastern Japan and the Sannai Maruyama site. In *Hunter-Gatherers of the North Pacific Rim*, ed. Junko Habu, James M. Savelle, Shuzo Koyama, and Hitomi Hongo, pp. 173–186. Senri Ethnological Studies 63. Osaka: National Museum of Ethnology.

Okada, Yasuhiro, and Junko Habu. 1995. Public presentation and archaeological research: a case study from the Jomon period Sannai Maruyama site. Paper presented at the 1995 Chacmool Conference, Calgary.

Okamoto, Akio. 1961. "Sake/masu" to "tochi-donguri": shuryo shakai kenkyusha e no shitsumon ["Salmon" and "acorns": questions to researchers of hunting societies]. *Kokogaku Kenkyu [Quarterly of Archaeological Studies]* 7(4): 2–4 (in Japanese).

Okamoto, Isamu. 1956. Jomon jidai no seikatsu: maiso [Lifeways of the Jomon people: mortuary practices]. In *Nihon Kokogaku Koza III: Jomon Bunka [Lectures in Japanese Archaeology, vol. III: The Jomon Culture]*. Tokyo: Kawade Shobo (in Japanese).

1959. Doki keishiki no gensho to honshitsu [The nature and meaning of pottery styles]. *Kokogaku Techo [Archaeology Notes]* 6: 1–2 (in
Japanese).

1975. Genshi jidai no seisan to jujutsu [Mode of production and ritual during the prehistoric period]. In *Iwanami Koza Nihon Rekishi I: Genshi oyobi
Kodai [Iwanami Lectures in Japanese History*, vol. I: *Prehistoric and Protohistoric Periods]*, ed. Yoshiro Kondo and Yokoyama Koichi, pp. 75–112. Tokyo:
Iwanami Shoten (in Japanese).

1986. Sendoki/Jomon jidai no shokuryo seisan [Food production during the
Preceramic and Jomon periods]. In *Iwanami Koza Nihon Kokogaku III: Seisan
to Ryutsu [Iwanami Lectures in Japanese Archaeology*, vol. III: *Production and
Circulation]*, ed. Yoshiro Kondo and Koichi Yokoyama, pp. 33–56. Tokyo:
Iwanami Shoten (in Japanese).

Okamoto, Takayuki. 1999a. Sekkan, ishinoko, katsuobushi-gata sekki [Stone
"crown," stone saws, and katsuobushi-gata stone tools]. *Jomon Jidai [Journal
of Jomon Period Studies]* 10(4): 91–97 (in Japanese with English title).

1999b. Dokko-jo sekki (Dokko-ishi, Shirakawa-gata sekki) [Dokko-ishi or Shi-
rakawa type stone tool]. *Jomon Jidai [Journal of Jomon Period Studies]* 10(4):
83–89 (in Japanese with English title).

Okamura, Hideo. 1995a. Chozoketsu to mizu sarashi-ba: Nagano-ken Kurib-
ayashi iseki [Storage pits and water-leaching area: the Kuribayashi site in
Nagano Prefecture]. *Kikan Kokogaku [Archaeology Quarterly]* 50: 43–48 (in
Japanese).

1995b. Jomon jidai no teishicchi riyo-rei: Nagano-ken Kuribayashi iseki [The
use of low, waterlogged areas by the Jomon people: the Kuribayashi site
in Nagano Prefecture]. *Kikan Kokogaku [Archaeology Quarterly]* 50: fron-
tispiece, p. 3 (in Japanese).

Okamura, Michio. 1992. Kaimuki to seien sagyo-jo [Shellfish processing and salt-
making sites]. *Kikan Kokogaku [Archaeology Quarterly]* 41: 8 (in Japanese).

1996. Kita e no michi, umi no michi [Trade routes to the north and over-
seas routes]. In *Jomon no Tobira [A Door to the Jomon Period]*, ed. Jomon
Mahoroba-haku Jikko Iinkai [Jomon World '96 Committee], pp. 66–69.
Tokyo: NHK Shuppan (in Japanese).

Okuno, Mitsuru, and Toshio Nakamura. 2000. Koseido ^{14}C nendai to sokutei
shiryo no taphonomy [High-precision ^{14}C dating and taphonomy of
specimens]. In *Nihon Bunkazai Kagaku-kai Dai 17 kai Taikai Kenkyu Happyo Yoshi-shu [Abstracts of the Papers Presented at the 17th Annual Meeting of
the Japanese Society for Scientific Studies on Cultural Properties]*, pp. 6–7 (in
Japanese). Sakura: Nihon Bunkazai Kagaku-kai (in Japanese).

Omoto, Keiichi, and Naruya Saitou. 1997. Genetic origins of the Japanese: a
partial support for the dual structure hypothesis. *American Journal of Physical
Anthropology* 102(4): 437–446.

Ono, Miyoko. 1999. Dogu (soron) [Introduction to clay figurine studies]. *Jomon
Jidai [Journal of Jomon Period Studies]* 10(4): 107–117 (in Japanese with
English title).

Osaka Furitsu Yayoi Bunka Hakubutsu-kan [Museum of Yayoi Culture]. 1998.
*Heisei 10 nen Shunki Tokubetsu-ten: Jomon no Inori Yayoi no Kokoro [Special
Exhibition in Spring 1998: Ceremonial Practices of the Jomon People: The Spirit*

of the Yayoi People]. Izumi: Osaka Furitsu Yayoi Bunka Hakubutsu-kan [Museum of Yayoi Culture] (in Japanese).

O'Shea, John M. 1984. *Mortuary Variability: An Archaeological Investigation.* Orlando: Academic Press.

Ota, Yoko, Yoshiaki Matsushima, and Hiroshi Moriwaki. 1982. Nihon ni okeru Kanshinsei kaimen henka ni kansuru kenkyu no genjo to mondai: "Atlas of Holocene Sea-Level Records in Japan" o shiryo to shite [Notes on the Holocene sea-level study in Japan: on the basis of "Atlas of Holocene Sea-Level Records in Japan"]. *Daiyonki Kenkyu [Quaternary Research]* 21(3): 133–143 (in Japanese with English title and summary).

Otaishi, Noriyuki. 1983. Shika [Sika deer]. In *Jomon Bunka no Kenkyu II: Seigyo [Studies of the Jomon Culture, vol. II: Subsistence]*, ed. Shinpei Kato, Tatsuo Kobayashi, and Tsuyoshi Fujimoto, pp. 122–135. Tokyo: Yuzankaku (in Japanese).

Otake, Sachie. 1998. Hoshikuso toge no gensanchi to iseki-gun [Obsidian source and archaeological sites at Hoshikuso Pass]. In *Dai 10 kai Nagano-ken Kyusekki Bunka Kenkyu Koryukai Happyo Shiryo [Proceedings of the 10th Workshop of the Association for Palaeolithic Studies in Nagano Prefecture]*, pp. 29–43. Suwa: Nagano-ken Kyusekki Bunka Kenkyu Koryukai [Group of Palaeolithic Studies in Nagano Prefecture] (in Japanese).

———. 2000. Jomon jidai no kokuyoseki kozan [Obsidian quarry of the Jomon period]. *Shiroi Kuni no Uta [Essays on Northern Land]* 529: 18–21 (in Japanese).

Otani, Toshizo. 1983. Kanjo dori [Burials with circular embankment]. In *Jomon Bunka no Kenkyu IX: Jomon-jin no Seishin Bunka [Studies of the Jomon Culture, vol. IX: Mortuary and Ceremonial Practices]*, ed. Shinpei Kato, Tatsuo Kobayashi, and Tsuyoshi Fujimoto, pp. 46–56. Tokyo: Yuzankaku (in Japanese).

Otsuka, Hisao. 1955. *Kyodotai no Kiso Riron [The Basic Theory of Communities]*. Tokyo: Iwanami Shoten (in Japanese).

Oyabe-shi Kyoiku Iinkai [Board of Education of Oyabe City]. 1998. *Sakuramachi Iseki [The Sakuramachi Site]*. Oyabe City: Tourism Association of Oyabe City [Oyabe-shi Kanko Kyokai] (in Japanese).

Ozeki, Kiyoko. 1996. *Jomon no Koromo [Clothing of the Jomon People]*. Tokyo: Gakusei-sha (in Japanese).

Parker Pearson, Michael. 1982. Mortuary practices, society and ideology: an ethnoarchaeological study. In *Symbolic and Structural Archaeology*, ed. Ian Hodder, pp. 99–113. Cambridge: Cambridge University Press.

Patterson, Thomas C. 1995. *Towards a Social History of Archaeology in the United States*. Fort Worth: Harcourt Brace.

Pearson, Richard J. 1992. The nature of Japanese archaeology. *Asian Perspectives* 31(2): 115–127.

Pearson, Richard J., Gina L. Barnes, and Karl L. Hutterer, eds. 1986a. *Windows on the Japanese Past: Studies in Archaeology and Prehistory*. Ann Arbor: Center for Japanese Studies, University of Michigan.

———. 1986b. Editors' comment on "Clay figurines and Jomon society" by Mitsukazu Nagamine. In *Windows on the Japanese Past: Studies in Archaeology and Prehistory*, ed. Richard Pearson, Gina L. Barnes, and Karl L. Hutterer, p. 255. Ann Arbor: Center for Japanese Studies, University of Michigan.

Pearson, Richard J., and Kazuc Pearson. 1978. Some problems in the study of Jomon subsistence. *Antiquity* 52: 21–27.

Peebles, Christopher S., and Susan Kus. 1977. Some archaeological correlates of ranked societies. *American Antiquity* 42(3): 421–448.

Polanyi, Karl. 1980. *Ningen no Keizai [The Livelihood of Man]*, vol. I (translated by Yoshiro Tamanoi and Shin'ichiro Kurimoto, into Japanese). Tokyo: Iwanami Shoten.

Price, T. Douglas 2002. Afterword: beyond foraging and collecting: retrospect and prospect. In *Beyond Foraging and Collecting: Evolutionary Change in Hunter-Gatherer Settlement Systems*, ed. Ben Fitzhugh and Junko Habu, pp. 413–425. New York: Kluwer Academic/Plenum.

Price, T. Douglas, and James A. Brown. 1985a. Aspects of hunter-gatherer complexity. In *Prehistoric Hunter-Gatherers: The Emergence of Cultural Complexity*, ed. T. Douglas Price and James A. Brown, pp. 3–20. Orlando: Academic Press.

eds. 1985b. *Prehistoric Hunter-Gatherers: The Emergence of Cultural Complexity*. Orlando: Academic Press.

Price, T. Douglas, and Gary M. Feinman, eds. 1995. *Foundations of Social Inequality*. New York: Plenum Press.

Renfrew, Colin, and Stephen Shennan, eds. 1982. *Ranking, Resource and Exchange: Aspects of the Archaeology of Early European Society*. Cambridge: Cambridge University Press.

Renfrew, Colin, and Ezra B. W. Zubrow, eds. 1994. *The Ancient Mind: Elements of Cognitive Archaeology*. Cambridge: Cambridge University Press.

Rosenberg, Michael. 1998. Cheating at musical chairs: territoriality and sedentism in an evolutionary context. *Current Anthropology* 39: 653–684.

Saga Kenritsu Hakubutsu-kan [Museum of Saga Prefecture]. 1975. *Sakanoshita iseki no Kenkyu [Studies of the Sakanoshita Site]*. Saga: Saga Kenritsu Hakubutsu-kan.

Sagawa, Masatoshi. 1998. Archaeological new discoveries of the Pleistocene–Holocene transition in China. In *Abstracts of the Papers Presented at the Symposium on the Comparative Archaeology of the Pleistocene–Holocene Transition*, ed. Akira Ono, pp. 32–34. Sakura: National Museum of Japanese History (in English and Japanese).

Sahara, Makoto. 1979. *Nihon no Genshi Bijutsu, II: Jomon Doki, II [Ancient Art of Japan*, vol. II: *Jomon Pottery, Part II]*. Tokyo: Kodansha (in Japanese).

1987. *Taikei Nihon no Rekishi I: Nihon-jin no Tanjo [A New History of Japan*, vol. I]. Shogakkan: Tokyo (in Japanese with English title).

Sahara, Makoto, Hiroko Koike, and Nobuyuki Nakai. 1986. Zanzon shibo bunseki-ho to genshi kodai no seikatsu kankyo fukugen [Lipid residue analyses and the reconstruction of the prehistoric/protohistoric living environment]. In *Nihon Kokogaku Kyokai Dai 52 kai Sokai Kenkyu Happyo Yoshi [Abstracts of the Papers Presented at the 52nd General Meeting of the Japanese Archaeological Association]*, p. 22. Tokyo: Nihon Kokogaku Kyokai (in Japanese).

Sahara, Makoto, and Masuo Nakano. 1984. Shibosan bunseki to kogaku [Lipid analyses and archaeology]. In *Nihon Kokogaku Kyokai Dai 52 kai Sokai kenkyu Happyo Yoshi [Abstracts of the Papers Presented at the 52nd General*

Meeting of the Japanese Archaeologica Association], p. 33. Tokyo: Nihon Koko-gaku Kyokai (in Japanese).

Saitama-ken Kyoiku Iinkai [Board of Education of Saitama Prefecture]. 1984. *Juno Deitanso Iseki Hakkutsu Chosa Hokoku-sho [Excavation Report of the Juno Waterlogged Site]*. Saitama: Board of Education of Saitama Prefecture (in Japanese).

Saito, Sachie. 1985. Kokuyoseki no riyo to ryutsu [Use and distribution of obsidian]. *Kikan Kokogaku [Archaeology Quarterly]* 12: 27–30 (in Japanese).

Sakamoto, A., and W. Nakamura. 1991. Jomon kaishin-ki no jukyoshi fukudo-nai kaiso: Yokohama-shi Nishinoyato kaizuka J30 go jukyoshi to so no kaiso ni tsuite [A shell-midden associated with a pit-dwelling from the Jomon marine transgression period: Dwelling J30 of the Nishinoyato site, Yokohama City and its associated shell-midden]. In *Chosa Kenkyu Shuroku [Excavation and Research Results]* 8, ed. Yokohama-shi Maizo Bunkazai Center [Archaeological Center of Yokohama City], pp. 61–130. Yokohama: Yokohama-shi Maizo Bunkazai Center (in Japanese).

Sakatsume, Nakao. 1957. Nihon genshi nogyo shiron [A tentative theory on primeval agriculture in Japan]. *Kokogaku Zasshi [Journal of the Archaeological Society of Nippon]* 42(2): 1–12 (in Japanese with English title).

——— 1959. *Nihon Kaizuka Chimei Hyo [A List of Shell-Middens in Japan]*. Tokyo: Doyokai (in Japanese).

——— 1961. *Nihon Sekki Jidai Shokuryo Sosetsu [An Outline of Stone Age Food in Japan]*. Tokyo: Doyokai (in Japanese).

Sannai Maruyama Iseki Taisaku-shitsu [Preservation Office of the Sannai Maruyama Site], ed. 1999. Sannai Maruyama iseki no jiki-betsu tateana jukyoshi-su [Number of pit-dwellings from each phase of Sannai Maruyama occupation]. In *Sannai Maruyama-jin no Shigen Riyo Model no Kochiku: Aomori-ken to no Sannai Maruyama Iseki ni kansuru Kyodo Kenkyu: 1998 nendo Hokoku [Resource Utilization at Sannai Maruyama: Collaboration with Aomori Prefecture on the Study of the Sannai Maruyama Site: Report of the 1998 Fiscal Year]*, p. 35. Aomori Prefecture: Aomori-ken Kyoiku Iinkai [Board of Education of Aomori Prefecture] (in Japanese).

Sasaki, Fujio. 1993. Wajima shuraku-ron to kokogaku no atarashii nagare [Wajima's settlement studies and new approaches in archaeological studies]. *Ibo* 13: 46–123 (in Japanese).

Sasaki, Komei, and Toshio Matsuyama, eds. 1988. *Hatasaku Bunka no Tanjo: Jomon Noko-ron e no Approach [Origins of Dry Field Cultivation: Approaches to Jomon Agriculture]*. Tokyo: Nihon Hoso Shuppan Kyokai (in Japanese).

Sasaki, Masaru. 1994. Iwate-ken ni okeru Jomon jidai no hottate-bashira tate-mono ni tsuite [On the *hottatebashira tatemono* (building with pillars embed-ded directly in the ground) in Jomon period in Iwate Prefecture area]. *Iwate Kenritsu Hakubutsu-kan Kenkyu Hokoku [Bulletin of the Iwate Prefec-tural Museum]* 12: 29–44 (in Japanese with English title).

Sasaki, Yoji. 1996. Ondashi Iseki no chosa keika to sono igi ni tsuite [Excavation of the Ondashi site and its implications]. In *Ondashi Iseki [The Ondashi Site]*, ed. Yamagata Kenritsu Ukitamu Fudoki no Oka Koko Shiryo-kan [Archaeological Museum of Yamagata Prefecture], pp. 32–33. Yamagata: Yamagata Kenritsu Ukitamu Fudoki no Oka Koko Shiryo-kan (in Japanese).

Sato, Hiroyuki. 1992. *Nihon Kyusekki Bunka no Kozo to Shinka [Structure and Evolution of the Japanese Palaeolithic Culture]*. Tokyo: Kashiwa Shobo (in Japanese).

Sato, Masahiko, and Masaru Kumagai. 1995. Shukyo no mondai [Jomon rituals]. *Kikan Kokogaku [Archaeology Quarterly]* 50: 75–80 (in Japanese).

Sato, Masanori, Mitsuru Mimura, Takayasu Koezuka, and Kazuo Yamazaki. 1999. Shutsudo kohaku no sanchi suitei ni kansuru kihon mondai [Sourcing of amber recovered from archaeological sites]. In *Nihon Bunkazai Kagaku-kai Dai 16-kai Taikai Kenkyu Happyo Yoshi-shu [Abstracts of the Papers Presented at the16th Annual Meeting of the Japanese Society for Scientific Studies on Cultural Properties]*, pp. 32–33. Nara: Nihon Bunkazai Kagaku-kai Dai 16 kai Taikai Kenkyu (in Japanese).

Sato, Yo-Ichiro. 1997. Mori no Bunmei, Jomon no sekai [Civilization of the forest: the Jomon world]. In *Jomon Toshi o Horu [Excavating a Jomon City]*, ed. Yasuhiro Okada and NHK Aomori, pp. 163–178. Tokyo: NHK (in Japanese).

1998. Sannai Maruyama iseki dai 6 tetto chiku shutsudo no kuri no DNA bunseki [DNA analysis of chestnuts recovered from the Sixth Transmission Tower Area of the Sannai Maruyama site]. In *Sannai Maruyama Iseki, IX dai 2 bunsatsu [The Sannai Maruyama Site, vol. IX, Part 2]*, ed. Aomori-ken Kyoiku-cho Bunka-ka [Cultural Affairs Section of the Agency of Education of Aomori Prefecture], pp. 141–146. Aomori: Aomori-ken Kyoiku Iinkai [Board of Education of Aomori Prefecture] (in Japanese).

Sato, Yo-Ichiro, Junko Habu, and Aoi Hosoya. 2002. Comparative studies of early agricultural societies [Sekai no Genshi Noko]. In *New Perspectives on Jomon Plant Cultivation* [Jomon Noko o Torae Naosu], ed. Y. Sato, pp. 107–128. Science of Humanity Bensei, No. 41. Tokyo: Bensei Shuppan, Tokyo (in Japanese).

Sato, Yo-Ichiro, Shinsuke Yamanaka, and Mitsuko Takahashi. 2003. Evidence for Jomon plant cultivation based on DNA analysis of chestnut remains. In *Hunter-Gatherers of the North Pacific Rim*, ed. Junko Habu, James M. Savelle, Shuzo Koyama, and Hitomi Hongo, pp. 187–197. Senri Ethnological Studies 63. Osaka: National Museum of Ethnology.

Schalk, Randall F. 1981. Land use and organizational complexity among foragers of northwestern North America. In *Affluent Foragers, Pacific Coasts East and West*, ed. Shuzo Koyama and David H. Thomas, pp. 53–75. Osaka: National Museum of Ethnology.

Schmidt, Peter R., and Thomas C. Patterson, eds. 1995. *Making Alternative Histories: The Practice of Archaeology and History in Non-Western Settings*. Santa Fe: School of American Research Press.

Seido, Kazunori. 1977. Jomon jidai shuraku no seiritsu to tenkai: Kokubu-dani shuhen kuiki ni okeru Zenki, Chuki o chusin to shite [Establishment and development of Jomon settlements, with special reference to the Kokubu-dani area during the Early and Middle Jomon periods]. *Chiba-ken Bunkazai Center Kenkyu Kiyo [Bulletin of the Archaeological Center of Chiba Prefecture]* 2: 1–36 (in Japanese).

Serizawa, Chosuke. 1960. *Sekki Jidai no Nihon [The Stone Age of Japan]*. Tokyo: Tsukiji Shokan (in Japanese with English title and table of contents).

1974. Sekki seisaku giho no hatten [Development of stone tool production technique]. In *Saiko no Kariudo-tachi [Ancient Hunters]*, ed. Chosuke Serizawa, pp. 38–50. Tokyo: Kodansha (in Japanese).

Serizawa, Chosuke, and Takashi Suto. 1968. Tazawa Iseki chosa yoho [Preliminary report of the excavation of the Tazawa site]. *Kokogaku Journal [Journal of Archaeology]* 27: 6–8 (in Japanese).

Shanks, Michael, and Christopher Tilley. 1987. *Reconstructing Archaeology*. Cambridge: Cambridge University Press.

Sherratt, Andrew. 1997. Climatic cycles and behavioral revolutions: the emergence of modern humans and the beginning of farming. *Antiquity* 71: 271–287.

Shibuya, Takao. 2000. Teishicchi Jomon iseki no shin-hakken: Yamagata-ken Ondashi iseki [New discoveries at a waterlogged Jomon site: the Ondashi site in Yamagata Prefecture]. *Shiroi Kuni no Uta [Essays on Northern Land]* 526: 22–25 (in Japanese).

Shiga-ken Kyoiku Iinkai [Board of Education of Shiga Prefecture]. 1973. *Kosaisen Kankei Iseki Hakkutsu Chosa Hokoku-sho [Archaeological Excavations prior to the Construction of the Kosai Line]*. Shiga: Shiga-ken Kyoiku Iinkai (in Japanese).

Shimizu, Yoshihiro. 1973. Jomon jidai no shudan ryoiki ni tsuite [On group territory in the Jomon period]. *Kokogaku Kenkyu [Quarterly of Archaeological Studies]* 19(4): 90–102 (in Japanese).

Shinoda, Ken'ichi, and Satoru Kanai. 1999. Intracemetery genetic analysis at the Nakazuma Jomon site in Japan by mitochondrial DNA sequencing. *Anthropological Science* 107(2): 129–140.

Shinto, Koichi. 1997. Minami Kyushu no shoki Jomon bunka [Incipient and Initial Jomon Cultures in southern Kyushu]. In *Kagoshima no Jomon Bunka [The Jomon Culture in Kagoshima]*, ed. KTS Kagoshima Television, pp. 24–25. Kagoshima: Kokubu Uenohara Symposium Jikko Iinkai [Committee for the Symposium on the Uenohara Site] (in Japanese).

Shiraishi, Hiroyuki. 1980. *Terao Iseki [The Terao Site]*. Yokohama: Kanagawa-ken Kyoiku Iinkai [Board of Education of Kanagawa Prefecture] (in Japanese).

2000. Jomon Jidai Sosoki no yoso [Characteristics of the Incipient Jomon culture]. In *Symposium: Kyusekki kara Jomon e: Iko to Kukan Riyo: Happyo Yoshi [Papers of Millennium Symposia at Kagoshima by the Japanese Archaeological Association: From Palaeolithic Age to Jomon Period – Structural Remains and Space-Utilization]*, ed. Nihon Kokogaku Kyokai 2000 nendo Kagoshima Taikai Jikko Iinkai [Executive Committee of the Convention at Kagoshima, the Japanese Archaeological Association, October 22], pp. 32–35. Kagoshima: Nihon Kokogaku Kyokai 2000 nendo Kagoshima Taikai Jikko Iinkai, Kagoshima (in Japanese with English title).

Shitara, Hiromi. 1983. Dosei mimi-kazari [Clay earrings]. In *Jomon Bunka no Kenkyu IX: Jomon-jin no Seishin Bunka [Studies of the Jomon Culture, vol. IX: Mortuary and Ceremonial Practices]*, ed. Shinpei Kato, Tatsuo Kobayashi, and Tsuyoshi Fujimoto, pp. 206–217. Tokyo: Yuzankaku (in Japanese).

1999. Maiso to haka no iroiro [Variability in mortuary practices]. In *Jomon Sekai no Ichiman-nen [Ten Thousand Years of Jomon]*, ed. Takura Izumi and Yasutami Nishida, pp. 22–24. Tokyo: Shueisha (in Japanese).

Soffer, Olga. 1989. Storage, sedentism and the Eurasian Paleolithic record. *Antiquity* 63: 719–732.

Sowers, T., M. Bender, L. Labeyrie, D. Martinson, J. Jouzel, D. Raynaud, J. J. Pichon, and A. Korotkevich. 1993. A 135,000 year Vostok-Specmap common temporal framework. *Paleoceanography* 8: 737–766.

Spencer, Robert F. 1959. *The North Alaskan Eskimo: A Study in Ecology and Society.* Washington, D. C.: Smithsonian Institution.

Stewart, Henry. 1982. Kaishin, kaitai [Transgression and regression of sea level]. In *Jomon Bunka no Kenkyu I: Jomonjin to sono Kankyo [Studies of the Jomon Culture, vol. I: The Jomon People and the Surrounding Environment]*, ed. Shinpei Kato, Tatsuo Kobayashi, and Tsuyoshi Fujimoto, pp. 130–142. Tokyo: Yuzankaku (in Japanese).

Stuiver, Minze, and Pieter M. Grootes. 2000. GISP2 oxygen isotope ratios. *Quaternary Research* 53(3): 277–284.

Stuiver, Minze, Pieter M. Grootes, and Thomas F. Braziunas. 1995. The GISP $\delta^{18}O$ climate record of the past 16,500 years and the role of the sun, ocean, and volcanoes. *Quaternary Research* 44: 341–354.

Stuiver, M., and P. Reimer. 1993. Extended ^{14}C data base and revised CALIB 3.0 ^{14}C age calibrating program. *Radiocarbon* 35(1): 215–230.

Stuiver, M., P. J. Reimer, E. Bard, J. W. Beck, G. S. Burr, K. A. Hughen, B. Kromer, G. McCormac, J. van der Plicht, and M. Spurk. 1998a. INTCAL98 radiocarbon age calibration, 24000–0 cal BP. *Radiocarbon* 40(3): 1041–1083.

Stuiver, M., P. J. Reimer, and T. F. Braziunas. 1998b. High-precision radiocarbon age calibration for terrestrial and marine samples. *Radiocarbon* 40(3): 1127–1151.

Sugawara, Masaaki. 1972. Jomon jidai no shuraku [Settlements during the Jomon period]. *Kokogaku Kenkyu [Quarterly of Archaeological Studies]* 19(2): 47–63 (in Japanese).

Sugihara, Sosuke, and Chosuke Serizawa. 1957. *Kanagawa-ken Natsushima ni okeru Jomon Jidai Shoto no Kaizuka [A Shell-Midden from the Beginning of the Jomon Period at Natsushima, Kanagawa Prefecture]*. Tokyo: Meiji University (in Japanese).

Sugitani, Masaki, Nakagawa Akira, and Nishide Takashi. 1998. Mie-ken Iinan-gun Iinan-cho Kayumi Ijiri iseki [The Kayumi Ijiri site, Iinan town, Iinan County, Mie Prefecture]. *Nihon Kokogaku Nenpo [Archaeologia Japonica]* 49 *(Annual Report of the Japanese Archaeological Studies and Excavations: Fiscal Year 1996)*, pp. 524–527 (in Japanese with English title and summary).

Sugiura, Shigenobu, ed. 1987. *Higashi Rokugo 1, 2 Iseki [The Higashi Rokugo nos. 1 and 2 Sites]*. Furano: Furano-shi Kyoiku Iinkai [Board of Education of Furano City] (in Japanese).

Suzuki, Hideo. 1974. Hypsithermal ni okeru sekai no kiko [World climates in the hypsithermal]. *Daiyonki Kenkyu [Quaternary Research]* 13(3): 99–105 (in Japanese with English title and summary).

Suzuki, Jiro. 1983. Dasei sekifu [Chipped stone axes]. In *Jomon Bunka no Kenkyu VII: Dogu to Gijutsu [Studies of the Jomon Culture, vol. VII: Tools and Technology]*, ed. Shinpei Kato, Tatsuo Kobayashi, and Tsuyoshi Fujimoto, pp. 48–59. Tokyo: Yuzankaku (in Japanese).

308   References

1985. Sekifu no tairyo seisan [Mass-production of stone axes and adzes]. *Kikan Kokogaku [Archaeology Quarterly]* 12: 31–34 (in Japanese).

Suzuki, Kimio. 1979. Jomon Jidai ron [A study of the Jomon period]. In *Nihon Kokogaku o Manabu III: Genshi-Kodai no Shakai [Studying Japanese Archaeology*, vol. III: *Prehistoric and Ancient Societies]*, ed. Hatsushige Otsuka, Mitsunori Tozawa, and Makoto Sahara, pp. 178–202. Tokyo: Yuzankaku (in Japanese).

1986. Volumetry and nutritional analysis of a Jomon shellmidden. In *Prehistoric Hunter-Gatherers in Japan*, ed. Takeru Akazawa and C. Melvin Aikens, pp. 55–72. Tokyo: University Museum, University of Tokyo.

ed. 1988. *Kodaishi Fukugen II: Jomon-jin no Seikatsu to Bunka [Reconstruction of Ancient History*, vol. II: *Lifeways and Culture of the Jomon People]*. Tokyo: Kodansha (in Japanese).

1992. Prehistoric *urushi* (lacquer) manufacture in Japan. Paper presented at Art, Technology, and Society in Ancient Japan, Arthur M. Sackler Gallery, Smithsonian Institution.

Suzuki, Masahiro. 1993. Doki seien to kaizuka [Salt production and shellmiddens]. *Kikan Kokogaku [Archaeology Quarterly]* 41: 47–51 (in Japanese).

Suzuki, Masao. 1969. Fission track ho ni yoru kokuyoseki no funshutsu nendai to uran nodo no sokutei dai I po (Fission track dating and uranium content of obsidian (Part I). *Daiyonki Kenkyu [Quaternary Research]* 8(4): 123–130 (in Japanese with English title and summary).

1970a. Fission track ho ni yoru kokuyoseki no funshutsu nendai to uran nodo no sokutei dai II ho [Fission track dating and uranium content of obsidian (Part II)]. *Daiyonki Kenkyu [Quaternary Research]* 9(4): 1–6 (in Japanese with English title and summary).

1970b. Fission track ages and uranium contents of obsidians. *Journal of the Anthropological Society of Nippon* 17(1): 50–57.

1973. Chronology of prehistoric human activity in Kanto, Japan. Part I. *Journal of the Faculty of Science, University of Tokyo, Section V: Anthropology* 4(3): 241–318.

1974a. Butsuri kagaku donyu ni yoru nendai sokutei [Dating methods using physics and chemistry]. In *Saiko no Kariudo-tachi [Ancient Hunters]*, ed. Chosuke Serizawa, pp. 151–159. Tokyo: Kodansha (in Japanese).

1974b. Chronology of prehistoric human activity in Kanto, Japan. Part II. *Journal of the Faculty of Science, University of Tokyo, Section V: Anthropology* 4(4): 395–469.

Suzuki, Toshiaki. 1989. Moroiso b shiki kara c shiki e no doki hensen [Changes over time from Moroiso-b to Moroiso-c style pottery]. *Saitama Kenritsu Hakubutsu-kan Kiyo [Bulletin of Saitama Prefectural Museum]* 15: 29–48 (in Japanese).

Tainter, Joseph A. 1996. Introduction: prehistoric societies as evolving complex systems. In *Evolving Complexity and Environmental Risk in the Prehistoric Southwest*, ed. J. A. Tainter and B. B. Tainter, pp. 1–23. Reading, Mass: Addison-Wesley.

Takahashi, Mamoru. 1958. Doki to sono keishiki [Pottery and style]. *Kokogaku Techo [Archaeology Notes]* 1: 1–2 (in Japanese).

1965. Jomon jidai ni okeru shuraku bunpu ni tsuite [Settlement distribution during the Jomon period]. *Kokogaku Kenkyu [Quarterly of Archaeological Studies]* 12(1): 16–20 (in Japanese).

Takahashi, Mitsuru. 1996. Doki seien no kotei to shudan [Social groups behind various stages of salt-making]. *Kikan Kokogaku [Archaeology Quarterly]* 55: 38–43 (in Japanese).

Takahashi, Osamu. 1998. Hokkaido ni okeru Jomon jidai no shokubutsu saibai to noko no chihei [Jomon plant cultivation in Hokkaido and the origins of agriculture]. *Kokogaku Journal [Journal of Archaeology]* 439: 4–9 (in Japanese).

Takahashi, Ryuzaburo. 1999. Haka to bochi kozo: Higashi Nihon: Kanto Chiho ni okeru Jomon Koki zenhan no bosei [Burials and cemetery structures: eastern Japan: mortuary practices during the Late Jomon period in the Kanto region]. *Kikan Kokogaku [Archaeology Quarterly]* 69: 55–59 (in Japanese).

Takano, Mitsuyuki. 1979. Gyobutsu sekki [Gyobutsu stone bars]. In *Sekai Kokogaku Jiten [Encyclopedia of World Archaeology]*, ed. Heibonsha, p. 285. Tokyo: Heibonsha (in Japanese).

Takayama, Jun. 1974. Sake/masu to Jomon-jin [Salmon and the Jomon people]. *Kikan Jinruigaku [Anthropology Quarterly]* 5(1): 3–54 (in Japanese).

Takeda, Akiko. 1996. Ondashi iseki shutsudo urushi seihin ni tsuite [Lacquered artifacts recovered from the Ondashi site]. In *Ondashi Iseki [The Ondashi Site]*, ed. Yamagata Kenritsu Ukitamu Fudoki no Oka Koko Shiryo-kan [Archaeological Museum of Yamagata Prefecture], pp. 40–41. Yamagata: Yamagata Kenritsu Ukitamu Fudoki no Oka Koko Shiryo-kan [Archaeological Museum of Yamagata Prefecture] (in Japanese).

Takei, Norimichi. 1990. Nanbori kaizuka [The Nanbori shell-midden]. In *Kohoku New Town Chiiki Nai Maizo Bunkazai Chosa Hokoku, X: Zen Iseki Chosa Gaiyo [Excavation Report of Recovered Materials from Kohoku New Town Area vol. X: Overview]*, ed. Yokohama-shi Maizo Bunkazai Center [Archaeological Center of Yokohama City], pp. 16–18. Yokohama: Yokohama-shi Maizo Bunkazai Center (in Japanese).

Tamada, Yoshihide. 1996. Sei to Jomon doki [Life and Jomon pottery]. In *Rekishi Hakkutsu II: Jomon Doki Shutsugen [Excavation of the Past, vol. II: Emergence of Jomon Pottery]*, ed. Takura Izumi, pp. 74–109. Tokyo: Kodansha (in Japanese).

Tanaka, Migaku. 1984. Japan. In *Approaches to Archaeological Heritage*, ed. H. Cleere, pp. 82–88. Cambridge: Cambridge University Press.

Taniguchi, Yasuhiro. 1999a. Archaeological research at the Odai Yamamoto I site: summary. In *Odai Yamamoto I Iseki no Kokogaku Chosa [Archaeological Research at the Odai Yamamoto I Site]*, ed. Odai Yamamoto I Iseki Hakkutsu Chosa-dan [Odai Yamamoto I Site Excavation Team], pp. 135–144. Tokyo: Odai Yamamoto I Iseki Hakkutsu Chosa-dan [Odai Yamamoto I Site Excavation Team] (English summary of the report).

1999b. Chojakubo Bunka-ki no shomondai [Problems of the Chojakubo culture period]. In *Odai Yamamoto Iseki no Kokogaku Chosa [Archaeological Research at the Odai Yamamoto I Site]*, ed. Odai Yamamoto I Iseki Hakkutsu Chosa-dan [The Odai Yamamoto I Site Excavation Team], pp. 84–99. Tokyo:

Odai Yamamoto I Iseki Hakkutsu Chosa-dan [The Odai Yamamoto I Site Excavation Team] (in Japanese).

1999c. Doki [Pottery]. In *Odai Yamamoto I Iseki no Kokogaku Chosa [Archaeological Research at the Odai Yamamoto I Site]*, ed. Odai Yamamoto I Iseki Hakkutsu Chosa-dan [The Odai Yamamoto I Site Excavation Team], pp. 26–33. Tokyo: Odai Yamamoto I Iseki Hakkutsu Chosa-dan [The Odai Yamamoto I Site Excavation Team] (in Japanese).

Terakado, Yoshinori. 1983. Seien [Salt production]. In *Jomon Bunka no Kenkyu II: Seigyo [Studies of the Jomon Culture, vol. II: Subsistence]*, ed. Shinpei Kato, Tatsuo Kobayashi, and Tsuyoshi Fujimoto, pp. 239–251. Tokyo: Yuzankaku (in Japanese).

Terasawa, Kaoru, and Tomoko Terasawa. 1981. Yayoi jidai shokubutsu-shitsu shokuryo no kiso-teki kenkyu [Basic studies of plant foods of the Yayoi period]. *Kashihara Kokogaku Kenkyu-jo Kiyo Kokogaku Ronko* 5: 1–129 (in Japanese).

Teshigawara, Akira. 1988. Jomon jidai shuraku o meguru mondai [Current issues in Jomon settlement archaeology]. *Rekishi Hyoron [Critiques in History]* 466: 112–125 (in Japanese).

Tochigi-ken Kyoiku Iinkai [Board of Education of Tochigi Prefecture] and Oyama-shi Kyoiku Iinkai [Board of Education of Oyama City]. 1994. *Terano-higashi Iseki [The Terano-higashi Site]*. Oyama: Tochigi-ken Kyoiku Iinkai, and Oyama-shi Kyoiku Iinkai (in Japanese).

Togashi, Yasutoki. 1983. Seiryuto-gata sekki [*Seiryuto*-shaped stone tools]. In *Jomon Bunka no Kenkyu IX: Jomon-jin no Seishin Bunka [Studies of the Jomon Culture, vol. IX: Mortuary and Ceremonial Practices]*, ed. Shinpei Kato, Tatsuo Kobayashi, and Tsuyoshi Fujimoto, pp. 197–205. Tokyo: Yuzankaku (in Japanese).

Toi-machi Kyoiku Iinkai [Board of Education of Toi Town]. 1993. *Toi Kaizuka III [The Toi Shell-Midden, vol. III]*. Toi: Toi-machi Kyoiku Iinkai (in Japanese).

Toizumi, Gakuji. 1998. Sannai Maruyama iseki dai 6 tetto chiku shutsudo no gyorui itai (I) [Fish remains recovered from the Sixth Transmission Tower Area of the Sannai Maruyama site (I)]. In *Sannai Maruyama Iseki, IX, dai 2 bunsatsu [The Sannai Maruyama Site, vol. IX, Part 2]*, ed. Aomori-ken Kyoiku-cho bunka-ka [Cultural Affairs Section of the Agency of Education of Aomori Prefecture], pp. 61–97. Aomori: Aomori-ken Kyoiku Iinkai [Board of Education of Aomori Prefecture] (in Japanese).

Toizumi, Gakuji, and Hiro'omi Tsumura. 2000. Iseki no hoshasei tanso nendai to reki nendai [^{14}C dates and calendar dates of archaeological sites]. In *Nihon Senshi Jidai no ^{14}C Nendai [^{14}C dates from Japanese Prehistoric Periods]*, ed. Nihon Senshi Jidai no ^{14}C Nendai Henshu Iinkai [Editorial Committee of "^{14}C dates from Japanese Prehistoric Periods"]. Tokyo: Daiyonki Gakkai [Japan Association for Quaternary Research] (in Japanese).

Toma, Seita. 1951. *Nihon Minzoku no Keisei [The Origins and Formation of the Japanese People and Culture]*. Tokyo: Iwanami Shoten (in Japanese).

Torrence, Robin. 1986. *Production and Exchange of Stone Tools: Prehistoric Obsidian in the Aegean*. Cambridge: Cambridge University Press.

Toyoshima, Y. 1978. Postglacial sea level change along San'in district, Japan. *Chirigaku Hyoron [Geographical Review of Japan]* 51: 147–157 (in Japanese with English summary).

Tozawa, Mitsunori. 1989. Kaizuka o hakkutsu suru [Excavating shell-middens]. In *Jomon-jin to Kaizuka [Jomon People and Shell-Middens]*, ed. Mitsunori Tozawa, pp. 11–56. Tokyo: Rokko Shuppan (in Japanese).

Trigger, Bruce G. 1967. Settlement archaeology: its goals and promise. *American Antiquity* 32(2): 149–160.

   1968. The determinants of settlement patterns. In *Settlement Archaeology*, ed. Kwang-chih Chang, pp. 53–78. Palo Alto: National Press Books.

   1995. Romanticism, nationalism and archaeology. In *Nationalism, Politics, and the Practice of Archaeology*, ed. Philip L. Kohl and Clare Fawcett, pp. 263–279. Cambridge: Cambridge University Press.

Tsuboi, Kiyotari. 1962. Jomon bunka-ron [On the Jomon culture]. In *Iwanami Koza Nihon no Rekishi I: Genshi oyobi Kodai [Iwanami Lectures in Japanese History*, vol. I: *Prehistoric and Protohistoric Periods]*, ed. Yoshiro Kondo and Koichi Yokoyama, pp. 109–138. Tokyo: Iwanami Shoten (in Japanese).

Tsuji, Seiichiro. 1996. Shokubutsu-so kara mita Sannai Maruyama iseki [The Sannai Maruyama site seen from its floral assemblage]. In *Sannai Maruyama Iseki, VI [The Sannai Maruyama Site*, vol. VI], ed. Aomori-ken Kyoiku-cho Bunka-ka [Cultural Affairs Section of the Agency of Education of Aomori Prefecture], pp. 81–83. Aomori: Aomori-ken Kyoiku Iinkai [Board of Education of Aomori Prefecture] (in Japanese).

   1997a. Sannai Maruyama o sasaeta seitaikei [The ecosystems that supported Sannai Maruyama]. In *Jomon Toshi o Horu [Excavating a Jomon City]*, ed. Yasuhiro Okada and NHK Aomori, pp. 174–188. Tokyo: NHK (in Japanese).

   1997b. Jomon jidai e no ikoki ni okeru rikujo seitaikei [A land ecosystem in the transition to the Jomon age]. *Daiyonki Kenkyu [Quaternary Research]* 36(5): 309–318 (in Japanese with English title and summary).

   1998. Sannai Maruyama iseki: Jomon jidai zenki no taiseki butsu no naiyo to kankyo fukugen [The Sannai Maruyama site: contents of Early Jomon sediments and environmental reconstruction]. In *Sannai Maruyama Iseki, IX, dai 2 Bunsatsu [The Sannai Maruyama Site*, vol. IX, Part 2], ed. Aomori-ken Kyoiku-cho Bunka-ka [Cultural Affairs Section of the Agency of Education of Aomori Prefecture], pp. 27–28. Aomori: Aomori-ken Kyoiku Iinkai [Board of Education of Aomori Prefecture] (in Japanese with English title and summary).

   1999. Koseido ^{14}C nendai sokutei ni yoru Sannai Maruyama Iseki no hennen [Chronology at the Sannai Maruyama site using a high-precision ^{14}C dating method]. *Gekkan Chikyu Special Issue* 26: 32–38 (in Japanese with English title and summary).

Tsukada, Matsuo. 1986. Vegetation in prehistoric Japan. In *Windows on the Japanese Past: Studies in Archaeology and Prehistory*, ed. Richard Pearson, Gina L. Barnes, and Karl L. Hutterer, pp. 11–56. Ann Arbor: Center for Japanese Studies, University of Michigan.

Tsukamoto, Moroya 1993. Shokuryo chozo [Food storage]. *Kikan Kokogaku [Archaeology Quarterly]* 44: 62–66 (in Japanese).

Tsunoyama, Yukihiro. 1971. Shokko [Textile production]. In *Shinpan Kokogaku Koza VIII [Lectures in Archaeology: New Edition*, vol. VIII*]*, ed. Iwao Oba, pp. 175–182. Tokyo: Yuzankaku (in Japanese).

Tsutsumi, Takashi. 1998. Human adaptation system in the last glacial–postglacial transition in Japan. In *Abstracts of Papers Presented at the Symposium on the Comparative Archaeology of the Pleistocene–Holocene Transition*, ed. Akira Ono, pp. 35–53. Sakura: National Museum of Japanese History (in English and Japanese).

Ueki, Hiroshi. 1999. Ibutsu kenkyu: dogu (kino-ron, yoto-ron) [Function and usage of clay figurines]. *Jomon Jidai [Journal of Jomon Period Studies]* 10(4): 133–138 (in Japanese with English title).

Umitsu, Masatomo. 1976. Geomorphic development of the Tsugaru Plain in the Holocene period. *Chirigaku Hyoron [Geographical Review of Japan]* 49: 714–735 (in Japanese with English abstract).

Ushirono Iseki Chosa-dan [Excavation Team of the Ushirono Site], ed. 1976. *Ushirono Iseki [The Ushirono Site]*. Katsuta: Katsuta-shi Kyoiku Iinkai [Board of Education of the Katsuta City] (in Japanese with English abstract).

Ushizawa, Yuriko. 1981. Isarago kaizuka shutsudo no gyorin [Fish scales recovered from the Isarago shell-midden]. In *Isarago Kaizuka Iseki [The Isarago Shell-Midden Site]*, ed. Isarago Kaizuka Iseki Chosa-dan [Excavation Team of the Isarago Shell-Midden Site], pp. 422–439. Tokyo: Minato-ku Isarago Iseki Chosa-kai [Committee for the Excavation of the Isarago Shell-Midden Site] (in Japanese).

Vita-Finzi, Claudio, and Eric S. Higgs. 1970. Prehistoric economy in the Mount Carmel area of Palestine: site catchment analysis. *Proceedings of the Prehistoric Society* 36: 1–37.

Wajima, Seiichi. 1948. Genshi shuraku no kosei [The organization and composition of prehistoric settlements]. In *Nihon Rekishi-gaku Koza [Lectures in Japanese History]*, ed. Tokyo Daigaku Rekishigaku Kenkyu-kai [Historical Association of the University of Tokyo], pp. 1–32. Tokyo: Tokyo Daigaku Shuppan-kai [University of Tokyo Press] (in Japanese).

     1958. Nanbori kaizuka to genshi shuraku [The Nanbori shell-midden and settlements of the prehistoric period]. In *Yokohama Shi-shi I [History of Yokohama City*, vol. I*]*, pp. 29–46. Yokohama: Yokohama-shi [Yokohama City] (in Japanese).

     1962. Josetsu: noko-bokuchiku hassei izen no genshi kyodotai [Introduction: primitive communities before agriculture and animal husbandry]. In *Kodaishi Koza [Lectures in Ancient History]*, pp. 1–16. Tokyo: Gakusei-sha (in Japanese).

Wajima, Seiichi, T. Matsui, Y. Hasegawa, I. Okamoto, K. Tsukada, Y. Tanaka, Y. Nakamura, T. Komiya, T. Kurobe, K. Takahashi, and T. Sato. 1968. Kanto Heiya ni okeru Jomon kaishin no saiko kaisuijun ni tsuite [On the highest sea level of the Neolithic transgression in the Kanto Plain]. *Shigen Kagaku Kenkyu-jo Shuho [Bulletin of the Institute for Scientific Studies of Resources]* 70: 108–129 (in Japanese with English title and summary).

Warashina, Tetsuo. 1999. Sekki to tama no genzai sanchi bunseki [Sourcing of stone tools and beads]. In *Nihon Bunkazai Kagaku-kai dai 16 kai Taikai Kenkyu Happyo Yoshi [Abstracts of the Papers Presented at the 16th Annual Meeting of the Japanese Society for Scientific Studies on Cultural Properties]*, pp. 68–73. Nara: Nihon Bunkazai Kagaku-kai (in Japanese).

2001. Hatanai iseki shutsudo kokuyoseki-sei sekki no genzai sanchi bunseki [Sourcing of obsidian tools recovered from the Hatanai site]. In *Hatanai Iseki, VII, dai 2 bunsatsu [The Hatanai Site, vol. VII, Part 2]*, ed. Aomori-ken Kyoiku Iinkai [Board of Education of Aomori Prefecture], pp. 3–10. Aomori: Aomori-ken Kyoiku Iinkai [Board of Education of Aomori Prefecture] (in Japanese).

Warashina, Tetsuo, and Takenobu Higashimura. 1983. Sekki genzai no sanchi bunseki [Sourcing of raw materials of stone implements]. *Kokogaku to Shizen Kagaku [Archaeology and Natural Science]* 16: 59–88 (in Japanese with English title).

Watanabe, Hitoshi. 1964. Ainu no seitai to honpo senshi-gaku no mondai [Ecology of the Ainu and problems in the prehistory of Japan]. *Jinruigaku Zasshi [Journal of the Anthropological Society of Nippon]* 72(1): 9–23 (in Japanese with English title and summary).

1966. Jomon jidai jin no seitai: jukyo no antei-sei to sono seibutsugaku-teki minzokushi-teki igi [Ecology of the Jomon people: stability of habitation and its biological and ethnohistorical implications]. *Jinruigaku Zasshi [Journal of the Anthropological Society of Nippon]* 74(2): 73–84 (in Japanese with English title and summary).

1972. *The Ainu Ecosystem: Environment and Group Structure*. Tokyo: University of Tokyo Press.

1983. Occupational differentiation and social stratification: the case of northern Pacific maritime food-gatherers. *Current Anthropology* 24(2): 217–219.

1986. Community habitation and food gathering in prehistoric Japan: an ethnographic interpretation of the archaeological evidence. In *Windows on the Japanese Past: Studies in Archaeology and Prehistory*, ed. Richard J. Pearson, Gina L. Barnes, and Karl L. Hutterer, pp. 229–254. Ann Arbor: Center for Japanese Studies, University of Michigan.

1990. *Jomon-shiki Kaisoka Shakai [Jomon Stratified Society]*. Tokyo: Rokko Shuppan (in Japanese).

Watanabe, Makoto. 1967. Nihon sekki jidai bunka kenkyu ni okeru "sake/masu" ron no mondai-ten [Problems with the "salmon-fishing hypothesis" in the study of the Japanese Stone Age culture]. *Kodai Bunka [Cultura Antiqua]* 18(2): 33–36 (in Japanese).

1970. Aomori-ken Ruike kaizuka ni okeru shizen ibutsu no kenkyu [Analysis of faunal remains from the Ruike shell-midden in Aomori Prefecture]. *Kodaigaku Kenkyu [Studies of Prehistory and Protohistory]* 17(3): 82–87 (in Japanese).

1973a. Jomon jidai no donguri [Note on acorns in the Jomon period: an approach to the gathering economy]. *Kodai Bunka [Cultura Antiqua]* 25(4): 127–133 (in Japanese).

1973b. "Sake/masu" ron hihan [Criticism of the "salmon-fishing hypothesis"]. In *Jomon Jidai no Gyoryo [Fishing during the Jomon Period]*, pp. 206–212. Tokyo: Yuzankaku (in Japanese).

1975. *Jomon Jidai no Shokubutsu-shoku [Plant Food during the Jomon Period]*. Tokyo: Yuzankaku (in Japanese).

Watanabe, Naotsune. 1966. Jomon oyobi Yayoi jidai no C^{14} nendai [Radiocarbon dates of the Jomon and Yayoi periods in Japan]. *Daiyonki Kenkyu [Quaternary Research]* 5(3–4): 157–168 (in Japanese with English title and summary).

Watanabe, Yoshimichi, Akira Misawa, Kimio Izu, and Jiro Hayakawa, eds. 1936. *Nihon Rekishi Kyotei dai 1 satsu- Genshi Shakai no Hokai made [Textbook of Japanese History, Part 1: Up to the Collapse of the Primitive Society]*. Tokyo: Hakuyosha (in Japanese).

Weninger, B., Olaf Jöris, and Uwe Danzeglocke. 2002. CalPal for Windows. Available from: http://www.calpal.de/

Willey, Gordon R. 1953. *Prehistoric Settlement Patterns in the Viru Valley, Peru.* Washington, D.C.: Smithsonian Institution.

Winterhalder, Bruce. 1981. Optimal foraging strategies and hunter-gatherer research in anthropology: theory and models. In *Hunter-Gatherer Foraging Strategies*, ed. Bruce Winterhalder and Eric A. Smith, pp. 13–36. Chicago: University of Chicago Press.

Wylie, Alison. 1991 Feminist critiques and archaeological challenges. In *Archaeology of Gender*, ed. Dale Walde and Noreen D. Willows, pp. 17–23. Calgary: Archaeological Association of the University of Calgary.

1993. A proliferation of new archaeologies: "beyond objectivism and relativism." In *Archaeological Theory: Who Sets the Agenda?*, ed. Norman Yoffee and Andrew Sherratt, pp. 20–26. Cambridge: Cambridge University Press.

Yamada, Masahisa. 1983. Mokusei-hin [Wooden artifacts]. In *Jomon Bunka no Kenkyu VII: Dogu to Gijutsu [Studies of the Jomon Culture, vol. VII: Tools and Technology]*, ed. Shinpei Kato, Tatsuo Kobayashi, and Tsuyoshi Fujimoto, pp. 263–283. Tokyo: Yuzankaku (in Japanese).

1997. Jomon shuraku no okisa to shikumi [The size and structure of Jomon settlements]. In *Jomon Toshi o Horu [Excavating a Jomon City]*, ed. Yasuhiro Okada and NHK Aomori, pp. 127–148. Tokyo: NHK (in Japanese).

Yamada, Yoshikazu, ed. 1986. *Ishikawa-ken Noto-machi Mawaki Iseki [The Mawaki Site, Noto Town, Ishikawa Prefecture]*. Noto: Noto-machi Kyoiku Iinkai [Board of Education of Noto Town] and Mawaki Iseki Hakkutsu Chosa-dan [Excavation Team of the Mawaki Site] (in Japanese).

Yamamoto, Teruhisa. 1979. Sekibo saishi no hensen [Transitions of the religious meaning of stone-rods in Jomon period, Japan]. *Kodai Bunka [Cultura Antiqua]* 31 (11) and 31 (12): 651–691, 713–736 (in Japanese with English title).

1983. Sekibo [Stone rods]. In *Jomon Bunka no Kenkyu IX: Jomon-jin no Seishin Bunka [Studies of the Jomon Culture, vol. IX: Mortuary and Ceremonial Practices]*, ed. Shinpei Kato, Tatsuo Kobayashi, and Tsuyoshi Fujimoto, pp. 86–94. Tokyo: Yuzankaku (in Japanese).

Yamanaka, Shinsuke, Yasuhiro Okada, Ikuo Nakamura, and Yo-Ichiro Sato. 1999. Shokubutsu itai no DNA takei kaiseki shuho no kakuritsu ni yoru

Jomon jidai zenki Sannai Maruyama iseki no kuri saibai no kanosei [Evidence for ancient plant domestication based on DNA analysis of plant remains: chestnut domestication in Sannai Maruyama sites]. *Kokogaku to Shizen Kagaku [Archaeology and Natural Science]* 38: 13–28 (in Japanese with English title).

Yamanashi-ken Kyoiku Iinkai [Board of Education of Yamanashi Prefecture]. 1994. *Tenjin Iseki [The Tenjin Site]*. Kofu: Board of Education of Yamanashi Prefecture [Yamanashi-ken Kyoiku Iinkai] (in Japanese).

Yamanashi-ken Maizo Bunkazai Chosa Center [Archaeological Center of Yamanashi Prefecture]. 1989. *Kinsei Iseki II: Jomon Jidai hen [The Kinsei Site II: Artifacts and Features from the Jomon Period]*. Kofu: Board of Education of Yamanashi Prefecture [Yamanashi-ken Kyoiku Iinkai] (in Japanese).

Yamanouchi, Sugao. 1932a. Nihon enko no bunka 1: Jomon doki bunka no shinso [Ancient culture of Japan, Part 1: Overview of the Jomon pottery culture]. *Dolmen [Dolmen]* 1(4): 40–43 (in Japanese).

1932b. Nihon enko no bunka 2: Jomon doki no kigen [Ancient culture of Japan, Part 2: Origin of Jomon pottery]. *Dolmen [Dolmen]* 1(5): 85–90 (in Japanese).

1932c. Nihon enko no bunka 3: Jomon doki no shumatsu [Ancient culture of Japan, Part 3: The end of Jomon pottery]. *Dolmen [Dolmen]* 1(6): 46–50 (in Japanese).

1937. Jomon doki no saibetsu to taibetsu [Classification and sub-classification of Jomon pottery]. *Senshi Koko-gaku [Prehistoric Archaeology]* 1: 28–32 (in Japanese).

1964a. Nihon senshi jidai gaisetsu [The outline of Japanese prehistory]. In *Nihon Genshi Bijutsu I: Jomon-shiki Doki [Primitive Art in Japan*, vol. I: *Jomon Pottery]*, pp. 135–158. Tokyo: Kodansha (in Japanese).

1964b. Jomon shiki doki kakuron [Typological chronology of Jomon pottery]. In *Nihon Genshi Bijutsu I: Jomon-shiki Doki [Primitive Art in Japan*, vol. I: *Jomon Pottery]*, pp. 159–173. Tokyo: Kodansha (in Japanese).

1968. Yagara kenmaki ni tsuite [Arrow shaft smoothers in world prehistory and their bearing on the chronology of Jomon pottery]. In *Nihon Minzoku to Nanpo Bunka [Interaction between the Japanese and Southeast Asian Cultures: In Honour of Prof. Dr. Kanaseki Takeo on the Occasion of His Seventieth Birthday]*, ed. Kanaseki Takeo Hakushi Koki Kinen Iinkai [The Committee for the Commemoration of Prof. Dr. Kanaseki's Seventieth Birthday], pp. 63–87. Tokyo: Heibon-sha (in Japanese).

1969. Jomon jidai kenkyu no gen dankai [Current status of Jomon archaeology]. In *Nihon to Sekai no Rekishi I [World History and Japanese History*, vol. I]*, pp. 86–97. Tokyo: Gakushu Kenkyu-sha (in Japanese).

Yamanouchi, Sugao, and Tatsuo Sato. 1962. Jomon doki no furusa [The antiquity of Jomon pottery]. *Kagaku Yomiuri [Yomiuri Science]* 12: 18–26, 13: 84–88 (in Japanese).

1967. Shimokita no mudoki bunka: Aomori-ken Kamikita-gun Tohoku-machi Chojakubo Iseki chosa hokoku [Pre-pottery culture of Shimokita: Excavation Report of the Chojakubo site, Tohoku Town, Kamikita County, Aomori

Prefecture]. In *Shimokita: Shizen, Bunka, Shakai [Shimokita: Nature, Culture, and Society]*. Tokyo: Heibonsha (in Japanese).

Yane, Yoshimasa. 1996. Jomon doki no Shuen [Final Jomon pottery and culture]. In *Rekishi Hakkutsu II: Jomon Doki Shutsugen [Excavation of the Past*, vol. 2: *Emergence of Jomon Pottery]*, ed. Takura Izumi, pp. 134–154. Tokyo: Kodansha (in Japanese).

Yasuda, Yoshinori. 1995. Kuribayashi ga sasaeta kodo na bunka: kafun ga akiraka ni shita iseki no hensen [Prosperous culture supported by chestnut forest: changes in site occupation seen from pollen analysis]. In *Jomon Bunmei no Hakken: Kyoi no Sannai Maruyama Iseki [Discovery of the Jomon Civilization: New Findings at the Sannai Maruyama Site]*, ed. Takeshi Umehara and Yoshinori Yasuda, pp. 118–152. Tokyo: PHP Kenkyu-jo (in Japanese).

Yesner, David R. 1987. Life in the "Garden of Eden." In *Food and Evolution*, ed. Marvin Harris and Eric B. Ross, pp. 285–310. Philadelphia: Temple University Press.

Yoffee, Norman, and Andrew Sherratt. 1993. Introduction: a source of archaeological theory. In *Archaeological Theory: Who Sets the Agenda?*, ed. Norman Yoffee and Andrew Sherratt, pp. 1–9. Cambridge: Cambridge University Press.

Yokohama-shi Furusato Rekishi Zaidan Maizo Bunka Center [Archaeological Center of Yokohama City], ed. 1995. *Hanamiyama Iseki [The Hanamiyama Site]*. Yokohama: Yokohama-shi Furusato Rekishi Zaidan Maizo Bunka Center (in Japanese).

Yoneda, Konosuke. 1984. *Hyojo Yutaka na Dogu [Clay Figurines with Various Facial Expressions]*. Tokyo: New Science-Sha (in Japanese).

Yoshiasa, Noritomi. 1999. Ibutsu kenkyu: gyobutsu sekki [*Gyobutsu* stone bars]. *Jomon Jidai [Journal of Jomon Studies]* 10(4): 98–106 (in Japanese).

Yoshida, Itaru. 1965. Seikatsu yogu [Tools for daily use]. In *Nihon no Kokogaku II: Jomon Jidai [Japanese Archaeology*, vol. II: *The Jomon Period]*. Tokyo: Kawade Shobo (in Japanese).

Yoshida, Kunio, Yumiko Miyazaki, Keiichi Ohara, Naohiro Abe, Shigeomi Hishigiki, Ayako Oono, and Hiroko Iijima. 2000. Jomon doki ga motsu jikan joho [Chronological information contained in Jomon pottery]. In *Nihon Bunkazai Kagaku-kai Dai 17 kai Taikai Kenkyu Happyo Yoshi-shu [Abstracts of the Papers Presented at the17th Annual Meeting of the Japanese Society for Scientific Studies on Cultural Properties]*, pp. 8–9. Sakura: Nihon Bunkazai Kagaku-kai (in Japanese).

Yoshikawa, Masanobu, and Seiichiro Tsuji. 1998. Sannai Maruyama iseki dai 6 tetto standard column no kafun kaseki gun [Pollen data obtained from the standard column of the Sixth Transmission Tower Area of the Sannai Maruyama site]. In *Sannai Maruyama Iseki, IX, dai 2 bunsatsu [The Sannai Maruyama Site*, vol. IX, Part 2]*, ed. Aomori-ken Kyoiku-cho Bunka-ka [Cultural Affairs Section of the Agency of Education of Aomori Prefecture], pp. 11–14. Aomori: Aomori-ken Kyoiku Iinkai [Board of Education of Aomori Prefecture] (in Japanese).

Yoshizaki, Masakazu. 1995. Nihon ni okeru saibai shokubutsu no shutsugen [Origins of plant domestication in Japan]. *Kikan Kokogaku [Archaeology Quarterly]* 50: 18–24 (in Japanese).

Yoshizaki, Masakazu, and Kyoko Tsubakisaka. 1992. Aomori-ken Tominosawa (2) iseki shutsudo no Jomon Jidai Chuki no tanka shokubutsu shushi [Carbonized plant seeds excavated from the Tominosawa (2) site, Aomori Prefecture]. In *Tominosawa (2) Iseki VI [The Tominosawa (2) Site*, vol. VI], ed. Aomori-ken Kyoiku Iinkai [Board of Education of Aomori Prefecture], pp. 1097–1110. Aomori: Aomori-ken Kyoiku Iinkai (in Japanese).

Zhushchikhovskaya, Irina. 1997. On early pottery-making in the Russian Far East. *Asian Perspectives* 36(2): 159–174.

Index